/\/\/\/\/\/\/\

End of the Spear is a compelling book. Steve brings the reader into the Waodani culture and into their lives—a life unknown to all but a few.

LARS AND ELISABETH (ELLIOT) GREN
www.elisabethelliot.org

End of the Spear is a fascinating inside story that only Steve Saint could tell. The affection and respect of Steve and his family for the Waodani ("Aucas") and especially for the delightful Mincaye, once a killer of Steve's father and now a lover of God's Son, capture the heart and power of the gospel. This book is a page-turner, right through the heart-gripping epilogue. Read it. You'll never be the same.

RANDY ALCORN
Author of *Safely Home* and *Heaven*

End of the Spear is a fantastic adventure that takes the reader deep into the Ecuadorean Amazon for an unbelievable encounter with a violent Stone Age tribe. Steve Saint guides us on this journey with sensory detail and emotion that only come through living this adventure himself. Experience an amazing transformation that leads to an incredible reconciliation. Learn how a "culture bent on killing" becomes a "people of the Book." This is a true story our world desperately needs to hear.

BILL EWING
President, Every Tribe Entertainment

This book really gripped me. It is incredibly intimate and t
through some of the remarkable experiences and equally gr
sorrows Steve Saint and his family have been through. To
evidence that God is in control, even when the world has g
and when everything falls apart.

GARY WITHERALL
Operation Mobilization and author of *Total Abandon*

I commend Steve Saint's *End of the Spear* to anyone who has experienced pain in their lives and has wrestled with seeds of bitterness as a result. It offers a compelling portrait of authentic human grace. His incredible story makes it clear that he is able to see the sovereign hand of Providence, even in the most challenging of circumstances.

FRANK WOLF
Congressman

END OF
THE SPEAR

A TRUE STORY

END of THE SPEAR

STEVE SAINT

SALT**RIVER**®

AN IMPRINT OF
TYNDALE HOUSE PUBLISHERS, INC.

Visit Tyndale's exciting Web site at www.tyndale.com

TYNDALE is a registered trademark of Tyndale House Publishers, Inc.

SaltRiver and the *SaltRiver* logo are registered trademarks of Tyndale House Publishers, Inc.

End of the Spear

Designed by Beth Sparkman

Library of Congress Cataloging-in-Publication Data

Saint, Steve
  End of the spear / Steve Saint.
    p. cm.
  ISBN-13: 978-0-8423-6439-3 (hc)
  ISBN-10: 0-8423-6439-0 (hc)
  ISBN-13: 978-0-8423-8488-9 (sc)
  ISBN-10: 0-8423-8488-X (sc)
  1. Saint, steve. 2. Huao Indians—Missions. 3. Missionaries—Ecuador—Biography. 4. Huao Indians—
Religion. 5. Huao Indians—Social life and customs. I. Title.
  F3722. 1.H83S34 2005
  986.6—dc22   2005021966

Printed in the United States of America

12 11 10 09 08 07
8   7   6   5   4   3   2   1

The author has used a mixture of orthographies in spelling Waodani names and words in order to most accurately reflect Waodani pronunciations for English-speaking readers.

IF MY LIFE WERE AN AIR SHOW, I know just the act that would best represent it. In this act, two skydivers take off in separate planes that fly about a quarter of a mile apart, right in front of the crowd. On cue, both jumpers exit their planes and join up in the air. Once they meet, they deploy one large chute and descend to a happy landing, together.

No big deal, you're thinking. But I've left out one important detail: The skydivers have only one chute between them. If anything goes wrong and they do not join up, one of them is a goner.

If I were you, reading this, two questions would probably come to mind: First, how did they decide who jumped without a chute; and second, what does this have to do with a book dedication? I can answer only the second of those questions.

You see, I was like the guy free-falling without a chute. I knew where I was headed. I was going fast, and life was exciting, to be sure. But it did not hold great promise for staying that way for long. Then, at just the critical moment in my rapid plunge, I found a bosom buddy, who suggested we join our solo acts into one really good one. Well, actually, I suggested we join up, but she had the same idea.

I dedicate this book to my best and longest friend, without whom my part in this story would have been very different—probably much shorter and certainly not nearly as much fun. You'll understand what I mean a whole lot better when you get to the end of this story.

I first met Virginia Lynn Olson in 1973. It took me only three months to realize that I couldn't live long without her, although it took a bit longer to convince Ginny and her family that she should quit her job and return to Ecuador with me. And another three months to convince everyone in both families that we should join acts. Not everyone believed that six months was a sufficient trial period, but thirty-two happy years later, I think we've about got them won over.

Now, since I can write my life story only once, I would also like to dedicate this book to a growing group of little jumpers who have joined our act in the last few years—and a whole bunch more whom Ginny and I are looking forward to working into our act over the next few years.

To our eight really *grand*children, one little boy still waiting to be born, and several more who are just a sparkle in our children's eyes: This book is for you, too. This is the preface to your story.

Contents

Prologue: Amazon Guide xi

1: Back to the Stone Age 1

2: Can Cowodi Hunt? 11

3: Operation "Auca" 27

4: Friendly Friday 37

5: Did They Have to Die? 49

6: What We Do for Love 61

7: Thatched Huts and G-Strings 71

8: Swiss Family Saint 85

9: A Critical Decision 95

10: Trial by Trail 101

11: Terminal City 113

12: Could This Be Home? 123

13: Get Ready 147

14: Get Set 173

15: We're Gone 183

16: It's a Jungle Out Here 199

17: The Fateful Day 221

18: End of the Beginning 239

19: Another Spearing 251

20: Between Two Worlds 265

21: The Foreigners' Place 281

22: On the Road 295

23: Now I See It Well 307

24: Cloud of Witnesses 323

Epilogue: Maybe They Knew 333

PROLOGUE

Amazon Guide

When I entered the cheap rooming house in Quito, I could tell that the group of students I was about to lead into the Amazon jungle had little idea of the genuine adventure they were launching into. From the casual way they were sprawled around the low-budget hostel, I was also convinced they did not realize the risks involved.

An adjunct professor from the University of Washington had asked me if I would take a group of college students into the territory of the notorious Waodani tribe. The U.S. Embassy had told him he could no longer take student groups into the northern Ecuadorean jungles because of the increased threat of kidnappings by Colombian terrorists.

The professor had read somewhere that I was living with the Waodani tribe further south, in an area that was much more isolated. Even Colombian terrorists did not dare invade Waodani territory. Not just because of their isolation but also because of their notorious past.

My only interest in taking visitors deep into the rain forest was my desire to help the Waodani find a means of creating a desperately needed economy. This group was going to be extremely large: over thirty students plus the director and a couple of assistants. In order to make sure they stayed within their budget and were still able to compensate the Waodani, we had to eliminate the expense of flying the group into the jungle. They would have to spend days walking the steep, muddy trails; fording rivers; and fighting the unique flora and fauna that make the Amazon so intriguing to the uninitiated.

I would have said no. I had no standing with this group. With other groups I'd led, I had known the leaders or members of the group. I knew that they would respect the parameters the Waodani and I had established for tours like this. But the decision was really up to the Waodani. They surprised me with their enthusiasm to guide, host, and teach these *cowodi*, or foreigners, about life in their dynamic world.

As we boarded our chartered bus for the daylong ride to the edge of the immense Amazon rain forest, I could tell that I was going to have to earn any respect I would get from this group. They weren't exactly disrespectful; there just seemed to be some kind of a barrier between us. (Perhaps they had heard that I was a missionary.) Compared to life in the Amazon, North American society is very faddish. Fashions change every season, and what is considered politically correct changes almost as rapidly. At that time, two favorite whipping boys of the politically correct crowd were missionaries and oil companies.

I was quite sure this group had no idea I had spent time in the oil and gas business. So they couldn't hold that against me. But they had probably heard that my parents were missionaries, which would explain why I was intimately familiar with the Amazon and consequently why I was serving as their guide. If my parents were missionaries, they probably figured I was one too. I wasn't. I had not been sent by North Americans to help people of the Amazon with their medical, educational, political, economic, and spiritual needs. I was born here. Though my "shell" looked North American, my heart and thinking processes were quite Latin American. And my passport said I was just as Ecuadorean as the president of the country.

After spending a day outfitting the group with some necessary equipment, whittling down their personal effects to a fraction of what they'd expected to take with them, and buying provisions, we were as ready as we were going to be to leave the world of roads, stores, hospitals, radio, TV, public transportation, restaurants, and English—or any other major language.

I was not going to be trekking into the jungle with the group. I was going to turn them over to three friends from the tribe. I was the group's pilot. While they were slogging over muddy trails, ever on the lookout for giant anacondas, poisonous snakes, and tarantulas, I would be flying our provisions and their personal belongings into the last Quechua village before we entered Waodani territory.

The journey into Pitacocha should have taken about six hours. The Quechuas and Waodani make the trip in less than four hours, even when they are carrying big loads. I left the students at the end of the road at seven in the morning. I expected them to arrive in Pitacocha between noon and one o'clock. About the time they should have arrived, I was busy trying to reinsert a little boy's large intestine into his rectum after about three inches of it blew out due to a prolonged episode of severe diarrhea.

When I finally got the little fellow to quit screaming by giving him a piece of candy, the pressure on his abdomen decreased enough that I could wash off the section of inside-out bowel and push it back where it belonged. It was past three-thirty in the afternoon. A torrential rain inundated our part of the jungle in a deluge that left water standing inches deep on the short grass runway. An hour later, the sun was starting to dip behind the huge mountain peaks that towered just seventy miles to the west. Worried, I took off in my little bush plane in a desperate attempt to find out what had happened to thirty-three gringos and three Waodani guides.

The jungle was too dense to see anything from a plane. Since there was nothing more to do until daylight, I landed and decided to string my hammock, finally drifting off to sleep. I was awakened at ten o'clock by strange sounds and what looked like an army of giant lightning bugs. The group had not taken the wrong trail; it had taken them fifteen hours to make a four-hour trek. Fortunately, Doug, their director, knew better than to let them separate. They had arrived at the pace of the slowest member of the group, but at least they had arrived.

The next morning, I flew them in twos from Pitacocha to Caenawaeno, the nearest village in Waodani territory. The students were so pumped that they had overcome the myriad of obstacles the previous day to make it to Pitacocha, they were game for anything. The only way I could take off from the short village airstrip at Pitacocha was to carefully match the heavier members of the group with the lighter members. The airstrip there ends with a bump followed by a hundred feet of stumps and then falls off over a two-hundred-foot cliff. I would use the bump to get airborne long enough to clear the cliff, where I would dive to pick up airspeed. Everything in this world was so new to the foreigners that most of them seemed not to notice.

At Caenawaeno, a delegation of Waodani was waiting with dugout canoes to pole the group and our provisions down the Ewenguno River (the Curaray

River on maps) to the primitive Waodani-style village they had built for the group. By the time we arrived at "Camp Waaponi," or "Camp I-like-it," these sophisticated intellectuals from a distant world were clearly in awe of the fearsome virgin paradise they had entered. They were also awed by the Waodani, who patiently and without condescension fed them, protected them, and warmly welcomed them to their ancestral home—all without being able to speak an understandable phrase to them.

I had flown the cargo that needed to stay dry from Caenawaeno to a small village located just a forty-minute trail hike further downriver, where I lived with some of the Waodani who were hosting the group. I walked back up to the camp in the late afternoon to be sure that the hammocks were hung properly in the thatched longhouse that would be our home for five days. No matter how hard I tried, I could not convince the Waodani that foreigners don't know how to do something as basic as stringing a hammock. I also needed to make sure that the biggest *cowodi* got the largest hammocks. The Waodani are giants in strength and heart, but they are short in stature.

By the time the sun was beginning to set and night creatures and insects were tuning up for the evening symphony, I joined a group of students and Waodani who were sitting together by a fire. One of the girls in the visiting group turned to me with a question.

"In preparation for coming here," she began, "I did some research for the paper I have to do about this trip. I discovered that there is a notoriously violent tribe of people living someplace out here. Would you ask the Waodani if they know who those people are?"

I thought she was putting me on. The Waodani had once been called "Aucas," a derogatory term that means "naked savage" and carries with it the connotation of questionable humanity. The name "Auca," given to the Waodani by the Quechuas with whom they historically warred, is a demeaning (though perhaps not undeserved) term that I never use except to clarify that the "Aucas" and the Waodani are one and the same group of people. They have been classed by anthropologists as probably the most violent society ever studied. Before missionaries made peaceful contact with them, the homicide rate within the tribe was over 60 percent.

The young lady who had asked the question informed me that in addition to the incredible homicide rate within the tribe, these people viciously killed other tribespeople, rubber hunters, adventurers, and anyone else who trespassed onto their territory or lived near its borders. It was obvious she was referring to the Waodani. I told her, "The people you are describing would be the Waodani."

She clearly thought I didn't know what I was talking about. I was apparently still fighting the "ignorant missionary" stigma. "The people I'm referring to became world famous for killing five North American missionaries who tried to befriend them in 1956," she said. "That story was broadcast around the world by radio, appeared in a series of newspaper articles around the United States, Canada, and Europe, and even made it into *Life* magazine and *Reader's Digest*."

It was apparent she wasn't going to accept my word for it, so I suggested she ask the Waodani themselves. "Just ask any of the adult Waodani here where their fathers are," I suggested. I told her how to say "Bito maempo ayamonoi?" which means, "Your father—where is he being?" She seemed to wonder what this had to do with her question, but she picked out one of the Waodani men who was enjoying our English gibberish and asked him. He answered simply, "Doobae." I explained to her that the word means "Already." His father was already dead. I added, "Did he get sick and die, or did he die old?"

The warrior snorted at my ridiculous question and clarified with dramatic gestures that his father had been killed with spears.

"Did he just say what I think he said?" the girl asked. "Was his father speared to death? Who would do such a terrible thing?" I informed her that the only people I knew of in Ecuador who had speared anyone in the twentieth century were Waodani. I didn't expect her to take my word for it, and she didn't disappoint me.

One of the other students picked a Waodani woman and asked her the same question. Same answer. After one more try with similar results, two girls in the group asked me to ask Mincaye's wife, Ompodae, the question. From the whispering I overheard, I gathered that they were sure someone as loving and sweet as Ompodae couldn't have been traumatized by something as horrible as the vicious murder of her father. But Ompodae answered, "My father, my two brothers"—she counted them on her fingers—"my mother, and my baby sister . . ." There seemed to be more, but she stopped there. "All of them were speared to death and hacked with machetes!" Then she pointed at the oldest warrior in camp, who was quietly sharing a stump with one of the young male visitors. "Furious and hating us, Dabo killed us all."

As soon as I got the translation out, the young man sitting with Dabo jumped to his feet as if he had been stuck with a pin and blurted out, "My God, I was sitting with him!"

By this time it was getting pretty dark. The tree frogs were well into their nightly concert, a sound that is hardly noticed by jungle dwellers but can be unnerving to visitors. One of the students pointed out, "Guys, we are now four for four!"

My feisty tribal grandmother knew what the question was, so she decided to give her answer. She told how her family had been ambushed by another clan of Waodani. When the spearing was over, only she and another girl who was just reaching marriageable age were left alive in their clearing. When she finished her narrative, which I hardly needed to interpret because her pantomime was as clear to the students as her words were to me, she pointed to one of the warriors I was sitting with and stated matter-of-factly, "He killed my family and made me his wife!"

One of the girls in the group stammered, "How could she possibly live with the man who had killed her whole family?" I explained that the other girl who was kidnapped with Dawa was overheard complaining about her family being speared. One of the raiders ran a spear through her, and they left her on the trail to die an agonizing death alone, with no one to even bury her body. I explained, "It wasn't like Dawa had much of a choice."

Then it occurred to me that these young people did not know what my relationship was to the tribe. I was sitting between Dawa's husband, Kimo, and Mincaye, who had adopted me into his Waodani family when I was a boy. Both of them had speared those missionaries to death back in 1956. Dyuwi was sitting across the circle from me. He had been part of that killing raid too.

"They speared my father too," I informed the group. I had my arm around Kimo, and Mincaye was leaning on me and holding my hand in the familiarity that Waodani men feel free to express. "My father," I told the young lady who had started this dramatic conversation, "was one of those five missionaries you referred to."

1

Back to the Stone Age

November 1994

The head flight attendant had given us the customary briefing before takeoff. It was obvious that her first language was not English. I couldn't help but feel a sense of excitement as the powerful engines on the 757 pushed me back in the seat.

We were a cosmopolitan bunch. Experience (and numerous Goofy hats) told me that some on board had been to Disney World. Others, apparently from the upper socioeconomic end, had probably come to the land of malls and shopping extravaganzas to update their wardrobes. But there were also some who had the coarse hair and weathered skin of the mestizo, those born from the mingling of Spanish conquistadores and descendants of the Inca Empire they conquered.

I love to fly, but not back where I was sitting. I like the front left seat, where I can select my destination through the smallest manipulations of the controls. My stomach goes queasy every time a pilot I don't know—with my life in his hands—pulls back the power levers and we begin to decelerate while still pointed up at an alarming angle. In the small aircraft I fly, reducing power with the nose pointed at the sky is an invitation to stall and spin. But my mind was on other things this night. I tilted the seat back and closed my eyes.

On the other end of this flight I would spend a short night in the Andes Mountains. I hoped I would not get that crazy, suffocating sensation that had kept me awake in Quito's thin atmosphere on recent visits. Years before, when I lived and went to school almost ten thousand feet up in the mountains, I could play a full game of basketball and feel fine. Now, twenty-five years later, I had begun to understand what tourists complain about: "I can't catch my breath" or "I wake up gasping for air."

If they have Aunt Rachel's body ready, I should be on my way down to the jungle early the next morning, I thought.

Just the day before, I had been sitting at home after a long day of the same old, same old—driving around, talking on the cell phone, haggling over a few cents now that could make a difference of thousands of dollars down the road—the usual knockdown, drag-out life of a businessman. When the phone rang, I almost didn't answer. At home, Ginny answers the phone. She is a lot nicer to telemarketers, and after a day with my hand to my ear, I didn't want to talk into a machine anymore.

We had been expecting the call, but I still was not ready for it. "Hi, is this Steve?" I could tell the voice on the other end was calling from outside the United States. "I'm sorry to have to tell you that your aunt Rachel died this afternoon. I think it would be good if someone from the family could come down. Remember, down here we have to bury within twenty-four hours. I can ask the doctor if he can do some embalming, but that will only buy us a few hours. If we take too long, the authorities will make us bury her in Quito."

Aunt Rachel had been in Quito to receive treatments for cancer. But I knew she had wanted to be buried at home in the jungle, with the people she loved—the Waodani. Mom and my stepdad, Abe, were out of town. I knew they wouldn't be able to get down to Ecuador in time. I would have to represent the family and help bury "Star," as the people there called her.

As we cruised high over Cuba, I wondered how to best get my dear old aunt's body down to the jungle. And I contemplated how I could keep the Waodani who had loved her from being overwhelmed by "outsiders" wanting to get in on this historic event.

I woke up to the same voice that had put me to sleep: "Pleeze fosten yur-e seat bels fur ourr londing in Quito." Now I was glad I wasn't sitting in the left front seat. Quito lies in a tight valley rimmed by Andean mountain peaks. The city spreads right to the runway threshold, and on this night there was a heavy fog hanging over the valley floor. If we couldn't make a landing on our first couple of tries, we would have to divert to the coast and spend the night in Guayaquil, and I would almost certainly miss the reason for which I was coming. But thankfully, we made it.

/\/\.·/\·/\·/\·/\·/\.·/\/\

By the time I got to the Quito airport early the next morning, Aunt Rachel's body, wrapped in sheets, was already lying on the floor of the Cessna bush plane that would take us home. I took the seat beside her body. As we flew down the Avenue of the Volcanoes, regal snowcapped peaks rose above our flight altitude and disappeared into the overcast sky above us. Normally, we would have made a fuel stop on the edge of the great Amazon rain forest, but we were in a hurry. I heard our pilot request that another plane deliver the casket and bring extra fuel for him. I watched as we flew over the little town where I had spent my most formative years. Aunt Rachel had been a big part of those years. I felt a yearning to tell her just once more how much I loved her and respected her willingness to risk everything for what she believed. She was the most humble, but also the most stubborn, person I had ever known. Without the humility, she never would have been willing to live in a thatched hut in the middle of nowhere. Without the stubbornness, she never could have survived the violent cultural chaos that characterized life among the Waodani, known to the outside world as "Aucas"—savages. Without her, it is possible that there would have been no one left to welcome us at our destination.

The Waodani heard the plane coming and were standing by the short gravel-and-grass strip when we landed. The makeshift runway was surrounded on all sides by a sea of dense jungle. Dayumae, Aunt Rachel's closest living "relative" in the tribe, was the first one I saw after I opened the plane door. She greeted me and then saw what was left of the *cowodi*— foreigner—she had adopted as her sister more than four decades before. Her reaction was chilling. She began to wail, taking me by surprise. The Waodani, her own people, don't do that. But Dayumae had spent fifteen years living with the Quechua, a neighboring tribe, and had adopted much of their culture. Their death wail is a dark window into the excruciating agony of a human soul that has little control over its own destiny. The rest of the group retreated from Dayumae's grief.

Finally, the pilot and a couple of Waodani and I unwrapped Aunt Rachel's shroud and lifted her body from the plane into the simple plywood box that would serve as her coffin. It seemed appropriate for this old Saint who had never worried about luxuries or her own comfort. Its rustic simplicity matched her house, which sat just a hundred yards down the trail. We carried her there for final preparations.

No one had thought to tie Aunt Rachel's mouth shut before rigor mortis set in. So the doctor had tied a head scarf around her head and under her chin to keep it closed. The Waodani women surrounded the coffin to get a last glimpse of this woman who had become as much one of them as her ruddy complexion and white skin would allow. Immediately, they began an animated discussion. They spoke much too rapidly for me to catch the details of what they were saying, but it was clear that they were not pleased with the doctor's choice of scarf. They untied it to find a replacement, but when they did, Aunt Rachel's mouth opened just as though she were going to speak. A gasp ran through the crowd, and they instinctively recoiled. But not even mismatched accessories were going to bring Star's eighty-two-year-old, cancer-ravaged body back to life.

I retied Aunt Rachel's mouth shut with the piece of bright cloth that the Waodani women finally settled on. We carried her body over to the rustic little church just a few feet away. I was surprised to see that there were quite a few foreigners mixed in with the Waodani. But these were Aunt Rachel's close colleagues and friends, who had made flights for her, kept her two-way radio working, and helped her help the Waodani. I could not object to their presence, although I did ask them to let the Waodani bury Star their own way.

The Waodani, however, have no chief or other recognized authority. Over the past forty years, they had become accustomed to giving decision-making power to the *cowodi*, who can fly and make little metal boxes talk, who have little seeds that make diseases go away, and who perform a myriad of other unimaginable feats. I realized they were waiting for one of the foreigners to take charge. I stepped in.

I handed a nail for the coffin lid to each of the people who constituted Star's closest family.

Brave, impetuous Dayumae had adopted Star and given her the name of her young sister, Nemo, who had been hacked to pieces in a spearing raid when she and Dayumae were just girls. It was because of Dayumae that the tribe had invited Aunt Rachel to live with them, along with Elisabeth Elliot, whose husband, Jim, had also been speared when my dad was killed. Aunt Rachel and "Aunt" Betty were the first outsiders ever to receive such an invitation.

I also handed nails to handsome Kimo and nubile Dawa, the first ones to believe what Aunt Rachel and Dayumae taught them about a new way to live, a way without hating and killing. Kimo had taken a big risk in building a house for Aunt Rachel. Others in the tribe had been displeased and told him it would be his grave.

I gave a nail to Mincaye, who didn't take well to allowing foreigners in Waodani territory. He had threatened to spear Aunt Rachel and Aunt Betty. Then one day, Mincaye mysteriously had a change of heart and told Aunt Rachel that he had decided to follow God's trail. After that, Mincaye became jovial and almost happy-go-lucky.

Old Dyuwi also received a nail. When Dayumae had first returned from the outside world with the two foreigners, he was already a seasoned killer at age twenty. But he went from hating and killing to peacemaking almost instantaneously.

I kept the last nail for myself.

Just before we carried Star out to the hole that had been dug between her house and the little tin-roofed church with chicken-wire windows and chainsawed boards, Kimo offered an impromptu eulogy.

"Waengongi Taado ante odomoncaete ante Nemo pongantapa"—*Teaching us to walk God's trail, Star came.*

Aunt Rachel was large by Waodani standards and had grown stouter as she aged. When we reached the burial site, several of the Waodani men jumped into the grave to help lower her coffin. I was moved to see the care and almost reverence with which they handled the old shell that had been so precious to those of us gathered in that little clearing. This was the second member of my family to be buried here.

Dyuwi missed the signal to jump out of the grave and found himself alone, under the coffin, as it was lowered the last couple of feet. In desperation, he struggled to extricate himself. In doing so, he tipped the coffin, and we all stood horrified as we heard Aunt Rachel's body roll to the side. With all the weight on one side, the box fell to the bottom of the grave with a thud. No one moved.

I could almost hear Aunt Rachel giving instructions, with Dayumae passionately countermanding them. At first, we reacted like schoolkids whom the teacher had caught cheating. Were we in trouble again? But I could tell that Mincaye was trying to keep from bursting out laughing. Finally he let out a little involuntary snort, and we all broke up. Even Star would have enjoyed the irony of her mourners laughing at her interment.

/\/\/\/\/\/\/\/\

Strange circumstances, combined with providence, had led this silver-haired old woman to spend half of her long life in the wilds of the Amazon jungle with an egalitarian and once violent Stone Age people. Aunt Rachel's mother had been a daughter of wealth, growing up with luxury and pampering. Her father was a well-known stained-glass artist.

Rachel was Lawrence and Katherine Saint's third of eight children and only daughter. Because her mother was frail, Rachel became something of a second mother to her younger brothers, including my dad, Nate.

As a young girl, Rachel caught the attention of a wealthy Philadelphia widow who had no children of her own. That woman lavished Rachel with the accoutrements of prosperity that Katherine had rejected but her daughter had never tasted. Coming home from a summer in Europe—as was the custom of the old moneyed families in New England—the wealthy dowager informed a teenage Rachel that she had decided to make Rachel her heiress.

Such an inheritance would have ensured the care her mother so desperately needed for tuberculosis, fine educations for her brothers, and the opportunity for Rachel to be the financial protector and provider for the family she already nurtured.

But Rachel refused the offer because it would require her to be a companion to her wealthy benefactress until her death. "I have already made a prior commitment to do whatever God wants with my life," she told the woman. "I cannot make any commitment that might cause me to compromise what I have promised to God."

Unaccustomed to rejection of any kind, the wealthy mistress scolded Rachel harshly for her lack of gratitude and her idealism. She summarily cut off any hope of help for Rachel and her family. "You will not receive a cent from me, you ungrateful girl," she informed Rachel; and she meant it. When she died years later, she had her executor send Rachel a set of inexpensive cuff links. "It was the only cheap possession she owned," Aunt Rachel told me.

Feeling rejected, and uncertain about what her family would think of her hasty but principled response, Rachel sought privacy in the bow of the passenger liner on which they were voyaging home. In the mid-Atlantic she poured out her heart to the One to whom she had betrothed herself emotionally and spiritually.

"This never happened to me before or since," she told me on one of my extended visits with her in the jungle, "but while I was in the bow of that ship, I had a vision of a dark-skinned tribe of people who had never heard that the Lord Jesus loved them. And God promised me that if I continued to be faithful to Him, He would one day allow me the privilege of being the one to take His precious Word of love and peace to them."

She went on to finish high school and then spent the next twelve years working in a Christian center for drug and alcohol addicts. The family needed help financially if her brothers were to get adequate educations. She was content that when her responsibility to them was satisfied, God would keep His promise to her.

Although Rachel was past the normal age limit, Wycliffe Bible Translators accepted her as a translator candidate and sent her to Peru to temporarily replace a translator who had been working with a head-hunting tribe there. On the way, she stopped in Ecuador to visit my parents, Nate and Marj, who were missionaries there. Dad flew her to several jungle stations, carefully skirting "Auca" territory in the process. Rachel was keenly observant and asked why Dad avoided flying over that area.

"That part of the jungle is inhabited by people who have killed everyone from the outside world who has ventured inside their borders," Dad explained. "If we had a forced landing there, we might survive the crash, but we would not survive the 'Aucas.'"

"As soon as Nate told me that, I knew that they were the very ones God had promised to let me take His Good News to," Aunt Rachel told me. She never wavered in her confidence, even when tragedy struck several years later and the "Aucas" speared the little brother she loved like a son.

·∧·∧·∧·∧·∧·∧·∧·∧·

I watched as the Waodani filled the grave. Kimo and Dyuwi were watching me.

I had been near this spot years before. Kimo and Dyuwi had been watching me then, too. I was only fourteen. Of course, there was no village and no airstrip back then. We had trekked over from the next valley to the south with a group of Waodani.

My sister, Kathy, had decided she wanted to be baptized. Because our own dad was dead and could not do it, Mom suggested that Kathy choose a couple of men who had influenced her life spiritually. Only two years younger, I decided it was time for me to take this step too.

I understood that baptism was a symbolic, though important, gesture that signified my determination to live by a standard that *Itota*, the Creator's Son, had established for His followers. My hunting buddy, Iniwa, and Oncaye, a Waodani girl about Kathy's age, said they wanted to be baptized as well.

Mom had always wanted to see where my dad and his four friends had been killed, so she and Aunt Rachel decided to do so on this trip. We would trek over to the Ewenguno River to visit Dad's grave for the first time in the nine years he had been gone. And we would be baptized there.

We slogged over muddy jungle trails for several hours and then poled down the Ewenguno in dugout canoes, arriving just before dark. There was a set of jaguar tracks on the beach to inspire my imagination, and there was dinner to be caught. I helped with the fishing while the Waodani demonstrated their jungle skills, gathering materials to make shelters for the night. I never ceased to be impressed by how little the Waodani took with them and how much they had when they arrived.

Since Aunt Rachel had started living with the Waodani, I had looked for every chance I could to stay with her and the tribe. That is, after Aunt Rachel figured I could visit without being killed. The Waodani had a long history of killing outsiders and being killed by them. I was just a nine-year-old kid when

I first visited Waodani territory, but I was almost as tall as some of the adults in the tribe, though pitifully skinny.

By the time the evening mist began to settle over our little encampment and the night sounds began their serenade, the shelters had been made, the fires were going, and fish and monkey were in the pot. It didn't get much better than that in my book—and there was always the possibility that the jaguar would come back. That would add some excitement for sure.

The next morning, after drinking the Waodani's customary breakfast of plantain mashed in warm water and finishing the meat from the last night's meal, we were ready for the baptismal service. Kathy wanted Kimo and Dyuwi to baptize us. They were both warriors I had learned to respect, and they treated me like family. Kathy's choice was good by me.

Kimo spoke to *Waengongi*—God—as some of us bowed our heads: "A long time ago we came to this place to do a bad, bad thing. But now, speaking Your name well and keeping You in our hearts, we have come back to do a good thing. Taking these four young people into the water, they will die to the old way of living and will show that they truly want to walk Your trail now, following *Itota*, Your only Son, who marked Your trail for us."

It didn't occur to me until Kimo was praying that he and Dyuwi knew this sandbar well. The men we had chosen to baptize us were two of the very same men who had speared my father and the others—at this very same place. It seemed strangely out of character that such kind and gentle men whom we all liked so much and who obviously liked us could have done such a terrible thing. I hadn't forgotten the pain of losing Dad, but I couldn't imagine not loving Kimo and Dyuwi and all the other Waodani who had come to visit this terrible, wonderful place with us.

Then Kimo and Dyuwi took Kathy, Oncaye, Iniwa, and me into the water and lowered us into it as though they were burying us. When they lifted us back up, they told us to live happily and at peace, following God's trail.

We all gathered back on the beach while Dyuwi prayed. Dyuwi, normally a man of few words, covers a lot of territory when he talks to *Waengongi*. I opened my eyes, wondering why we should keep them shut when there was so much to look at. On the sand, right in the middle of our circle, was a bright yellow butterfly that looked an awful lot like my dad's little Piper Cruiser.

When Dyuwi finally finished his address to our Creator, the butterfly was still there, in the exact place where "56 Henry," as Dad's plane was called, had died. I wanted to ask Kimo and Dyuwi why they had destroyed the plane, but I didn't know how. And I was sure Aunt Rachel would disapprove. I also wanted to know why they had speared my dad and our other friends. But again, I remained silent. I was too young to realize how strange it would seem to other people that Kathy and I were baptized at the same place and by the same men who had speared our dad and hacked his body with a machete. These were people Aunt Rachel loved and Mom had been praying for since before they killed Dad and the four others. Following their example, it had never even occurred to me to hate them.

When we finished praying, the Waodani warriors took the four of us into the jungle beside the beach to show us the stump of the tree where "the five foreign God followers built their sleeping house when they came to bring us God's carvings and teach us how to live well." The bodies had been buried right here. We had no idea at the time, however, that one of us would also die and be buried in this same place. Nor did we have any clue that 56 Henry would one day reappear here.

As we prepared to leave the grave site, Mom noticed four bright red flowers clustered together nearby. It seemed almost odd that there were not five of them. Then Aunt Rachel noticed one more just a short distance farther back. I remembered then that Ed McCully's body had not been buried with Dad, Jim, Roger, and Pete. His body had been found too far downriver to safely bring back for burial. Surely that fifth bloom was for "Uncle" Ed.

2

Can Cowodi Hunt?

The Mission Aviation Fellowship planes left, taking all the visitors with them. I was finally alone with the Waodani. There was a group of Aenomenani in the village, members of the downriver part of the tribe, whom I had never met. They were technically part of the same tribe, but they and the upriver Waodani had killing vendettas that went back as far as anyone could remember. Apparently, the Aenomenani had heard that the foreigner who was Star's "son" was visiting. They wanted proof that I was that foreigner, the one called "Babae."

No problem! Mincaye grabbed one of the Aenomenani's nine-foot blowguns and prepared to give them proof. I could understand only a little of what he was saying, but it was clear that he was bragging about what a great hunter I was. "Just like one of us, only with white skin," he said. They all laughed. Using the blowgun as a prop, he started demonstrating how I could creep up on the wiliest of jungle fauna. But the Aenomenani did not want to hear Mincaye's stories; they wanted to see me prove myself.

While I was busy thinking of excuses that would work in this particular setting, a young boy returned from hunting. He had a tiny bird tucked under his G-string. One of the Aenomenani warriors grabbed the little bird and climbed up a nearby tree, where he tied it to a limb. I could see what was happening and began to protest. My authenticity and the credibility of my mentors were about to be tested. I could hardly see the bird way up in the tree, and most of what I could see was just feathers. Unless I happened to hit the scrawny body hidden under all that feather fluff, the dart would fly right through. Besides that, I had not been blowgun hunting for about twenty-five years. I had a blowgun at home in Florida that I used to discourage raccoons and other varmints from getting into our garbage. The poison on my darts was too old to be very effective, but the varmints in our neighborhood quit patronizing our garbage. Still, I hadn't used a blowgun for serious hunting since I was a boy.

The Amazon jungle covering the six thousand square miles of Waodani territory is like a sea of green poured over the Badlands of North Dakota. The terrain is rugged and wet. The precipitation there can reach thirty feet per year as the warm, humid ocean of Amazon air pushes up against the Andes Mountains to the west. Some of the moisture is carried up those steep slopes, forming glaciers on the perpetually snowcapped peaks that overlook the jungle. There, the air is cold and dry enough that Incas buried on those high slopes can still be found in amazingly well-preserved condition—freeze dried.

In these rain forests the foliage is so dense that the jungle floor is a world of semidarkness. It is in this mysterious and wonderful world that I learned to hunt the exotic animals that make up a significant portion of the Waodani's diet.

The Waodani impale large animals that live in and on the jungle floor with hardwood spears they have developed into highly effective weapons. But a warrior must be swift enough to get within a few feet of a tapir, wild pig, or deer in order to spear it. It takes a powerful thrust to plunge a pointed hardwood shaft deep enough through tough skin and muscle to make a kill. Pride and hunger are a Waodani hunter's greatest assets.

Young boys in the tribe who are not yet strong enough to spear start their hunting careers with the ingenious and inspiring Waodani blowgun. When I was a boy, my first challenge had been figuring out how to maneuver a nine-foot blowgun through dense foliage at a dead run. Whenever I tried to creep up noiselessly on a nesting toucan or a large macaw, I always seemed to bang one end or the other against something. My ineptitude frequently scared away my intended prey.

Monkey hunting presented another challenge. We could usually hear monkeys long before we could see them, because they yell and scold each other as they graze in the upper canopies. I would follow the Waodani boys through the jungle, and when we heard game nearby, they would begin to talk in their special hunting voices that carried well but, surprisingly, would not startle jungle wildlife. Their voices became high-pitched as they called to each other in clipped staccato outbursts of sound rather than individually identifiable words. I learned to discern what they were communicating from pitch and inflection before I actually understood what they were saying.

Once we were in position, our next challenge was to drive a poison-tipped dart a hundred feet or more on a straight trajectory toward the bird or animal. This requires much practice and incredible skill. The dart, made from a soft palm frond stem, must be whittled aerodynamically. Heat from the fire hardens the darts, which look like sharp, foot-long toothpicks. Monkeys and other tree-dwelling animals are much too large to kill with a single dart. For them, the dart is merely the vehicle for delivering *oomae*—poison.

The Waodani taught me to make the poison from shaving the thin bark of a special vine. The poison, which causes muscle paralysis, is the same drug used for surgery in many developed countries. Once a patient is put to sleep, this "poison" is used to temporarily paralyze the patient, ensuring that he or she won't twitch or move during surgery.

The Waodani boys were patient and persistent. I'm sure I provided great entertainment for them. And in exchange for what they taught me about hunting, I taught them about airplanes, screws, paper, radios, and other mysteries from the "outside world."

In the outside world I was always chosen in the first round for pickup softball, football, or basketball. In the jungle, it was embarrassing to be such a klutz. But after much patient coaching by my young Waodani friends, I finally started to get the hang of hunting. I only now realize that they never would have allowed me to scare off so much game if they didn't like me. I also realize now that Mincaye, especially, encouraged his boys to teach me these critical jungle skills. I think he was hoping, even way back then, that I would choose to stay and live with him and his family. He was certainly treating me like a member of the family.

During one particular hunt, we shot a fairly large monkey. A monkey can reach almost fifteen pounds, which provides a lot of meat, though it tends to be a bit tough. (People often ask me what monkey tastes like. To be perfectly candid, it's a lot like chicken.) The monkey reacted to being shot by screeching and dramatically clawing at his side. The dart broke off almost immediately, leaving the poisoned tip to do its work and paralyze the monkey.

The tip didn't just happen to break off. My Waodani friends had taught me to twist the dart in a piranha jaw that hangs from every authentic blow-gun dart-holder. This creates a groove that weakens the dart right behind the poisoned tip so that when a monkey tries to pull the dart out, it breaks off.

Instead of running, the other monkeys gathered around their injured companion to see what had happened to him. By the time the monkeys realized they were under attack, we had hit three or four of them. With a thrashing of leaves and rapidly diminishing crashes, the troop of monkeys fled, jumping from the branches of one tree to another. The boys disappeared after the fleeing monkeys, and I found myself completely alone.

I was scared and helpless. I didn't know it yet, but these were feelings I would get used to. This sense of dependence would help me understand how my tribal friends would feel years later when they had to learn to deal with another world as strange to them as theirs was to me. When confronted with elevators, moving sidewalks, bathrooms, cars, and grocery stores, they would feel helpless too. Remembering what it was like to be lost in the jungle, I would determine never to let them feel that way when I understood the surroundings and they didn't.

When my friends disappeared after the monkeys, I didn't have the vaguest idea of how to get back to the village. Even if I could have found the trail, I still could not have found my way back. The Waodani waste little effort in unnecessary tasks. Their trails are merely the elimination of obvious obstacles that require the expenditure of unnecessary energy to efficiently move from one part of their domain to another. They don't actually cut a trail. They just use it, and if it gets used often enough, a path eventually becomes distinguishable from the surrounding tangle of undergrowth. Hunting trails never became that apparent.

The first few times I was left behind, I feared for my life. Even the Waodani don't like to spend a night alone in the jungle. If it intimidated them, with their PhDs in jungle survival, it sure as anything was too much for me. I was just in kindergarten, but I knew enough to realize that if they didn't find me, I would never find them.

Finally, it dawned on me that it would actually be almost impossible for them *not* to find me, no matter where I went or what I did. If they could follow the trails of animals that wanted to elude them, surely the signs that this barely initiated *cowodi* left behind would be like a map from AAA.

/\/\/\/\/\/\/\/\

Now, I knew that my standing with the downriver members of the tribe hung on the impossible challenge of hitting a tiny bird with a blowgun. I had never used this blowgun before. Each blowgun, like everything else made by the Waodani, is one of a kind. I didn't even know the size of the hole running through this particular weapon. That would determine how much cottonlike kapok I would have to twist on the dart so the explosion of breath I was about to release into the blowgun would propel the dart through the long barrel, then through the air, and into the meager flesh of my tiny target.

I prepared my dart, adding kapok until the fit felt just right. I remembered to choose a fairly straight dart, flexing it to take out a slight curve. I think the Aenomenani were surprised to see that I at least knew how to properly spin the kapok on the dart. Even this minor step in the process requires practice. If the wad of kapok is not aerodynamic in shape, the dart won't fly straight or far.

When I had stalled as long as I could, I gave in to the inevitable. I held the long weapon as I had learned to do long ago, with my hands only about eight inches apart. This seems awkward but is necessitated by the fact that we almost always shoot up at a forty-five-degree angle or greater. My audience realized that I had done this before. Maybe they would give me the benefit of the doubt if I at least came close to the target.

I took a huge breath, cheeks puffed out, both eyes open, and let go with all the pressure that my out-of-practice diaphragm could muster. "Tae, tae, woo-tae." Mincaye immediately started jumping around, exercising the traditional "I hit it, I hit it" bragging rights used by Waodani hunters. I hadn't even seen where my dart hit. It didn't appear to be sticking in the bird, but it must have come very close, because the tiny fowl was spinning slightly on the string used to secure it. Then it twisted back, and I saw what Mincaye was bragging about. My dart was sticking right through the center of the bird's scrawny neck.

It is not the Waodani way to be modest at a time like this. Showing the traditional arrogance, I handed the blowgun back to its owner and challenged him, "Bito diae?"—*What about you?*

A half hour later, everyone was still trying his hand at duplicating my feat of marksmanship. They kept offering me more tries, but I wasn't going to tempt fate. It seemed providential that I hit it the first time. There was no way I was going to take a chance on ruining a perfect score.

The Waodani do share one characteristic with all other hunters of the world. The more they tell their stories, the bigger and more dangerous the quarry gets and the more magnificent their own role in bringing it down. I could only imagine what was going to be told around the Aenomenani cooking fires that night. Chances were, Mincaye would make the rounds to ensure I received adequate credit for my incredible shot—and that he got credit for teaching this white-skinned foreigner to be so *Waodani-bai*—Waodanilike.

/\·/\·/\·/\·/\·/\·/\

Many of the Waodani from the original Gikitaidi clan had gathered at the Toñampade village to bury Star.

While the younger men were finishing the blowgun tournament, members of the clan I had belonged to invited me to Dayumae's cooking hut to eat some wild pig and manioc. They seemed to have something serious on their minds. I thought maybe it was just the somber occasion of burying Aunt Rachel. Finally, my tribal grandmother, Dawa, raised the issue that was on their minds: "Now Star, who is dead—being buried, we say you come live with us!"

What was this all about? I thought I might have misunderstood part of what she said, but I did understand the part about "come live with us."

It was a nice gesture, but I realized that these people who had become like a part of my family could not possibly know what they were asking. I couldn't just leave my business; I had struggled for twenty-some years to learn how to live in North America. After years in Ecuador, it really had been tough for me to get an education and compete against contemporaries who grew up in business families with connections and venture capital. And what about my wife, Ginny? Her biggest adventure had been leaving Minnesota at age twenty-two to visit South America for a two-week excursion with a singing group. Dawa and my *iñanani*—jungle family—could not possibly know what Ginny and our four children would think of such an outlandish request. Shaun was starting college. Jaime was finishing high school. Our youngest son, Jesse, and only daughter, Stephenie, had well-established friends and were busy in high school jazz band and other activities. *No. What you just asked me to do is impossible, but thank you for asking,* I thought to myself.

"You sending a message to me, I will come and visit," I countered, quite sure that this would end the conversation. I couldn't have been more wrong.

"We say come again to live with us, bringing your wife and children." I tried sweetening my offer: "Star, who is dead, being gone—her house is now mine. You calling me, I can come and live here with you from time to time when you need me."

Dawa was intransigent. "Bringing your family, we say come and live here."

I was surprised. Adult Waodani don't tell other adults what to do. They rarely tell small children what to do in a demanding way. They are probably the most egalitarian people on earth, with everyone doing whatever he or she wants. So what was Dawa, obviously coaxed by the others, doing? Surely she was not telling me what to do. But there could be no mistaking that she was telling, not asking.

Then I realized what was happening. Aunt Rachel had once explained to me that when an individual Waodani clearing, usually consisting of two warriors and their families, felt an attack against them was imminent, they would move to another part of the jungle to elude their enemies. The alternative was to invoke a cultural mechanism that allowed one family group to demand relatives from another clearing to temporarily live with them. The increased concentration of warriors in one house reduced the risk of being attacked.

The group being asked to join could refuse, but in doing so, they risked severing familial ties that are important to the Waodani both emotionally and practically. When families stuck together against their mutual enemies, their life expectancy increased. Even when they did stick together, extreme, unimaginable violence within the tribe made their life expectancy unbelievably short. No one would invoke the right of assimilation lightly, but neither would anyone object without a very good reason.

It finally sank in: The Waodani weren't asking me to come. They were telling me to! They were also paying me a high compliment in doing so. They considered me to be family. But none of that could eliminate the fact that I had another life with another family who knew little of the Waodani and their unique culture.

I couldn't deny my Waodani family's demand lightly, but neither could I casually accept. I decided to use an old excuse: "Speaking to *Waengongi*, if He sees it well, then I will come live with you." English translation: "I'll pray about it." But what I really meant was, "I don't want to do what you have asked, but I don't want to say no either, so I'll pretend to seek God's will in the matter and give you *my* answer later—which I hope you actually believe is God's answer, to which you can hardly object."

The Waodani show their cleverness in a thousand ways living off the unforgiving land they know as home. But I had learned the obfuscating ways of the foreigner, where sleight of speech, like sleight of hand is a skill much to be prized.

They were not deterred by my prevarication, however. Dawa merely turned to the group gathered in the little smoke-filled hut and declared, "Already having spoken to *Waengongi*, I know He sees it well." How could I, of all people, have so easily underestimated my Waodani relatives? Just because Dawa and most of the others could not read the Book, it did not mean they were not a people of the Book. Nor did it mean they couldn't understand what it taught about the Creator and His desire to talk with His creation. I felt bad about my condescending attitude. It was unintentional. But I still needed a good reason to turn down what they wanted me to do.

"Speaking to *Waengongi* and my wife, Ongingcamo (Ginny), if they both see it well—then I will surely come." The Waodani might be able to talk to God, but I knew none of them could get in touch with Ginny. The nearest telephone was days away by trail, and no one would know how to use it if they got there. Nor did they have phone cards or money to pay for it.

I felt relieved and slightly smug at my ability to handle such a sensitive cross-cultural situation.

Dawa was neither intimidated nor stumped. "Ongingcamo, being a God follower," she declared to the gathering, "if God sees it well that Babae come, how can Ongingcamo not see it well?" I was taken aback, but I was also moved. I remembered what a close friend would often say when faced by a difficult decision: "A hundred years from now, who will care how successful we were or how comfortable our lives were? What will matter then is what we invested our lives in."

I couldn't imagine how I would explain to my gentle and loving, but unadventurous, wife and our four children that I was even contemplating what the Waodani wanted. I wasn't about to give in, but neither could I think of any way to resist. The clan's demand put me in a precarious position between my two worlds. Either choice would surely alienate people who were critically dear to me. And if I wasn't careful, I could alienate both sides. *God only knows,* I thought, *how I can come out of this dilemma a winner.*

~~~~~~

I needed to get away. But where? I knew the jungle around the Tiwaeno village where I had lived with Aunt Rachel, but I didn't know any of the trails around Toñampade, where we had buried her. *Hey,* I thought, *no one has told old Gikita that Star is dead.* Gikita needed to know. In the tribal kinship, Gikita was Aunt Rachel's uncle. He was also the warrior who had led the spearing raid at "Palm Beach." I could get Mincaye to trek over there with me to tell him. I hadn't seen this charismatic and imposing old warrior for a long time, but I knew he lived at the headwaters of the Tzapino River, just north of where we were.

There was a group of young bucks standing around between Dayumae's house and Aunt Rachel's—no, it was my house now. I noticed that some of them were wearing *nenkinga*—sun things, watches. I had only one full day before the plane was scheduled to come back to fly me out of the jungle. If I was going to tell Gikita about Star, I would have to be sure that I could make it there and back the same day.

Time means little to the Waodani. They don't divide life up into segments of work and play. They don't have weekends off. They don't take vacations, either. There is nothing in their lives to take a vacation from. For them, everything is simply *cae*—doing. Asking the Waodani if I could make it to Gikita's house and back in one day would seem like a ridiculous question. In their mind, it would depend solely on me: how fast I could walk or run and how long I was able and willing to keep at it. They would want to know if I was going to be carrying a heavy load or just taking food and my *tiamo*—killing stick.

But since these young guys had watches, I knew they must be attending the high school there in Toñampade. I was sure they could tell me how many hours it would take.

"Aepodo nenki, Gikita weca, gote pomoi?" I asked, pointing to my watch. They looked at each other, building up the courage to answer my inquiry. Finally, one of them bravely answered as spokesman for the group. He raised his arm, fingers outstretched, to a forty-five-degree angle above the horizon.

That is the way the Waodani indicate where the sun will be when something happens. But I didn't want Waodani time; I wanted to know how long it would take in "gringo time." I tapped my watch and asked again. They whispered nervously, glancing at their watches, and then lifted their hands in concert and pointed to where the sun would be at about three o'clock in the afternoon.

I wanted to know how many hours it would take to get to Gikita's house and back. Besides, they had not asked what time I was going to leave. How could they know what time it would be when I returned? They looked so sure of themselves and so proud that I had asked them, I hated to reveal what I was really feeling.

How can you all spend so much time going to school without even learning how to tell time? I wondered critically. I had already noticed that Waodani young people who attended high school at Toñampade seemed to have a cocky attitude that was an aberration of Waodani comportment. I had also realized that around Toñampade, the young people let the old people do all the heavy work. But a nagging feeling told me that my frustration was due to something I had forgotten rather than their poor answer. Then it occurred to me. They *did* know what time I would leave.

Waodani wake up at about six and bathe quickly in the river while it is getting light. By six-thirty, they are having their breakfast of manioc or plantain drink and whatever might be left in last night's cooking pot.

If you are going anywhere, you are on the trail when the sun is "there," just over the eastern ridges—seven o'clock.

They were telling me that if I left at seven in the morning, I would be back from Gikita's house at about three in the afternoon. But now I realized that I needed some clarification. The Waodani have three trail speeds: Fast, which is about as fast as foreigners walk when they are late to catch a plane. They use this speed when they are carrying a heavy load and going a long distance with lots of climbing and descents along the way. Faster is approximately a slow trot, which they use to cover two days' worth of walking in one day. All-out is what they do when word comes that there is a herd of wild pigs or a fiesta someplace off in the jungle. It is a run that they can keep up from sunup to sundown. This speed requires powerful legs, the stamina of a marathoner, and a high pain threshold.

I asked more questions, determined to find out which speed and how much pain would be required to get back by three o'clock the next day. The old people who had taught me to walk their trails weighed in on our conversation, claiming that I would have no trouble making the trip. I reminded them that I had lived like a foreigner for a long time. But I got the impression that they were bragging again about how much I was like them. With the blowgun, their boast just required a lucky shot. On this test, proving them right might kill me.

Mincaye said he would go with me, and I was grateful. Since he was twenty-some years older than I was, I mistakenly figured that I would finally be able to keep up with him.

I was up with the sun the next morning, ready to hit the trail. Half an hour into our excursion, we came to our first big ridge. I was tired within five minutes of climbing and slowed down. A few minutes later I was totally winded. It was so steep that I could as easily pull with my arms as push with my feet—and I was hardly bending over. The last couple of hundred feet up "heartbreak ridge" brought sheer agony. At the top, I swallowed the remnants of pride that were poking through the pain in my muscles and lungs and asked Mincaye to carry my pack.

By the time we started the long descent into Gikita's valley, my legs were quivering. Climbing down ridges under such circumstances is just as painful as climbing up. By the time we saw Gikita's house nestled on a triangle of land where the Tzapino and another small river join, I was numb with exhaustion. *The plane might come,* I thought, *but I'm not going to be there unless Mincaye can drag me back.*

Gikita's wife, Mangamo, handed me a gourd full of plantain drink as soon as I plunked down in one of their hammocks. I started to drink just to be polite. But I quickly remembered why the Waodani don't go anywhere without drinking manioc or plantain and why they always drink as soon as they arrive. By the time I had downed a full quart, I was feeling better. Not good, just better. Mincaye was on his third quart, and he and Gikita laughed when I made it only partway through my second. The Waodani can drink nearly four quarts of the thick drink. I was ready to explode after my first.

Gikita showed no emotion when I informed him that Star had died and we had buried her. This old warrior had spent his life as head killer of the Gikitaidi clan that bore his name. He grew up in a culture of death and had achieved its highest accomplishment. He had become *tempo*—a remorseless killer. By the time the two *cowodi*, Star and Woodpecker (the tribe's name for Aunt Betty), came with Dayumae to live with his clan, Gikita had outlived every other man in the tribe. He was the old man—in his early thirties.

The only way to reach such a ripe old age was to kill your enemies before they killed you. Gikita had distinguished himself in that. But I had come to know him just after he gave up killing and forgave the vendettas he had yet to avenge. I looked up to Gikita in the jungle like one might look up to the chairman of a large corporation in the outside world. In his world, Gikita was top dog, the best at what mattered most in Waodani life: killing.

After digesting the information about Aunt Rachel, Gikita responded. "Babae, being old I, too, am soon going to die. Going to live, then, in God's place, I will wrap my arms around your father whom I speared first. There we will live happily together.

"Before, we lived very badly, hating and spearing all the time. Now, the young people, well, they are living badly again. Wanting many things and not sharing, they, too, are living angry.

"Star already dying, and me dying soon, I say, you come and teach the young people how to live well." End of speech. Short and sweet, for him. Difficult and convicting for me. One of my reasons for making this grueling trek was to get away from the turmoil caused by the demand that I return to the jungle. Now Gikita had added to it.

Mincaye picked up my pack for the return trip to Toñampade without my even asking. Fortunately, we surprised a badgerlike animal on the return trail, and since my hands were free, I hit it. We would return with meat. I felt a bit wimpy having Mincaye carry my gear for me, but by bringing game back to the village, I felt my honor was at least partly redeemed. Mincaye carried my animal, too.

I asked Mincaye why Gikita lived way over on the Tzapino, so far from everyone else. He explained that two of Gikita's daughters had been married to a young warrior. One day, the husband killed two pigs while out hunting. He carried one of the pigs to his clearing and told his older wife to fetch the other. She refused, demanding that he send the younger wife. As she stormed off, he became angry and shot her in the back with his muzzle-loading shotgun. "She bled, threw up, and died," Mincaye finished.

Gikita had had enough. He had grown up hating and killing. Then, after becoming a God follower, he gave up all the hatred and fear that had haunted the first half of his life. Seeing the old ways creeping in again in a new form, he moved deeper into the jungle with his wife, Mangamo, and sister, Mintake.

There seemed to be no end to the chaos and violence contained within this small, isolated tribe of people. I had learned to love them before I reached the age when I felt I had to understand them. Now I wondered if I ever would. It would be several years before I would see the Waodani struggle with the same thing as they tried to understand the "civilized world," a world in which the *cowodi* kill each other with great killing machines.

As Mincaye and I neared Toñampade, the sun was somewhat lower than the young Waodani men had estimated. I had forgotten to tell them I wanted to drink plantain and talk. All they had factored in was the time needed to trudge there and back.

A half hour out, I heard a bush plane land at Toñampade. Oh, no! They had come for me early. There were no flights planned into Toñampade that Mincaye knew of, so I coaxed my rebelling body into one final agonizing sprint, knowing that the pilot would not be able to wait long.

When Mincaye and I reached the airstrip, the Waodani told me that the plane was parked at the other end of the strip. Four hundred extra yards to go.

I grabbed my things and walked to the strip, followed by a small entourage of Waodani. As we walked down the strip, we met a couple of obvious gringos coming the other way. The plane had not come for me. It had come to bring visitors. Clean clothes and lack of proper jungle attire made it obvious that this was their initiation into the world of mud and mildew.

I was too tired to expend unnecessary energy on elaborate greetings. "Hi, who are you?" I asked.

"Who are you?" they asked back, as though *I* were the intruder. I was sure they would be embarrassed when I told them who I was. I belonged here, after all. I answered, "I'm Steve Saint."

They might not know who I was, but surely they would recognize my last name and its association with the Waodani. I was wrong. They continued on past us before turning around. "Did you know that these are the people who killed the five missionaries?" they asked me. "We just came back from the beach where they did it."

I was aghast at what I had just heard. *How dare such callous people come here and strut around like they own the place!* I thought. They had apparently come to see a sandbar and add an adventure badge to their experience vest. They would go home and tell their friends that they had visited the famous Palm Beach, where savages had killed the missionaries. They probably had even taken some sand home as a memento.

"Who let these *cowodi* come?" I asked the Waodani. "We don't know," they responded with shrugs. "Always coming, they just want to see the sand where the missionaries died," they informed me. But I could see the resentment and frustration behind their response. What they hadn't said was, "To the foreigners, we will always be the people who killed the missionaries," but I could tell they were thinking it.

I was seething with emotion. I was feeling protective. Someone had just threatened my family, and the fight-or-flight reaction had automatically kicked in. If I felt this much emotion, how must the Waodani feel? What the Waodani had done made sense within their warped culture of hate and fear. What they had done to the five foreigners was reasonable in their minds. At the time, they couldn't understand the extravagant overtures of friendship these foreigners had made. But I know my other world is just as warped, and just as full of hate and fear. In the outside world, we just have more rules to keep the killing in check. And we have a lot of police and soldiers to enforce those rules. Otherwise, both worlds are pretty much the same.

The Waodani's reasons for telling me to return and live with them were probably as complex as the group that was asking. But when I asked them why they wanted me to come, I was given three reasons. They wanted me to help them protect themselves; they wanted me to teach them; and they wanted me to help them to get medicine. None of those reasons had seemed urgent or had made much sense to me when I first heard them less than twenty-four hours before. But now the reasons had become personal. Someone needed to put a stop to people rubbing my "family's" face in the fact that members of their tribe had killed my dad and uncles. They needed to be protected from this type of insensitive intrusion.

What the Waodani had meant for evil, God used for good. Given the chance to go back and rewrite the story, I would not be willing to change it. Sure, it was painful, but over time I have begun to see the pain of Dad's death in a different light. If I could have changed things, I could have kept my dad. But then Mincaye would not have adopted me. Dyuwi and Kimo would not be my spiritual mentors. I would not have been part of this mysterious and wonderful Waodani world. Dawa would not be my grandmother, and Dayumae would not be my aunt. And in the outside world, thousands and thousands of people would not have dedicated their lives to helping take teachings of peace and hope and comfort to people like the Waodani in frontiers scattered all over the world.

I would soon find out that the Waodani's requests were a lot more complicated than I could have guessed that afternoon in Toñampade. What I realized, however, was that if I couldn't help, who could? And if I wouldn't, who would?

Palm Beach was about people, not sand. It was about giving life, not death. Without knowing it, I had just crossed the fine line of decision.

3

Operation "Auca"

My body ached all over after my trek to Gikita's house and back. I had small cuts on my legs and arms. I couldn't wait to clean up. I thought about the fly in the jungle that lays its eggs inside cuts in people's skin. I remembered, as a boy, seeing the Waodani "clucking" maggots out of one another's bodies. With an unpoisoned blowgun dart in hand, they would put their mouths close to the red mound on the other person's body and begin making a sound like you might make to get a horse going.

It is hard to believe, but it actually works. As the person clucks, the maggot sticks its head out of the host person's flesh. In a flash, the Waodani skewer it with the dart and pull it out.

I did not want maggots in my legs so I walked down to the little stream that ran behind Dayumae's and Aunt Rachel's houses. Dayumae was there, and she could tell from the way I was walking that I was exhausted and in pain. "Tengo nanta biimo"—*I have hurting medicine*—she informed me, in a mixture of Spanish and Wao-Tededo. Imagining some exotic jungle remedy, I told her I would like her *biimo.*

Dayumae came back from her house with the magic potion wrapped in a leaf. Carefully unwrapping it, she handed me a tube of Ben-Gay and a small bottle of ibuprofen. I took Dayumae's pills and liberally coated my aching muscles with the precious Ben-Gay she had been carefully hoarding. The medicine did wonders for my aches and pains, but it forced me to realize in a personal way how difficult it was for the Waodani to have to depend on foreigners for medicines that could stop infection, cure malaria, kill parasites, and treat other physical problems. I realized that although the exotic world of the Waodani had become inextricably linked with the outside world, the Waodani did not control the link.

I hated to see that the Stone Age Waodani world I had loved so much as a boy was changing. On the other hand, I was glad that it now included at least one bottle of pain medicine and some muscle ointment. And I was glad that there was a little solar-powered radio to let me know if and when the plane was coming for me. My only other way to get out of the jungle was to spend days slogging up and down steep, muddy ridges on foot. With the pain of my short trip to Gikita's house, I dreaded even the thought of spending days, not just hours, on the trail. Late that afternoon, as I poked through Aunt Rachel's earthly belongings with Dayumae and her husband, Komi, other members of the Gikitaidi clan began to gather with us. These people were my jungle family. It soothed me to realize that they were grieving for Aunt Rachel just as I was.

One of the women pulled a little booklet off the only shelf in the small shack and began carefully sounding out the words represented by the strange markings. I stopped to see what she was reading. It was the first book ever written in the Waodani language. As we continued to go through Star's things, the Waodani began to reminisce about how Aunt Rachel had labored to put their "talk" into little marks on paper so they could learn to read the "carvings that marked God's trail."

Kimo's reminiscing went even further back. He started to talk about their first contact with my dad, Jim, Ed, Pete, and Roger. Sitting in a hammock in Aunt Rachel's shack as the jungle night sounds began their haunting nightly performance, I listened carefully to Kimo. Even though it had been almost forty years since my dad had been killed, we had never really talked about that day. I really wanted to know more about what had happened.

∧∨∧∨∧∨∧∨∧∨∧

I remembered standing on the grass-covered bank of dirt that separated our tin-roofed house from the sand-and-gravel airstrip in Shell. That was where I watched my dad take off to fly into the jungle each morning. I always tried to be back there again in the afternoon to watch him come back. It seemed perfectly normal to me that we lived on the edge of the jungle and had a plane in our "garage" instead of a car. I didn't realize how unique our circumstances were until much later.

Actually, my parents' lives had started out fairly normal. My mom grew up in Idaho. My dad's family lived in Pennsylvania. They met in California, where my mom was studying nursing and my dad was in the U.S. Army Air Corps. They had both individually decided that they wanted to make careers of helping people less fortunate than themselves.

They joined a new organization called Mission Aviation Fellowship and were assigned to the little country of Ecuador, which straddles the equator on the bulging west coast of South America. My older sister, younger brother, and I were all born there. To me it was home, and I loved it.

Each morning, Dad would pull his little Piper Cruiser out of the hangar, loading cargo and passengers who needed to reach destinations deep in the endless jungle to the east. Mom would prepare packages of medicine for missionaries who lived with the different tribes in "our" jungle. Along with a hardworking Ecuadorean friend, she would buy meat and vegetables and other supplies and package them for Dad to deliver.

As Dad took off in his little four-place, fabric-covered plane, I would wave good-bye from the dirt bank and then anxiously wait for him to come back, since that was the really exciting part.

When Dad returned each afternoon, he was often loaded with exotic cargo sent by missionaries and members of the various tribes he visited. One tribe, the Shuar, were headhunters. They would cut off their enemies' heads, remove the skull, and then shrink what was left using hot sand and herbs. They called these ghoulish trophies *tzantsas*. They would proudly wear their shrunken heads or display them in their longhouses to prove their skill as warriors. The Quechuas, another large tribe descending from the Inca Empire, were less volatile. However, they, too, had a history of violence and an ongoing hatred and fear of the dreaded "Aucas"—the Waodani.

The word "Auca" started coming up regularly in guarded conversations around our house. And Dad spent quite a bit of time practicing his "bucket drop." He had mounted a reel of heavy cord in the plane where the right front seat had been. The line from the reel fed through a fitting attached to the wing strut. Someone in the backseat, usually Ed McCully, would reel the line out while Dad flew. When Dad circled, while trailing about twelve hundred feet of line, I could see the bucket on the end of the line drop toward the center of the circle Dad was flying.

After about three complete turns, the canvas bucket would hang motionless in the air as Dad's bright yellow plane flew circles around and above it. Uncle Ed would reel out more line, and the bucket would come straight down until it hovered just above the ground. A person on the ground could just walk over and grab onto it.

Dad would then climb or fly wider circles, putting tension on the line. When the person holding the bucket let go, the cord would shoot straight up and then begin a lazy arc until it was again following the plane as it flew off.

Dad had initially developed the bucket drop because there were many small villages in the jungle that had no airstrips. Dad could drop cargo by parachute in those clearings, but the villagers almost never had a radio. He couldn't communicate with them or retrieve anything from them until he invented the bucket drop. He even considered the possibility of actually lifting people who were fatally sick. (He practiced for such an occasion by using my sister's pet dog.) He also experimented with two-way communication by tying a portable, battery-powered telephone into the bucket and using the telephone wire as the bucket line.

I know now that the flurry of unusual activity just before Christmas of 1955 was part of a plan Dad had devised with Ed McCully, Jim Elliot, Pete Fleming, and Roger Youderian to make the first-ever friendly contact with the violent "Aucas." The Quechuas, their historic enemies, called them "Aucas," or "naked ones," because they wore no clothes. The term became synonymous with "savage," because the "Aucas" frequently killed Quechuas who ventured into their game-rich territory. The "Aucas" also raided Quechua villages to steal metal axes and machetes, spearing anyone they encountered in the process.

The killing was not one-sided, however. It was just as common for Quechuas to shoot "Aucas" with their muzzle-loading shotguns as it was for "Aucas" to spear Quechuas. But the ongoing violence was not the only reason my father and the others wanted to reach the "Aucas."

The Shell Oil company had just pulled out of the Ecuadorean rain forest, where they had spent a great deal of effort and money proving that there were significant oil reserves hidden deep beneath the rugged jungle's surface. One of the frustrations that motivated the company's departure was the constant threat of attack on their employees by the cunning Waodani—or "Aucas."

The giant company, with all of its technology and resources, was no match for the spear-wielding jungle nomads whose territory they were invading. In the rain forest, the Waodani had home-court advantage. However, the need and greed for oil made it imperative that Shell—and the Ecuadorean government—find a solution. Rumors were flying that both Shell and the government wanted to do away with the tribe or, at the very least, drive them deep into the jungle and away from the presumably oil-rich territories.

Dad and his friends had grown to respect and love many of the jungle tribes—the Quechuas, the Shuar, the Atshuar, and the barely surviving Zaparos. Motivated by compassion for the little-known "Aucas" and a desire to give them a chance to live, both temporarily and eternally, they decided to attempt friendly contact before these people were exterminated or driven deep into the jungle beyond the possibility of contact.

First they had to find them. The "Aucas" were seminomads, living in small clusters and moving frequently from one part of the jungle to another. This ensured a constant supply of game. It also allowed time for their gardens in one area to mature while they were harvesting and eating from those in another area. But there was another important reason to move regularly. Staying in one area for an extended period made them vulnerable to their enemies within their own tribe.

Dad started making excursions over Waodani territory, which he had always previously avoided. Even at five years old, I knew this was a huge risk. If Dad had a forced landing there and survived the crash, chances were good that the "Aucas" would kill him.

Dad started stockpiling fuel at the McCullys' place in Arajuno. Uncle Ed and his family had moved into one of the Shell Oil company's abandoned bases just on the border of Waodani territory. The Quechuas who lived in the nearby village would visit them during the day, but none of them would sleep or build houses on that side of the river. The McCullys had taken the risk of living there because it was near the oil company's airstrip. They also thought that living on the "Auca" side of the river might prompt these violent people to attempt friendly contact of their own.

After making his regular flights, Dad would pick up Ed, and they would fly up and down the many rivers and streams in "Auca" territory looking for houses. They found one clearing that had been abandoned but had an active garden way up on the northern part of Waodani territory. Unfortunately, it was too far away to be a practical contact possibility. Ed knew there had to be "Aucas" living closer because of the frequent spearing raids made on Quechuas near Arajuno. The Quechuas also frequently found "Auca" footprints around the McCullys' house. The threat was so real that Dad put in a little battery-powered electric fence to discourage "Aucas" from getting close enough to the house to spear someone inside.

One day Dad was flying Pete Fleming and two Quechuas to a Bible conference just south of "Auca" territory. Flying from Arajuno, they had to either fly far out of their way to go around "Auca" territory or take the short-cut over it. Dad uncharacteristically took the shortcut.

About halfway to their destination, the Quechuas started yelling, "'Auca' houses, 'Auca' houses." Sure enough, there was a small clearing below them on a little river. This clearing was only about fifteen minutes by air from Arajuno. This is what Dad and his friends had been looking and waiting for.

Operation "Auca" was on!

I was just a little boy, certainly not part of the planning, but I was my dad's shadow, and I overheard enough to know that this was the big adventure.

I was never scared of poisonous snakes or boa constrictors or flesh-eating piranhas or stingrays or airplane accidents. I regularly witnessed the results of these jungle threats. But an "Auca" spearing was never an accident. Now my "uncles" and my very own dad were going to try to meet these people. I was excited about what was going on, but I was also scared of what might happen.

One day, a week after Christmas, Dad loaded up the plane and flew into the jungle. But this time he did not come back. "Aunt" Olive, Pete's wife, had come to stay with us while Pete was with Dad.

It was not unusual for Dad to spend a night in the jungle. But this time Dad didn't come back for several days. I did not realize he was using Arajuno, where the McCullys lived, as a temporary base. But I knew he was okay, because Mom talked to him by radio each day and marked where he was on her map whenever he was in the air, just like she always did. The names of the places they were talking about were strange to me, but such details did not seem important to me at that age.

They kept talking about "the neighbors," "Terminal City," and "Palm Beach." Johnny Keenan, a new pilot who had recently come to help Dad, was doing all of Dad's regular flying while he was gone. As Mom did the flight following for Dad, she used a different frequency that none of the people in our radio network were using. Kathy and I had been told not to talk about what Daddy was doing. It was all a big secret.

What I didn't know at the time was that there were people who didn't want us to make a peaceful contact with the "Aucas." Simply put, if friendly contact was established, the "Aucas" could no longer be considered savages, and the popular perception that "the only good 'Auca' is a dead 'Auca'" would no longer hold. As long as they could be considered hostile, they could be dealt with more quickly and permanently.

/\·/\·/\·/\·/\·/\·/\·/\

While we continued to go through Aunt Rachel's possessions after her funeral, the Waodani reminisced nostalgically about her and all that she had done for them. Then the conversation turned to my father. I listened closely, wanting to soak up as much information about my dad as I could.

While Aunt Rachel was living, she never asked the Waodani about the events surrounding Dad's death. Aunt Rachel never wanted the Waodani to think that she was trying to figure out who had speared my dad. Dayumae had told her that the people were afraid that if she found out who had killed her brother, others in her family might come to avenge Dad's death. The Waodani divulged some information on their own, but it was always of a general nature, with only the barest of details.

When the Waodani realized Aunt Rachel was avoiding the subject, they avoided it too. But now that we had buried Star, they put the subject back on the table. They had unresolved questions, and so did I.

They told me how scared they had been when the yellow "wood bee" first flew over their village and how a long string had dropped from the plane, leaving presents.

Dad had known that the "Aucas" would probably be scared, so he had cut the handle off of one of Mom's brooms and put a hook into one end of it.

This he attached to the bucket line. When the broom handle with presents tied to it hit the ground, it would fall off, and Dad and Uncle Ed could retrieve the line.

Dad's journal notes tell that on the second or third gift delivery, one of the Waodani rushed out from hiding and grabbed the bucket. "Who was the one who did that?" I asked the Waodani.

"Mincaye grabbed the wood bee string," they replied. He had figured out that if he got there first, he would get to distribute the gifts, making him the "big man."

On one of the gift drops, they said, the wood bee brought them a chicken. Before I could ask what they did with it, Dawa informed me, "Happily we ate it!"

Mincaye informed me, "Receiving an ax head and another ax and a machete and another machete and another, we also received knives, a chicken, aluminum pots—two of them, and ribbons and buttons," Mincaye remembered. "We also got a shirt of white cloth as we had seen a Quechua wearing when we speared him, but we didn't know how to put it on."

The Waodani assumed that if they wanted to keep receiving gifts, they should give some in return.

"We sent to the wood bee a *yoweta* (toucan headdress), smoked woolly monkey meat, some combs, and a parrot," someone told me. I had known about the parrot, because Dad had given it to me for a pet. It had been my companion for a long time.

Dad and Ed McCully had carried out most of the gift drops. The Waodani told me that they figured my dad was the *tempo* one—the oldest and most experienced warrior—like Gikita was for them.

The Waodani asked me if my dad and his friends truly had killing sticks with them. *Why would they ask me something they already know?* I wondered. Pictures and movie footage that Dad and his companions took on Palm Beach showed that they had at least one pistol, a shotgun, and Dad's survival rifle. I was quite sure that each of the five men had at least one gun. But I knew the men had determined that none of them would use the guns against the "Aucas," even in self-defense. They had heard that the "Aucas" were afraid of guns and always ran when a gun was fired. So it seemed prudent to take them. If they had guns, they didn't have to shoot "Aucas," but if they didn't have them, they would have given up the option to use them to scare the "Aucas" if they attacked.

Besides that, guns might be needed for hunting and for defense against other jungle threats.

"Yes, they had *tiamo* with them," I responded, affirming what they already knew. Aunt Rachel and Dayumae had long ago explained why the foreigners had not killed them: "Because they were God followers who knew that although they were ready for heaven, the 'Aucas' were not." But even after all these years, hearing me confirm it once more sobered the Waodani.

/\·/\·/\·/\·/\·/\·/\

Opening the subject of Palm Beach was extremely emotional for the Waodani who had gathered with me in Aunt Rachel's house. It was emotional for me as well. I remembered waiting day after day for my hero to return. After Dad had been gone for a few days, lots of people started arriving at our house. Big planes that I had never seen before landed on our airstrip. But all I wanted was for my dad to come back.

Finally, one afternoon my mom called me into the house and took me into her room. "I'm sorry, Stevie Boy," she told me. "Daddy is never going to be able to come back and live with us again." My world started to cave in as my little mind filled with all sorts of questions.

Why would my daddy not come home? He loved me, and us, just as much as we loved him. Besides, where would he go without us?

"He has gone to live with Jesus," my mom explained.

Oh wow! I thought. That was different. That was what Dad had told me we were looking forward to: one day going to heaven to live with the One who loved us so much that He was willing to die so we could live. I just did not understand why Dad didn't take us with him.

As the years passed, I often wondered what exactly had happened when Gikita, Kimo, Dyuwi, Nampa, Nimonga, and Mincaye attacked Dad and his friends. How, after exchanging gifts for three months, could they still hate the five men enough to kill them?

As a little boy, I had seen pictures of Dad's plane all torn apart on Palm Beach. It seemed to be standing naked and dead on the sandbar. The fabric skin from its wings and fuselage hung in tatters from its skeleton like a maimed bird with one wing resting on the sand. Machete strikes had scarred the metal frame. If they had expended that much energy in "killing" the wood bee, I could only imagine what they had done to Dad and my uncles.

Now, thirty-eight years later, I realized I could ask them my questions. *They* had raised the subject, and it was clear that they had been haunted by questions as well. Now I could finally find out why my dad and uncles had died. Had they actually allowed themselves to be killed so the Waodani could live?

4

Friendly
Friday

Aunt Rachel's death marked the end of an era for us all. The years she lived in Waodani territory were a time of learning and growth, as the Waodani finally began to interact peacefully with the outside world. It was also a time when the Waodani culture of death came to an end.

Certainly, Aunt Rachel had not been solely responsible for the changes that took place during this time. But I knew that no other single person, Waodani or *cowodi*, symbolized the changes more than she did.

Now as the Waodani and I sat together in the days following her death, we all wondered what was going to happen. The Waodani had decided that I should return. In an effort to convince me, they were reminiscing about the times when I had lived with them as a boy. I think they wanted me to remember how close we had been. Smart strategy on their part. After Dad was killed, I learned to love the Waodani's natural and uncomplicated way of living. I think they must have known that they had been a major influence in my life.

It only made sense that I would respect, admire, and love them. Even if I had not naturally been inclined to feel a kinship with them, Aunt Rachel's unreserved affection for everything Waodani would have won me over.

All of us sat together in Aunt Rachel's house, remembering this supremely loyal, stubborn woman who had left her world to become as much Waodani as she could be, considering her vastly different background and complexion. Star had been more than a personality. She was an institution. We were all feeling the vacuum her death had left suddenly in our worlds.

Reminiscing about the old days led to other topics, which finally led to this discussion among the Waodani about what had happened when my dad and his friends had burst into the Waodani's reclusive world and paid with their lives for doing so.

I looked around the room. Sitting with me were Dyuwi, Mincaye, and Kimo—three of the four living warriors who had carried out that spearing raid. Grandmother Dawa, one of two living women who had been at Palm Beach, was also there.

Mincaye asked a question that I'm sure had haunted all of those involved in the Palm Beach attack for almost four decades. I knew they had been given the answer by Aunt Rachel, but I guess they wanted me to verify it. "Why did the foreigners not kill us with their *tiamo*?" I was listening closely, following just enough of the conversation to know what they were talking about. They had been talking animatedly among themselves. Suddenly all eyes were on me. They were expecting me to answer this important question that Mincaye had posed on their behalf.

Before this question was posed, I hadn't understood all of what had been said, but I knew it was something about Nampa spearing one of the men in the back and then that man acting as if he were going to spear Nampa. I asked Dayumae to repeat the question, but even in her broken Spanish, I couldn't quite understand what they were referring to. It seemed to be a crucial dilemma for them, so I started asking them questions, hoping I could help them settle the issue.

This was a big step between the Waodani and myself. Aunt Rachel had told me that we could never ask the Waodani what led to the killings at Palm Beach. Nor could we ask about how it was carried out. She explained that if we did, they might suspect that we were trying to find out who was responsible so men from our families could avenge our Palm Beach losses. Over time, I knew that the trust between the Waodani and us had grown much too strong for those suspicions to survive. I had just assumed that the rule against bringing up the subject still held.

But now I told myself, *Aunt Rachel's rule does not cover someone else bringing up the subject.* As I looked out at the fresh mound of reddish clay covering the hole where we had buried her, it occurred to me that Aunt Rachel was no longer able to interject her thoughts on the matter. As the Waodani tried to clarify their questions for me, I became less reserved about asking questions of my own. With our inhibitions lowered, we were finally able to talk about what had happened and why.

The Waodani had lots of questions, but I was able to figure out that they had four primary concerns:

1. Why did one of the foreigners raise his arm as though he was going to spear Nampa after Nampa had speared him?
2. Why was there no door on the plane so Nimonga could spear the foreigner who climbed into the plane after the spearing started?
3. Why was that foreigner trying to eat something in the plane during the attack? Surely it was strange even for foreigners to stop to eat when they were being attacked.
4. Why did one of the foreigners stand on a log and call to them instead of fleeing so he could live?

For the most part, these questions left me even more confused. I needed more information. I needed to know what had preceded these actions of my dad and his friends if I hoped to answer the Waodani's questions. Many of the connecting details were missing.

I knew that the people had wondered where the wood bee came from four times each moon to give them gifts. They told me they decided to go look for its living place. They could see that it always flew toward the place where they believed the spirits of the foreigners congregated: somewhere in the direction of the Quechua village where the Waodani periodically speared people in order to steal precious metal machetes and axes.

To find the wood bee's nest, a whole delegation of the Damointado clan hit the trail, traveling northeast toward Arajuno. They crossed the Tiwaeno River, then the Ewenguno River, and finally, by midafternoon, they made it to the Tzapino River near where Gikita now lived. There they spent some time spearing fish to smoke for food for the rest of their trip.

While they were spearfishing, they heard the wood bee making its distinctive noise. But it wasn't ahead of them; it was behind them, someplace in the Ewenguno River valley gorge. As they listened, it got higher and higher, and its sound became clearer and clearer. Then it flew off toward Damointado, and they could no longer hear it.

They decided to head back toward the Ewenguno River the next day. It was too late to try making it there the same day unless they were willing to be on the trail after dark. The Waodani don't like to do that; it is dangerous to walk jungle trails at night. They believe snakes, large predators, and evil spirits are more active at night and more difficult to avoid.

The next morning, the little band that included Mincaye, Nampa, Nenkiwi, Mintake, Gimade, and a few others arrived at the Ewenguno shortly after the mist was rising above the ridges. They were trying to decide how to find the wood bee when they heard it coming toward them from the same direction they had just come from. First it flew over them in the direction of Damointado. Then it returned.

It came back much lower this time, and they figured it was going to find a beach to land on. Sure enough, it did just that. They could hear it buzzing a short distance up the river, and most of the group took off through the jungle so they could find it before it flew off again. I figured that they must have gone off in a hurry with no planning or discussion about what they would do if they found the plane. Mincaye told me he had gone off to have a bowel movement, and they just went off and left him. Of course, planning and organization never have been Waodani traits, so I wasn't surprised at this part of their story.

When they rounded a large bend in the river, the group found the place where the wood bee had landed. The group, hidden from view, peered out of the jungle and saw the bright yellow wood bee sitting on the sand on the far side of the river—the side toward Damointado next to a big slough full of swamp palms.

I had always wondered why the group of Waodani had appeared on the north side of the river when their village was on the south side. Now I knew. I wondered, though, how they could have heard the plane all the way over on the back side of the steep ridge. Then I remembered reading something in Dad's journal about how he had decided to circle high over Palm Beach to see if he could view Terminal City from that location. That must have been the day the Damointado search party was out looking for the plane's nesting place. They would have been able to hear the plane as it circled.

Looking through the cane that still grows thick on the frequently flooded banks of the Ewenguno River, the group saw the five foreigners walking around the plane.

Suddenly, Gimade said in a typical Waodani huff, "If I can't marry, I'll just go over there to the foreigners and let them kill me." She wasn't bluffing. Gimade was like her mother, Akawo, and her older sister, Dayumae. They were all feisty and willing to step out from the crowd. Dayumae had certainly done it when Moipa speared her father and she fled to live with the outsiders.

I realized that this was a critical piece of information about what had prompted the friendly contact on Friday, January 6. Dyuwi had been promised Gimade as his wife. But now I realized she had wanted to marry Nenkiwi. No doubt, if Dayumae's sister was supposed to marry Dyuwi, one of his sisters was probably promised to her brother, Nampa. That would have given Nampa reason to object when Nenkiwi wanted to take Gimade for himself. I was beginning to understand how everything fit into place.

As Mincaye answered my questions and told me more of the story, he explained how Nampa had said, "I, too, will go to the foreigners." But then Nenkiwi said, "No, *I* will go also to the foreigners." As Mincaye explained how Nenkiwi had contradicted Nampa, he was clearly nervous, even after all these years. Waodani etiquette doesn't allow one adult to tell another adult no. That kind of confrontation could be settled only one of three ways: Nampa could give in and lose face, Nampa could kill Nenkiwi, or Nenkiwi could spear Nampa.

At Nenkiwi's insult, Nampa turned and headed for Damointado in a rage. The others in the group followed, except for Nenkiwi, Gimade, and Mintake. Old Mintake realized that now the gauntlet had been thrown down. Nampa and Akawo had said no to Gimade marrying Nenkiwi. If they were left alone, everyone would assume that the marriage had been consummated. Then there would be no way for Nampa to overlook Nenkiwi's insult. Besides that, it might well have jeopardized Nampa being given the wife intended for him. And, of course, that would leave Dyuwi without a wife while Nenkiwi had two, in addition to the two he had already had.

So Mintake stayed with the couple to act as a chaperone.

From the other side of this dramatic story, I knew that my dad and the other fellows on the beach had been waiting for the Waodani to find them. For three days they had waited, calling out the few Wao-Tededo phrases Dayumae had taught them into the seemingly empty jungle.

By this time, Aunt Rachel had been living on the jungle hacienda with Dayumae for several years. Jim Elliot had waited until he knew Aunt Rachel would not be there and then trekked over to talk to Dayumae about these phrases, which Dad and his friends considered critical to letting the Waodani know they were coming in peace. Aunt Rachel could have easily taught the men these phrases, but then she would have known they were planning contact with the "Aucas." Dad was sure she would have felt a responsibility to tell her superiors what he, Jim, Ed, Roger, and Pete were planning. And he was worried that they would feel a need to tell government authorities, who might well try to stop them.

On Friday morning the five young men waiting on Palm Beach were surprised to hear a male voice suddenly call to them from across the river. They looked in the direction of the voice and saw Mintake and Gimade standing just outside the cane on the sandbar.

It was obvious that neither one of them was male, and yet they were sure it had been a male voice they had heard. Then "George," as they would nick-name Nenkiwi, stepped out of the jungle. As I listened to Mincaye retell the story, I understood a little detail now that had not occurred to me before. Nenkiwi had stepped out of the jungle behind the two women because he wanted to see if the foreigners' reaction predicted a peaceful encounter or a violent one. If the foreigners looked like they were going to attack the women, Nenkiwi would flee. If the foreigners shot guns at them, the women's bodies would protect him.

To Waodani men, it makes sense to let a woman walk ahead of them. If an enemy is laying an ambush for a man, or if there is a poisonous snake on the trail, it is always best to have a woman clear the way.

The five men started up the beach to meet the small delegation of "Aucas." But then it must have occurred to them that maybe it would be best if they did not all barge out onto the river to greet the trio. Better not to take any chances of frightening them.

From pictures taken by several of the five men, as well as movies taken with my dad's sixteen-millimeter movie camera, it is clear that this historic event appeared to be as casual as an everyday get-together between people from different planets could have been.

Several of the five men documented the day's happenings in their journals. From these accounts, I had been able to piece together many of the details of what had happened. Now, with Mincaye's additional information, I was finally able to answer many of the things I had been wondering about.

The two groups were unable to talk with one another. One of the men remarked in his journal that Gimade talked a blue streak. He called her "Delilah," probably because she seemed to be provoking sensual interest from Nenkiwi like the biblical Delilah provoked from Samson. Mintake mostly hung back by the fire, enjoying the strange food that the foreign men shared with her: lemonade, peanut butter sandwiches, cookies, and other treats not found in the Waodani "grocery store."

Nenkiwi was mesmerized by 56 Henry. He tried to talk to it but found that it wasn't alive. He tried to talk to Dad about it, but Dad could not understand what he was saying. Finally, while "Delilah" rubbed her bare body on the plane's smooth fabric and inspected it, Nenkiwi climbed into the cockpit. He wanted to go for a ride.

As a pilot who has done quite a few landings and takeoffs on unimproved strips, I know Dad must have been hesitant to take Nenkiwi up in the plane. Dad had no way of explaining to Nenkiwi why he shouldn't touch the controls. Nenkiwi would have to sit in the backseat since Dad had taken out the right front seat, along with the copilot's control stick, in order to save weight and to make room for the prefabricated tree house and other materials they needed on the beach.

Besides Dad's concern over making unnecessary takeoffs and landings on Palm Beach, he surely would have assumed there was also the danger that Nenkiwi would get violent and hurt Dad or distract him during the critical tasks of taking off or landing. Operating an airplane from a soft six-hundred-foot strip surrounded by towering jungle left no room for even a slight wrong move or a second of distraction.

On the other hand, Dad knew the plane might be a way to establish rapport with "George." So he decided to take Nenkiwi up for a short flight. When they were safely back on the beach, Nenkiwi was excited but not yet satisfied. He would not get out of the plane and kept insisting on something that Dad could not understand.

Dad finally figured out that he wanted to fly over to Damointado. Knowing now that Nenkiwi was embroiled in a major controversy with the others who had gone back from the Ewenguno River to Damointado, I realized that flying over the village was probably Nenkiwi's way of raising his standing in the clan. Being seen in the foreigners' wood bee would be the equivalent of adding another *tempo* notch in his spear. When they got over the village, Nenkiwi started climbing out the open doorway and shouting to the people in the clearing below. They must have realized it was Nenkiwi, because Dad wrote that everyone in the clearing started running around excitedly.

When they landed back at Palm Beach for a second time, Nenkiwi got out and started giving Gimade and Mintake a dramatic account of what he and Dad had just done.

But Gimade seemed antsy. She tried hard to communicate with the five fellows on the beach, but they couldn't understand her. It seemed that perhaps she was a bit upset by Nenkiwi's enthusiasm about his flights in the wood bee. In midafternoon, Gimade went off into the jungle. Nenkiwi left at about the same time.

My guess is that they had decided to ditch Mintake, because by late afternoon they still had not returned to the sandbar. Dad took off with Pete late in the afternoon and headed for Arajuno. He didn't dare risk losing the plane and their ticket out of Waodani territory if the river flooded during the night.

Ed, Jim, and Roger climbed up into the tree house for the night. Mintake camped out by the fire under the tin shelter on the sand. The men had given her a blanket, which must have seemed luxurious to her. When the three men in the tree house woke up the next morning, Mintake was gone. But the coals from her fire were still warm, so they knew she had been there until first light. I had always wondered if she left the blanket or took it with her. I know that the Waodani concept of "borrowing" is not like that of outsiders. As a boy, I borrowed things from my *iñanani*, but they seemed to think I was upset when I returned the things to their owner. Apparently, they expected me to keep what I had borrowed. I have also had experience lending things to Waodani, thinking it was a temporary transfer of use. It usually became apparent that they were just thinking *transfer*.

Nenkiwi was speared later that same year, as closely as I can tell from what the Waodani have related to me. They aren't very concerned with timing of events. Gimade died in childbirth years after I first went to live in Tiwaeno. So I can't ask either of them what went on after they left the beach.

I do know, however, from our conversations after Aunt Rachel's funeral, that the next day they were on the trail back to Damointado and ran into a group coming to find out about the *cowodi*. Nampa and Akawo were in the group. As soon as Nampa realized that Gimade and Nenkiwi had been alone together, he blew up and started talking "wild." It was clear that there was going to be trouble within the Gikitaidi clan. Nenkiwi knew he had crossed the line. He had given both Nampa and Dyuwi reasons to spear him, so he tried to redirect the group's animosity away from himself.

"The foreigners attacking us, we had to flee," Nenkiwi lied. Akawo and Dawa just laughed. They challenged his testimony, saying, "If the foreigners wanted to kill you, why didn't they just do it when you were in the wood bee?"

But Gikita took Nenkiwi's side. He began to remind the people of all the instances in which foreigners had killed Waodani. The ancient ones had even told them about a place where outsiders had taken some captured Waodani and made them work on the gum trees. He told them that foreigners ate human flesh, which explained why they had such light skin. And the foreigners had a little house from which horrible sounds could be heard, he said. Blood would seep out from under the board walls in that terrible house.

I couldn't imagine what Gikita could have been referring to, so I asked Mincaye to describe it for me. It sounded like it might have been a diesel engine or something similar that was leaking red lubricating fluid.

The Waodani are no different than any other humans in conflict. Everyone sees his or her own side of the issue. The Waodani didn't classify outsiders. They were all *cowodi*—not quite human. In their minds, a dead foreigner was the only safe foreigner. And there were plenty of foreigners who thought the same of the Waodani.

From the Gikitaidi clan, Dayumae had gone to the foreigners' place and had never returned. Nemonta had seen her father harpooned in the Todobodo River by Quechuas while she watched from the foliage on the Waodani side of the river. Others had been shot by oil company employees.

But the five wood bee foreigners did seem different. They had given and accepted gifts. They had entered Waodani territory without doing the people any harm. Nenkiwi said they had attacked the party of three, but it was clear that at least Nenkiwi and Gimade had not been hurt. The little group who caught them together on the trail had every reason to believe that Nenkiwi and Gimade had just gone off to be together, without Mintake.

Strangely, only Gikita seemed to accept Nenkiwi's preposterous story. Nenkiwi was a known troublemaker. Now it seemed he was threatening to destroy the one peaceful contact the tribe had ever had with *cowodi*. Mintake could settle the issue, but Nenkiwi said that she, too, had fled from the foreigners. He said she had just used a different trail to flee on.

The group seemed content to wait for Mintake to verify that Nenkiwi was speaking *ononki*—without reason. But Gikita kept reminding the group that foreigners had always hated and killed Waodani. "If we are going to spear, let us spear the foreigners," Gikita said.

I am convinced that Gikita did not believe Nenkiwi. He had not become the oldest man in the tribe by being easily deceived. But he also, no doubt, felt that they had no choice. If they speared the foreigners, Nampa and Dyuwi would have an opportunity to vent their anger, and the bad blood between them and Nenkiwi might be remedied by bleeding the foreigners.

I remembered a story Kimo and Mincaye had told me of a planned spearing raid downriver. The spearing party got themselves all worked up until they were furious and ready to kill. But as they trekked to the place where they planned to ambush their enemies, they ran into a herd of fat *odae*—wild pigs. "Spearing the *odae* and smoking lots of meat, we came back from spearing," he told me. Apparently once they had speared the wild pigs and had meat to eat, their anger was gone.

As Gikita led the group back to Damointado, he continued to talk, working up the men's natural anger at foreigners until it exceeded their fear.

Fear and hate are very much the same in every respect except in what they motivate one to do. In Waodani society, the secret to staying alive was to convert fear to hate, which motivates one to kill rather than flee. Waodani warriors always worked themselves into a frenzy of hatred before setting out to spear people. When their hatred for their enemies reached critical mass, they would carry out their spearing raids. But once the deed was done, that extreme hatred quickly turned to blind fear. Even while their surviving enemies were fleeing from them, they were often fleeing themselves—back to their clearing, where they would burn their own houses and scatter, trying not to leave tracks for the avengers to follow.

I had never heard of a retaliatory killing taking place immediately after a spearing raid. So why would they burn their houses and flee to another part of the jungle? It seems to me that the real reason for the perpetrators to flee when they had the upper hand was irrational fear emanating from unreasonable hatred. That was the Waodani way of life. They lived to kill and die.

Surprisingly, in between these two occurrences, many of them seemed almost happy-go-lucky. Of all the Waodani killings I have ever heard about, only the psychopathic killer Moipa did not become afraid after he killed. He would use his victims' fear to recruit them to help him kill others. Instead of burning his house and abandoning his gardens, he would eat from his victims' gardens and use their clearings to stage his next killing raid.

The pieces to the violent puzzle that had wrenched my hero from me at such an early age were fitting into place. Now I knew *why* my dad and our four friends had been killed, but I still did not know *how* Gikita, Mincaye, Dyuwi, Kimo, Nampa, and Nimonga had carried out the attack that changed my life forever.

5

Did They
Have to Die?

I desperately wanted to ask how my dad and uncles Jim, Roger, Pete, and Ed had actually been killed. Gracia Burnham, whose husband, Martin, was killed by terrorist rebels in the Philippines in 2002, was quoted by news networks as saying, "[Martin] was a good man, and he died well." I wanted to know if the men who defined most of my world had died well. At the same time, I was hesitant to find out details about how they died. I knew it would be a gruesome tale. I had heard plenty of Waodani killing stories. It would also be emotionally devastating to hear details about how these kind, loving men, who had become family to me, had so cruelly and irrevocably destroyed my life as a little boy.

I didn't have to ask. Once the subject was opened, the Waodani who had stayed behind with me after we buried Aunt Rachel just kept talking. It almost seemed like the ultimate catharsis for them to finally be able to openly discuss—with someone from the other side with whom they felt safe—what they had done. This is the story they told me.

When Gikita said, "If we are going to spear, let us spear the foreigners," the group turned around and headed back to their Damointado village. Gikita kept up a litany of atrocities that outsiders had perpetrated against the Waodani.

He had plenty of material to work with. It is true that the "Aucas" had speared plenty of Quechuas living along their borders for reasons as inconsequential as stealing a machete or a knife. They also killed anyone they found invading their tribal territory. But outsiders were as willing to kill "Aucas." The very term "Auca"—*naked savage*—attributed almost animal-like status to the Waodani. Quechuas, colonists, adventurers, rubber hunters, oil company workers, and maybe even conquistadores had killed these nomadic jungle dwellers without feeling any need to justify their atrocities. My dad and his friends knew they would be risking their lives if they tried to contact the "Aucas," but they believed that if they didn't, outsiders would inevitably destroy these people who had never had friendly contact with the outside world. Dad, Jim, Roger, Pete, and Ed believed they had a responsibility to give these people a chance to go on living, both temporally and spiritually.

More than once I've been asked whether the "Aucas" were actually in serious danger of being wiped out. They were. By their own admission, they were on the verge of killing themselves into extinction. And there was also the threat of being annihilated by outsiders.

Just recently, I received a letter from the wife of a Shell Oil company pilot documenting the oil company's and the Ecuadorean government's involvement. She included an article written by her husband that detailed deadly encounters between Shell Oil and the "Aucas."

Captain Johns wrote, "In this remote section of the world, murder by the Aucas was just another everyday occurrence. It had been going on for years. Twenty-one of our people, not to mention the many colonists and their workers, were brutally killed by these vicious aborigines who roamed the jungle like wild animals, strip-stark naked with the exception of a skimpy G-string." He continued his narrative, describing what happened when the company began building their airstrip at Arajuno—the very place where the McCullys would later live and where "Operation 'Auca'" would be launched.

"Though vigilant armed guards were posted, the workers lived in daily fear; and it was for good reason, for the savages, as everyone was well aware, would wait for hours, even days, watching for an off-guard moment to strike their adversaries. Their method of attack was complete surprise, kill, and retreat immediately.

"The stumping of trees and building of the airstrip progressed for many weeks without incident. Then one afternoon at approximately 3 p.m., it happened!

"Auca warriors descended suddenly and swiftly from a small wooded hill east of the runway. They pounced upon the startled workers with such cunning accuracy, thrusting their dreaded barbed lances through the running, screaming victims, that even the guards were dazed from the sudden, violent attack."

Johns went on to describe how three victims, "Klinger, the foreman, and two workers, José Chacon and Jorge Cadena, pinned to the ground with two to three spears in each mutilated body," were killed in that raid.

Johns also recorded that the violence was not one sided. "The mounting loss of human life, taken by Auca raids, caused much controversy in Quito among government officials. Several dignitaries, including President Velasco Ibarra and the Ministerio del Interior, visited Shell Mera, our base camp. It was my assignment to fly them on this special mission over Auca territory for them to evaluate, as they put it, future strategic defenses against our formidable foe."

Captain Johns wrote that the official Ecuadorean government position was not to retaliate against the "Aucas" except in self-defense. I have seen documents, however, that suggest there was another less formal government policy that included trying to wipe the Waodani out or drive them deeper into the Amazon rain forests, away from their ancestral lands.

I have read and heard countless other stories about Waodani atrocities and killing habits. Most of them were obviously contrived by people who did not know what they were talking about.

Most people who write about the Waodani don't know them. Captain Johns, on the other hand, obviously knew what he was talking about. As I read further into his account, I was surprised to find that he had actually been part of a group that was attacked by Waodani. He was flying one of the company's planes over Waodani territory when he had trouble with one of his engines. He made an emergency landing on a river in Waodani territory to make repairs.

Johns's account continues. "I entered the cockpit to try out the starboard engine. It purred like a kitten, and I gave orders for everyone to come aboard. Sexto was standing in the front hatch, holding the plane against the balsa raft by taking up slack in the rope when, suddenly . . . Auca warriors swarmed out of the jungle, screaming their bloodcurdling yells as they heaved, with all their might, their deadly barbed spears.

"I saw one swish over Sexto's head as he ducked down into the hatch. In the next instant the lance was shattered by the swirling propeller that slammed pieces of the broken spear into the water and against the side of the hull with resounding force. As I turned to see if everyone was aboard, I heard another spear slam against the rear of the plane and then a heavy thud and an anguished moan, 'Dios mio.'"

One of the passengers had been speared in the chest. Another spear penetrated the plane's fuselage and dangled there until the increasing airflow tore it loose. The plane survived. The passenger, Bericimo Acebo, did not.

But the part of Johns's account that interests me most is that he was an eyewitness to the fact that oil company employees, perhaps with the blessing of the government, committed atrocities against the "Aucas." The *cowodi* were not always innocent victims on the receiving end of Waodani attacks.

Johns wrote, "Through the months that followed, it was one hit-and-run raid after the other against the seismograph parties that had penetrated deep Auca territory." Then he documented a retaliatory raid against the "Aucas." He had previously mentioned that some oil company people had talked of bombing the Waodani.

"It was early morning, low ceiling with solid overcast, as I turned the nose of the G-21 to the usual heading for the river and our daily reconnaissance flight over Auca country. Some twenty minutes later, as we passed over the Rio Curaray [Ewenguno River], not far above the trees, I could not believe my eyes. The large Auca house near Arajuno was in shambles. It had been blown to smithereens, its remnants burned and charred. The pilot and his cohorts had made good on their boast!

"As to how many survived the explosion, it was never known. But it was easy to reason that the survivors would spread the word to the other Auca tribes (clans) throughout the jungle.

"Several months went by, and all was quiet. And then one of the most brutal raids in Ecuadorean history took place! I find it difficult to find adjectives strong enough to describe it in its fullest. The Capricho raid was one of the cruelest, most vicious, most cold-blooded of them all!"

ʌ·ʌ·ʌ·ʌ·ʌ·ʌ·ʌ·ʌ

The Waodani sitting with me in Aunt Rachel's little rustic house went on to tell me that while Kimo, Dyuwi, Nimonga, Nampa, Gikita, and Mincaye were making "man-killing" spears, Mintake finally showed up. When she was asked to confirm Nenkiwi's accusations that the five foreigners had attacked Gimade, Nenkiwi, and herself, she derided them for believing such an obvious lie. She told how Nenkiwi and Gimade had snuck off into the jungle to be alone. "Didn't we eat their sweet food and drink their foreigners' drink?" she scolded. "Have they not given us many presents that we all have seen very well? Did I not sleep by their fire with a warm cloth they gave me? Now, why are you going to spear them for no reason?"

As I thought about Mintake's words, I was sure everyone knew Nenkiwi was lying to direct animosity away from himself. But old Gikita, the only truly *tempo* member of the group, would not let the younger men back out. This was happening during the "moon," or month when the *dagaenga* fruit was ripe and the rivers were at their lowest. They could expect to be raided at any time by the downriver clans they had speared the year before. If either Nampa or Nenkiwi speared the other one, the retaliatory vendetta killings would badly weaken the clan just when they needed to be strong against imminent attack.

Early the next morning, the six warriors, along with Dawa, Miimo, Akawo (Nampa's mother), and Mintake, headed for Palm Beach with machetes and spears. When they got to the sandbar, the women went upriver to the head of the beach to act as decoys, with the purpose of separating the five men. Gikita, along with Mincaye, Dyuwi, and Kimo, approached the sandbar near the base of the tree house, directly in from where Dad's plane sat on the sand. When three of the four women stepped out from the cover of the jungle foliage, two of the foreigners started walking toward them. The Waodani described them as the "biggest one" and the "smallest one." I assumed that Jim was the "biggest one," because the Waodani measure big in terms of strength rather than height, and the "smallest one" would have to be Pete.

Nimonga and Nampa quietly shadowed them, keeping out of sight behind the dense border of jungle growth along the flanks of the sandbar. Gikita told his three fellow attackers that he would spear each of the other three men (Dad, Ed, and Roger) first, and then the three younger warriors could finish them off. It seems clear to me that Kimo, Dyuwi, and Mincaye were probably afraid of attacking five foreigners who had guns, in broad daylight. Nampa was not as reticent. He had been insulted by Nenkiwi, who had then publicly defied him by leaving camp with his sister Gimade. Although Nampa's fury was not directed at the five foreigners, he wanted to kill someone in retaliation for his rebuke by Nenkiwi. The foreigners would have to do.

Gikita grabbed his bundle of spears and gave the signal for the attack to begin. He started to charge out onto the beach in typical, explosive Waodani fashion. But in the process, he slid on a slippery log hidden under the jungle floor vegetation. He fell, and his spears banged into the log, making a terrible racket. Dyuwi, Kimo, and Mincaye realized that surprise, their only remaining advantage, had now been lost. They told me that the men on the beach, hearing the clatter of Gikita's spears, turned to see what had made that noise. They turned to flee, but Gikita grabbed his spears and yelled, "Let's kill them or die!" charging out from hiding onto the beach.

At the same time, Nampa and Nimonga charged onto the beach from behind Jim and Pete. Nampa speared Jim through the abdomen from the back.

As I listened to the Waodani describe in such great detail something that had happened almost forty years earlier, I couldn't believe they remembered specific details after so many years. But for the Waodani, killing was a matter of life or death. They told stories of their spearing raids over and over, like football teams reviewing past games against strategic rivals. The best way to predict how future victims would react to their spearing raids was to study how past victims had reacted. But these five foreigners had not followed typical victim responses. First of all, none of them shot the attackers.

Kimo asked, "Nampa spearing the biggest one, he clawed at his side like a *gata* monkey that has been shot with a poison-tipped dart. Why was he doing that?" Jim clearly had been speared through his abdomen from the back, so it didn't make sense for him to be clutching at his side. He had to have been doing something else. "Turning, he raised his hand as if he was going to spear Nampa in return; but he had no spear," they said. When Jim turned toward Nampa, Akawo thought he was going to spear her son. She slashed at him with her machete and then grabbed his upraised arm so he could not do whatever he was planning to do to her son.

"Grabbing the foreigner's arm, Nampa fell on the sand like he was dead," they remembered. By that time, Nimonga had speared Jim also. "What happened to the smaller foreigner?" I asked. "Running into the river, he crossed to the other side," they answered.

Then they started to describe what was happening at the other end of the beach, by the plane. They said Gikita speared my dad first because he was the one they always saw in the plane and "he was the oldest one."

When Gikita speared Dad, they told me, one of the foreigners grabbed

Gikita so he couldn't spear Dad anymore. I assumed this must have been Roger. He was a veteran of the second World War and had been under enemy fire at such hot spots as the Battle of the Bulge. It would take great resolve to grab an adrenaline-pumping, spear-wielding Waodani warrior instead of giving in to instinct and shooting him. That sounded like Uncle Roger.

"Not being able to spear that foreigner while he was holding Gikita, we cut him with the machete." They showed me where Roger had been slashed from his shoulder, diagonally across his back, with one of the machetes that the five had recently given to the Waodani.

About this time, I was beginning to wonder if they really accurately remembered what had happened. I was having trouble reconciling what I was now hearing with two pieces of information Aunt Rachel had overheard and passed on to me. The first one was that one of the five men ran and got into the plane when the attack started. I was sure that was my dad. Why would any of the other men run to a delicate, fabric-covered plane? They couldn't fly it, and it certainly would not have offered any protection. The other bit of information that did not jive with this account was that Uncle Roger had not been slashed on the back with a machete. One of the most poignant pictures taken by the search party shows Roger's body being pulled behind a canoe, facedown in the river, with a spear protruding at a shallow angle from his hip. Frank Drown, the leader of the search party, had told me himself that he knew it was Roger's body because he was the only one wearing blue jeans. I remembered seeing in the picture that his back had not been slashed in the manner the Waodani were describing.

At this point in the incredibly emotional story, Mincaye asked a question that made everyone quit talking. Up to this point, in typical Waodani fashion, three or four people had been simultaneously telling their own stories in a commotion of descriptive words, punctuated by dramatic sound effects of spears hitting flesh, guns going off, the yells of the attackers, and the cries of the men being speared.

"The foreigners, being speared, one of them ran to the wood bee and started eating something. Why, being speared, would he be eating?" The very suggestion sounded preposterous. Mincaye showed me how my dad—I assumed it was him, anyway—leaned into the door of the plane, grabbed something in the palm of his hand, and seemed to take a bite of it. That is when it occurred to me that it hadn't been my dad after all.

I had always wondered how Uncle Roger had been speared in the back with the spear running parallel to his body rather than perpendicular to it. Having hunted with the Waodani and knowing how they use their spears, I could not figure out how someone could be speared the way the canoe picture indicated. Someone almost had to have been standing in a hole for the spear to enter the way the picture showed. Now I finally realized what had happened.

The man in the airplane was not my dad; it was Uncle Roger. He had been speared while he was leaning into the plane. He must have been trying to use the plane radio to let Mom or his wife, Barbara, know what was happening.

That meant that my dad could have, in fact, been the first one speared by Gikita. The pieces of the puzzle were finally falling into place. Uncle Roger hadn't been the one to hold Gikita back. When the search party had found Ed's body, only his clothes were keeping his body from separating into two pieces. Quechuas in the search party had told me that he had been cut with a machete—in exactly the same place the Waodani had just described to me.

I explained to the Waodani that the foreigner in the plane was not eating but probably trying to talk into the radio. I could see on their faces that they suddenly realized now what should have been obvious to them before. They had all held a radio microphone in their hands as one holds an apple to take the first bite.

With what seemed like an intense yearning, they asked me a new question: "Babae, all other wood bees having doors, why did your father's not have one?" Dad had left the door off of 56 Henry to make it easier to get cargo in and out of the little cockpit. He also needed the door off if he wanted to drop gifts. I tried to explain Dad's thinking, but I had no idea why the Waodani cared about the door. They explained.

"If your father's wood bee had a door on it, the one who got in the plane would have lived." That seemed unlikely to me. A sharp chonta-wood spear would have gone right through that flimsy door without even slowing down. But the Waodani explained to me that if there had been a door on the plane, Nimonga would not have speared Roger. I still don't fully understand their reasoning, unless they thought the plane was a spirit, in which case they would have hesitated to spear Roger if they had to spear the plane to get to him.

They sadly shook their heads. They still thought it to be almost miraculous that they managed to kill all five of the foreigners. In their new way of thinking, they wished desperately that they had not been so successful on that fatal day.

I still wasn't sure why Jim had been clawing at his side after he was speared. I asked them to show me exactly what he had done and which side he was grabbing at. They were all sure that it was his right side. I vaguely remembered seeing a picture in which one of the men was wearing a pistol and holster on his belt. The holster had a snap-down cover on it. That had to be it. They told me that after he clawed at his side, he raised his arm as if he was going to spear Nampa. At the same time, they heard a gun going off, but none of them saw Jim or Pete holding a shotgun or rifle. *Because it was a pistol,* I realized. Nampa must have been grazed by a bullet that temporarily knocked him out. I asked them several times to tell me, "Truly, truly," if Akawo grabbed Jim's arm before or after Nampa fell on the beach.

All those who had been there vehemently agreed that, "First cutting him with the machete and then pulling his arm down, *then* Nampa fell on the beach." I knew Nampa had been grazed by a bullet. That, and the fact that Dawa, who was too scared to watch the attack and stayed hidden just out of sight, had been hit in the leg by a nearly spent shotgun pellet, had let the Waodani know that if the foreigners had wanted to shoot them, they could have.

I finally asked who killed my dad. I knew he had been slashed in the face with a machete and had been speared multiple times, but I wondered who had been the one to deal the final blows. Frank Drown had told me that he probably died from a spear that entered his right temple. He mentioned that the tip of the spear had broken off in Dad's head.

Several years ago, my dad's brother Sam died. His daughter told me he wanted me to have a spear that had been found in Dad's body. She gave me several but did not know which one it was. When I got them home and was alone, I finally looked at them closely. It was hard to do, but one of them caught my attention. The tip had been broken off. I noticed a speck of white near the tip. I examined it closely and saw that it was a tiny fragment of a New Testament that had been taken from the beach. It is customary for Waodani warriors to decorate the spears they are going to use on their enemies with something that belongs to that enemy or something that would be associated with that enemy. There was little doubt that I was actually holding the spear that took my dad's life.

As soon as I asked who had finished killing Dad, I regretted asking. I had only been worried that *I* might not be able to handle the answer, but now it occurred to me that whoever it was might not be able to deal with having me know.

No one answered my question, but everyone looked at Mincaye. The most agonizing look I had ever seen crossed his dear, handsome face. Now I knew. I'm glad I know, but I wish he didn't know that I know. I don't think I could have loved my own father any more dearly than I have come to love *Maemae Mincaye.* What is more, I can't imagine that my own dad could have loved me and Ginny and our children and grandchildren any more than our adopted grandfather does.

The Waodani had one more burning question for me, and then we were all anxious to change the subject. One of the men who had not been part of the spearing party asked me, "All the other foreigners being speared, the smallest one got to the far side of the river; what about that?" *What about what?* I wondered. "What did he do?" I asked. Another warrior answered, "Not fleeing, he just stood there and called to us, 'We see you well; why are you spearing us? We see you well; why are you spearing us?'"

I knew that the men had learned the phrase, "Biti, miti punimupa." I think they were actually trying to say something more like, "Bite emite waa ponemopa"—*You yourselves well, we are thinking of you.* I don't know how Pete would have known to say, "Why are you spearing us?" but they seemed sure that was what he was saying.

But that was not what the Waodani wanted to know. Their question was, "Being on the far side of the river, why was he not fleeing?"

"Surely fleeing, you would have just tracked him down and speared him anyway?" I said. I meant it as a question, but I know the Waodani are all expert trackers. Even I could probably track someone wearing tennis shoes.

The Waodani said, "Baa"—*No.* One of the warriors told me, as though he was revealing a dark secret, "When we speared, first we were furious. Then, having speared, we were afraid. The foreigner going to the far side of the river, we were already afraid. If he had fled just a little, surely he would have lived."

I could see the pain on their faces. They were all wishing that at least one of the five had survived their hatred. I think they would have liked to have been able to explain to at least one of the men that they had gone to spear them because hatred was the only way they knew to live then. As Mincaye says, "We acted badly, badly until they brought us God's carvings. Now, seeing His markings and following His trail, we live happily and in peace."

It is only my conjecture, because none of us can know the will of God, but I think it fit God's plan that all five men died. I know that might offend some who have a narrower opinion of the parameters within which God must operate, but I don't think what happened to my dad and his four friends caught God by surprise. Nor do I think God simply allowed it. No, after learning in detail what happened on January 8, 1956—while I was so anxiously waiting to see the speck of my dad's little 56 Henry airplane appear over Penny Ridge—I believe God was much more involved in what happened than merely failing to intervene.

Pete could have fled. If he had, the Waodani said they would not have followed him. One of the men could have climbed up into the tree house and called from there on the extra radio to let the world know what was happening. Dad could have gotten into the plane and taken off. Kimo, Dyuwi, and Mincaye could have run away like they started to do. What if the only beach in all six thousand square miles of Waodani territory had not been near a Waodani village and right on a commonly used hunting trail? The Waodani probably would never have found Dad and his friends. What if Nenkiwi and Nampa had not been feuding? What if it had not been January when Gikita was expecting a raid from the downriver part of the tribe? It is unlikely that he would have been willing to risk their once-in-a-lifetime—no, their once-in-all-time—chance for friendly contact with the outside world, just to keep Nampa or Nenkiwi from spearing the other one.

There are too many factors that all had to work together to have allowed the events to happen as they did. Too many for me to believe it was just chance. I have come to the conclusion that God did not look away. He did not simply allow this to happen. I think He planned it. Though this has not been an easy conclusion to come to, I believe it is the right one.

I have personally paid a high price for what happened on Palm Beach. But I have also had a front-row seat as the rest of the story has been unfolding for half a century. I have seen firsthand that much good has come from it. I believe only God could have fashioned such an incredible story from such a tragic event.

I could not begin to record the thousands of people who have told me that

God used what happened on Palm Beach to change the course of their lives for good. Besides, it is enough for me that because Mincaye killed my father, my family now has the privilege of loving him and being loved by him. And because my dad and Jim and Ed and Pete and Roger were willing to die, Kimo and Dyuwi and Gikita and Ompodae and Tementa and Gaba and Odae and Tidi and Dawa and Cawaena and Coba and Gaacamo and their children and their grandchildren and their great-grandchildren and many others will all have a chance to live. If I could go back now and rewrite the script, I would not change a single scene. I have come to understand that life is too complex and much too short to let amateurs direct the story. I would rather let the Master Storyteller do the writing. I don't say that casually. What happened to Dad was extremely traumatic for me, but even so it has not been the most difficult event in my life.

6

What We Do for Love

It was time to go home. After burying Aunt Rachel and spending several days with my jungle family, I felt some confusion about where home really was. I had been born and raised in Ecuador. During college, my first extended time living outside Ecuador, I began to realize that I wasn't like everyone else. I looked the same and I spoke English without an accent, but I knew I was different.

As a kid, when we would arrive in the United States from Ecuador, I would look out the windows of the old piston-engined Pan American airliner as we made our approach into Miami. I could see huge highways lined with late-model cars. There were neon signs everywhere. In the terminal you could buy a "stateside" candy bar and real root beer right out of a machine. The people around me seemed to take these things for granted. I determined that I would never get used to it, and to a certain extent, I haven't.

But as much as I missed the "good life" when I was in Ecuador, I quickly learned that I also missed the "real life" when I was away. In Ecuador, life was slower. People really got sick, and when they died, we saw them dead—not all dressed up, their cheeks rosy, lying in a beautiful bed made of oak. The market didn't just have food in it, it smelled like food too. When we bought chicken, we had to cut off its head and pluck it ourselves. When we saw someone we knew on the street, we didn't just say hi and keep on going. We crossed the street, gave him a big *abrazo* (hug), and spent some time finding out how he and his family, and his business, and the rest of his life were.

Where was home for me? When I was a kid, I didn't exactly know whether the United States or Ecuador was where I really belonged. But when that old question began to haunt me out in the jungle after we had buried Aunt Rachel, I realized that the deciding factor was Ginny.

We had met in Ecuador after college. I had just returned to South America and was trying to figure out where I belonged. A short time after returning, I was asked to act as tour guide for a singing group sponsored by a Swedish Covenant church in Minnesota. I was asked to accompany them to the jungle, one leg of their tour. Ecuador is sometimes called the Switzerland of South America because of its beautiful snowcapped mountains. However, over half of the country is actually covered by dense Amazon rain forest. Few people know this half of the country. It is a mysterious world of emerald green beyond roads and beyond the reach of those who have not been trained in its ways.

The night before we left for the jungle, the singing group gave a concert in the capital city of Quito. At the concert, I sat with the missionary woman whose husband had organized the tour. I knew Mrs. Kelly well. She was the mother of a good buddy from school, and she was usually quite reserved, even shy.

But this night she was in rare form. She, along with most of the group, was of Scandinavian descent. All during the concert, she kept telling me what great wives Scandinavian girls made. "They can milk cows in the morning and then dress up and look stunning at night," she assured me. She was acting so out of character that I was perplexed. But when she suggested that I should pick one of the girls to marry, I was really shocked. Finally, to get her to leave me alone, I jokingly told her I would marry the girl who was singing a solo part at that moment.

The next day, when I showed up to start my duties as tour guide, Mrs. Kelly marched me over to one of the tour buses. From about ten feet away, she pointed to a young lady sitting at one of the bus windows and informed me that she was the girl I had chosen.

Mrs. Kelly had her arm extended, index finger aimed right at Virginia Olson. I could feel my face flush. But when the young lady turned toward us, my heart did something it had never done before. I should have looked away to prove I wasn't party to this overt intrusion, but I couldn't bring myself to do it. Over the next three days, I fell "face-forward in love," as we say in Spanish.

You can think you're in love and not be, but you can't be in love and think you're not. Everything around me seemed suddenly clearer. Colors were brighter. I found myself disinterested in all but one thing. I wanted to be with Ginny. Thirty-two years, four children, thirteen moves, three continents, a precious gaggle of grandchildren, and five businesses later, I still feel more alive inside when I am with Ginny. My heart still does funny things when I'm around her. Yes, home is where Ginny is; and now it was time to go home.

I called Ginny from Quito to tell her I was out of the jungle and to let her know that I had decided to keep Aunt Rachel's apartment in the city. Aunt Rachel had used it while she was recovering in Ecuador from cancer surgery she had undergone in the United States. When I finished talking to Ginny, there was a long silence on her end of the line.

Somehow, women have an uncanny intuition about coming change. Maybe it is just that Ginny has lived with me for so long. She somehow knew that my mind was in turmoil about something. I had no intention of even hinting over the phone at what the Waodani had told me to consider. But Ginny figured it out.

It is embarrassing to admit, but it took me years to realize that Ginny not only has a good head and a heart that is sensitive to God's leading, but that God can direct her just as He does me. I knew I couldn't make a decision this momentous without Ginny's input. Our four teenagers would no doubt want to weigh in on the decision as well. Although I had not made a decision, Ginny knew something was happening, and I could tell by her uncharacteristic coolness that she was really scared.

When I landed in Orlando, the nearest major airport to our home in Ocala, Florida, Ginny was there to meet me. She kissed me, but it seemed more of a chore than heartfelt relief at having me home safe and sound. She was still the girl of my dreams, but there was a wall between us now.

I knew I had to start tearing down this invisible barrier. Unfortunately, I made the mistake of trying to talk it down when I should have just shut my mouth and held Ginny in my arms until it melted away.

"Really, Ginny," I started in. "I haven't made any decision, either in my head or in my heart, to move back to Ecuador, regardless of what the Waodani think they want. I don't even know if they are serious about it. Maybe it's just a small group of Waodani who want me to go back. If that is the case, it would be useless for me to even consider going back. They said they want me to teach them to fix teeth, cure sickness, repair outboard motors, establish their own source of medicine, and start their own school.

But if what they really want is just one more person to give them things, then I wouldn't go even if I wanted to. Even if they insisted that they wanted me to be a part of that, I couldn't."

I loved the Waodani too much to be a willing party to the destruction of their independent and self-sufficient way of life. I had watched these "nomads of the rain forest" become practically a beggar society. The blame was partly "outsiders" who introduced medicines, metal tools, and other goods and services that the Waodani wanted but could not provide for themselves. Part of the blame was the Waodani's, for being so willing to sit around and wait for outsiders to do things for them instead of working to figure out how to do it themselves. But for me, the important issue was not who was to blame. For me, it was the pain of watching the process take place. I didn't think I could change their slide down the slippery slope of dependence. I definitely didn't want to be part of that.

I sounded convincing to myself. But Ginny could tell that my thinking had progressed even further than I thought it had. She could tell that my head was still evaluating the Waodani's request, but my heart was moving south.

"I don't think you realize it yet, but you are going to want to move back to the jungle in Ecuador, and I don't think I can!" Ginny told me.

At the time, I couldn't imagine the depth of Ginny's despair. She simply could not imagine trying to be a mother and a wife in a place where she couldn't understand the language, where she had to hunt and gather the "groceries," and where she would have no appliances or electricity to run them.

Ginny continued, "When your dad's plane suddenly appeared after all these years and you showed me that little Piper nameplate, I knew something was going to happen. I didn't know what it was then, but I do now."

I thought about my dad's plane and how excited we had been just a few months earlier when the Waodani had found 56 Henry and I had gone to help them salvage its precious remains.

∕·∖∕·∖∕·∖∕·∖∕·∖∕·∖∕·∖

I had driven down to meet Aunt Rachel at the airport in Orlando when she came to the United States for cancer surgery. She had learned of her illness years before, but she chose to ignore the diagnosis until it weakened her enough that she could no longer live at home with the Waodani. Now she wanted to get well so she could go back to the jungle, even if only to die there.

After living with the Waodani for so long, Aunt Rachel had become very much like them. When I met her at the airport, she didn't waste any time with polite greetings. Instead, in typical Waodani fashion, she skipped traditional North American small talk and gave me some information that stunned me.

"The Waodani radioed Quito from Toñampade this morning and told me that they found your daddy's airplane!"

How could that be? More like a member of the family than just a machine, 56 Henry had been left "dead" and stripped naked on Palm Beach. I remembered the pictures in the *Life* magazine article that came out on my fifth birthday, January 30, 1956. On one page was a picture of my dad, very much alive, standing in front of 56 Henry with a big smile on his face. He was holding a feather headdress and handmade comb that the "Aucas" had just given him in exchange for the gifts he and Uncle Ed had delivered to them via the bucket drop. On the next page, side by side, were the crushing pictures of the remains of good old 56 Henry on the beach and my dad's body caught on a snag in the river like so much flotsam.

The plane's remains had disappeared within days of my dad's death. There had been no question in my mind about what had happened. The river had flooded, as it did on a regular basis. The rushing torrent had dragged the carcass of that fragile little plane off the beach. I was sure that after almost four decades, whatever was left of 56 Henry had been reduced to flakes of rusted steel and bits of aluminum. I imagined that these plane particles had been spread and buried across hundreds of miles of riverbed between Palm Beach and the Atlantic Ocean on the other side of the continent.

I asked Aunt Rachel for more details, but she had told me all she knew. She couldn't tell me how much they found or where they found it. All she knew was that Cawitipae and his wife had been poling up the river, returning from fishing and hunting for turtle eggs. His wife found a strange, hollow stick protruding from the sand. Curious, they tried to pull it loose but couldn't. They could wiggle it freely, but they couldn't pull it out, so they dug down to find out what was holding it. There they found the remains of Dad's plane.

I made a phone call to Ecuador to see if I could get details and learned that a significant portion of the cabin fuselage had been found. I tried to imagine what it looked like but couldn't. The next day, joined by my brother, Phil, and my second son, Jaime, I was on my way to Ecuador, armed with metal detectors and enough excitement to keep us awake for days.

In less than twenty-four hours, we landed at the little airstrip in Toñampade, way out in the virgin Amazon jungle where Dad had found his Palm Beach airstrip in "Auca" territory.

Dayumae, her husband, Komi, and a group of Waodani met us at the plane and then led the way to a thatched hut beside the airstrip. There we found what we were looking for. From a distance it looked like just a bunch of rusted, brown tubes stuck together in a jumbled mass. But as we approached, I could see what Cawitipae's wife had seen protruding from the sand. It *was* a hollow metal tube—56 Henry's control stick.

The Mission Aviation Fellowship pilot who had flown us into the jungle reached out and touched the joystick.

"Just think," he said. "The last person to hold this stick was your dad."

The seat supports, landing gear, and lower fuselage—from the fire wall where the engine attached to the rear of the cabin area—were pretty well intact. In fact, the bungee cords, which were simply a bundle of rubber bands sewn into a fabric housing that served as shock absorbers on early fabric airplanes like this Piper PA-14, were still in place. They even had some snap left.

I noticed the pedals. Dad used those to steer the plane. Attached to each rudder pedal was an independent brake that worked one of the plane's front wheels. I pushed one of the brakes, engrossed in the incredible realization that this was the same plane I had watched carry my dad out of my life when I was a little boy.

When I pushed on the brake, it moved. As it did, a little bit of brake fluid shot out of the broken brake line. I couldn't believe it. And I couldn't wait to find more of old 56 Henry, so we headed down to the river. When the Waodani saw how excited my brother, son, pilot friend, and I were about the discovery, they dropped what they were doing and joined the shovel-wielding salvage operation. We hoped the sand that had once been Palm Beach would yield more of this precious discovery.

Our metal detectors indicated the presence of ferrous metal in numerous locations on the beach. We fell to digging with enthusiasm, and before long, we discovered more fuselage tubing. It turned out to be the mounting structure for the backseats of the plane, and it fit with the parts Cawitipae and his wife had found. However, in spite of all our enthusiastic efforts, we didn't find much more.

Weary from our long trip, lack of sleep, and finally coming down from the extended adrenaline rush that had kept us practically bouncing off the walls, we decided to head back to the village, almost a mile away.

As I walked along the beach with Coba, one of my boyhood friends, his son walked with us. Suddenly, the boy reached down into the shallow water at the edge of the beach and grabbed for something. I saw a flash of silver and thought he had grabbed at a fish. He reached out his hand to Coba and asked, "Does Babae want this?"

In his hand was a little trapezoidal piece of aluminum with five letters embossed onto its delicate surface—*PIPER*—the nameplate from Dad's plane! That settled beyond any shadow of a doubt that this was, in fact, 56 Henry itself.

As I held that little piece of aluminum in my hand, I felt like I was reliving history. It would be difficult to overstate the significance of Dad's little Piper. Even its registration number (assigned by the U.S. Federal Aviation Administration) seemed fated to predict its status as a symbol of twentieth-century missions: 5156—the plane took five men to die in the first month of 1956. This piece of aluminum had been stamped in a press, making the letters stand out. The background had been painted black. After almost forty years in a wild and moody jungle river, that precious nameplate looked just like it did the day I last saw Dad taxi his little plane over to the airstrip and out of my life. I couldn't believe it; even the paint was still intact. This unlikely discovery, after so many years, was a miracle, and I knew it.

/\/\/\/\/\/\/\/\

Ginny was right. When Coba had handed me that little piece of metal, I knew it was more than a wild coincidence. I knew something was happening, and I could feel God's hand in it. I hadn't thought of this when the Waodani startled me with their demand that I return to live with them, but Ginny had.

She was right—finding 56 Henry had been the first step in the process of making me receptive to the major upheaval that was about to change the rest of our lives.

My heart may have already turned the corner about going to live with the Waodani, but my head was still struggling to make sense of what it would require: giving up my business career in order to try to help my jungle family out of a virtually impossible situation. I had been successful in business, and Ginny and I had always spent a lot less than we earned. In the last few years, I had been making more than I had ever dreamed possible. If the Waodani needed someone to help them, I could afford to pay someone to do it. But I had tried that excuse, and they made it clear that they wanted more than that. They wanted someone who had a relationship with them and loyalty to them. They didn't want me to send someone; they wanted *me*.

The more we talked about the decision, the more desperate Ginny became. She simply could not imagine how she could be a mother in a hut in the middle of the Amazon jungle.

That raised another major issue: What would our four children think about going to live in the rain forest?

Ginny and I have always been open with our kids about almost everything. We display our affection for each other quite liberally around the house. And when we have a fight, we don't hide that either. We also let the kids know about our finances and other earthly aspects of our lives, from the time they could barely comprehend those kinds of details.

The day came when I decided to tell Shaun, Jaime, Jesse, and Stephenie what we were considering. But then something happened that made me hesitate. I was just getting dressed when I heard Stephenie scream from the living room. It was not unusual for Steph to be overly dramatic, but this sounded urgent. I rushed out of the bedroom, thinking maybe she had fallen with a glass and gashed herself or something. But when I reached the living room, she was standing on the couch with one hand over her mouth and the other arm above her head like she was warding off an attacker.

Crawling across the living room carpet was a palmetto bug, which is a type of large cockroach. My heart sank. If Steph thought Florida bugs were menacing, she would have an immediate coronary in the jungle. Down there we would have real cockroaches that could measure almost six inches in length. There are beetles that fill the palm of your hand and grasshoppers that you could make a meal of if you were really, really hungry.

In spite of my hesitation, I told all four of our children what we were considering, "though it is just a remote possibility," I assured them. The result was mystifying.

"All right, let's do it," Jesse immediately responded. Shaun and Jaime thought it was a great idea as well.

Stephenie, however, was the real surprise. She squealed and then clapped her hands together five times really fast, a nerdy thing she often did to irritate me or get my attention. When I gave her "the look," she grabbed me and started dancing around. "Yes, yes Papa, promise me we'll go. I don't fit around here anyway, and life is sooo boring." This from my almost-fifteen-year-old daughter who thought cockroaches were life threatening?

I could not have imagined then that in less than a year Jesse would be asking if he could take off on a five-day jungle trek with no one but a young Waodani friend or that I would have to tell Steph that she couldn't keep a vampire bat as a pet.

7

Thatched Huts and G-Strings

I knew that if we agreed to what the Waodani were asking, it was going to be a gigantic transition. We would be moving from the tail end of the twentieth century back to the periphery of the Stone Age. But we still had not decided if we should pack up and move to the jungle. First, Ginny and I would need to make at least a short visit to the jungle together to verify that the Waodani were really serious. I also wanted them to realize that taking responsibility and authority over their own futures was going to be almost as traumatic for them as it was going to be for us to help them do it. And I needed to give Ginny a chance to see if she could face the incredible upheaval all this would mean in our lives.

Thinking about what Ginny might face on our upcoming visit made me think back to my first entry into the mystical and magical world of the Waodani rain forests.

/\/\/\/\/\/\/\/\

My first visit with the Waodani when I was nine years old was incredibly exciting. I had heard Aunt Rachel and Mom talking about it. "I think it is safe for a male to come in and stay now," Aunt Rachel told Mom. "They know that they killed Stevie Boy's father, and several of the men might worry that he will want to avenge Nate when he grows up. But the majority of them are convinced that we don't want vengeance. Most of them have given up their vendettas, so they can understand that we have done the same thing."

I could not believe that my mom, who was scared to even let me have a pellet gun, would actually allow me to go live with Aunt Rachel. Out there, I would be surrounded by people who might want to kill me so I wouldn't kill them later on. I was surprised, but I wasn't going to say anything. I couldn't wait to go.

We drove down from Quito to Shell, where we had lived when Dad was alive. It was exciting just to be back on the edge of the jungle. But going deep into the jungle was even more exciting. We weighed ourselves and our baggage at the hangar where the JAARS (formerly Jungle Aviation And Radio Service) plane was kept in Shell. We would fly into the jungle in a Helio Courier, a short takeoff and landing (STOL) airplane that uses really short airstrips. We were going to need it. I had flown into lots of jungle strips, but I had never seen one as short as the one in Tiwaeno, where Aunt Rachel now lived.

When I looked down at Tiwaeno from the plane, all I saw was a narrow clearing near a few thatched huts. It just looked like a big tree had fallen over and knocked down a narrow strip of jungle as it fell. Most of the clearing was actually the little airstrip, which measured about six hundred feet in length. But with trees on one end and a drop-off into a river at the other end, it appeared impossibly short from our vantage point. I remembered my dad describing this kind of a landing: "It's like parking a car in the garage at seventy miles an hour," he would say. It seemed to me that dropping out of the sky onto a postage-stamp sized clearing would be an appropriate start to my great adventure.

As we headed toward the tiny opening in the trees, something on the plane's wings began to make a banging noise as if it was going to fall off.

"Don't worry about that," the pilot assured me. "It's just the slats coming out because we are slowing down. *Tell Aunt Rachel,* I thought. *I'm not scared. If it flies, I want to ride in it—or fly it.*

When we were safely on the ground, the pilot taxied in front of one of the thatched houses and shut down the engine. The pilot stayed close to the plane. I figured that Aunt Rachel didn't want him to get too far away in case he had to make a quick exit. But I did not know what I was supposed to do after I got out.

Aunt Rachel must have gone to the pilot's side of the plane. I could not see her, but I did see a whole bunch of Waodani standing nearby. When I took a couple of steps toward them, several young kids started to scream and ran away. The older people laughed nervously, talking a mile a minute—about me, I supposed. They seemed to be intrigued.

I was intrigued myself. Most of the people checking me out were completely naked. I didn't notice the strings they all wore around their waists. A few men had on little shorts, but one of them was wearing the shorts on his head. A couple of the women had cloth wrapped around their lower bodies like skirts, and a few others had blouses, but no one seemed to have both.

Every culture has its own rules of modesty. Back then, in the early sixties, Ecuador had few, if any, public restrooms, even in the cities. It was common for Ecuadorean men from the lower classes to urinate right in public, even in the capital city. The women were not self-conscious about nursing babies anywhere, anytime. And they did not worry about covering their breasts while they did it. But most Ecuadorean women were very modest about other parts of their bodies, careful to always dress very conservatively.

The Waodani had a totally different sense of modesty. I was about to learn that modesty, for them, was not about being naked but about how one acted when naked. They had a carefully defined cultural taboo against sexually provocative behavior. Besides, they weren't really *undressed*, since they had never been dressed in the first place. They lived naked. This was their natural costume.

Both men and women wore only a multiple-stranded string around their waists. I found out later that women could wear theirs around their legs if they wanted to, because the G-strings served no obvious purpose for them as they did for the men. The men used the strings they wore to hold their uniquely male anatomy in place. I still don't know if this Waodani custom served any purpose in terms of modesty. I do know that it served a practical purpose, one that any man would understand if he had to run quickly through the thorn-infested jungle while completely naked.

The group of Waodani that met our plane in Tiwaeno was actually dressed up for the occasion. They were wearing all the clothing they had. To me, they looked pretty naked. I would normally have been self-conscious about staring, but they were looking me over pretty carefully, so it seemed to be okay. Somehow I just felt at ease with them.

It did make me feel bad that most of the children were obviously scared of me. They apparently thought the black rings around my eyes that extended behind both ears were growing out of my face. The older people seemed to be perplexed by other features of my anatomy.

I had white skin, like Star, and white hair, like Woodpecker's daughter. I even had hair on my arms and legs. At nine, I was not much shorter than some of the Waodani adults, but I had no outstanding physical attributes of either a man or a woman yet.

The group decided to send old Miimo over to check me out. In the Waodani culture, the *piquianani*, or "old ones," held a special place. More than anything, I think they were considered fortunate just to have lived to old age in a culture so violent and earthy that surviving to even thirty qualified a person as "old." Everyone in the tribe had to carry his or her own weight, hunting and gathering food and then preparing it. When they reached an age where they couldn't contribute, their existence became tenuous. The Waodani had no concept of retirement and no mechanism for supporting old people who no longer worked. Old women were unique in another way. They posed no threat to anyone, nor could they help defend the community against the threat of violence from others. So they were considered quite dispensable.

That was probably why the welcoming party by the plane sent Miimo over to check me out. If I took offense at what they wanted her to do, well, they were only risking old Miimo.

Miimo walked up to me and pulled at the hair on my arms as though she thought maybe it was just lying there and not really attached. Then she felt my glasses and discovered that they weren't growing out of my head. Everyone laughed as if that was what they had thought all along, but it sounded like they were relieved. Then she began to feel the hair on my head, rub my ears, and look at my strange yellow-green eyes.

Finally, the group egged her on to what they quite obviously were most curious about. She patted my shirt to see if there was anything special under there. If I was a girl, I was either young and very tall or a late bloomer. But maybe I wasn't a girl at all. My muscles weren't well developed for a boy my size in the tribe, but if I was one, it would be easy enough to verify. That is just what Miimo had in mind. She grabbed the elastic waistband of my pants, pulled it out, and looked inside.

We were both embarrassed; I, because a total stranger was looking down my pants, and old Miimo, because I wasn't wearing a G-string. No male my size would be caught dead without a G-string.

Miimo let everyone know that I was skinny, white, and male. The ice was broken. The Waodani broke ranks and surrounded me in welcome. Now everyone was pulling my hair, smudging my glasses, and patting me. But I held on to my pants. I had had all the inspections in that region that I could handle. Dayumae's mother, Akawo, went into her house and came back with a soft, cottonlike ball of string. Miimo had obviously made known her discovery of no G-string. She wanted to be sure that no member of 'her' family was out in public without being properly dressed.

Looking back now, it seems that I was immediately accepted into the Tiwaeno community. Dayumae had adopted Aunt Rachel as her sister long before. That made Akawo one of my tribal grandmothers and old Gikita a great uncle. Dawa became my closest grandmother. Mincaye, Dayumae's cousin, seemed to take a special interest in me right from the start. He lived so close to Aunt Rachel that I could hear him telling stories at night as he lay in his hammock and I was on my cot. I would quietly call his name at night and he would respond with "Woooo" or with a little whistle, meaning, "I'm listening." After I had been there a short while, he even told his boys that I could use his blowgun, a Waodani warrior's prized possession. I knew I was beginning to belong.

Mincaye decided one day that I needed a tribal name. He decided I should be named for Dawa's older brother, Babae. Many of the Waodani are named for jungle creatures. Mincaye, for example, means "wasp." I wish I had known that when someone behind me on the trail ran past me, excitedly calling, "Mincaye, mincaye." I stopped to see why he so desperately wanted to catch up with Mincaye, only to painfully realize he wasn't running to Mincaye. He was running from a swarm of angry *mincayes* that had been stirred up by our passing.

When I asked what *babae* meant, the Waodani simply said that old Babae was an Aenomenani warrior who had killed a lot of people. Babae, with the first *a* nasalized, sounds like their word for "wild." I think that is where the name came from, and it would fit their description of my namesake. But if you don't nasalize the *a*, it means "lie," as in "liar."

Now that I had a G-string, a name, and an instant tribal family, it was time for fun.

Waodani life is centered around a few special places. One of them is the cooking fire, for obvious reasons. Another is the river. The Waodani love to be clean, usually bathing at least twice a day. Besides that, they often get into the river to fish with long spears. And they frequently butcher their meat there. The water is also the best place to cool off and get away from biting insects if the Waodani don't want to be in their smoke-filled longhouse.

Several times each day, my friends would yell, "Babae, aepae pantatae gokimba"—*Babae, water swimming, let's be going.* They would then promptly run to the ten-foot-high Tiwaeno riverbank, just a few feet from the village houses, and jump into the river. I wanted to be like my Waodani friends, but somehow I always felt the need to change into my bathing suit first. I didn't feel comfortable just tearing off my shorts and T-shirt to go skinny dipping in public like they did.

When the tribe realized that I was going to put on special *weicoo*—cloth— just for swimming, they all wanted to watch me change.

The walls of Aunt Rachel's house had been made from large bamboo trunks that had been split with a machete. These crude walls had about as many gaps as they had solid places. If anyone wanted to see what was going on inside, he simply had to peek through the wall.

So every time we went swimming, my friends would call to everyone in the village to come see Babae *duranibai*—without clothes. For some reason, it never bothered me to have an audience watching me change clothes through the wall of my bedroom, but I could not bring myself to go outside the house naked. I'm sure the Waodani thought this was strange.

The modesty thing was indicative of substantive differences among the three cultures I had grown up in. I remember when the plane brought Aunt Rachel's Sears catalog. My new Waodani friends and I looked through it. When we got to the underwear section, I knew I should probably skip some pages, but I didn't. I just assumed that the Waodani boys would be curious, just as I was. But they weren't. Then it dawned on me. Why should they think anything of seeing girls wearing just underwear when we were surrounded by a whole tribe wearing nothing?

I was being exposed to a lot of new things in the Waodani world, but I was young enough that I didn't think through most of them. I simply absorbed and accepted the Waodani way of life and grew to love it. As an adult, I have often thought about the things that the Waodani culture taught me to view in a different light: issues such as nudity, polygamy, the spirit world, generosity, the dangers of competition and materialism, and the extreme value of relationships.

All of those subjects that the Waodani treated in their own unique way affected me as I grew into adulthood. The one that most caught my attention, however, was the contrast between the relationships of boys and girls in the tribe and those same relationships in my North American world.

Back in the world I had come from, nine-year-old boys were just starting to discover girls. There was a great deal of pressure to figure out how to talk to these strange creatures who giggled and twittered to get our attention. In the Waodani world, however, boys didn't even seem to know that girls existed. Boys and girls didn't talk to each other unless they were brothers and sisters. And they didn't do things together. It wasn't like they had to stay away from the opposite sex. It was more like boys didn't realize girls existed, and vice versa. As I look back now, I realize that in the world I had come from, most of a boy's interest at that age in girls was simple curiosity. Girls were like caterpillars in the rapid process of morphing into butterflies. The Waodani world left nothing to wonder about. It happened out in the open, right in front of everyone. No sneaking and peeking necessary. This natural approach also saved Waodani parents from needing to have any kind of "facts of life" talk with their pubescent children.

I was also fascinated by other aspects of everyday Waodani life. On a typical day, the Waodani men would wake up just before sunup and announce from their hammocks what they were going to do that day—no calendars, appointments, or meetings for them. And definitely no time clocks to punch. Usually they would just announce that they were going spearfishing or hunting, specifying what they were going to bring home to eat that night. I was awestruck by their keen knowledge of the natural world they lived in and their mastery over it. Sometimes men in the tribe, especially Mincaye, would take me hunting with them. But these men were serious hunters; their stamina on rugged trails was incredible. Even little Waodani kids never seemed to tire.

It was exciting to go with the adults and watch them spear wild pigs and other animals. They were always on the lookout for fruits and honey, they could catch fish with their bare hands or with small nets, and they were always animated. They never seemed to tire of teaching me how to do what they did so naturally. But going with them was also exhausting and painful. There were times when I got so hungry and tired I just wanted them to go off and leave me.

The boys my age were getting to the stage at which they preferred to hunt by themselves. They were trying to prove their ability to function on their own, since some of them would be married about the time I was just getting started in high school. I'm sure they were amazed at how difficult it was for me to follow animal tracks, use a circle of vine to climb incredibly tall trees with no branches, and follow a trail. I felt like a clumsy baby most of the time, but I tried to make up for it at night. I couldn't read tapir tracks on mud trails, but I could read the "signs" on paper that Aunt Rachel was trying to teach the Waodani to read.

School in Tiwaeno was purely voluntary, and it was always a social event. A group of Waodani would come to Aunt Rachel's house when it got dark and there wasn't much else to do but sleep. By the light of Aunt Rachel's candles, the men would whittle darts while the women made string or wove mesh bags and fishing nets. While everyone was working, Aunt Rachel would try to teach them the sounds represented by the strange markings she was making on a little blackboard.

At night, I would sit in the middle of the "class" and tutor the friends who had been my teachers during the day. After a little practice, I could read the literacy primers that Aunt Rachel and Dayumae had created. I could read it, but I could not understand it. So I would teach everyone the sounds and words the strange markings represented, and the Waodani would teach me what the words meant.

I really wanted to master the skills necessary for living in the jungle. The Waodani wanted to master reading so they could study for themselves what Aunt Rachel was translating about the outside world. They especially wanted to read the stories and information about *Waengongi's* creation of the world and how to follow His trail. Their ancestors had taught them that when they died, they would come to a boa constrictor on the afterlife trail. They believed they would have to jump the boa in order to continue on the trail. If they failed, they would turn into termites. The idea that the Creator had

marked His trail for people to follow and that He had sent His own Son to
jump the "boa" for us was intriguing to many of them.

Many of the Waodani wanted to learn to read so they could find out about
how to live with *Waengongi* when they died and, in the meantime, how to
live with foreigners. They built a special hut they called *Waengongi onco* or
"the Creator's house," where they could gather to hear about *Waengongi* and
discuss His teachings.

The Waodani church building was a small thatched hut that sat on stilts
and had no walls. This design allowed whatever breeze there was to flow
through the building when it filled with people and assured us of good lighting during the day. It also provided the congregation with some entertainment during long "talking times," because tame birds, monkeys, and other
exotic pets would regularly join us.

During the service, the women would make string and weave net bags
while nursing their babies or even an occasional pet. The men usually
whittled blowgun darts or had young people inspect their hair to remove lice
eggs. While the people talked about *Waengongi*, I usually had one or two
people picking irritating grass chiggers out of my legs with thorns or darts.

On one of my earliest visits to the Waodani, Aunt Rachel and Dayumae
had just finished translating the book of Mark into Wao-Tededo, the
Waodani language. It was ready for distribution to those who had learned to
read the foreigners' markings.

The JAARS plane came in, bringing a missionary couple from Wycliffe
Bible Translators and boxes of precious little books. The Waodani knew that
the arrival of the books with markings in their own language made this a
special occasion. Those who had clothes brought them. When it was their
turn to climb the notched log into the elevated church hut, those with clothes
would nonchalantly put them on. I couldn't help but imagine that happening
in other churches I had visited. I imagined how people getting dressed corporately in the vestibule would change the traditional formality of the typical
North American church.

Then the Waodani began to celebrate. They were excited. Very few of
them could read God's carvings, but they knew that the markings on the thin
bark in these little books could lead them along the very good trail that
Waengongi's Son, *Itota*, had marked for them. I didn't know it at the time,
but more than three decades later, I would translate for Mincaye as he

explained the significance of that trail and God's carvings to hundreds of thousands of *cowodi* in the United States, Canada, and Europe.

"We acted badly, badly," he would tell the foreigners, "until they brought us God's carvings. Then, seeing His carvings and following His good trail, now we live happily and in peace."

On the far side of the little, crude platform under a thatched roof, my brother Phil was cradled on Kimo's lap. He had his arm lazily draped over Kimo's powerful shoulders and was pulling at the big hole in one of Kimo's ears, where he sometimes wore a large balsa earplug. It seemed totally natural that Phil and I should be there with the people who killed our dad while Aunt Rachel and Dayumae distributed the Good News that our dad and his friends had died trying to deliver.

/\/\·/\·/\·/\·/\·/\·/\

Now Ginny, Shaun, Jaime, Jesse, and Stephenie might learn to live in the world that had claimed my heart as a boy. I went to sleep at night and woke up early in the morning contemplating what we would need to get done in order to join the Waodani in their world.

It would have been fairly easy to move into Aunt Rachel's house, next to Komi and Dayumae, in Toñampade. But I knew that would never work. Toñampade had become to Waodani territory what Tijuana and other border towns are to Mexico. It was the gateway through which the most deviant and dangerous outside influences entered Waodani culture. Although it was part of Waodani territory, it was not representative of Waodani culture or most of its people. I considered Toñampade to be the seedy underbelly of Waodani communities. I think most Waodani thought of it as "the big city." It did, after all, have a population of between two and three hundred people, which was a huge community by Waodani standards.

New Waodani communities typically start when a couple of families have conflict with other families in their community. Or they may decide that the hunting is no longer good in a certain area. Sometimes, they simply become restless.

Many Waodani communities now have small elementary schools with one or two outsider teachers. Some teachers exert a fair bit of influence in those communities; others very little. But Toñampade had a full high school with many buildings and numerous outsiders serving as teachers and administrators.

In the days before Waodani communities had schools, they were quite nomadic. Usually families would form an alliance with another family, and they would live together for mutual benefit and protection. Most of these alliances were based on some relationship between the parents, but sometimes the families stayed together just because they got along well, as with Mincaye and Nimonga.

A two-family group would find a place in the jungle where they felt safe from their enemies and where the fishing and hunting were good. A second family couplet would often start a clearing within about a half hour's walk. I am no anthropologist, but it seemed to me that this gave each family grouping a place to flee from the frequent spearing raids that characterized the old culture.

The Waodani seemed to start new communities without much hesitation or planning, but it wasn't an easy process. In order to build a community where people from other family groupings could come to get medicine and medical attention, borrow tools, and learn to fix their few outboard motors, the Waodani would need to settle in a central location.

The Waodani are extremely egalitarian; people are free to do what they want, how they want, and when they want. Even today in their territory, there are no laws, no property ownership, no building codes, no taxes, no police, and no courts to enforce laws even if they existed. I knew that the Waodani were picking up some nonbeneficial ideas from the outside, however. Most communities had begun selecting presidents. They didn't vote, really; they just agreed that this person or that one would serve. The president of the community didn't necessarily have a formal function or authority, but people could use the president as an excuse to do or not do something as they desired. If someone did not want to have the community airstrip lengthened, he could say, "But the president has not said yes to this." Or if they *did* want the airstrip lengthened and wanted to pressure someone else in the community into helping with the work, they could say, "The president saying yes to this, why aren't you helping?"

The more I thought about what the Waodani were asking me to help them with, the more I realized that it would have to be started in a new location. They were asking me to help them learn the skills and develop the economy necessary to take care of their own needs. This was going to be a major undertaking. I knew that it could not happen in an existing community with a dominant family in place. To be successful, some Waodani were going to have to work for the good of the tribe, at the expense of their own family and clan. Such a new idea needed to be planted in a new village free from the control of any given family.

To start a new village, we would have to clear virgin jungle, build houses, and start gardens. Then we would have to build an airstrip. In the rugged rain forest of Waodani territory, this would be a huge undertaking that could take a couple of years or more. But without an airstrip, we would have to walk or canoe in and out of the community. We would have no access to medicine, no mail, and no efficient way of getting supplies.

I didn't know how long it would take to do what the Waodani wanted me and my family to help them do. I was quite sure that they assumed we would stay like Aunt Rachel had—until we died. In fact, one of them had even said to me, "Your father being buried here, and your 'mother' (Aunt Rachel) being buried here too, I say we should bury you here too!" This old warrior would have had plenty of scalps on his belt, if he had had a belt. Hearing him say he wanted to bury me would have made me nervous, had I not known and loved him since boyhood.

I did know that in order to really help the Waodani, we couldn't stay more than two or three years. Doing so would only compound their dependence on outsiders. Looking back over the years that Aunt Rachel had lived with the Waodani—1958 to 1994—was like reading a case study on the dangers and challenges of a culture undergoing rapid change. What distinguishes the Waodani from other societies whose cultures face drastic change is that their lack of authority structure makes it difficult to establish a consensus for change. When I tell people what we eat in the jungle, they always comment about how impossible it would be for them to eat monkey meat or tree grubs. In reality, it would be much easier for the typical North American to learn to enjoy gnawing on a smoked monkey head than it would be for them to learn to live in a society with no structure and no authority system.

In a culture where people are free to do as they please, there is no fundamental penalty for stealing or killing or kidnapping.

In safe societies such as the United States, people tend to think that the more freedom we have, the better it is for us. Having lived with the Waodani, I realize that freedom is a precious commodity that has to be measured publicly, not privately. That is why we have stoplights. We don't like red lights, but we tolerate them because we realize that our freedom has to be limited for the benefit of others, and vice versa. The ideal is to limit everyone's individual freedom just enough to maximize the liberty for all.

That takes police to enforce rules and a court system for settling differences. It requires laws to let us know what we can and cannot do and a penal system in which those who break the rules are punished. We may not like these impositions on our personal freedom, but we call the result of their existence "civilization." We celebrate personal freedom without realizing that, really, total freedom is no freedom at all.

The Waodani have no written code of conduct. Ecuador considers the Waodani to be citizens, but it doesn't enforce the law in Waodani territory. I had to consider this when I was trying to decide if I dared to accept the Waodani's invitation. I wasn't exactly scared that any of us would be killed, but when there is no penalty for killing, it is certainly more likely. I knew some of the people loved me and would want to protect my family. But I wondered how they would protect us in a society that had always killed to live. The people who we would have to count on to protect us had given up killing long ago. As I thought about the issue of safety, I began to realize that when people are not willing to kill, it's easy for them to become slaves to those who will—unless God intervenes. The Waodani had been killing themselves into annihilation when my dad and his four friends tried to establish friendly contact with them. As far as I can tell, the Waodani in those days had only a short list of generally accepted rules, most of them dealing with killing:

1. If someone does something you don't like, ignore it.
2. If you can't ignore it, kill the person.
3. If someone kills someone in your family, it is your right and duty to kill someone in that person's family in retaliation.
4. It is best to kill everyone you can in the families of those you have vendettas against so there will be fewer of them to retaliate against your family.

The Waodani were a killing society. They were a culture of death. But with just a few exceptions, I'm convinced that the Waodani didn't like to kill. They simply knew that they could kill and live or be killed and die. They felt they had no choice.

When Aunt Rachel and Aunt Betty went to live with them, the Waodani almost completely gave up their killing and vendettas. Some did it in order to follow God's trail. Others just used *Waengongi*'s authority as the Creator as reason enough to stop doing what they otherwise could not stop. While this was generally a good thing, it also created new problems. When they gave up killing, the Waodani no longer had a means of controlling deviant behavior. This left a serious void in Waodani culture.

On some level, every society has to be willing to kill in order to exist. During my lifetime, there have been five "international conflicts" in which American soldiers have been required to kill and die under the assumption that they were doing it so the rest of us could live. The perpetuation of a society requires that some have to be willing to give up all their liberty so that others can go on living and be free and happy. That is why we celebrate Memorial Day in the United States and keep a flame lit at the Tomb of the Unknown Soldier. We celebrate those who sacrifice their lives and fortunes and honor for others.

My dad gave up his life so the Waodani could go on living. Now I had to decide if I was willing to give my life to help them figure out what the continuation of their lives was going to look like. I felt that my chances of helping the Waodani develop the skills and attitudes necessary to build a meaningful life out of the chaos and dependence that had taken deep root in their society were slimmer than their prospects of surviving the threat of violence from the outside world when my dad first tried to contact them. My motivation, however, was similar.

My dad felt compelled by his love for God to help the Waodani. I was moved by a similar love for God, but I also loved the Waodani themselves. This was not an altruistic love. I loved them simply because I had been loved by them. I could not help myself.

8

Swiss Family Saint

Living in limbo was fatiguing. My growing desire to move back to the jungle just didn't make sense to me. It was not part of any plan I had ever dreamed of or contemplated. But I found myself wanting to go, and I was feeling more and more that God wanted us to go. Although I did not have a clear idea of what I needed to do, I still wanted to take the plunge.

Our four kids were ready to go and excited about it, even though they really didn't realize what we would be getting ourselves into. So although their enthusiasm didn't serve as a reason to go, they certainly weren't holding us back.

Ginny, however, was petrified. I had just reached the stage in life at which I had started to figure out that men are from Mars and women are from Venus. It was even more complex for Ginny and me. I was naturally adventurous and had grown up triculturally. Ginny had grown up in a small agricultural community in west-central Minnesota and had very little desire for adventure. In fact, she had probably used up her quota of adventure early in our marriage. It had taken a lot out of her to leave her family, work, and familiar surroundings in order to marry me and live in Ecuador where I was developing land and starting a construction company on the outskirts of Quito.

If there was any adventure in Ginny after that, it had then gone into helping me start and sell a couple of businesses in construction and land development in Minnesota. Then we joined some friends in the oil and gas business, which took us to Dallas, with its highly competitive, transient, and glitzy lifestyle. From there, we went to live in Mali, West Africa, as volunteers with the same organization that had sent my parents to Ecuador. Ecuador had been a stretch for Ginny, but living in Africa in a staunchly Muslim and animist society in the middle of a major drought that was killing thousands was a stretch even for me.

So now the thought of going to live in the middle of the Amazon jungle was more than Ginny could bear.

Ginny is the love of my life. We are more than marriage partners; we really are best friends. I knew she trusted me, so I tried to convince her that I would take good care of her. But that wasn't her concern. The only thing Ginny had ever dreamed of was being a good wife and mother. She didn't want big houses or fancy cars; she didn't have great ambitions of taking expensive vacations or becoming powerful or famous. She wasn't worried that I couldn't take care of her. She was more worried that she would not be able to take care of me or Shaun, Jaime, Jesse, and Steph.

"So soon old and so late smart" is certainly true of me. I didn't understand how desperately dependent I had grown on Ginny, not only for friendship and affection, but for the stabilizing influence she was in my life. She inspired me to pass up the temporary "glitter" life offered in favor of doing something significant.

The old saying "If mama ain't happy, ain't nobody happy" is true in our family. But it isn't because Ginny makes the rest of us miserable when she is. It is because Ginny is the life of our party. When she isn't in the party mood, there isn't a party in our home.

I knew that God had brought Ginny and me together in an explosion of love and happiness because He had chosen us for each other. I also knew that if God was telling me to accept the Waodani's invitation to return to Ecuador, He could somehow make Ginny want to go too.

But seeing Ginny's despair at the mere thought of living in the jungle was painful for me. I didn't try to convince her that we should go. In fact, part of me actually hoped she would refuse. I still harbored thoughts that maybe I could stay in business and help the Waodani at the same time. Ginny and I decided to make a quick trip to Ecuador to visit the Waodani. I told Ginny that if during that trip God didn't do in her thinking what I was convinced He was doing in mine, we would know that my desire to go was probably just an early case of midlife crisis.

A couple from our church, Rick and Teresa, offered to go with us. It seemed like a good idea to have another couple along so Ginny would not feel alone when I got busy with making the complicated arrangements necessary to get us into and out of the jungle, and when the Waodani started bombarding me with requests to do things for them. Besides that, Rick was a physician's assistant, and I hoped he would help me evaluate what I could do to help the Waodani learn to meet their own medical needs.

The trip started out fairly smoothly. We flew to Quito, nestled high in the Andes between beautiful snowcapped peaks, right on the equator. From there we drove a couple of hundred miles south and then east, to the little town where my parents had lived when I was born. Finally, the bush aviation operation my dad had started for Mission Aviation Fellowship flew us into Toñampade, where Aunt Rachel and Dad were buried.

After three days of traveling, we finally arrived at Aunt Rachel's rustic little cabin between Dayumae's house and the tin-roofed building that served as the Toñampade God followers' meetinghouse. It was obvious word had gotten out that we were coming. Most of the Waodani who had been Aunt Rachel's closest friends in Tiwaeno were there. They had walked over or canoed in from the various outlying communities where they lived.

Ginny and I both realized we were at a major crossroads in our lives. This was a critical juncture for us, and we felt the usual turmoil that accompanies huge direction-of-life decisions. If we stayed in the United States, I would probably remain in business, we would finish raising our children in central Florida, and we would continue to blend in with the North American way of life.

But what would become of us if we moved to the rain forest to live with the Waodani? I had no idea, and that uncertainty gnawed at me. Now that we were in the jungle, isolated from meetings and telephones and my car and my airplane and a secretary and restaurants and grocery stores and movies and radio and air-conditioning, I started to have grave misgivings. I found myself feeling relieved that Ginny would probably say that she just could not do what the Waodani were asking of us, letting me off the hook from having to make the final decision.

Ginny had actually told me that although she thought I should go, it made her physically sick to think of going with me herself. The thought of being totally and completely helpless to do what gave her life meaning—of living in a place where she would be isolated from everything that was familiar, where she could only imagine the dangers that threatened her family, and where she couldn't even communicate with anyone who might try to help her—was too much for her to contemplate rationally.

My position was easy. If our decision wasn't unanimous, we wouldn't go. That night, as Ginny and Rick and Teresa and I sat in Aunt Rachel's house listening to the cacophony of nighttime jungle sounds, Rick started to play a small guitar he had brought with him. Before long, the four of us were singing some praise and worship songs we knew from church. As we sang, I thought I heard an animal or something under the house. I grabbed a candle and opened the door to see if anything was out there. I was amazed to find the dirt porch packed with Waodani men, women, children, and babies. Only the Waodani can congregate a group like that and hardly make a sound.

"Hearing your chanting well, we have come to listen," someone in the group said. "Tomorrow, chanting in God's house, we will all come back, doing it again."

So we did. After eating an early supper the next evening, we were escorted the few steps over to the *Waengongi onco* by a delegation of Waodani. The small building was already filled with Waodani families, and more were coming.

It took us a little while to get going. I remembered that Dayumae's favorite song was "Jesus Loves Me," so I asked her if she wanted to sing that. "Ooo, sí," she answered enthusiastically in Wao-Tededo and Spanish. She knew the words in Spanish and English, and she joined in enthusiastically when we sang it in both languages. Next, I asked if the Waodani would chant like the "ancient ones" for Rick and Teresa. Their response was a chorus of "Ooo."

They started out with one of their favorite chants about how *Waengongi* created everything. They would chant a phrase such as "*Waengongi* created everything, *Waengongi* created everything, *Waengongi* created everything," over and over in a three-note, pulsating style that is purely Waodani. After about five to ten repetitions of one phrase, they would move on to another one that built on the first. In this way, their chants slowly weave a story. Some have historical or spiritual significance. Other chants tell about hunting exploits and about how the birds and animals act when they are speared or shot with a poison dart.

When the Waodani had chanted in their own style for a while, they wanted us to sing for them in English again. We tried a little song with hand motions, and the Waodani watched carefully and then started to join in.

We sang a song about Moses' confrontation with Pharaoh, a story Aunt Rachel had taught Dayumae and she had taught many of the others. It isn't very deep spiritually, but the hand and body motions are fun.

Watching the Waodani try to do these hand motions was both hilarious and pretty much characteristic of what happens every time they try to copy outsiders. Everyone seems to fixate on a different part of what they see outsiders doing, rarely coordinating in any semblance of uniformity—which is almost always critical to success in the outsiders' world.

Some of the people really liked the "yea, yea, yea, yea" part of the song. In fact, an entire segment of our ensemble simply ignored the rest of the song and just kept enthusiastically singing the "yea, yea" part. Others never seemed to make it past the opening line, and there were some who got so confused at the strange Egyptian-like hand motions that they never got past "Pharaoh, pharaoh" (which they pronounced, "Pa-da-oo, pa-da-oo").

If someone had brought some manioc drink, we would have had a full-blown Waodani party. Fortunately no one did, because Waodani parties can go all night.

After a while, I noticed that Ginny was missing. I left Rick and Teresa to lead the choir and went to check on her.

I found her standing just inside the door of Aunt Rachel's house, sobbing. "Steve, I just can't do this. I'm sorry. I know we ought to come try to help the Waodani, and I know you love them, but I just can't do it." Ginny was crying so hard that her whole body was convulsing with her sobs. I knew it was time to pull the plug.

Some people can't stand snakes; others are afraid of the dark or of heights. For me, it is the boredom of uninterrupted routine with no challenge that I can't abide. Ginny was most afraid of living helpless and dependent in the Amazon jungle.

"The decision is made," I told her. "Not your decision, but my decision. We aren't going to move down here. If this was what God wanted me to do, then He would want both of us to do it, or He wouldn't have made us a team. Maybe the Waodani just needed to see that I was willing to come and that I really do care about what happens to them."

Ginny's crying subsided, and I talked her into going back to the party with me for a little while longer. When we got there, Ginny's eyes were obviously red, even by candlelight. If the Waodani asked, I would explain how scared Ongingcamo was of living in a place she didn't understand.

I knew Dawa and a few of the others would understand. They had visited the outside world and told incredible stories of the horrors they had encountered there. I remembered them telling of their adventures outside the *Wao omae*—Waodani territory. "There are strange noises all the time, and everything goes very fast. They have huge trails everywhere, but if you try to walk on them without a foreigner holding on to you, the *autodi*—things people ride in—will just kill you."

They also understood how hard it is to eat strange foods. Most of those who had been to the outside really liked to eat the foreigners' food, but it usually made their stomachs hurt. They liked Coca-Cola that felt like it was burning you when you drank it. But it was no substitute for mashed plantain mixed in warm water.

With the weight of the decision lifted, Ginny had rejoined the party with a bit more enthusiasm. I watched her from across the room as she was surrounded by Waodani who were enthusiastically trying to mimic what she was singing and the motions she was making. I was tired, so I snuck out and headed for my hammock in Aunt Rachel's house. Rick saw me checking out and followed me. He had started out playing the guitar for our singing, but the Waodani had long since drowned out any possibility of hearing him play, so he decided to put away the guitar before it got smashed in the melee of bodies jammed into *Waengongi*'s house next door.

Swinging gently in a Waodani hammock in the cool humidity of the Amazon night is extremely conducive to sleep, and I was out in no time. I must have slept for an hour and a half, maybe even two, judging by how far the candle had burned down, before I awoke. I wondered where Ginny was and went to see if she was in Aunt Rachel's little room. Empty!

Rick was in the house, but there was no sign of Ginny and Teresa.

I could still hear singing coming from next door. I couldn't imagine that Ginny was still over there, but I didn't have any other ideas of where to look, so I put on my boots and headed outside.

Sure enough, there were Ginny and Teresa, surrounded by Waodani young people who were insisting, "Ayae, ayae"—*More, more*—every time they finished a song. Ginny saw me standing in the doorway of the one-room structure and gave me a clear "I'm exhausted" look.

When I tried to rescue Ginny, the Waodani countered, "Ayae wedengi"— *just a little more*. That wasn't a surprise, but when I realized that Ginny didn't really want to be rescued, *that* was a surprise. Her hair was wet with perspiration, and it was clear she was enjoying being with the Waodani.

When we finally got back to the house, Ginny wanted to talk. "You told me that the Waodani young people are so mesmerized by the clothes and customs and technology of the outside world that they are usually indifferent to spiritual issues," she said. "If that's true, why were they so interested in singing songs about *Waengongi* tonight?"

"They are like young people all over the world," I explained. "They love music. Maybe even more than other young people because they don't have any music or instruments in their culture—just chanting. The old people's chanting about hunting and killing enemies is something most of the young people want to forget. Outsiders have looked down on the Waodani because they were naked and violent and 'primitive.' The very name 'Auca' that outsiders have always called the Waodani is a derogatory term that means 'naked ones' or 'savages.'"

I reminded her that when Aunt Rachel and Dayumae had told the Waodani about *Waengongi* and His desire that people should live without hating and killing, they had saved these people from certain annihilation.

"But it didn't solve all the problems," I said. "They were still an insignificant tribe without money or education, surrounded by a world that wanted to force them to either give up their personal identity and become 'civilized' or stay as they were—like animals in a zoo—so the rest of the world could observe them and study them anthropologically. No in-between."

It didn't take much to get me riled up about what I had seen happen to the Waodani as outside forces began to dominate them. These outsiders refused to accept them as equals or to treat them with dignity and respect.

Aunt Rachel and Dayumae had gained substantial fame in Ecuador as they acted as intermediaries with these feared and mysterious killers. These two dynamic women, along with Dayumae's charismatic son, Caento (Sam), had convinced the Ecuadorean government to grant the Waodani a protected territory, much like the reservations the U.S. government gave to Native American tribes. The Waodani were pleased at first that the government was willing to recognize their right to at least a small part of their ancestral lands. They thought this meant that they would not have to protect their territory themselves. But soon they realized that the same people who had signed a paper to give them land could just as easily sign another paper that would take it away.

The Waodani's specific interest in me, I realized, was not that I was more capable than the many other foreign adventurers, writers, anthropologists, environmentalists, oil company representatives, government workers, and missionaries who had offered—and sometimes even tried—to help them. I think what they saw in me was someone who knew how the outside world functioned but who also understood and respected them. And more important, my aunt was the one who had become one of them through learning their language, adopting their customs, and showing her obvious love for and loyalty to them. The Waodani who accepted Aunt Rachel as part of their tribe knew that they had influence through her. They also believed that I would do what they told me to do, just as I had obeyed Star. They felt they had a right to expect me to teach them what they needed to know to survive in the outside world. After all, hadn't they taught me what I needed to know to survive in *their* world?

I wanted to help them, but knowing the complexity of the outside world and its intolerance for protecting weak, defenseless members, I didn't think there was much I could do. One of the great drawbacks of Waodani reality was that they had become famous. Everyone wanted to help them. I would have to get in line. The Waodani were already divided into a multitude of factions, each one with its own champion. Because the Waodani had known me since I was a boy, I had more of a history with them than perhaps any other outsider. I was also an Ecuadorean citizen, which gave me standing with the government. But possibly the most important fact to the Waodani was my claim to live in their territory. My dad and my "aunt/mother" were buried there. In their eyes, that gave me a significant claim to be part of them.

I would have some advantages in trying to help the Waodani, but I knew I also had a couple of huge liabilities. My advantage was that I had known the Waodani since they first had contact with the outside world; and they had known me since I was a little boy. We had standing with each other. But this advantage made me an obvious target for outsiders who wanted to have influence over the Waodani. The Waodani who wanted me to help them believed

I could help them defend themselves against powerful outside forces. Those forces did not want that kind of interference. But all of that didn't make any difference if I couldn't accept their request to return to live with them. And I couldn't give in to the demands of my extended Waodani family at the cost of my immediate family. I think I was willing to sacrifice almost anything else, but not my love and commitment to Ginny and our children. If Ginny couldn't live in the jungle, neither could I.

Ginny just stood there watching me while my mind wandered. When I finally rejoined the conversation, she said, "I'm not ready to say I can live out here, Steve, but tonight I discovered one little thing that I might be able to do for the Waodani. I can at least teach them how to sing."

Ginny seemed at peace. Now she was ready to go to sleep. I was suddenly wide awake. I had been sure Ginny would be my excuse not to take this gigantic leap back in time. Now the decision felt like it was back on my shoulders.

I knew I wasn't going to get much sleep that night—and I didn't, although not just because I had a lot on my mind.

I was just sitting down on the bed beside Ginny when suddenly it felt like someone powerful was grabbing me around the waist and trying to squeeze the life out of me. The pain was so intense that I would have cried out if I could have, but I couldn't breathe.

Ginny called Rick, who thought it might be kidney stones. He gave me some strong pain reliever he had with him, and eventually the pain subsided.

Whatever caused that pain temporarily disabled me. And it forced me to face the fact that similar unanticipated calamities could, and probably would, happen when there was no one from the outside world around to save the day. If I was going to take my family to live with the Waodani, I would have to be willing to share their isolation and helplessness.

9

A Critical Decision

The next day the plane would come to take us out of the jungle and back to Quito, where I planned to visit a doctor before saying good-bye to Ginny and Rick and Teresa. They would head back to the States, but once I knew what was causing my pain, I wanted to return to the jungle so I could make sure the Waodani were really serious about what they were asking me to do.

Once the medication began to take effect, Ginny and I talked late into the night about the decision to move back to the jungle.

"Steve, I have been feeling that you should do what the Waodani are asking you to do. I just knew I couldn't. Now I think I could survive in the jungle," Ginny told me. "I still think I might be more of a hindrance than a help, but I'm not afraid anymore." Now it was time for *me* to be cautious.

I had pointed out to my *iñanani*—those in the tribe who constituted my extended family—that there were many other people who were trying to help them.

"What can I do for you that they haven't already done for you?" I asked.

Grandmother Dawa answered by scolding me. "We don't say come do for us; we say, you teaching us, we will do for ourselves."

What they were asking for seemed impossible. How could these people—who couldn't read and didn't understand the concept of money—possibly run a pharmacy or manage a clinic? How could two thousand Waodani gain enough political clout to sway the Ecuadorean government to consider their interests against those of the powerful oil companies?

On the other hand, I told myself, at least they were ready to try something other than waiting for another handout. The Waodani were not naturally beggars, but with people from all over the world wanting to help them, they had become largely a welfare society.

The Waodani were used to living off the land in their own territory. Whenever they tried to leave the jungle, they had to have money to buy food and shelter. But they didn't have marketable skills, and they weren't used to doing what other people told them to do. Nor had their culture prepared them for the daily planning that life in the outside world demands.

I had told my Waodani family that I would drop off Ginny and our friends and then return to the jungle alone. If they truly wanted to "do for their own people," I told them we needed to talk to Waodani in other villages to see if they were in agreement.

I thought about hiring a plane to take me around from village to village, but that would have been expensive and difficult to plan. No pilots wanted to overnight in jungle villages. The alternative was to have the plane drop me off in one village and then return to pick me up and drop me at the next village. That didn't seem to be a good idea either. I would be paying hundreds of dollars for the plane to dead head—to use it for just a few minutes between villages.

Besides that, I had been gone for a long time. I knew that spending a week on the trail would force me to remember both the physical and the emotional inconveniences of living in the jungle. I had grown very used to the North American Disney World way of life.

On the way up to Quito, however, I started to get cold feet. I hadn't walked more than short distances for years. It isn't very far from my back door to my car. The only place I had to do much walking was at the mall, and I tried not to do that more than once a year. I was worried that physically I might not be able to make it from village to village, especially in cheap rubber boots, the standard jungle footwear. All other shoes get wet and full of mud and then stay that way.

Ginny, Teresa, Rick, and I spent the day in Quito, visiting the school I had attended from second grade through high school. Then we went next door to the compound where World Radio Missionary Fellowship prepared programs in Russian, German, Czechoslovakian, Japanese, Portuguese, and many other languages. These multilanguage broadcasts were then transmitted by shortwave all around the world.

After my dad had been killed, Mom kept us in Shell for a year while another pilot and his family prepared to replace Mom and Dad in their supporting roles for the missionaries and various tribes of the eastern jungles in Ecuador.

Then we spent a year in California. Kathy, Phil, and I lived with Mom's parents while she traveled and told the story of what had happened to us in Ecuador. Millions of people had read bits and pieces of the "tragedy" in *Life* magazine, *Reader's Digest,* and hundreds of newspaper articles across the country. Audiences—both Christian and secular—were captivated by the thought of the twentieth century coming into contact with the Stone Age. The thought of spear-wielding "primitives" massacring white men who had guns but refused to defend themselves gave the story even more allure.

I attended first grade in California, and there I discovered how small the world was for my peers. None of them could speak a second language. They all were white kids from similar middle-class neighborhoods. They didn't even know what a jungle was. Their world extended from Disneyland to the beach, neither one more than a short distance from their homes. That had been my first experience living with people I looked like but shared little in common with.

I was thinking about these things while Ginny and I waited outside the radio station for Rick and Teresa. Suddenly, with no warning, I had another terrible attack of pain. I was standing next to a parked car and just collapsed onto it. The pain was so intense I could not stay standing, even with Ginny's help.

As soon as I could move, Ginny helped me hobble across the street to the hospital. They got me right in to see an Ecuadorean doctor. We talked while he had X-rays taken and lab tests run, and I discovered that he was the little boy who had once run around the piano while I took lessons from his mother—a reminder that I was no longer a young kid in prime physical condition.

Early the next morning, Ginny and our friends prepared to head back to the United States. I was really apprehensive by now. The medical exam wasn't conclusive, but the doctor agreed with Rick that it could be kidney stones. He also sobered me by explaining that the pain I had felt was nothing compared to what could be coming. The only good news was the advice he gave me: "If this is kidney stones, the best thing you can do is to walk lots and drink plenty of water."

If I went on with my plan to spend a week trekking from village to village, I would be doing more walking than I had done since I was a mountain climber in high school. I would be sweating and drinking the whole way. But if I suffered from another attack, I knew that I could also end up stuck out in the jungle with no doctor or medical help.

I really didn't know what to do. The only thought that seemed to tip the balance was this one: If God really was intervening in our lives and wanted us to leave our home and career in favor of obeying Him in an undertaking that was at best uncertain and at worst a painfully futile exercise, we should probably expect some obstacles and tests along the way.

I wanted to give up and go to my U.S. "home" and a lifestyle that had become familiar. But I realized I feared living a safe but mediocre life even more than I feared suffering beyond the reach of help in the rain forest.

I decided to do the hard thing, which I've found is usually the right thing, and head back to the jungle.

⋀⋁⋀⋁⋀⋁⋀⋁⋀

While I was in the hangar before our flight into Toñampade, I asked if any of the pilots had a handheld Global Positioning System. I had purchased some very accurate geodetic survey maps in Quito that covered the geographic area I would be trekking across. A GPS would help me to know where I was and allow me to find and mark the coordinates of a potential building site for a Waodani tribal center—if I could make it that far.

Unfortunately, none of the pilots could help me out. But a stranger who had overheard my request approached me as I was leaving. Without any introduction he asked me, "Do you love Jesus?"

If the stranger's question seemed a little radical, he certainly looked the part. He was tall, with receding hair but a full beard.

My answer was yes, but I wasn't used to being asked that question, in that way, by a total stranger—out in public, no less. He went on, "Do you tell people that you do?"

"Well, yes," I replied. I really felt on the spot, though I wasn't sure why. I guess I was just used to trying to make my spiritual beliefs seem a little more sophisticated. I didn't know it then, but this stranger was going to help me get over that.

"Well then, you can borrow my GPS," he said.

"Why do you have a GPS?" Not a very diplomatic question on my part, but he didn't seem like much of a diplomat.

"I use it to navigate when I'm flying my plane out in the jungle. Do you want to see the plane?"

I had never known anyone with a private plane in Ecuador. I had heard that there was a missionary who had an ultralight aircraft; maybe this was that fellow.

The man led me up the service road that paralleled the runway and passed right by the little bank where I had once watched my dad fly into the jungle and back each day. Just a few hundred yards up the road from our old house, the stranger turned into a small hangar. There was only one plane in the place, an old Cessna 172. I had owned one like it when Ginny and I lived in Minnesota. Without thinking I took a guess, and ventured, "Looks like about a '68 172."

"Sixty-seven," he answered. "But how did you know?"

"Oh, I used to own one."

A lot of old planes are so meticulously maintained that they can be twenty or thirty years old and still look new. This plane, called HC-BTS, was not one of those. While I inspected the plane, the fellow carried the conversation.

"You are probably my answer to prayer," he said. "I've been working on getting this plane, bringing it down here, and doing all the necessary paper-work for over a year. Now I have to go to the States for a year, and I don't have anyone to look after BTS for me. I've been praying for someone who could keep it flying and in shape for me and I think you are God's answer to my prayer."

Wow! No way! I thought. This couldn't actually be happening. As I had been considering the possibility of living back with the Waodani, one of my biggest concerns was how isolated and helpless I would be without an airplane. I dreaded the thought of having to beg for rides and wait for others to fly me in and out of the jungle, and around from village to village. And I knew that walking was a very poor and painful alternative to the cost and frustration of having to depend on others.

The fellow with the plane went on like it was a done deal. "You've got to come over to the house to read an article that some people in California gave to me. It was this article that motivated them to make this plane available to me," said the man, whose name, I finally learned, was Rick. "That was a miracle. Come on, I'll introduce you to Sharon and you can read it. I'll get you the GPS and some batteries and a special antenna I use out in the jungle."

While we walked to where Rick lived, he continued telling me about the story he wanted me to read. When he produced a copy and handed it to me at the house, my suspicions were confirmed. "To the Ends of the Earth," the title read. I knew this story. It was about a young man who found himself at the end of a series of strange circumstances in the fabled city of Timbuktu, in West Africa. All alone in a scorching, dry climate and surrounded by fanatic Muslims, this young man had a spiritual experience that made him long for the father who had been taken from him as a boy. It also proved to him that God's promise to be a "Father to the fatherless" was true.

I had written the article. But I didn't know how to convince my enthusiastic but overbearing potential benefactor of this. It seemed too great a coincidence, even to me. When I finally got through to him that the article that had played a key role in getting his plane was *my* article, he was as incredulous as I was. He told me he would plan on my keeping the plane for him, even though I told him I wasn't even sure I would be in Ecuador while he was gone. Rick assured me that he was confident I was his answer to prayer. We would just have to work out a couple of details. I took his GPS and left.

If I was going to be his answer to prayer for someone to keep the plane, he certainly was going to be the answer to mine of having a plane available. Even if I had decided to buy one myself, I realized I didn't have a year to do all the paperwork. Now it seemed that I was going to have a miracle plane handed to me. Not a luxury model, for sure, but at least flyable . . . or so I thought.

10

Trial by Trail

When I finally arrived back in Toñampade, the Waodani were surprised I had returned. The people confided that only a few outsiders ever did what they said they would do. Most of the Waodani expected the same of me, especially since I had said I was going to walk from village to village.

I got out my maps and started to plan which villages I could get to before the plane came for me. The Waodani were intrigued by the maps. They never used maps, and most of them had no idea what my big sheets of paper were for. Maps of Waodani territory show just rivers and ridges—the only identifiable landmarks. The jungle is a drastically undulating continuum of deep chasms and steep ridges covered by an uninterrupted canopy of giant-leafed plants and huge trees.

As I looked at the maps, I realized that the locations of the villages were wrong. Toñampade was listed by a name I had never heard. Tiwaeno was in about the right place, but at least one other village I was familiar with was on the wrong river.

When I explained to the Waodani that the blue lines were rivers and the funny elevation lines were ridges, they started crowding around and pointing to where the various communities actually were. They also showed me where various trails went. They knew their ridges and rivers like we know the streets and avenues of our hometown. They could all read the map at the same time too, because it didn't matter what angle they were looking from. They were just as happy to look at the map upside down as right side up.

When we had placed about twenty villages in the right spots on the proper rivers, we were able to pick out one spot that would be accessible to about two-thirds of all the Waodani. We discussed that area as a possible location for the new community we could build, where people from various villages could go for medical and dental services and where they could fix their guns and a few other pieces of equipment. It would be a place where they could learn skills that would allow them to integrate slowly into a partnership with the outside world on equal footing.

Coba, my old childhood friend, became excited. He asked me to point again to the rivers on the map. I was trying to figure out how to explain the obvious fact that water is blue, so the blue lines represent rivers. Then I realized the Waodani had never seen water clear enough or deep enough to look blue. I had been out of the jungle for so long that it was going to take a while to start naturally thinking like the Waodani.

Coba looked over the prospective area for the new community with intense concentration and suddenly stabbed the paper with his finger. "In this place," he said, "the ground is hard even when it rains. I see this place well for building an *ebowei* (airstrip)." I doubted if the place he was pointing to on the map was the place he was thinking of, and I wondered how he could know that the soil there was hard. But I carefully marked it on my map and made a note of the latitude and longitude coordinates.

If we trekked from Toñampade to the village of Damointado, and from there to Tzapino, where Kimo and Dawa lived, we would trek right through the prospective area for the new community.

As we began to plan our trip, I remembered the grueling trek Mincaye and I had made from Toñampade to Gikita's place and back. On the trail, distances are of little consequence. How long a trip takes depends much more on how frequently the trail has been traveled and how many major ridges have to be crossed to get to the destination. I was thinking in terms of pain per day, using the trip to Gikita's as my baseline.

I asked over and over, "Leaving here *baneki* (in the early morning), where will the sun be when we get to Damointado?" Every answer I got was different. Waodani kept feeling my legs and talking about how slowly foreigners walk and how much they cried climbing ridges. Mincaye kept assuring them that I was strong just like they were. I appreciated Mincaye's loyalty, but his praise and high esteem weren't going to increase my stamina. I wanted to know the painful truth.

Finally one of Dawa's nephews said, "Going to Damointado, carrying lots, the sun will be there." His arm pointed to the sun's position at maybe one or two o'clock in the afternoon. That would be about six or seven hours of traveling. "Not carrying, and walking fast, the sun will be there," he said. This time he pointed to about eleven o'clock—four hours. Then he added one more possibility. "When they say that there are pigs to hunt and I am hungry for meat, running fast, I will be there then," and he pointed to nine o'clock.

That was my answer. The Waodani, depending on the need for speed, could make the trip to Damointado in two to seven hours. I realized that neither they nor I had a good idea how long it would take me.

Once I figured out where I was going, I had to find out who would go with me. Coba seemed to be the most knowledgeable about the general area we were considering for the tribal center.

"Coba, do you see it well to go walking with me?" I asked. He answered simply, "Yes, let's be going together."

Paa, another boyhood friend, offered, "You seeing it well, I too will go!" In a tribe in which everyone over the age of ten is a master of the rain forest, Paa stood out as a super-expert. And we were old friends.

"Augh, bito gote waa abopa," I said. *You going, I see it well.*

One young man who had been hanging around caught my attention. I realized it was Gaba, my old friend Toñae's son.

When I had lived with Aunt Rachel in Tiwaeno, Toñae was the quickest of the Waodani young people to catch on to outsider concepts. He was the best new reader in the tribe, and Aunt Rachel had hoped that he would be the first Waodani teacher. I had been more impressed with his ability to make balsawood airplanes.

When Toñae figured out that I liked airplanes, he started making models for me. I tried to make some too, but I couldn't come close to getting the proportions as accurate as Toñae did. He possessed incredible dexterity that seemed to be a genetic trait of the Waodani.

One day Toñae showed up with a beautiful scale model of the Wycliffe Helio Couriers, which flew in and out of Tiwaeno every month or so with supplies for the tribe. What really caught my attention was that Toñae had carved the propeller with pitch, like a real propeller. He had mounted the propeller on his Helio with a blowgun dart. As I studied this special propeller Toñae had carved, he blew on it and it turned.

I had plastic models with similar propellers, and I had played with pinwheels that spun when I ran with them. But Toñae had discovered that the strange "arms" that flailed around on the front of foreigners' wood bees had pitch. He had experimented in carving model propellers just like they were on real planes, with no understanding of why they were made like that. How he figured out to mount it on a loose-fitting dart, I have no idea. I often remembered this years later when *cowodi* would marvel at the ability of the Waodani to make sophisticated blowguns.

People tend to think that Stone Age people are low-tech because they are somehow inferior. But the Waodani, for sure, weren't lacking in intelligence. They just lived in a world that did not promote skill specialization or reward long-term planning. The Waodani lived from day to day. Their primary occupations were hunting, growing or gathering food, and staying out of the reach of their enemies.

My friend Toñae had not originally been part of this Waodani community. He had been kidnapped in a spearing raid when people from the upriver Waodani speared his family downriver. Although the upriver Waodani had raised Toñae like one of their own, he had worked hard to develop his skills as a jungle warrior so that when the time was right, he could avenge his old family by killing those who had taken him in.

Toñae was about eleven when my aunt Rachel went in to live with the People. When he heard that *Waengongi* decreed that people should not kill their enemies but should "see them well" in spite of the bad things they had done, something happened to this bright young jungle nomad. Not only did he lose his desire to take revenge on his enemies, he also decided that he wanted to help teach them God's carvings so that everyone could live well.

One day when the People were meeting in *Waengongi*'s house, Toñae stood up and informed the Waodani living in Tiwaeno that *Waengongi* had spoken to him in a vision while he was sleeping. He said the message had come to him in the form of a question: "Why should you be living happily and in peace while your own *nanicabo*—family—is living in the old way, hating and afraid all the time?"

Toñae said *Waengongi* had told him that he should go teach his own family to walk God's trail.

The Waodani who heard his pronouncement were aghast. "Being bad, bad killers, those people will spear you without remorse," they responded, trying to reason with him. But Toñae then announced that in his dream, *Waengongi* told him that He was going to tell someone else to go to the downriver People with him. This stunning announcement silenced the group. They wondered which of them was the appointed one.

Old Dyuwi finally stood up and announced that what Toñae had said was true. *Waengongi* had told him to go as well.

The people who had been part of the spearing raid that killed Toñae's family described where they had found Toñae's clan. With no more information than that, Toñae and Dyuwi set off for what everyone believed would be their death—at the end of a spear.

Their first attempt to make contact with Toñae's family group was unsuccessful. They spent weeks trying to follow and reopen long unused trails while scavenging for food along the way. They encountered unseasonably high water in the rivers they had to constantly cross and suffered recurring fevers that eventually forced them to turn back.

Toñae made the next attempt on his own. Aunt Rachel knew that the oil companies had been trying to penetrate the general area inhabited by Toñae's family group. She convinced company officials that if they helped Toñae contact his family, it might reduce the likelihood of future spearing raids against their employees.

The company agreed, and they delivered Toñae by helicopter to the general vicinity he and Dyuwi had spent weeks trying to reach by trail. Toñae hiked the last part of the journey, carrying a portable two-way radio Aunt Rachel had convinced him to take.

It wasn't long before Toñae found the downriver People and, in fact, discovered the remaining members of his own long-lost family. After the initial surprise of seeing him again, fifteen years after the raid in which he had disappeared, his family quickly warmed to him. They wanted him to show them where the upriver People lived so they could spear them in revenge for the family members the upriver People had killed. When Toñae refused, they tried to marry him to a young girl in their group. They probably thought that marriage into his old family would change his allegiance.

Toñae refused the marriage. He explained that *Waengongi*'s carvings, though they don't rule out polygamy, definitely advise against it. Toñae already had a wife who had borne two children: a little girl who shared my mother's tribal name, Ongimae, and a son, Gaba.

This refusal did not sit well with Toñae's clan. Toñae used his radio to call Tiwaeno, and he informed the people there of his suspicion that his family was planning to spear him.

The people in Tiwaeno insisted that Toñae wait until everyone was asleep and then flee with his radio to a nearby river. They promised to tell Star to send the oil company *dayinim* to pick him up at the river.

The growing tension seemed to make Toñae nervous, but he was not afraid. "*Waengongi* sending me here to teach my *nanicabo* His carvings, speaking to Him tonight, I will see if He sees it well that I flee. If not, I will stay. If they kill me, they kill me. I will die and go to live in *Waengongi*'s place with Him. Then He will send you to teach my family to live well." Toñae prayed all night. In the morning, he called the Tiwaeno group and told them he was staying.

That was the last message we heard from Toñae. I found out later that Toñae's uncles and a couple of brothers or cousins told him they had found a herd of wild pigs nearby. They all grabbed spears and ran into the jungle to give chase. But it was just a trick to get Toñae out where they could easily spear him. And that is just what they did.

I got word of Toñae's death shortly after I went to college in the United States. While Toñae was bravely risking his life in order to carry out *Waengongi*'s instructions, I was living in a dorm with a dining room card that guaranteed me all the food I wanted, anytime I wanted it. I was required to do nothing more strenuous than attend a few classes a day and do a little bit of homework—and even then, my contemporaries and I complained as though it was more than should be expected of us at this stage of life.

When Ginny and I were first married and living in Ecuador, the tribe named our first son Toñae. It was clear that the tribe considered Toñae's son,

Gaba, and me to be part of the same family, especially since his sister and my mom shared the same name.

Now, as we planned our trip to the various villages, I felt a responsibility to Gaba and asked if he would like to go with us.

Gaba agreed. Our trekking party was complete: shy but steady Coba, with feet so widely splayed that even I could recognize his footprints; super-jungleman Paa; and Toñae's lonely son, Gaba. I rounded out the group as the wild card.

Early the next morning, Komi called me over to his house, where Dayumae made me banana drink. She mashed two huge boiled plantains into a quart of warm water. Once I got it down, she made me another. I told her I was tight and thumped my stomach to prove it. The fact that Paa, who was drinking with me, had finished three gourds full should have prompted me to try to get down at least one more. I had forgotten what it had been like for me as a boy, trying to keep up with Waodani hunters, who could go hard all day without eating anything. All I could think about was the pain I knew was coming.

Our little party left Dayumae and Komi's house just after seven. As we passed Waodani houses on our way down to the river, people from inside spoke casually to my companions. They had no windows in their houses, but news travels fast, and everyone knew we were heading for Damointado, *yaipodingi*—walking. The people seemed to be surprised but pleased that I was going to travel like they did. I did hear a few people comment, "Yaipodingi gokimini. Babae woody," or "By trail going, Babae is dead" (as in, "Steve's a gonner if he's going by trail"). In the back of my mind, I was thinking about the two attacks I had suffered just a few days earlier—attacks that had made it impossible for me to move, much less walk.

Once we reached the river, we borrowed someone's dugout boat and poled across the water. I could tell Paa and Coba were pleased that I stood up, as they did. It had been years since I'd spent much time in the tribe, but I, too, was surprised at how quickly I was beginning to feel at home. Although the finer parts of most learned skills are lost without constant practice, the foundational feel for those skills can be recalled even after years of disuse. But I soon encountered a phenomenon I did not remember having to deal with before. As we started down the trail, I kept banging my head on vines and branches that crossed the trail. I also ran into cobwebs that stuck to my face and made the skin on my sweating face and hands sticky. I was carrying a machete, the universal jungle tool, but it slowed me down to chop the vines and branches that kept hitting me in the face. I wondered why Paa, who was leading the way, wasn't cutting them for the rest of us. That is what the trail leader is supposed to do.

Then it dawned on me: Paa wasn't clearing the trail overhead because he wasn't hitting anything. Neither was anyone else. At six feet, I was a head taller than my three companions. When I was a kid, I was about Waodani height, so I hadn't faced this problem. The Waodani aren't little people, but they are short. The tallest person I had ever known in the tribe was Kenta. He would have been the Shaquille O'Neal of the tribe if the Waodani played basketball. I still think of Kenta as being taller than I am, but I doubt he was actually more than five feet seven or eight at the very most.

Following my buddies on the trail, I quickly remembered why I admired their physical prowess. Paa, Coba, and Gaba walked as if they were just out for a leisurely stroll. With the benefit of my longer legs, I was keeping up pretty well until we got about halfway up the ridge, just across the river from Toñampade. My three companions were chatting while they climbed—no heavy breathing or any other indication that they even noticed how incredibly steep the trail had become.

That first ridge was almost as tall as the Washington Monument (and just as steep as those winding stairs I had once climbed nonstop on a dare). I knew I couldn't do the ridge nonstop. I gladly gave Coba my pack as soon as he offered to carry it. I wanted to give him my half-gallon canteen too, but I found myself needing a drink so often I knew I couldn't take a chance on being separated from it.

By the time we finally made it to the top of the first ridge, my legs were quivering from exhaustion. Fortunately for me, part of the dense foliage on the Toñampade side of the ridge had slid down the steep slope in a landslide. That gave us a rare opportunity to rest and look down at the valley below. I could see Toñampade just a mile in the distance. Closer to us, I could see the bend in the river where Palm Beach had been. Since jungle rivers are dynamic and change course frequently, I knew the current beach was only approximately the same one Dad and my uncles had landed on to meet the "Aucas." Paa and Coba had been part of that first community whose members had killed Dad. I wondered if they, too, were thinking of the dramatic event that had taken place on that little bend in the river below us—an event that changed all of our lives forever.

Once we topped that first ridge, I hoped it would be all downhill from there. But I had forgotten that ridges in this territory are steep on both sides, and the coming down part is sometimes even more difficult than going up. After two hours of hard walking, I was in a daze of pain. I didn't try to talk or joke with my companions anymore. I just kept sucking on the hard candies I had found in Aunt Rachel's tiny storeroom, hung my head, and put one foot ahead of the other as quickly and evenly as I could.

Coba and Paa tried to point out animals or other objects of interest in the canopy overhead, but it was useless for me to even try to look. I was so hot that my glasses fogged up as soon as I stopped moving and looked up. Besides that, the sweat from my forehead was running into my eyes and making them water, so I couldn't have seen much even if my glasses had been clear. It was pointless to ask if we were getting close, since I knew my friends would just say, "illiqui," or "close," no matter how much of the trek was left. If I could just gut it out and keep going. We would get there when we got there.

We continued our trek, often having to cross streams and small bodies of water along the way. Paa, Coba, and Gaba walked right across. Coba was barefoot, because his big toes stick out almost perpendicular to his other toes, making his foot too wide for boots. Paa and Gaba had boots, but they wore no socks. After walking through a river or stream, they would just lean forward and lift their leg behind them to let the excess water run out, and they were ready to go on.

My feet were much too tender for me not to wear socks. So at each stream, I had to sit down to take off my boots and socks, then very carefully cross, trying not to injure my feet on rocks or thorny vegetation in the water. After a while, Paa offered to carry me across the streams, and I accepted. A day earlier, it would have been too humiliating to accept such a thing. But I was so tired and sore that humiliation was way down on my list of undesirables.

Finally, after crossing what turned out to be our final stream, we followed the trail over a small rise and cut through a small canyon near the top. There below us was a stretch of grass about a hundred feet long. We had made it to Damointado! Although we were just a few hundred feet from our destination, I wasn't sure if my worn-out feet could make it. The only thing I wanted to do was collapse into a hammock.

No such luck. When Paa made the customary "Woooo" call to let the people of Damointado know we were coming, they met us and led us straight into the little schoolhouse at the east end of the airstrip. I had my heart set on a wonderfully comfortable string hammock, but rough boards would do.

I collapsed onto the floor with my back against the rough wall and hoped no one would want to do anything but stare at me until I woke up the next day. That wasn't going to happen.

I didn't recognize anyone at Damointado except for one old warrior, Peque, whom I had met at Aunt Rachel's funeral. I remembered him because his leg had been extremely swollen, infested with the maggotlike larvae of a jungle fly. Peque's leg was now healed, and he was deep in conversation with Gaba about something. I caught the word for stingray. It seemed Peque wanted us to look at the leg of a young girl who had been poisoned by the barb on a stingray's tail. I had stepped on a stingray once at the coast, and I remembered the excruciating pain.

This girl was long past the initial pain of her injury. As is often the case where there are no antibiotics, the stingray venom had caused necrosis around the wound. The flesh had rotted, leaving a deep, puss-filled hole in the girl's leg.

I had brought a little tackle box of medical supplies from Aunt Rachel's house. Everyone seemed to expect me to do the honors, so I had the girl lie face down on her mother's lap so I could bend over her leg. I was trying to act as if I really knew how to help her. As soon as I knelt down, my legs started to knot up. I grabbed a chunk of wood nearby and sat on it with my legs stretched out in front of me. I held the girl's leg on my lap and started to probe the wound with a long curette that looked like an oversize Q-tip.

The pus kept sticking to the curette, and I had to wipe it over and over on a piece of bandage. As I did this, the hole grew bigger, finally being big enough that I could have inserted the whole end of my thumb into it.

While I was cleaning her wound, I had to fight the urge to throw up at the smell of rotten flesh. I was concentrating so hard that it didn't even occur to me that the girl must have been in terrible pain. Amazingly, she never flinched or made a sound.

While I was in the middle of this minor operation, I heard loud footsteps coming up behind me at a rapid clip. Before I could see who was descending on me, someone grabbed both my shoulders and repeatedly banged my head into his chest. My hands were full of puss and junk, and the brim of my ball cap was too low for me to see anything higher than my attacker's breastbone. I did get a clear look at the wording on his soiled T-shirt, however. It said "Jordache."

Finally, the old warrior held me at arm's length. His empty earlobe holes hung within inches of his shoulders, and his hair was unusually gray for a Waodani. It was obvious that he was very old. From the look on his face, I could tell he was glad to see me. The chest banging with my head was his way of greeting me. He didn't wait to introduce himself but immediately started a long discourse on something of obvious interest to him—something the audience was finding hilariously funny.

It turned out that he had heard stories about a tall, skinny foreigner who had become like a Waodani in ways that did not include appearance. He told me that even though I had become old like him, he was still glad to see me. He wanted me to know that although he had killed people before, he had given that up, so I didn't have anything to worry about. Besides, he had assured Aunt Rachel that he wanted to meet me and would not spear me or let any other people from his downriver clan spear me either.

Cawaena, as I later learned was his name, obviously didn't think head banging violated his commitment not to hurt me. I was much too tired to make an issue of it.

Knowing that I could not repeat our six-and-a-half-hour trail trot without a day to rest, I accepted old Cawaena's invitation to drink plantain and eat howler monkey with him the following day.

11

Terminal City

Peque's family brought us boiled manioc and fish wrapped in leaves for our evening meal. I added a healthy dose of salt I had brought with me to help replace what I had lost in perspiration along the trail.

I have always liked most Waodani food, with a few exceptions, such as large, live, wriggly tree grubs. I'm also not terribly fond of premasticated manioc drink. To make this staple beverage, the women boil manioc roots and then mash them as we do potatoes. During the mashing process, the women put balls of the mash into their mouths to collect their saliva. Then they spit the saliva-laden mashed manioc back into the mixing bowl to start the digestive process while they fill their mouths with another load. The objective is to create a food source that will give quick energy. That is the good news. The bad news is that it produces an unusual taste, and I just prefer to do my own digestion. There are a few other delicacies that stretch my culinary imagination, but I like monkey and eel just fine.

As we were eating, I remembered a conversation I'd just had with Komi the night before while we were in Toñampade. Komi told me that Dyuwi and Nimonga had speared Nenkiwi. Then he added, "I went with them to learn to spear-kill too."

His dramatic revelation seemed like a random one. Komi, who was old Gikita's son, was not a whole lot older than I was. I had always assumed that he had not been involved in any killings. I was wrong. Now I suddenly realized that Damointado was the village where Nenkiwi had been speared.

Komi, knowing I was going to trek to Damointado, apparently decided it was time to tell me this story.

At that time the old warriors had just started to train Komi how to ambush and spear his enemies. Apparently, rumors were circulating that Nenkiwi was planning to kill Gikita, so a spearing party was organized to spear Nenkiwi before he could spear Gikita.

"At night, taking our spears, there was no moon," Komi remembered. "Quietly walking to Nenkiwi's clearing, we waited, listening. While the People in Nenkiwi's house were still making a little noise, we moved quietly around the house to the place where they urinated at night. Waiting there, without moving for a long time, I was shivering in the cold." Probably with fright too, I imagined.

"Sleeping a little," he went on, "Gimade had to urinate, but she was afraid to go out by herself, thinking maybe Nenkiwi's enemies might be waiting to spear her. So Nenkiwi said he would urinate too. Waiting and waiting, I heard them coming close, but I could not see anything. First, Gimade started to pass water. Then Nenkiwi started to pass water too, and Dyuwi touching my spear, I knew it was time to kill Nenkiwi. Dyuwi and Nimonga both spearing, Nenkiwi said 'yea-ea-ea' and fled. We heard him fall off the bank and run across the river very fast.

"Nenkiwi crying out, all the People in his house fled into the jungle. Taking fire from his house, we went to finish Nenkiwi off. Finding his blood, we followed his trail for a while. But thinking maybe he was not wounded too badly and maybe having his spears hidden out there, we decided to wait until early morning to spear him more."

Komi went on to tell me how they tracked Nenkiwi down the next morning. He was still alive, but both spears had gone right through his abdomen. No doubt he had made the wounds much worse by charging through the jungle to get away. The eight- or nine-foot spears that remained in him would have caught on vegetation, and his flailing around certainly would have exacerbated the damage they had done.

"Doing like this," Komi said, raising his arm in the typical hand motion that Waodani warriors use to signify spearing, "I was going to spear Nenkiwi more. But Nenkiwi said, 'Seeing I am truly dying, let me die like a real person.'" I understood what Komi was telling me. Nenkiwi wanted to be buried alive, in old Waodani tradition.

"Letting him go back to his clearing, they called his sister to dig his *wodido* (grave) so he could die."

I remembered Aunt Rachel telling me that Nenkiwi had been buried alive, although as a boy, I had never understood why someone would be so afraid that he would climb into his own grave and be covered to die. Nor could I imagine being so angry that I could actually drive a spear through another person's body. The Waodani said it felt just like spearing a banana tree trunk. They had taught me to do that in preparation for spearing pigs, tapirs, and deer.

I listened to Komi's account, thinking that customs such as live burials were things of the distant past. I was soon going to find out that although many traditions from the old days had become the exception rather than the rule, they were still part of Waodani culture.

When Nenkiwi's grave was dug, the others helped break off the spears that were still skewering his body. He climbed into the hole voluntarily. But before the people put the split palm fronds over him to hold the dirt from falling directly on him when they covered the hole, Nenkiwi observed another Waodani tradition: He asked for his children to be buried with him.

Nenkiwi was just a young man, probably in his early twenties. But in the Waodani world he was considered an up-and-comer. A Waodani warrior's greatest aspiration was to be considered *tempo*—fearless, remorseless, cunning; able to overcome his enemies, hunting them down and killing them without concern for what others might do in retribution. A warrior who became *tempo* was willing to break tribal guidelines of conduct. Violation of these unwritten rules was cause for spearing, which was the Waodani's only mechanism for resolving conflicts among themselves. Nenkiwi had already violated several important standards within his clan. For one thing, he had openly demanded a wife before the "old ones" were ready to give him one. He was given an older woman who had been married to the dreaded Moipa, the psychopathic killer who had killed more Waodani than any other warrior in Waodani history.

It wasn't long before that first wife was speared by other warriors in Gikita's clan who were furious at Moipa and needed an outlet for their fury. I doubt if Nenkiwi missed the older woman much, but her death gave him reason to demand a replacement. The old ones gave him another girl, but Nenkiwi's mother disdainfully informed him that the "cousin" he had married was his own father's daughter. Waodani traditionally marry their cousins, but they have strict guidelines for determining which cousins are eligible. Waodani sexual habits made it important for a man to marry only his cross cousins: his mother's brothers' children or his father's sisters' children. They understood that marrying parallel cousins might result in their marrying a half brother or sister, the result of their father sleeping with their mother's sisters. They knew the genetic danger in doing that.

Nenkiwi took the wife who his mother said was his half sister out to the jungle with him to hunt. There he drowned her in a stream—or thought he did—and then went off and left her body unburied. The Waodani considered the idea of not burying her to be as bad as killing her. Nenkiwi had committed a double offense on that one.

Old Mintake, Gikita's lazy sister who had been married to Dabo until he found her to be reluctant to work and "threw her off," had been living in Nenkiwi's house. She was suspicious of Nenkiwi's intentions in going hunting. She followed him and his new wife into the forest. Mintake found the poor girl barely alive after the attempted drowning and helped her back home, where she did finally die.

Reluctantly, the old ones gave Nenkiwi a third girl, named Epa, who bore him two children. It was Epa's two children that Nenkiwi wanted buried with him. Epa's daughter was only about four at the time. Knowing Epa, as I have since I was a little boy, I find what happened next to be almost impossible to imagine.

Epa is a sweet, kind woman and a loving mother, as most Waodani women are. But she was caught in tribal tradition. The Waodani find it almost impossible to believe that *cowodi* women voluntarily give up their babies during the day to be raised by other women who already have plenty of other babies to keep them company. They can't conceive of a mother who would willingly give up the pleasure of nursing her children.

When Nenkiwi demanded that Epa's babies be buried with him, Epa strangled her little daughter and put her in the grave on top of Nenkiwi. Knowing Epa, I think she probably did it to save her precious daughter from the horror of a slow death by suffocation or dehydration locked in a dark hole in the ground with her groaning and bleeding father.

Epa did what was expected of her. But when Nenkiwi demanded that his son, Tementa, join him as well, Epa fled with her still-nursing baby. There is a limit even to the power of tradition.

/\/\/\/\/\/\/\/\

I was ready to call for lights-out as soon as it got dark that night. Actually, our only light was the candle we had brought with us. Most Waodani houses make do with light from their cooking fires, saving rare flashlights with working batteries for excursions on the trail after dark—especially for hunting night animals.

Coba took his blanket, curled up in it, and was asleep immediately. I took a few minutes to get settled. I put on my extra shirt, because it can get really cold at night in the jungle. The rain forest is like a huge swamp cooler, covering millions of square miles. The incredible evaporation of moisture from the wet jungle floor continues after the sun has set, sucking heat out of the muggy air. To be really comfortable, people need clothes on, a blanket over and under them in their hammock, and a warm fire by their feet. I can't imagine how the Waodani survived jungle nights when they had neither clothes nor blankets. I guess that is why they always slept several family members to a hammock and kept their fires going all night.

Paa and Gaba kept rustling around for a while after I was settled down for the night. I finally turned on my flashlight to see what they were up to. Those rascals were setting up a small tent inside our crude school building motel. *Oh no, the roof must leak and they are getting ready for it,* I thought at first. Then I realized the tent must be to protect them from being bitten by mosquitoes and getting *daicou*—fever.

I had intentionally not brought any equipment along that would distinguish me from my three traveling companions. I figured that if they were going to risk malaria on my account, I would risk it with them. So much for not wanting to show them up. I almost expected them to start blowing up air mattresses. After admiring Paa's tent, I queried, "Now mosquitoes can't bite you?" He answered, "Now the bats can't bite us."

I had forgotten all about vampire bats. I was a little upset that Paa had not offered to let me sleep with him in his pup tent. Then I realized that Paa would naturally think that if he had a tent, I would surely have one too. If I didn't bring it, it must have been because I didn't want to use one. So why offer to share his with me when I obviously didn't want one?

Paa told me there were a lot of vampire bats around Damointado, and people and animals there were constantly being bitten. That was nice information to get just before going to sleep unprotected. I had my socks on, so I hoped my big toes, a favorite place for bats to bite, would be safe. I put on my hat and slipped the legs of my spare pants over my head to protect that second favorite place for bites.

I don't know how long I had been asleep when Gaba woke me up to borrow my flashlight. He said he had to go to the bathroom, so I decided to go with him as long as I was awake.

On our way back into the one-room schoolhouse, I noticed dark footprints leading toward the door we had just come from. They started at Paa's tent, proceeded over to where I had been sleeping, then headed out the door. Gaba said "wepe"—*blood*—and then held out his foot. Sure enough, his right foot was covered in coagulating blood. It was everywhere. Even inside the tent. He had been the evening snack for a vampire bat. We noticed blood from Gaba's foot on the mesh of the tent door. He must have inadvertently put his foot against the mesh, and a vampire bat had skinned the flesh from the end of his big toe, right through the mesh tent door.

Bats don't sink their teeth into flesh. They use their razor-sharp canine teeth to peel off a layer of skin just deep enough to expose the capillaries underneath. That is why they like big toes and heads—both places have lots of blood flow just beneath the surface. After getting the bleeding started, vampire bats lick the blood as it flows from the wound. They have some kind of anticoagulant and anesthetic in their saliva that keeps the blood from clotting and the wound from hurting. Paa and Coba, in typical Waodani fashion, started laughing and telling of times when they had been bitten. Then Coba held up his own foot. Sure enough, the bat had tried to bite the side of his exposed foot as well. We could see where the little winged varmint had peeled away the outer skin. All the bat got was a thin layer of callus, because Coba's feet were as tough as leather. The bat probably figured that out and moved on to easier pickings.

I finally went back to sleep, waking a few more times when my back or side went numb from contact with the unyielding, rough boards that served as my mattress.

Too soon, it was morning.

After eating more of what we'd had for supper and drinking some manioc drink—which, as I said, I don't really like, but I know better than to turn down food when it's uncertain how long it might be until it is offered again—we went to visit Cawaena's house.

/\\·/\\·/\\·/\\·/\\·/\\·/\\

I was relaxing in a hammock, listening to Paa and Cawaena carry on a typically enthusiastic conversation about hunting that was going way too fast for me to follow, when I noticed an aluminum bell from some kind of loudspeaker in the corner of Cawaena's house. I picked it up and began to inspect it. It looked like one of those portable megaphones that are used for crowd control at school events when no PA system is available.

"Kinoi?" I asked—*What is it?*

"Well, we don't know," they replied.

"Where did you get it?"

"Out in the jungle, when I was hunting," Cawaena answered.

"Where did it come from?"

Paa answered this one. "Falling out of the plane, it was there where Cawaena found it."

I tried to figure out why someone would be flying over a Waodani village with a megaphone and how they could possibly have dropped it.

"Was it the *compania*?" I asked.

"Wii compania," Paa answered—*Not the oil company.*

"Then who?"

Paa looked exasperated. "Wasn't it your own father who flew over here in the wood bee long ago, calling to us with this thing? Didn't I see him with my own eyes? Him dropping it, Cawaena found it."

But why would my dad have ever been flying near Damointado?

"Flying around and around," Paa explained, as though he was talking about something I surely already knew, "your father gave us presents here before I had hair." He didn't mean hair on his head. He was referring to the fact that he was prepubescent at the time.

"My father gave you presents from the wood bee at this place?" It dawned on me then. This must be the place Dad and his friends had given the code name "Terminal City."

Just fifteen minutes by air from the abandoned Shell Oil company camp at Arajuno, this little clearing with a few thatched huts had been close enough that my dad and Uncle Ed could make weekly flights over it to drop gifts to the Waodani. They wanted to establish a relationship with the people before attempting a face-to-face meeting.

Paa started telling me in minute detail about Dad's flights over this village. Cawaena and his family listened intently as he talked. I wish I could have understood more of what Paa was saying. I had wondered since I was a little boy about this place where Dad made his weekly gift drops to the "Aucas." Those days had been so exciting. I had wished in the worst way that Dad would take me along. But he told me he couldn't let me fly with him until I learned how to swim. It's impossible to go any distance at all in the jungle without having to cross a river. If I was with Dad and we had a forced landing, I would have needed to be able to swim. Besides that, I now realize I would have been in the way, but back then I thought I was my dad's big helper. Now, thirty-nine years later, I was visiting the very place I had longed to see as a boy.

Paa recounted all the presents that the people got from the wood bee. I couldn't believe that he actually remembered what Dad and Ed had given them on each drop. Paa remembered how badly they all wanted to get close to the plane. They actually built a high platform with long poles for legs, so they could get nearer to the aircraft as Dad buzzed the clearing or circled overhead. I knew that was true, because Uncle Ed took pictures of the platform from the air.

"One time, the wood bee dropping the string," Paa told me, "Mincaye tried to climb up to the plane. But the string breaking, Mincaye fell down and we laughed. The wood bee string, being very long and falling on the ground, we were very happy." It takes a lot of work to make string from palm frond membranes. Having fifteen hundred feet of *cowodi* line fall from the sky would have been a windfall for the Waodani.

Paa went on to tell how one of the men in the village had grabbed Paa's pet parrot one day and put it in the bucket as a return gift to the plane. Paa went on, his voice growing sad as he told us, "Giving my very own *cawiae* to the foreigners, they just ate it."

Dad had given that special parrot to me! It had been my pet for years. In fact, I had been standing next to that very parrot, trying to process the fact that my dad was never coming back again, when the *Life* magazine photographer took a picture that has memorialized those sad days. When I explained to Paa what had happened to his parrot, he smiled as if it was a great relief to hear that his prized pet had not been eaten.

It was incredible for me to finally be in this special place that I had imagined as a little boy and wondered about as a man. I asked where Gikita's clearing had been. They told me it was a little ways upriver. The Damointado River and another little stream came together just downstream from the schoolhouse where we were sleeping. The Waodani took me out and showed me where his longhouse had been and exactly where Nenkiwi and Gimade had gone to relieve themselves. Then we walked to the bank of the river where Nenkiwi had fallen into the river while fleeing from Dyuwi, Nimonga, and Komi.

As I processed these little bits of information, I was beginning to better understand the big event that had blown my world apart as a little boy—an event that marked the lives of tens of thousands of other people as well. Over the years, numerous strangers have told me just how dramatically the killings of "those five young missionaries" affected them. They often say something like this: "There are three events that have marked my life that I will never forget. I remember exactly where I was and what I was doing when I heard that President Kennedy was shot and when the Twin Towers fell. And I still remember hearing the news that your dad and his friends were missing in 'Auca' territory. We sat glued to our radio and scanned the newspaper every day, desperate for news about their fate. We were devastated when we heard that they were dead." Then they frequently go on to tell me that they have prayed for me and my family ever since. It's an incredible experience to meet a stranger who has been praying for you for decades.

As I looked around the village and thought about all that had happened here, I couldn't help but feel that perhaps those very prayers had led me back to this place, a place that held so much of my own history.

12

Could This Be Home?

I felt surprisingly chipper after a second night sleeping on the schoolhouse floor. It really gave new meaning to "firm" in describing the quality of a mattress. I thought nothing could be more difficult to sleep on. I would find out I was wrong.

As we left Damointado, the people admonished us to watch for a big jaguar that had been menacing the village. When I asked if a *mini* would actually attack a human, Peque's sons explained that when jaguars get old and can't kill wild pigs, they often try to kill and eat village dogs or small humans. I had a difficult time believing that an animal as shy as a jaguar would attack a person. When they realized that I was skeptical, Peque's son told me that another old jaguar, probably the mate of the one that was still around, had taken a dog from inside his house while his family was sleeping in the same space. He said the cat had grabbed and killed the good-size hunting dog in one bite before running off with it.

Later they found half of the dog lying just a short way into the jungle. The jaguar had pulled it in two, taking half with him. They figured it would come back for the other half, so that night they laid a trap.

Peque and his two boys armed themselves with spears and two guns and settled into branches above what was left of their hunting dog. Sure enough, the jaguar came back for the rest of the dog. They told me they shot and speared it to death. One of them ran into the house next door and brought out a large, spotted jaguar skin that was obviously fairly fresh. It was so full of bullet and spear holes that it looked more like a sieve than a pelt. They clearly had no intention of losing any more dogs to that particular cat. I still don't believe jaguars pose much of a physical threat to humans in the jungle. But the story of the Damointado jaguar did give me something to think about in the painful hours just ahead.

As we left the clearing, Paa, Coba, and Gaba discussed the best route for us to take from Damointado to Tzapino. The Damointado consultants suggested that we go a day downriver to Quiwado and then take the trail from there to Tzapino. That would have taken us east and then north-north-west. I wanted to cut the corner, going straight toward Tzapino, which according to my geodetic survey map would take us right through the place Coba had recommended for the new centrally located community where we might live. Not only did it supposedly have hard dirt for a good runway, but it also lacked a nearby slough, which would reduce the risk of mosquito fever and vampire bats. No one had lived in the area for as long as anyone could remember.

Since none of the Waodani had maps and no one was making any notes, I got the idea that all we had to do was follow the trail straight to Tzapino. Not the best idea I've ever had. First, there is no such thing as straight in the jungle. Come to think of it, I don't even know a Waodani word for "straight." Nor was there any trail from Damointado to the area we were looking for. The people in Damointado were not describing the trail; they were describing the ridges and streams we would have to cross to get to where we were headed. I still can't imagine how jungle dwellers can find their way from a description of ridges, although I have learned to recognize rivers from their descriptions.

I should have known, from the length of the directions they gave us, that we weren't simply going to follow one ridge, as Paa had tried to tell me. With an unfounded optimism in my heart, I followed my three stalwart friends back into the jungle. The first ridge we climbed was gradual enough that it lulled me into the false belief that the trail walk two days earlier had gotten me into shape. Not so! This was just a sucker ridge. It wasn't steep, but after a while I wondered if it was ever going to end. Then we hit the hard stuff.

Besides the grueling topography, the trail petered out. Whoever was in front hacked at the dense undergrowth until he could squeeze through. On this trail my friends were ducking to keep from getting hit on the forehead by branches. Being significantly taller, I had to either bend over at the waist or walk on my knees. If I didn't, my head got so tangled in the jungle growth above that I couldn't move. So I chose to walk bent over, at least on the occasional level stretches. The rest of the time it was easier just to crawl up the ridges on my hands and knees. I needed all four appendages to get up most of them anyway. It occurred to me that my old mountain climbing crampons might have come in handy. Fortunately, I didn't have to climb down the ridges—I just slid down most of the time.

By noon, I had gone through almost a gallon of water. I put it in my mouth and it poured out my forehead. We picked up a tortoise that Gaba found along the way, but I would not have carried that shell-covered dinner if it had been a succulent steak. I could not believe Gaba would add it to what he was already carrying without giving it a second thought. I was trying to figure out how to get someone to carry my canteen and the candy in my pocket.

Finally, I decided that I couldn't go on anymore. I told myself I would make it up and down the ridge we were on, and then they could just leave me to die. We covered thirteen more of those "last ridges" before Coba suddenly pronounced that we had found the good dirt. I was in a daze by this time and just looked at him, stupefied. I had dirt all over me, and my limbs were quivering with fatigue. Coba looked at me and spoke again about the "good dirt." There was nothing good about the grime covering me.

Then I realized he was talking about the dirt under me, not what was clinging tenaciously to my person and clothing. We had reached the place he had pointed out on the map, or so he claimed. But there was no way in the world he could have known where we were. We had been wandering up and down and around the jungle for over eight hours, trying to follow a trail that didn't exist until we cut it. No way. The Waodani might be masters of the jungle, but I figured there was absolutely no chance that anyone could know where we were, within two or three miles.

But I didn't have the energy to discuss the issue. I had to keep staggering toward our elusive destination, or I was going to collapse. I was famished. I felt as if I had a fever, and I was so exhausted that my ears had plugged up. I couldn't get them to clear. It hurt to straighten up after walking bent over for so long. It was the only time I can ever remember wishing I were shorter than I am. Either I needed to shrink or I needed to find a Waodani giant to walk the trail with.

A few minutes' walk from where Coba pronounced that we had found good dirt, we broke out of the jungle onto a riverbank. There were sand beaches, and the water was yellowed with silt. We were back on the Ewenguno River. At least we were on the right river. All I cared about was finding a place to lie down. I collapsed onto the sand and was almost instantly asleep. When I woke up, the sun was going down. Gaba had caught some nice fish and had prepared the tortoise for the soup pot. Paa and Coba had built an impressive sleeping shelter right over me. I could have gone back to sleep without moving until morning. But I had to know if Coba really knew where we were. So I bathed in my clothes, figuring I'd clean my clothes and my body in one step. Then I dug out Rick's little GPS, hung the special antenna, and got set to write down our position.

As I had predicted, it did not match the coordinates on the map. But then I realized that just the south coordinate was off. I started to figure out how far off it was. A quarter of a mile, more or less. Coba had actually brought us to a place in the endless Amazon within one-quarter of a mile of the exact spot he had told me about and picked out on the first map he had ever seen. One measly quarter of a mile.

And then it dawned on me. Coba hadn't said that the beach was the place with hard dirt. He had pointed out a spot a quarter of a mile back in the jungle. He had been dead on. We had found the place that was to be our new home.

/\/\/\/\/\/\/\/\

I was glad Ginny wasn't there to see this spot in its very natural state. I was also thinking a great deal more about the possibility of borrowing Rick's old plane. On the ground, I had hacked, crawled, swum, slid, climbed, and walked to my last ounce of energy. In the air, even a slow old Cessna 172 could do in four minutes what had taken me over eight agonizing hours to do.

Lying on the beach with my three friends that night, though dead tired, I couldn't have been happier. They talked for hours, telling stories and sharing memories. I could only follow the conversation if I knew what the topic was and if they were specifically trying to explain it to me. But regardless, I enjoyed being with them again after being gone most of twenty-six or so years. I had been back for visits, but my connectedness had grown distant and stiff with time. Now I again felt that old exhilaration I had felt as a kid. I loved these people and the world they represented.

As a kid, I had been so impressed with the way the Waodani lived, the way they survived on their own without depending on all the "necessities" of the outside world. The people were independent, doing things that needed to be done, relying on no one but themselves. At least that was how it had been. Now, it seemed that everyone wanted boots, aluminum pots, machetes and axes, blankets, clothes, soap, and salt. All these things came from the outside and had to be purchased. I knew that with time, the perception of need would grow to include much larger things that could not be purchased so easily: things like chain saws to cut boards for permanent houses, outboard motors for the back of dugout canoes, and tin sheeting for roofs. Materialism is an insidious thing; the more you get, the more you expect.

I thought of what King Solomon had said a couple of thousand years ago: "Those who love money will never have enough. How meaningless to think that wealth brings true happiness!" (Ecclesiastes 5:10). I knew from experience that he was right. I thought of all the time-saving devices my North American society had devised: dishwashers, washing machines, dryers, lawn mowers, vacuum cleaners, carpet cleaners, sewing machines, automatic coffeemakers, microwaves, garbage disposals, and the biggest necessity of all—the personal car.

With all those time-savers, one would think that we would have lots of time to sit around and fine-tune our relationships with our friends and families. But that never happened. Despite civilization's handy time–savers, life has become such a rat race that we can't afford to stop even for a few days, much less a couple of months, without risking everything. The Waodani were the ones who had time to play with babies and tell stories about everyday occurrences.

I remembered a time when the only thing a Waodani couple needed to get started on their own was a stone ax. They believed that *Waengongi* seeded these critically shaped stones on the floor of their jungle home just for them. That may have been all they knew about *Waengongi*, but in some respects that simple understanding of God's provision surpassed the complicated relationship that most civilized people have developed with their Creator.

I really began to hope I could help the Waodani, if in no other way, at least to help them realize the futility of getting rich by getting more. I especially hoped that they would avoid the humiliating and debilitating dependence that had wasted Native American tribes. The better-armed soldiers of North America never could subdue some of those tribes, so they gave them reservations, houses, blankets, food, and let them grow bored and unable to do for themselves. Once the people became sufficiently dependent, they could be manipulated at the whim of federal government handlers.

I had read with incredulity how the government had decided to relocate the once-independent and brave Apache from their native lands to the hot, humid, mosquito-infested forests of Florida. Some of the Apache warriors decided to leave the reservation and fight. But they had grown too dependent on government handouts. Winter was coming, and they knew they would starve or die of cold. So they let the government take them to Florida, and half of them died there.

I realized that dependence was the greatest threat the Waodani faced. The greater their perception of need for outsiders' things became—and without an economy of their own to earn money to pay for those things—the more control those from the outside would have over them. I knew they would learn the hard way that "there is no free lunch." But by the time they learned this, it would be too late to turn back. When the once-proud Cherokee people were forced to move from Georgia to Oklahoma, the journey was called the "Trail of Tears." All indications suggested that the Waodani were well on the way to their own trail of tears. They weren't moving geographically, but they were moving culturally from almost total egalitarian independence to national beggarhood.

I didn't think I could do much to stop it, but I was glad I might be able to walk a short way with them—a lot further, as it turns out, than I ever expected back then.

When I saw schoolteachers from the outside world scolding once-proud Waodani warriors and telling them what to do, I began to understand the long-term reality that the Waodani world I was about to rejoin had become virtually unsustainable. For the moment, however, under the beautiful jungle night sky, back with my childhood friends on the Ewenguno River, everything seemed deceptively peaceful.

The night sounds were in full swing. There was no moon, and the nearest artificial lights were so far away that they couldn't corrupt the incredible panorama of stars above us. I remembered lying on the beach, just a few miles upriver, the night after we visited the beach where Dad had been killed and Kathy, Oncaye, Iniwa, and I were baptized. I had been watching the stars that night too. On this night, however, I was amazed when one of the stars visibly moved across the sky above me. I thought it was a shooting star, but it was moving very slowly. I could actually see it moving, more like a crawling star. I asked Coba and Paa and Gaba if they ever saw stars moving across the sky. "Yes," they said, and a few minutes later Gaba pointed to one. I realized that what I was seeing was actually a satellite. As I watched that bright, man-made star cross the heavens over Waodani territory, I realized that it was impossible for the Waodani world to stay the way it had once been. My challenge would be to help them understand the methods and practices of the outside world, those forces that would continue to try to dominate them. I didn't know if I could make a difference, but at least I cared about what was happening to them and could try to coach them in the knowledge they needed if they were going to have any significant say in deciding their fate.

The next day we had to climb only one major ridge. About the time I was getting my muscles limbered up, we crossed a gently flowing river and walked onto the short airstrip at Tzapino. Kimo and Dawa were waiting for us. I wondered how they could have gotten the news so quickly that we were coming. Then I remembered that there were two-way radios in both Damointado and Tzapino.

Tzapino was home to Omene, a man about my age who had been taken in by Aunt Rachel. He was the son of Babae, whom I had been named after. Babae was a known killer who had so many enemies in both the upriver and downriver clans that he had stayed away when the rest of his clan had congregated with the other clans at Tiwaeno. His son, however, had lived for a while in Tiwaeno before moving to the nearby Tzapino community.

Omene had been hoping to connect with members of his father's clan— people his father's prolific killings had separated him from. Instead, he learned that his father's enemies were determined to kill him. Dawa, his aunt, asked Aunt Rachel to take him under her protection. She did, making Omene and me something akin to brothers in the tribe.

Omene had always seemed to be something of an odd duck to me. He grew up in the old ways but was quick to catch on to outsider savvy. On the other hand, he was one of those people whose social timing always seemed to be just a little off. But there was one thing he was known for: He was a great hunter. When Omene went out to get meat, he always came back with meat.

When we arrived in Tzapino, Omene invited me to his house to eat tapir meat. A tapir is the biggest animal in the jungle. It looks like a giant pig with a short trunk. The meat was great, and there was lots of it, filling several cooking pots and weighing down the smoking racks. Omene tried to catch me up on years of happenings in the tribe. I got the feeling he wanted to recount all of the threats and abuse he had suffered while I had been out of touch with the tribe. He used such a mixture of Wao-Tededo and Waodani-ized Spanish that I couldn't tell what he was talking about most of the time. But I was enjoying myself. I just nodded my head and kept eating his tapir meat.

In our conversation, Omene referred to one of his sons who wasn't there. "Where is he?" I asked. "Doobae Oneidi gocandapa," he told me—*He has already gone to God's place.* He explained that his son had been playing soccer with some of the other schoolchildren on the airstrip. He hurt his foot, so he ran over to the house to put on his little rubber boots. When he did, a scorpion hiding in his boot stung him between two of his toes.

He sadly went on to tell me how his son cried and then started to swell, starting at the scorpion bite and moving up his leg. Omene told me that as his leg became swollen, it got cold as if it were already dead. He held his little boy as the poison crept higher and higher up his body. Finally, the child told him that he was going to *Waengongi*'s place. Omene told me his son said he could see people coming from *Oneidi* to take him with them.

"Then the cold reached here," Omene said, pointing to my heart, "and he was no more. I dug his grave right over there." He thrust out his chin to indicate the place his son was buried. Omene's eyes filled with tears, catching me by surprise. Waodani men can be tender with children, but they don't often show tender emotion. It was obvious that Omene still missed his son. I wondered what it would be like to lose one of my children unexpectedly. Although the thought sobered me, I knew that with proper medical care, Omene's son would still be alive. That was one of the primary things they wanted from me.

Cogi, an older warrior from one of the downriver clans, came to Omene's house to meet me. When I was full of meat and sure that I had sufficiently renewed my relationship with Omene, I followed Cogi to his house. Cogi had a smoking rack filled with whole fish about the size of large trout. He motioned for me to sit in a hammock by the fire and handed me a fish. I peeled back a flap of dried skin and began to eat the meat that I could easily pull off of the bones. Cogi seemed to be content just to watch me eat. I was already full, but it had been a long time since I had eaten smoked *kedemenae*. I saved the head until last, since it is actually the tastiest part of the fish. Smoked fish eyes are like hard peas. The gills and brain don't amount to much, but they really are tasty if you don't mind the idea of putting a fish head in your mouth and sucking on it.

As soon as I was well into sucking on the head, Cogi started jabbering to his family. I realized that I had just passed a test of some sort. Cogi had heard that I had lived with the Edomenani when I was young. He wanted to see if it was true. He knew that outsiders do not eat fish heads like the Waodani do. But I ate like the Waodani, picking the flesh off with one hand, licking my fingers a lot, and most important, sucking the head.

Before going back to Kimo and Dawa's house for the night, I met Cogi's son Wentae, a handsome young Waodani man with one of his legs amputated at the thigh, leaving almost no stub. The Waodani aren't shy about their curiosity, as Miimo had taught me on my first introduction to the tribe. However, I knew it was more proper to ask someone else what had happened to Wentae than to ask him directly. So I asked Cogi.

He told me that Wentae was spearfishing, using a metal tip that the Waodani make by heating and hammering a short piece of construction reinforcing rod. These metal tips have two big advantages over the typical Waodani dowel-like spears, which have points that are part of the palm-wood spear itself. The metal holds a point much longer and the metal point can be fashioned with a major barb, so the spear can be thrust into the fish and then retrieved without the fish falling off.

Wentae had accidentally thrust his metal-tipped spear into his upper thigh. He didn't want to have to work the entire spear through his leg, so he just jerked it out the way it went in. The barb caught a major artery on the way out, and Wentae's leg was bleeding so badly he had to tie it tightly with a vine. A mission plane came and got him, or he would have died. As it was, he lost his leg—a drastic handicap for a Waodani warrior with no alternate means of getting around than his remaining leg. When I mentioned that we had just walked over from Damointado, I felt bad for having raised the subject. I knew it must be painful for Wentae to hear people talk casually about something he longed to be able to do again. With his crutches, I assumed there was no way he could ever travel that far. But he didn't seem fazed. "I just came from there too," he replied, as though it was no big deal. I had struggled to make that grueling trek with two legs. How in the world had he done it on only one?

Again, I realized that different worlds develop different stamina. I remembered how exhausted the older people got at night in Aunt Rachel's house when they were learning to read. When they got ready to leave, they would stretch and groan as if they had been through a major ordeal. I wondered if I could become master of both of these worlds, able to work hard physically and mentally, or if trying to live in both would leave me perpetually exhausted.

Kimo and Dawa had the pot on when I returned to their house. Coba, Paa, and Gaba were squatting on the split bamboo floor eating tapir meat and manioc. I had already eaten two meals in two different houses. But we weren't carrying food on the trail with us. I knew I had better obey one of the key jungle rules: When there is food, eat. You never know when you will have the opportunity to eat again.

I thought of my other equally important jungle rules: Don't run when you can walk; don't walk when you can stand; don't stand when you can sit; and don't sit when you can lie down. Whenever you find a place to go to the bathroom, go. This rule has two parts. The second part is, "Unless you are a botanist, never be without toilet paper." And this second part has a corollary as well. "Treat all jungle leaves as though they are stinging nettles or have some other equally harmful characteristic when brought in contact with sensitive flesh."

∧∨∧∨∧∨∧∨∧

Kimo opened his "guesthouse" for the four of us to sleep in. There were a couple of half-rotten boards lying on the dark floor. He picked them up so they would not be in our way. I climbed up the notched pole, ready to settle in for a good sleep. It was too dark to see details inside the little ten-foot-by-ten-foot house.

As my foot came down on my first step inside the tiny hut, my ankle twisted painfully. I tried to catch myself with my other foot, but something was wrong with the floor. I fell onto my side and instantly realized we were in for a long, painful night. The floor was split palm, which usually has some give to it. But Kimo had only split his palm trunks in half. Each floor plank was the still half-rounded trunk of a hardwood tree. If only Kimo had not removed those little pieces of flat board. I tried lying parallel to the humps and then perpendicular to them. I tried to sleep sitting up and even considered just standing through the night. I stuffed my few clothes between the humps, but there were too few of them. They just disappeared into the chasms between those unyielding trunks.

The floor was made from the same palm wood the Waodani use to make their blowguns and spears. I knew there was no chance that the floor would break, but even that would have been a relief. And my misery had no company. While I rolled over and fidgeted from one agonizing position to another, my three buddies contentedly snored away. I was so miserable I even used their backpacks for extra padding. I thought of sneaking back to Kimo's big house, but I would have to wake him to get in.

I considered digging dirt to fill in the valleys in my "bed," but I couldn't break out of my foggy lethargy to actually do something that physical to ease my bruised body.

When my kids were small, Ginny frequently called me "the Princess," as in "The Princess and the Pea," because it bothered me when the kids dragged sand and dirt into our bed on their "footie pajamas." Here in Kimo's guesthouse, I knew I couldn't complain; I had just passed a few of the Waodani's tests, and I didn't want to hurt my reputation as something of a jungle man.

But it was an agonizingly long night. Though I'd hardly slept, when I heard one of Dawa's roosters crowing, I was relieved that daybreak was just minutes away. But after it had crowed for a couple of dark hours, I started to think about relieving my aching bones while getting some exercise and providing breakfast—all by killing that genetically defective rooster.

/\\/\\/\\/\\/\\/\\/\\

In the morning Paa announced that we couldn't go on to Huamono because there was no trail. We had to go by canoe, but there was no one to take us. I said I had assumed Kimo would take us. But Paa just shrugged. "Waa, enenamai"—*Well, I don't know.*

Kimo was family. Surely he would take us down to where the Tzapino and Ewenguno Rivers joined. That was where we would find the trail to Huamono, and I knew Kimo had another hut there.

I turned to Dawa and said, "I see it well to visit my old friend Odoki at Huamono, Kimo taking us." The next thing I knew, Kimo had his trusty paddle out and was heading for the river. We were right behind him.

A young man, his wife, two small children, and an old woman accompanied us in another canoe. The young man had an ax, which he used regularly to cut through trees that had fallen across the narrow river. I figured maybe that was why Kimo hadn't offered to take us at first. The river must have just flooded, and he knew there would be many obstructions. Or maybe it was something totally different. I never found out.

From Kimo's downriver house, it was just a couple of hours' walk from the Ewenguno to the Dayuno River. As we came down the last ridge through someone's garden, Paa gave the customary warning that we were approaching: "Woooooo." Someone ahead relayed the call.

When we arrived, I expected a welcoming party. Wrong again. One little boy stood waiting in the brush at the side of the trail. I didn't even see him until he stepped quietly in front of us and led us past the outsider's board schoolhouse to where Odoki and one of his wives lived.

I had not seen Odoki in about twenty years. He didn't even look up when we entered. He just kept whittling darts and said simply, "Babae, you?" I answered in the affirmative by inhaling quickly with my throat constricted so that it made a sound like a child who has been crying hard and is running out of steam. Odoki then observed, "Ayae kiwimi"—*You are still living.* I inhaled again, and we were all caught up.

Although Odoki had helped to spear the *wena-bai*'s son, he had always treated me like a little brother. It didn't make any difference that I towered over him physically. He still seemed like the bigger man. He was very quiet and didn't give orders or raise his voice, but everyone in the house seemed to relish being with him and doing his bidding.

One of Odoki's young teenage sons by his second wife (who was his first wife's sister) was sitting in a hammock with his foot bandaged. The "old people" had married Odoki to the second sister because there was no one properly related for her to marry. Odoki was expected to give her children and care for them until they were old enough to make gardens and hunt. Then he was relieved of his responsibility for this second family.

When I asked about his son's foot, Odoki just said he was waiting for the shot to come out of it. The handsome boy had been patiently sitting in that hammock for weeks since accidentally shooting himself in the foot with his father's muzzleloader. I asked to see his foot. Under an old cloth he had wound around the damaged foot was a pussy, festering wound.

If something wasn't done, it looked to me as if he would lose many more weeks waiting for it to heal. He might even lose his foot. I had some ointment made from sulfa powder and petroleum jelly in my bag. A doctor at the mission hospital had made it and given me some as a sort of topical, all-purpose antibiotic.

I soaked the boy's foot in hot water while I listened to Coba and Paa converse with Odoki. A small jungle wildcat called a *minidim* had been attacking Odoki's few chickens for several nights. They talked animatedly about the best way to kill it. Most of the vocabulary I had learned as a boy dealt with hunting and fishing, which is what I spent most of my time doing back then. I was quickly remembering what I had known of the language regarding those narrow but popular subjects.

After we had soaked the foot for a while, I began to inspect the wound. There was some dead skin in the wound that had a funny texture. I carefully pulled some of it loose and saw that it was part of the cloth wadding that had penetrated the boy's foot along with the shot. I realized that the wadding probably had more to do with the infection than the shot itself.

I did get a couple of tiny pellets out of his foot, along with the wadding. But I could feel some pellets just under the skin on the top of his foot. It would take them a long time to migrate down to the wound face, if they ever did. I asked Odoki if he wanted the boy to go to the hospital if we could get a plane to come for him. Odoki just deferred to his son. "He knows." *He knows what?* I wondered.

It didn't take long for me to figure it out. Odoki's son did not want to go to the foreigners' hospital. I packed the wound with the sulfa ointment and left some extra clean bandages. I suggested that he soak his foot several times a day to speed the healing. He just raised his eyebrows, a Waodani way of saying yes.

/\./\./\./\./\./\./\

Before going to sleep in the schoolhouse, we trekked down the flat but short airstrip and crossed to the house of Dawa's downriver brother, Bai. Kimo had been part of a spearing raid that had killed much of Dawa's immediate family. He had taken her back upriver as his wife, but they never had any children. Kimo must have had a tender streak in his heart even when he was living in hate and fear, because in spite of Dawa's infertility—or his own—he didn't spear her and never took another wife. He would have had to kill again to get one, because he had no available cross cousins to marry. It dawned on me that Coba's wife, her sister (who is Mincaye's wife), one of Dabo's wives, and Dawa were all downriver women who had been taken in spearing raids. Those men likely would not have taken wives from downriver unless they couldn't get wives any other way. This was another indication of the imminent demise of the Waodani as a sustainable and identifiable people. So many people had been killed that eventually warriors had to kill in order to get wives. The cycle of violence had almost reached the point of no return. If the killing had continued unabated, the tribe would have almost surely wiped itself out.

Old Dabo, who was part of the original Damointado clan, verified what I believed. He had talked to a husband and wife anthropology team that had studied the Waodani as representatives of the most violent people on the planet. He testified, "We were down to almost just two. If Nemo and Woodpecker (Rachel and Betty) had not come, there would have been none of us left."

Dawa's brother Bai was a gregarious old warrior with uncharacteristically gray hair. He was barrel-chested and, though old, still strong. Several of his sons came to meet me. They were bigger than average and appeared strong even by comparison to other Waodani. They had the legs of weight lifters.

Later that night, after we joined a Waodani party for chanting and their version of line dancing at a house across the river, Paa and Coba told me a story about Bai's sons. Apparently, Bai and his boys had previously lived on the border of Waodani territory. An extended family of the Shuar tribe lived across the river from them. It must have been near an oil company road, because the Shuar's tribal territory did not border Waodani territory. They must have followed oil company penetration into the northern borders of Waodani land.

Some members of Bai's family were going upriver to their clearing one day when they stopped off at a little store (another indication that they were near a road). The Waodani got back in their canoe to pole upriver. But one young girl, probably a young teenager, was somehow left behind.

The old man of the Shuar family was home and invited the girl into his house. He abused her and didn't want her to go home and tell. So, they told me, he beat her feet so she couldn't walk. Still determined to get home, she crawled. When she got there and told what the old Shuar man had done, part of which was plainly obvious, Bai's sons grabbed spears and set out to kill the old Shuar.

When they got to the clearing, they ambushed the people in the house and speared all of them—all except for the old patriarch who had caused the problem in the first place. Apparently he was out relieving himself. He lived, but everyone else in his family died.

From meeting Bai and his sons, I knew I wouldn't want to be in their part of "town" if they were out looking for me.

∕\/\·\/·\·\/·\/\∕

I slept like a baby that night. After a night in Kimo's guesthouse, that board floor in Huamono was by far the softest I had ever slept on. The next morning, after drinking banana drink until my stomach was tight, I was almost ready for the trail again. This last walk was going to be the longest one of the trip. But I was starting to realize that it only makes sense to measure distances in the jungle when flying. On the trail or by river, the only thing that matters is how long it will take you to get there—usually measured as half a day, a day, or sometimes several days.

From Huamono to Quiwado, the village downriver from Damointado, we would be walking mostly west, paralleling the ridges and rivers. That meant fewer ups and downs. It also drizzled all day long, which kept the temperature down. My perspiration washed away in the drops constantly falling from the canopy overhead. The trail was muddy in places but not too bad.

I was getting into this walking thing. Before I knew it, it was almost noon. When we got back to Kimo's downriver house, we poled farther down the Ewenguno and then partway up the Quiwado. We left our canoe and did the last several hours on foot again. We bathed as soon as we arrived in Quiwado. That was proof that I was getting used to trail walking; at least I had enough strength at the end of the day to stand in the river and clean up.

Another of my childhood friends was living in Quiwado. Tementa was my younger brother Phil's age. He was also Nenkiwi's son, the one Nenkiwi had wanted buried with him. I was looking forward to seeing what had become of Tementa. He had been a homely little potbellied fellow when I had first lived with the tribe, and that was still the way I remembered him.

Aunt Betty had told me that Tementa practically lived on her steps while she and her daughter, Valerie, lived in Tiwaeno. He was always asking in his whiny little voice, "Mangade pantate tum, pantate tum?"—*Valerie, do you want to go swimming; do you want to go swim?*

In typical Aunt Betty talk, she often described him as "that pathetic child, simply pathetic."

To make matters worse, when he was a little bit older, Tementa tried to take a piece of meat that one of the hunting dogs had laid claim to. The dog bit little Tementa in the face, almost tearing off the side of his mouth and leaving his face badly scarred.

But I was soon to find out that what Tementa lacked in looks, he more than compensated for with a keen intellect and a quiet way of drawing consensus from the individualists who made up his tribe.

When Aunt Rachel went in to live with the tribe, Epa often sent little Tementa to Aunt Rachel's house to listen to her teach Dayumae and others about *Waengongi*. Tementa would go home and teach his mother what he had heard.

It was through Tementa that Epa decided to follow God's trail. Years later, with his mother's coaxing and Aunt Rachel's challenge that he teach others, Tementa also decided to follow *Waengongi's* trail. Then he became a translation helper for Aunt Rachel as she put God's carvings into the People's own talk.

That night in Quiwado, we were invited to spend the night in Awa's house. We had just gotten there when a wiry old warrior exploded into the house. His eyes looked wildly about until he saw Gaba and me standing along the split bamboo that made up the walls of this home built high in the air on tall posts.

The little man came charging up to us, pulled his shorts down, and fell face-first onto the floor in front of us. He didn't get down on his knees and lay down. He just fell forward and bounced off the split-palm floor a couple of times.

Judging by the way he had come at us, I thought he might be planning some kind of bodily harm. He didn't say a word, however. He simply lay prostrate before us. When Gaba realized that I did not know what was happening, he told me matter-of-factly, "Wepe is wanting the thorn." I still did not catch on. "Injection-bai," he clarified.

What? Wepe wants a shot? What for? And how does Gaba know this? I wondered.

"He wants a shot to make him *taaemo*."

"What kind of a shot would make him strong?" I asked.

"B doce," Gaba explained. Someone must have given this old warrior some vitamin B_{12} shots in the past. They made a believer of him, and he wanted more.

Gaba took over. He took out a packet from his little backpack and started mixing powder with serum in preparation for injecting the concoction. Wepe just lay facedown on the floor, bare and exposed, as though he were dead. When Gaba's syringe was loaded, he expertly jabbed it into Wepe's wrinkled little butt cheek, aspirated the syringe by pulling back to make sure he wasn't in a blood vessel, and injected the medication.

As soon as he pulled the needle out, Wepe jumped to his feet, pulled up his elastic-waisted shorts, and began jabbering animatedly about something—as though he had not just been lying naked on the floor. If Gaba's medicine was that good, I could have used some B_{12} myself.

As I considered the drama that was playing out in front of me, I began to realize just how arrogant my thinking had become. Wepe hadn't come to me for help; he had come to Gaba. I had just assumed that I knew more about medicine than anyone else because, well, I was from the outside world.

I realized that on this trip alone, I had already doctored several people right in front of Gaba without even waiting to see what he might want to do. For that matter, how did I know that Coba and Paa didn't know more than I did in this area? They certainly knew more about everything else in their world.

.∧.∨.∧.∨.∧.∨.∧.∧.

In the late afternoon, someone turned on the little transceiver mounted on the porch of the Ecuadorean teacher's house. Mission Aviation Fellowship had a regularly scheduled contact with most of the communities they served in the jungle. Each station would report their weather conditions and then pass along flight requests. In the evenings, the people in the community just listened in on the frequency for any emergency news. I wanted to make sure that the plane was still scheduled to fly my three traveling buddies back to Toñampade before flying me back to Shell Mera.

I had really had a great time with Coba, Paa, and Gaba, but I was ready to leave. In each community we had visited, people had solemnly told me that if I would come show them how to do the things they needed help with, they would help build an airstrip at this new location. They convinced me that they liked the idea of doing things for themselves. There seemed to be an undercurrent of discomfort with always having to wait for others to help them.

However, I realized that the only way to measure their commitment was to start the experiment and see who would put their sweat where their talk was.

I called MAF in Shell a number of times that afternoon. They acknowledged my call, but they gave me the runaround about my scheduled flight the next morning. I attributed their elusiveness to the poor radio conditions. Whoever was on the other end was speaking Spanish, but I didn't know who he was and he did not seem to know who I was.

I got on the radio again the next morning and got the same runaround. They kept telling me to wait for them to contact me later. Finally, at about noon, they told me that the plane was on its way. I was perplexed by their lack of specificity and by the fact that no one who knew about my flight request and confirmation ever came to the radio.

Finally, the Waodani yelled, "Ebo, ebo"—words that had always sent a shiver of excitement through me out in the jungle. Nothing was more exciting in a jungle village than having the plane come. Gaba, Paa, Coba, and I waited by the airstrip as the plane made its approach.

It is common for planes to fly over the strip to check the wind sock and make sure there are no obstructions on the airstrip. This time, however, the pilot just made a straight-in approach. He seemed to be light on the brakes, because he was still moving pretty fast when he passed us at about midstrip. He should have been stopped by that point. Something strange was going on.

As the Cessna 206 flashed past us, we could see that the pilot was dressed in camouflage. He wore a flight helmet with a dark sun visor in place. My mind reacted even before I consciously realized what was going on. I yelled, "Sequestro!"—*It's a kidnapping!* I grabbed my backpack and ran for the jungle. Several of the Waodani were right behind me, though I was sure I was the target. I charged through someone's manioc patch on my way to a trail I had seen leading into the jungle behind Awa's house. I had heard enough stories about kidnappings of "gringos" in Colombia, and I was sure I was now the intended victim of one. Just as I was swallowed up by the giant green, I heard someone yell, "Capitan Henry, Babae; it is Capitan Henry."

I looked back at the airstrip and sure enough, there was Henry Orellana standing beside the Waodani, waving for me to come. Henry was an old friend whose parents lived in Shell and managed the hangar where Aunt Rachel had gotten her supplies.

My adrenaline level was so high and my heart was beating so hard that I didn't even mind all the people laughing at me for fleeing. I did feel foolish, though, until Henry explained what was going on.

While I had been innocently trudging from village to village, Ecuador had gone to war with Peru, our neighboring country to the south. Not one of the villages we had visited knew anything out of the ordinary was going on, proving that the Waodani really were isolated from the rest of Ecuador. There was no mail service to Waodani territory, they had no place to vote, and there was no news service in their language.

The Peruvians could have invaded Waodani territory and recruited them to fight against their own country, and most of the Waodani never would have known the difference. I felt my anger rising. If the Ecuadorean government wanted to claim sovereignty over the Waodani, it certainly owed it to them to treat them like citizens. Ecuador isn't a homogenous population outside of Waodani territory. There are a lot of other tribes—Quechuas,

Shuar, Atshuar, Zaparos, Cofans, and Colorados. And these are just the tribes living in the rain forests. Besides these, there are a number of mountain tribes such as the Otavaleños and the Salasacas. All indigenous people groups have long been discriminated against in Ecuadorean society. But the Waodani, though the most famous tribe in the country, have generally been treated like the bottom rung on the social ladder.

I knew someone needed to stick up for the Waodani's rights. But in the back of my mind, I remembered the story of Moses I had learned as a little boy. When he found out he was a Hebrew who had been raised in Pharaoh's house, Moses decided to stand up for his people. When he saw an Egyptian abusing a Hebrew slave, Moses killed the Egyptian. A short while later he found two Hebrews fighting and tried to help settle their quarrel too. But one of the quarreling Hebrews challenged him: "What are you going to do, kill us too?"

I knew it would be risky to attempt to aid this group of people I wasn't legally a part of. And the risk would skyrocket if I harbored any expectations of being appreciated for it. People were sure to assume that I was doing it for gain of some sort. I realized that if I really wanted to help the Waodani for their sakes and not mine, I could expect to become persona non grata among the Latin Ecuadoreans, for whom the Waodani were merely an obstacle in the way of oil revenues. I would probably be despised by environmentalists and anthropologists who wanted to use the famous Waodani with their uniquely egalitarian culture to publicize their causes. The oil companies saw the Waodani as an unpredictable headache that they just wanted to go away. And then there were the lumber interests coming across the border from Colombia who would exploit the Waodani when they could and kill them or drive them off if they couldn't.

I knew it would be the height of foolishness to expect the Waodani as a group to follow my recommendations. I didn't expect them to appreciate me, even if I did what they had asked me to do. The Waodani don't even have a traditional way of saying "thank you."

Even though I realized all of this, I had no way to fully grasp all the controversy I was about to become part of. I'm glad I didn't know. I was still coming from a long immersion in the North American mind-set, which assumes that the less friction there is in life, the better.

Henry explained to us that when war was declared just a few days earlier, the Ecuadorean Air Force commandeered all private aircraft. Henry, part of the Ecuadorean Air Force reserves, asked to be assigned to one of the MAF planes he flew regularly. Then he told the authorities that there was a "gringo" stranded in Waodani territory by the war. He convinced them that it could be bad news if anything happened to this gringo, whose family was so famous that his father's face had been put on an Ecuadorean stamp and whose mother knew a past president of Ecuador. Exaggerated, but appreciated.

They gave Henry the go-ahead to make a rescue flight to extricate me before the situation became an international incident. But he told me he only had authorization to take me. "What about Paa and Coba and Gaba?" I asked. I couldn't just leave them after taking them away from their families for a week. I tried to explain what was going on. Gaba understood; Coba accepted it as another of those mysterious things that happens in the outsiders' world. But Paa accused me of going back on my word. He was right. I considered staying simply to make the point: "We all go or no one goes." But I knew that was futile. Paa wasn't upset that I wasn't going to walk two more days with him to Toñampade. He was upset because I had told him we would fly back from Quiwado. He wasn't tired of walking, as I was, but he was tired of being away from his little hut and his own cooking fire.

It was a good lesson for me. There were going to be many circumstances in the months to come that the Waodani just wouldn't understand. I would probably be accused of tricking them or not keeping my word. And there would not be any way to explain myself to them, because they didn't have the foundational information to understand certain issues.

I gave them the little bit of food I had, some candy, extra medicine, fishing line and hooks, a pocketknife, and a few other items. Once I was on the plane, I realized that giving those things probably just made it look like I was trying to buy myself out of trouble for having misled them. I felt terrible at having to abandon them and upset that one or two of them might think I had planned to do this. How could they understand that Henry really could not take them?

I wanted them to understand my situation. But was I willing to accept theirs? They had been tricked plenty of times before. What I was doing to them was suspiciously similar to what others had done to them.

True love doesn't mean "never having to say you're sorry," as *Love Story* postulated. It means expecting the best of those you love and giving them every reasonable benefit of the doubt. I was still learning to do that with the Waodani.

ᐱᐱᐱᐱᐱᐱᐱᐱ

I felt terrible for abandoning my friends, but I really was ready to go home. My week on the trail had marked me. I did not realize it then, as is often the case when we are in the midst of a pivotal life lesson, but this experience had altered the course of my life. I had not radically changed my thinking, really. But over the course of the week, I had somehow been stripped of enough of my everyday life that I actually started, in a very small way, to look at circumstances and events from the other side of the fence. For just a few days, I was totally dependent on people who owed me nothing. Love was the only dependable tie between us.

I have long dreaded the thought of getting to the end of life and regretting that I allowed my own timidity or other people's expectations to determine the course of my life. I had decided at a much younger age that several of my beliefs should determine the course of my life.

I believe that what happens in the world and in my own life is not the result of mere chance, just as I believe that life itself is not the result of a chance encounter of critical compounds meeting by accident in some ancient primordial soup. I believe that the same Intelligent Designer who created me has given me the freedom to make choices within the script of my life. But I also believe that *Waengongi*, the Creator, has an epic script into which my minute presence has been written.

Heading back to the United States, I finally knew that returning to live with the Waodani was God's next chapter for my life. It was a huge stretch of faith for me to keep my hands off the pen, however. I knew there would be people who would think this was crazy. They weren't significant. I was much more worried about the people who would undoubtedly think this was some publicity stunt: "Son of martyred father returns in love to take God to his father's killers."

That is the kind of story we yearn for, the kind that ends with "And they lived happily ever after." But that never happens. After each chapter, life just grinds on, and we have to go on making choices and living with the consequences.

I did not have any illusions that I could do anything significant to alter the future of the Waodani. I understood that there would be no long lines of well-wishers on either side of this issue. The people already meddling in the Waodani world would see me as a competitor. Most of the Waodani would be primarily interested in the handouts they thought they could get from me. In that game, influence is given to the highest bidder.

The Waodani believed in the existence of *Waengongi* before Aunt Rachel, Dayumae, and Aunt Betty ever told them about Him. They saw evidence of the Creator in His creation. They knew He cared about them because of the stone ax heads they found on the jungle floor from time to time. Without those ax heads, they could not clear gardens, meaning they could not survive.

The world wanted to make gardens for the Waodani. If God was leading me to take my family and leave our home, schools, friends, and career, I knew my call was simply to be like an ax head. I could not guarantee Waodani survival, but I could offer myself as a tool if they wanted to use me to help clear the way to a future.

I knew there would be people who would try to make heroes of us for the sacrifices we were going to make for the Waodani. I also knew that our sacrifice would not be what those people were thinking of: leaving our world of ease for a world of deprivation and hardship. No, our real sacrifice would simply be to continue giving up control of our lives. Frankly, life in the rat race of the developed world, with all its time-saving technologies and civilized comforts, is not easy. Giving up that life would not be very difficult for me. I just needed to believe that there was a reason to do it. Obedience to God was the only reason that made sense to me. That would have to be our reason.

I had no idea what would come of this experiment. I didn't even know what I was supposed to do. This was not part of the plan I had laid out for my life. But I believed it was part of a much bigger plan that would eventually prove to make our lives significant. I yearned for that sense of significance, not just for myself, but also for Ginny and Shaun Felipe (Toñae), Jaime Nate (Mincaye), Jesse Abram (Yeti), and Stephenie Rachel (Nemo).

13

Get
Ready

When I arrived home and told Ginny and our kids about my trip, everyone was in agreement that we should go live with the Waodani. There was little discussion or worry over coming to a consensus; it just happened. It appeared that I wasn't the only one who had undergone change during the week I was on the trail. We were ready, excited, and apprehensive.

I had begun planning our return to live with the Waodani as soon as I got back to Shell with Capitan Henry. I started a list of the many "little" details I needed Ginny to help me fill in, such as how Jesse and Steph would continue their high school studies in the jungle.

The big things on my list included getting gardens started so we would have food and getting an airstrip built so we could use Rick's Bravo Tango Sierra (BTS) to get in and out and around.

Manioc takes at least nine months to mature to the point that it can be eaten. And really, it isn't fully mature for about a year. I was pretty sure that plantains take almost a year to produce as well. We would have to plant our gardens immediately. Being able to get around without depending on another pilot would be a huge benefit, but only if we had our own airstrip. As I remembered, the little one in Tiwaeno took a couple of years to build. I spoke with some of the pilots at MAF, and they agreed it would take at least a year to build an airstrip without some kind of tractor. I did not expect to have a tractor.

On my weeklong trek, I had noticed that none of the Waodani villages had God's houses. Tiwaeno had once had one, and so had Tzapino. Now they didn't. I asked the People why. They simply said that they couldn't build them. Of course they could, I told them. They could build a *Waengongi onco* in the same way they built their own *oncos*! They explained that they could only build *durani-bai*—like the ancient ones had—not "proper" churches.

As the conversation went on, I realized that when outsiders had built the crude little board church in Tonampade, with cement posts and a tin roof, everyone decided that this is what a "proper" God's house should be like. The Waodani didn't know how to make boards, they didn't know what that mush was that got so hard and supported the building, and they didn't have money to buy tin roofing.

The Waodani in Toñampade would not even attempt to fix the church floor, which had begun to rot. When I asked them why they didn't fix it, they said they couldn't because they did not have permission. "Permission from whom?" I asked. They didn't know the answer to that, but what they did know was that they had not built it or paid for it. They did not know whose it was, but they knew it definitely was not theirs.

I realized that if the community we were planning to build together was going to really be *theirs*, they would have to build it. That was especially critical of the airstrip.

In most communities, the Ecuadorean government provided financial help to clear an airstrip. The government helped by buying shovels, picks, and wheelbarrows, and they sometimes even provided rice for the people when they were away from their homes and gardens working on a new strip. That was a huge help, but it had one serious drawback, as I saw it. If a community accepted help from the government in building the airstrip, the government had a right to use it. According to the Civil Aviation authorities, if we accepted help from the government, we would not be able to control our airstrip. If the oil company wanted to use it, they could. If *colono* (land squatters and colonists) wanted to use it, they could, even if they were bringing in *agua ardiente* ("firewater") to sell to the Waodani. Just as with North American tribes, alcohol was already becoming a major problem among the People.

The airstrip would be a powerful first test of the Waodani's resolve to take charge of their own future. I knew it would be a huge task, but I would soon find out that even I was underestimating how difficult it would be.

I decided to get a couple of chain saws to help speed the process along. I knew that one of the serious challenges in building an airstrip was to find a piece of jungle floor level enough and long enough to accommodate at least a bush plane. In Tiwaeno, the tiny airstrip started at the river and ended at a slough, and there was no space for it to be lengthened. It was just long enough for the Helio STOL plane but not long enough for it to take off with a full load. More common bush planes could not use it all. After nearly two years had been spent building that first airstrip, it was still barely usable.

I went down to Jerry's Pawn and Gun in our hometown of Ocala to fish for ideas that would help in building our new airstrip. I found a pistol laser sight. Lasers are often used in construction. I experimented and found I could mount the laser sight on a level tied to a tree. It would show me straight and level for at least a couple of hundred yards. Two moves and we would have our centerline laid out.

We would need some way to stay in touch with MAF to call for supply drops. That would require a two-way radio and some sort of power source. We would need extra chains, links, files, two-cycle oil, and spare parts for the chain saws' engines. I could pick up gasoline and dynamite in Shell. I had never used dynamite, but I remembered Uncle Roger had used it once to blast out tree stumps so they could finish an airstrip. This was when Dad needed to deliver medicines quickly in order to stop a flu epidemic that was decimating the villagers near where the Youderians lived.

I knew I would also need a hardy soul who could keep the chain saws and an outboard motor running; someone who was familiar with a winch and understood how a lever works. I wanted someone who would be willing to hurt along with me. I knew the supremely conditioned Waodani would be immune from most of my discomforts. Misery loves company, and I was expecting to be miserable.

I called Ginny's sister's husband, Steve. He and his brothers are large-scale farmers in Minnesota. He is a hard worker and an excellent mechanic, and he has a soft heart toward spiritually and physically hurting people. Years earlier, Steve and I had helped build part of a dam and penstock high in the Andes Mountains for the World Radio Missionary Fellowship in Ecuador.

I knew Steve could usually get away for a while in the winter, so I took a chance and asked him. I never got around to explaining what we would be doing, how long it would take, what we would eat, or what the chances were of surviving this adventure. Before I could get to any of that, Steve just said, "Sure, I'll go with you."

He met me in Florida, and we set about packing the chain saws, outboard motor, solar panels, a communications radio, antennae, tools, batteries, and an essential frill: a combination TV/VCR. If we could buy a twelve-volt video player, we could show the Waodani videos about the outside world. The world outside the jungle seemed like science fiction to the Waodani.

We were going to need a big crew of Waodani, too—the bigger the better. The Waodani are all strong, and they are good workers when they are motivated. But they don't live to work. That is a unique trait common only to civilized people from the "developed" world. The Waodani work to live.

Having rice and sugar and coffee would be a real treat for the prospective airstrip crew. The Waodani seldom had access to such luxuries or the money to buy them. When we had all our duffels packed, we had a total of over six hundred pounds of baggage. We were allowed only two checked bags of seventy pounds each, per airline ticket. That would cover half of what we had. We could get about fifty pounds in our carry-ons. We couldn't take more than that on the plane because we also had to take the fragile pieces, such as the two-way radio, in our carry-ons.

It looked as if our luggage would be two hundred to three hundred pounds over the weight limit. My dad's oldest brother, Sam, had retired just a few years earlier as a senior 747 pilot with the same airline we were taking. I called him about the possibility of finding someone with enough authority to let us take the extra baggage. Finally, an executive with American Airlines called to inform me that the only one in the organization who could allow me to take extra bags was the agent at the ticket counter. If they charged extra for our luggage, it could be expensive. But what if they simply wouldn't take half of our equipment? And then there was the matter of the outboard motor. I stripped everything I could off of it without requiring complex reassembly on the other end. It still weighed just over a hundred pounds.

I already knew the baggage handlers' rules specify that they don't have to handle any bag over a hundred pounds. We really needed that motor to get up and down the river to the Toñampade airstrip. I did not realize it, but I was about to enter a unique relationship with American Airlines.

We needed a dual-axle flatbed trailer to get all our bags to Orlando International Airport. I took the porter's groans as a bad omen. We piled our bags in front of the counter, where they were painfully obvious.

I tried to figure out which agent would be the most likely to give us a break. I was still trying to decide when a sharp, efficient voice called, "Next." Before we even got to the counter, the agent asked, "Do those huge bags belong to you? If they are overweight, I'm going to charge you big time."

Perfect. We had way too many bags, far too much weight, and one piece of luggage that was over the absolute threshold of acceptability. And we really needed *all* of it. I could tell from the look on her face that our ticket agent, Connie, was the kind of woman you wanted managing your business and guarding your door. She was obviously no pushover. There was no use sweet-talking Connie.

"Where do you think you're going with all this stuff, anyway?" she asked. "We're going to the Amazon jungle," I informed her. "And if we can't take all of this with us, there isn't much use in us going."

She ignored the "no use going" part and exclaimed, "The Amazon? Oh, I've always wanted to visit the Amazon. I read everything I can get my hands on about the Amazon. If I let you go, can I come visit you?" I thought she was putting me on, so I told her sure. "If there's room on the plane, you're welcome to come with us."

She wasn't fooling. She really wanted to go with us. "I can't just go off to the jungle," she said, as though I needed to have the basics of life explained to me. I suppose she did have some grounds for assuming that, considering I had shown up at the airport with more baggage than everyone else on the whole plane combined.

Connie continued to chat with me about the Amazon, asking questions and telling me what she had read. She appeared to have forgotten that there was a line of passengers waiting on her and that the two overloaded Steves were going to miss their flight. Then all of a sudden, she told me to write down my phone number so she could arrange to visit us. Then she called one of the porters over to the counter by name.

I decided it was time to throw my hook into the water. "Connie, I have one problem here," I began. I felt like I was back in second grade asking to go to the bathroom ten minutes after recess had ended. "Unless I can take all of this stuff down with me, there won't be anyplace for you to visit."

"Okay," Connie told me. "Jay here is going to take your bags down for you. They won't fit down the chute." She saw Jay struggling to get the huge duffel with the outboard engine onto his cart. "What have you got in there anyway, a boat?"

"No, of course not!" I didn't tell her it was just the engine for the boat.

Steve was helping Jay while Connie and I continued our in-depth analysis of all things Amazonian. It was really getting late.

Steve surprised me by handing me two of the same luggage tags that Connie had given Jay. I couldn't believe it. She had given us extras. I carefully asked Connie, who was now working hard to upgrade us to first class, if she minded my putting a couple of carry-ons in a duffel. She just waved me to go ahead.

That was a relief. Our carry-ons had grown. They weighed almost seventy pounds each and had no wheels. We jammed all but the most fragile items into two spare duffel bags I had brought along, thinking we would need them to pack things we would have to leave behind. Jay took the bags and twenty dollars, which he was fully earning, and headed off for the secret places of airport terminals known only to the privileged few. Then Steve and I took off for our gate and our first-class, cushy seats.

I didn't know it then, but Jay was going to become almost a friend of the family, Connie would be more like a member of the family, and I was going to be the procuring cause for hundreds of people to buy seats on American Airlines to Ecuador.

Lest I give the impression that Connie was taking advantage of American Airlines, let me say that she won me over as the company's most loyal customer. As long as Connie was working the American counter in Orlando, I would never fly another airline.

/\/\/\/\/\/\/\/\/\

Steve and I rented a bus in Quito to take us and our things to Shell. We flew to Toñampade, hoping there would be some people there ready to build an airstrip.

Mincaye was there and ready to go, of course. There was also a small group of other stalwarts, mostly God followers from the old Tiwaeno community. But when word got out that we had rice, beans, and sugar to take with us, our numbers swelled. We were a motley crew, but we were now a *big* motley crew.

Some of the men had nice clothes and shoes. I even noticed some name brands. Those fellows had obviously been outside the jungle long enough to learn what was considered important in the outside world. Other men, even fairly young ones, had earlobes distended from wearing large earplugs. I knew that the only younger men with holes in their ears were Aenomenani. The upriver People had stopped that distinctively Waodani tradition as soon as they found out that most outsiders identified anyone with big holes in their ears as "Aucas." Some of the older men let their hair grow to cover their ears. The women stopped cutting the traditional bangs, which extended across their foreheads to behind their ears in order to show off their white balsa plugs against their handsome olive skin.

I also saw a number of poor-quality tattoos. Those men had probably spent some time in the oil company camps. It looked like a lot of the tattoos were intended to commemorate the recent war with Peru.

One man of about twenty-five gave evidence that he might very well have been separated from his source of oxygen at birth. He had that special look about him, laughed too often and too loudly, and had some peculiar mannerisms. I wondered to myself, *How many are going to work, and how many are coming along just for the food?* I am embarrassed to admit that now.

Once we got started with the work, I realized that some of the men did turn out to be jokers, but at least they kept the troops entertained. Waodani don't work and play, anyway. They simply *cae*, or "do."

Everybody, even the cutups, worked incredibly hard, except for Wimanae, the warrior who seemed to be missing a few marbles. He would watch the rest of us start to work, and then he would disappear. I arrogantly figured it was probably just as well that he didn't stay around and get hurt. I found out, to my shame, that he was going out every day to hunt meat for the rest of us. It took a lot of meat to feed the more than thirty men in our crew. Wimanae, with just a little help, saw to it that we were never without protein.

I was going to teach the Waodani some useful things about building the airstrip, but they were going to teach me a lot more. I was starting to get used to that.

∧·∧·∧·∧·∧·∧·∧·∧

The first thing we had to do was build a camp. We strapped our well-used twenty-five-horsepower Johnson on the back of a big dugout boat that belonged to Sam (Caento), Dayumae's son, who had been a good friend of mine since we were kids. The boat held a few of us, along with loads of plantain, manioc, and plantings for our new gardens downriver. When we were loaded, our huge canoe had hardly any room left. No one seemed to know how to run the engine, so I volunteered to do it myself.

I had run an outboard on a canoe only once before, when Sam and I were on an adventure up on the northern border of Waodani territory. We had caught a ride on a huge freight canoe heading up the Napo toward the nearest road. The engine on that canoe started sputtering and coughing, but the *motorista* didn't seem to notice. It was getting dark, and the river was swollen from recent rains, with huge tree parts floating toward us like battering rams.

At Sam's urging, I went to the back of the boat to see if I could lend a hand. I knew almost nothing about navigating a jungle river. I think it was our operator's first time too. As soon as I got close to him, he smiled and handed me the tiller. I was about sixteen at the time.

I may have been green, but at least I wasn't a first-timer anymore. On this trip, we were headed with the current. I would guess our canoe weighed about thirty-five hundred pounds empty. With fifteen men, our duffels, and all our stalks of bananas and plantain shoots, we probably weighed eight thousand pounds. It would not be difficult to push the boat downriver, but if the engine quit while I was maneuvering around one of the innumerable sharp bends between Toñampade and our destination, we could easily lose most of our belongings—and maybe some lives, too!

I had to pull the engine out of the water probably thirty times when we ran over sunken trees wedged into the river bottom by regular flooding. The one problem I had not anticipated was that every time the river changed direction, the current pushed to the opposite side of the river. As it was changing sides, the current became wider before bunching up where the far bank made it switch direction. In those shallow crossovers, our overloaded canoe would hit bottom. The nose would grind to a halt, and then the current would push the back end around until it was even with the nose and sideways to the current. At that point the whole forty feet or so of the boat would run aground while the current worked feverishly to roll it over. Meanwhile, all of us in the canoe were desperately trying to pry it loose before it did so.

The rest of our gang hopped into little dugouts and poled for all they were worth. We surged ahead on the deep stretches when the current was up against one bank or the other. But after the first couple of experiences with getting stuck, I tried to stay just ahead of the rest of the flotilla so they could help us push when we got stuck.

That seemed like a good plan: One for all, and all for one. But Waodani culture has an abbreviated version of this code. Their cultural standard is more like "One for one"—in other words, every man for himself. If we looked as if we were about to turn over and lose everything, those passing us would hoot and laugh and yell insults and advice. It didn't even occur to them to help us. And stranger still, it didn't seem to occur to the men in our boat who were struggling to save the ship to ask for help.

It was mid to late afternoon when we finally reached the place where Gaba, Paa, Coba, and I had spent the night on the beach under the stars. No one yelled instructions or divided us into teams or took charge; everyone just did what he somehow decided he should do. Within an hour, a sturdy shelter had been built, with a tarp for a roof and a ditch dug around it to keep the floor dry. Fires had been started in a thatched cooking hut, and some of the men were already fishing.

Steve and I hung our army surplus hammocks with attached mosquito nets. Before nightfall, some of the men had started preparing a site for our garden. They began by clearing jungle by the river where there weren't many big trees to cut down. I checked out the solar panel and connected it so we could show videos that night.

While I was doing that, Steve started to assemble the chain saws. Everyone was interested when they heard them start up. For about six of the men, the chain saws were like magnets. They watched every move Steve made. I already knew from past experience that I would not be able to sleep in my army hammock. So I asked Tidi, a member of the self-appointed chain saw group, if he could cut us a couple of thin boards to use as beds.

He asked me how to do it, but I didn't know what to tell him. I had never cut boards with a chain saw. I just knew that Quechuas and *colonos* cut boards freehand all the time. I had figured Waodani could too. Tidi took off to figure it out by himself. We soon heard the saw running, a big tree falling, and then more cutting. In no time, Tidi was back with the chain saw in one hand and several boards over his other shoulder. He cut some poles with Y's at one end and a point at the other. He drove in two of these on each end where we were going to sleep and joined each pair of Y's with a horizontal pole. Then he put one of his new boards across each horizontal pole and—presto—a bed. Our new beds were firm but springy. Steve and I slept on those beds for ten days and grew fond of them—not necessarily because they were so comfortable but because they were a lot better than sleeping on the damp ground or in our army hammocks that kept flipping over.

The next morning we were all up at the crack of dawn. We ate soup made from *panonae*, a large jungle rodent that Wimanae had shot with his muzzleloader while the rest of us were sleeping. Then we crossed the river, climbed the unusually steep bank on the other side, and headed for the stretch of jungle where I hoped the airstrip would one day exist. I noticed that from the top of that far bank we had a nice view up the river to the northwest and down it to the northeast. I knew I had found the place I wanted to put my house, if the bank was solid enough not to cave in every time the river flooded. Mincaye, who always stayed near me, agreed that this was the place for my new house. He pointed a short distance from the site and informed me, "That is where I will build my house." So Mincaye was planning to leave his house and gardens and children and grandchildren up at Toñampade to live with me and my family. I wondered how his family would react to that news.

I had seen some rock in the face of the bank, and Coba told me that this bank never broke off. It was settled. This little virgin piece of rain forest would soon be home. I tried to imagine it but could not. The whole idea of actually being out in the middle of the Amazon with plans of settling there was ethereal. I hurried to catch up with the gang. They were following Coba, who was following the barely discernible trail we had cut when we came through from Damointado.

Using the laser-gun sight taped to a level that I'd nailed to a tree, we started laying out a trail that we hoped would be the centerline of our new airstrip. On the first couple of tries, we were unsuccessful. In one direction, we started down into a bog. On the second try, the ground dropped into a small canyon cut by a small stream. Some of the men started off into the jungle, calling out their findings in the falsetto voices they use to talk to each other at a distance when hunting.

Finally, everyone seemed to agree that one of the men way off to the west, by my compass, had identified the best direction for the runway. We set up the laser again, and the men started cutting a trail. I chose one of the men with a light-colored T-shirt on to act as the target. He would walk as far as he could into the dense undergrowth until we could no longer see the red laser dot on his back. Then he would wait until the machete-wielding men caught up before taking off again. As soon as the cutters figured out what the light was for, they started hacking at any foliage their keen eyes saw the laser hit. It wasn't long until they were deep into the jungle.

Just over four hundred yards into the trees, our centerline trail ran into a stream. That was long enough for a runway—*just* long enough. We went back to the east end, where we started cutting the underbrush and dragging it out of the way. I figured we needed about forty feet of principal runway where all the stumps would need to be dug out, with forty additional feet on each side where the trees would be cut low enough that the high wing on our little BTS bush plane would clear it. After the first day of clearing, I realized that it would be easier for the pilot (me) to aim better than it would be for us to cut so much jungle. I altered the center section to thirty feet, with thirty more on each side. By day two, several of the men's wives had arrived. But they had not come to cook; they came to dig stumps. Grandmother Dawa was one of them. She seemed to be related to most of us, so she felt free to scold us as we worked. If someone who was not related to her did something she didn't like, she would scold one of us instead. Whoever she was upset with usually got the message.

Waodani scolding is like swearing in Spanish. It is much more than words—it is an art form, and Grandmother Dawa is an artist.

Waodani women often keep pets. Because Dawa and Kimo could not have children, she always kept pets. On this expedition she had a woolly monkey that could talk. Well, I never actually heard him say words, but Dawa would scold him and tell him what to do, and he actually seemed to understand. She also had a talking parrot. When she would start to scold the monkey or any of the rest of us, the parrot would pick up the message and carry on with near-perfect intonations.

On the second day, we got out the chain saws. We had helmets with mesh face guards and ear protectors. Tiwe just loved the chain saw. But he couldn't seem to get the hang of using it. He preferred to use it when it wasn't making noise, because the spinning chain made him nervous and the exhaust bothered him. He was really strong, but he finally realized that he couldn't make any progress when the engine wasn't running.

I finally convinced him that it worked much better when it did make noise. But I could not convince him that he didn't need to make a sawing motion with it. Steve was worried that Tiwe was going to cut limbs that weren't attached to trees. We decided we had to get him away from the lethal machine for everyone's good.

Finally, Tementa intervened to settle the matter. He didn't tell Tiwe what to do, he merely asked Tiwe if he would see it well to use an ax, keeping the helmet and ear protectors on. Tiwe saw that very well. It turned out that he was much more fascinated with the chain saw outfit than with the machine. Steve taught a couple of the other fellows to run the chain saws; these men understood the concept of letting the saw cut the tree while the operator merely guided it.

The new guys started cutting trees like crazy, but nothing was falling. The second canopy, where the medium-size trees top out, is festooned with vines that grow from one tree to the next. Frequently when you cut through one tree, it remains upright, held by the vines that connect it to the trees around it.

When word came that we could go drink *paenaemae* and eat meat, we all took off, happy for the break. But when we came back to the airstrip clearing, we had been joined by a couple of new fellows who had just walked over from Quiwado. One of them grabbed an ax and started cutting down a medium-size tree. I happened to see him as he started to walk away from it as it fell.

Unfortunately for him, he had just cut down the tree that was balancing the trees the others had already cut. I saw the newcomer glance up in fear. Then I saw what was happening. Trees all around the poor fellow began to fall. He didn't know what to do. He darted one way and then another. Any one of the trees could have crushed him.

I was tense with worry. But all the other warriors were howling with laughter and mimicking the man's panicked darting back and forth. The poor fellow, who had just barely missed being killed, laughed with them.

It struck me that no one passed any laws here about marking cut trees that hadn't fallen. No one called a safety meeting, and OSHA didn't make an inspection. This was a different world—kind of refreshing. We might be killed by falling trees, but at least we wouldn't die of red tape.

By that afternoon, the underbrush removal had progressed far enough down each side that we could start clearing the center, where the roots would have to be pulled. At the start of our strip, right down the middle, stood a huge old dead tree.

We couldn't burn it. Our rain forest didn't get that name by accident. I had personally measured rainfall of almost four inches in a half hour out there.

The Waodani women began to dig around the base of the tree, with old Dyuwi chopping away the roots as they went. Finally, they got underneath the base of the trunk, and what was left of the tree toppled over. All we had to do was pry a few thousand pounds of stump out of the hole and roll it off to the side of the runway.

About twenty Waodani men got down in the ground around the stump and tried to lift it, but it didn't budge. This looked like my chance to show that *cowodi* do know some things. I rolled a chunk of hardwood into the hole against the base of the stump. Then I found the biggest, strongest sapling I could carry and dragged it back to the hole. With help from one of my mystified Waodani compatriots, I lifted the far end into the air until I could jam the bigger end between my hardwood fulcrum and the huge stump.

Everyone watched, thinking this was *ononki cae*—"for no reason doing." Then, when I had my twenty-foot lever in place, I jumped and grabbed it as far from the stump as I could. I walked out from there, hand over hand, until I was almost at the end.

Now I was ready for the show. I started bouncing up and down. Sure enough, that huge old stump started to rock. I expected everyone to run and get a lever and fulcrum of their own or to at least grab onto my lever to add their weight to mine.

Instead, everyone started yelling, and they all jumped back into the hole to pull on the stump again. I thought I had been pretty clever; they thought I had performed magic. I had to prod and cajole a couple of other fellows to get levers of their own, and then the three of us pried that old stump out of the ground. Now they were starting to catch on. For hours after that, everyone carried around long poles, trying to find something to pry up. It reduced our productivity to almost a halt.

Finally the crew discovered that levers were a great way to roll the trunks of trees we had already cut off to the side of the strip. But rather than working in teams, which is very un-Waodanilike, when someone started to roll a huge log with his lever, everyone else would sit around and yell encouragement and support. I was going to have to work on the concept of "many hands make light work."

$$\wedge\!\!\wedge\!\!\wedge\!\!\wedge\!\!\wedge\!\!\wedge\!\!\wedge\!\!\wedge$$

We encountered another huge tree with a potentially giant stump, and I figured it was time for a lesson in the use of dynamite to make jungle airstrips. If we didn't dig out all the tree roots, they would rot underground. That would create a void, which would eventually collapse under the weight of the airplane tires. Such a hole could tear off a gear or cause the plane to swerve off the airstrip into the stumps and trees.

I had bought about twenty sticks of the explosive in a tiny hardware store in Puyo, the "big" town just beyond Shell. The eight- or nine-year-old boy who was helping me wrapped them together in some old newspaper and handed the bundle to me.

When I hesitated to take it from the little guy, he just looked up at me as if to say, "What's wrong with you?" He was handing me twenty sticks of dynamite with fuses and blasting caps all rolled together with newspaper for protection. I knew better than that. I looked around the hardware store. That wasn't too difficult, because it was only about ten feet by twenty feet by about fifteen feet high. It was small, but they had everything a neighborhood True Value would have—plus machetes and, of course, dynamite—but no dynamite lockers.

The proprietor's son figured out what he thought my problem was. He quickly tied the volatile bundle with a piece of string and handed it back to me. I walked away with it as nonchalantly as I could, but I felt very conspicuous and kept an eagle eye out for anyone near me who might be smoking. That's how the movie villains light their dynamite—with a cigarette, right?

I was hopeful that the dynamite would solve our stump problem. Otherwise, digging roots from a thirty-foot swath down the middle of the entire

My family in 1953. Nate Saint, my father, was an innovative jungle pilot. He poses here with my mom, Marj; my sister, Kathy; and me in front of his plane, 56 Henry.

While growing up in South America, I wanted a wagon like a friend had. Dad built me something much better: a truck. My younger brother, Phil, made a perfect load, and Kathy provided the push power.

Kimo and Dyuwi (in the river with Kathy) were in the party that speared and killed my father and four of his friends. Only a few years later, they became like spiritual fathers to my sister and me. Here, they are baptizing Kathy as Oncaye, Iniwa, and I await our turns.

From the time Dad's sister, Rachel, first went to live with the Waodani in 1958, she loved them like family. They soon reciprocated. Even the little children, who usually ran in terror at the sight of "foreigners," knew that "Star" was somehow different from other light-skinned people.

Waodani men lower Rachel's coffin into the grave they dug in their village.

Dayumae (lower right) places her hand on Aunt Rachel's coffin.

We engraved Kimo's tribute on Aunt Rachel's grave marker: "Teaching us to walk God's trail, Star came."

In the jungle, an airstrip is a crucial link to the outside world. The Waodani built this one in record time at a central location called Nemompade, where they wanted my family to live with them.

I was amazed to find the nameplate from Dad's plane. We discovered it in 1994 after it had been buried in the river at Palm Beach for nearly 40 years.

I flew supplies and medicine for the Waodani in this plane until Tementa learned to pilot their own aircraft.

The Waodani use traditional markings for tribal social events. Here Ompodae paints my arm with dye made from a jungle tree pod.

I was often the closest thing the local people had to a doctor. With the mother's life on the line, I helped deliver this baby in Quehueidiono, about 30 miles north of Nemompade. No God followers lived in this community at the time.

My wife, Ginny, washes our clothes in the creek despite the fact that a large anaconda was seen nearby. The Waodani were worried that she would be scared . . . or worse.

Odae painstakingly works on a dugout canoe. Mincaye takes a breather in the background.

Once the Waodani realized that outsiders lack the skills necessary to survive in the jungle, they took seriously the need to teach them those skills. Here, Mincaye demonstrates the proper technique for shooting poison darts with a full-size Waodani blowgun.

Decades after Kathy and I had been baptized by Dyuwi and Kimo, Shaun, Stephenie, Jesse, and seven Waodani teens were baptized in the same river by the same two men and Mincaye.

Ginny and I pose with our daughter, Stephenie, after a long climb up a ridge on our way home from Tiwaeno. Afraid of bugs in Florida, Stephenie mysteriously thrived in Waodani territory.

Stephenie and Jaime enjoy a get-together with *piquianani* (old ones), both formerly prolific killers, soon after our move from Florida to Nemompade.

Mincaye loves our children like he has loved me. He wanted them to be as much like the Waodani as possible. Here he fits Jesse with earplugs (held in place by strings) for an important Nemompade celebration.

Shaun and I are holding a jaguar that was just killed by Waodani hunters after it stalked two young girls. Apparently, it was having difficulty hunting pigs and deer and came to Nemompade looking for easier prey.

In keeping with a Waodani custom, Marga asked Ginny to be co-mother of her new baby to cement the bond and love she had for Ginny. We named the baby Ana Beth. The tribe still considers us her mother and father, even though the Ecuadorean authorities did not allow Ginny and me to bring her to the United States and raise her as Marga hoped.

Here, Waodani elders and I discuss community concerns. In Waodani culture, decisions are made by consensus, not mandate. Meetings often take a long time, but they serve the dual purpose of constantly reestablishing relationships and showing respect for one another.

The elders instructed me to build them a *wicota ebo* (cloth wood bee) and teach Tementa to fly it. He flew the plane into Waodani territory in 2000 to be put into service by Waodani for Waodani.

This Waodani delegation of God followers visited the Ecuadorean capital to lobby for formal recognition as a legal entity. With the help of U.S. Congressman Frank Wolf from Virginia, it was soon granted.

Mincaye and I travel and speak around the world, sharing the amazing ways God has transformed us and reconciled us to each other.

The same man who brutally killed Dad has been amazingly changed and is now filled with tender love for Mom. On Mincaye's first visit to the United States in 1997, he put his arms around her and went on and on trying to reassure her that he would pray for God to watch over her.

four-hundred-yard runway was going to be as much work as clearing all the tangled underbrush, felling two canopies of trees, and pushing the whole works out of the way.

I decided to start on our first big tree with a quarter of a stick of dynamite. I carefully pressed the blasting cap into the end of the piece of dynamite I had carefully cut off. Then I even more carefully inserted the end of a foot-long piece of fuse. I pressed the soft end of the cap around the fuse, and I got ready to insert my homemade clearing device under our offending tree.

I flicked my lighter on, made sure all the Waodani were standing back, and waved the flame under the end of the wick. Then I hightailed it for cover. Nothing happened.

The fuse hadn't lit. I tried to light it again. It wouldn't light. Finally, I cut another piece of fuse and tried that. I simply could not get the stuff to light. Tementa very carefully approached me. I was quite sure he was in awe of what I was undertaking. But he didn't say anything. He just picked up a little toothpick-size piece of wood from the ground and held it in the flame from my lighter until it was glowing red. Then he blew on the end of the stick and touched it to the end of the fuse.

I just smiled to myself. Anyone who has studied physical science knows that the hottest part of a flame is the end of the blue, just before the yellow starts. I had been holding the end of the fuse in that flame for almost a minute with no results. But I decided to let Tementa discover the hard way what I already knew. Unfortunately for him, the fuse lit immediately when he touched the end of his glowing stick to it. He was cheated from ever learning about the hottest part of the flame from me.

When the fuse lit, all the other men, in chorus, called encouragingly, "Manomai"—*Yes, just like that.* So much for *my* teaching them about the marvels of dynamite.

When I finally got the dynamite lit, I ran for cover again. The Waodani had formed a circle just fifteen or so feet away. When I ran, they all just stood there. I hated to see them injured, but I wasn't going to play the fool twice in such a short time.

I skidded to a halt and turned around just in time to hear a muffled bang. Smoke came out from under the tree, and I looked up, expecting to see that hundred-plus-foot Amazon giant start its plunge to earth. All I got was a tiny shaking of the leaves. It might have been a little breeze, but I prefer to think it really was the dynamite.

Everyone seemed concerned about my reaction. I smiled sheepishly and thirty Waodani men simultaneously attempted to explain to me how to put the blasting caps in, light the fuse, wrap it in leaves tied tightly with a vine, etc.

Tementa took a whole stick to demonstrate what they all seemed to already know. When he had it wrapped and bound, he inserted about three inches of fuse. He placed it under the tree and packed dirt around it to contain the blast and channel the energy into lifting the tree.

When the fuse was lit, I forced myself to stand where the rest of the crew was standing. This time the effect was markedly different. When the dynamite went off, dirt exploded from beneath the tree, smoke poured out, and I'm almost sure that this time the shaking of the leaves was slightly more than could be accounted for by the slight breeze that was blowing.

All the Waodani men seemed pleased. We had had our fun. Now they seemed to think it was time to go back to *cae*. Our noble and gigantic tree still stood.

I asked Tementa, "How about three sticks?" The bad guys in the movies always taped three sticks together, I remembered. "Well, how about if we use it for fishing?" he asked back. I took it as a suggestion. "Sure, fishing with dynamite would be good!" The Waodani knew what they were talking about. My dynamite put fish in the pot a lot more efficiently than it blew stumps out of the ground. Every recalcitrant, gigantic stump down the middle of that runway had to be dug out, with all its associated roots, by hand.

Mincaye got a lot of good material for laughs out of that one. He is probably still telling about my dynamite lessons. Every so often he would look at me, screw up his face in deep concentration, and then pretend he was lighting a fuse. Then he would make wild gestures as if he were running in fear of his life. I tried to be irritated with him, but I couldn't keep from laughing with him.

At noon that day, one of the Waodani men, showed me that the side of his old rubber boots had torn. "Wiwa imba," he told me. I agreed with him—*Not good, it is being*—and went back to eating. But he was not finished. He started grumping about how hard it would be to get another pair and wondered aloud how he could ever get the money to buy them unless he got paid for building this airstrip.

I had dreaded the day that this subject would come up. I had, after all, spent a week on the trail explaining that I would not come to do "my own thing." I tried to make it clear that I would come only to help them do "their thing."

The warrior with the slit in his boot obviously thought his request was reasonable. But surely word had gotten around that I was coming only to help them take charge of their own fate. That is what the "old ones" had asked me to do. I knew that this was a delicate situation. If I paid them to build the airstrip, they would see it as my airstrip. But I did not want an airstrip; I only wanted to do what I believed was God's assignment for me.

I knew I should not engage the warrior in direct conversation. That would be confrontational and un-Waodanilike. Instead, I started talking to Kimo, Dyuwi, and Mincaye, reminding them that they had told me the airstrip was to belong to the People, not to outsiders.

Everyone could hear what I was saying. And everyone could hear what I was being asked. Quickly, about a dozen other men started talking too. We had all these conversations going at the same time—a typical Waodani meeting.

I did not know how this critical conversation would end, and I didn't know how to end it. Suddenly Paa stood to his feet and said simply, "Eh!" Everyone immediately stopped talking and listened. "Eewa!" he said, looking off into the distance. *Howlers?* I wondered. *Where?* Sure enough, way across the river, beyond the airstrip, I could hear a far-off rumble, like traffic on a distant freeway. Paa grabbed his muzzleloader and ran toward the river.

I knew this drill. There was no time to explain to Steve what was going on. I grabbed my shotgun and ran after Paa, along with a handful of other fellows. We charged across the river and ran up the bank and out to the airstrip. By the time we got there, I was already breathing hard. My boots, full of water, sloshed as I ran. I considered letting the rest of the pack go—better to get left behind at the airstrip than someplace in the bush. Just then, Paa looked back and called to me, "Babae, quickly come and tonight we will eat eewa!"

We charged into the jungle and headed up the first ridge, toward Damointado. So far, we were on something of a trail, but I knew that wouldn't last. Every few minutes the group would stop suddenly and listen just long enough to gauge where the troop of monkeys was headed. In the jungle, the Waodani hunt first with their ears. No one walks jungle trails gazing up into the trees above. That would be a sure way to trip on tree roots, step on a snake, or fall into a hole or a gorge.

Suddenly the large monkeys, much closer now, changed direction. Now we were going to head off into the wilds. We started down the steep side of the ridge we had been following. I was charging after the group when my leg caught on a vine and I involuntarily dove headlong down what was left of the ridge.

When I caught up with the group, the monkeys were just ahead. They had stopped to graze on some fruit or something. Suddenly a muzzleloader fired just ahead. Everyone started to yell instructions. "One is hit. The other one went high in the tree." Then, "Babae, one is coming to your place. Shoot him and I'll help you eat him!"

Sure enough, a big male jumped from a nearby tree into the one right above me. He was moving fast. I got around the tree just in time to see him run along a limb. He was going to jump into another tree, and in seconds I knew he would be gone. This was the time to shoot. If I got him while he was running on the limb, he would fall to the ground. If I shot him near the trunk, he would dive into the dense foliage and we would have to dig him out.

My heart was beating like crazy. The Waodani love to hunt any edible animals, but monkeys are perhaps the most fun. Not only are they a challenge, they are also the best to eat. I fired and got my monkey. He let out a roar, grabbed the branch, and then fell sixty or eighty feet to the jungle floor in front of me. Mincaye, who had followed me on the hunt with his blowgun, yelled, "Wootae, wooootae," and grabbed the fallen monkey by the tail. He would be bragging about my hunting skills that night for sure.

He motioned with his chin and took off to lead me in the direction of a few more howlers. Suddenly everything went quiet overhead. The howlers that had been crashing through the canopy above us all hid, as though on cue. This started another fun part of the hunt. We knew that the monkeys were up there and they knew that we were down below. Now we had to scare them or entice them out of their hiding places.

One of the guys in the group pulled a thin vine from a tree, wound it around and around into a multistranded climbing vine, put it on his feet, and started climbing a large vine hanging from a high branch overhead. He was going to go into the canopy to get in shooting position with his blowgun.

As soon as he was about seventy or eighty feet up, everyone else started making noise. One warrior sounded like he was shooting a gun over and over.

He formed a fist, leaving an open hole in the top where his thumb and index finger came together. Then he placed leaves over the hole and clapped his other hand onto the leaf. The compressing air would burst the leaf, making a report like a gun.

Others were shaking vines and making sounds like a rampaging male howler. I just stood and watched the circus, remembering how much fun it had been learning to hunt with the Waodani as a boy.

One of the men had chased a couple of monkeys up the next ridge. He suddenly appeared with a good-size monkey under each arm. He had tied the monkeys' tails up over their backs to their necks. That made it possible to carry the monkeys over his shoulders like two purses. We had five monkeys so far, and from the sounds coming from farther down the gorge, there was a good likelihood that there would be a couple more in the pot that night.

When we made it back to the airstrip, everyone was pleased. Even I associated eating monkey with a party. The tension over pay for clearing the airstrip was long forgotten. Those monkeys had come along just in the nick of time to defuse an uncomfortable situation. It might have been a lucky coincidence. But I didn't think so.

Just after getting back to the strip, we heard a plane flying in the distance. The Waodani listened and said confidently, "Alas," referring to the Spanish name for Mission Aviation Fellowship (*Alas de Socorro*). I grabbed a portable aircraft radio I had in my pack and tuned to the air-to-air frequency MAF used.

Brian Shepson, one of the MAF pilots, had been heading to a nearby Waodani village and wondered where we were building the new airstrip. The Waodani had finally gotten our giant, dead stump to smolder, trying to make it easier to finally roll completely out of the way and at the same time hoping to drive away the sweat bees that were constantly pestering us.

Brian saw our smoke and came to scout it out. He said he had bad news: If we continued to build our strip in the direction we were headed, the west end of our strip would be perpendicular to a nearby ridge, making it a one-way-only strip. Worse yet, the other end of the strip was heading right for another high ridge on the far side of the river, to the east. That would not interfere with landing, but it would mean that I would have to turn shortly after take-off to avoid it, unless I was extremely lightly loaded and could climb over it.

"How much would we have to turn the strip to make our approaches and exits better?" I asked. He suggested we try for 240 degrees southwest by 60 degrees northeast. Rats, rats, rats!

I thanked him, but the news was extremely disheartening. I hated to tell Steve and the Waodani, but when I did, they took it in their characteristic no-big-deal fashion. They wanted me to point out the new heading. When we investigated, we found that we could move the east end of the strip south to the edge of a gully. We could move the other end just far enough north that the middle of the strip would skirt by another depression we would never have been able to bridge.

By this time we had cleared the side of the planned strip far enough that we could actually see for quite a distance. I stepped off the usable length on the new heading and found that we could actually increase the length by about sixty meters. That would give us a little more than 180 extra feet. If we could fill in a narrow bog, we could eventually extend the runway several hundred feet on the other side.

After four days, we seemed to have settled into a routine. Several of the men, especially Tidi, were learning to operate the chain saws. Steve had also taught Tidi to clean both saws each night and sharpen both blades. Wimanae continued to bring in meat every day, so we always had plenty to eat.

We had several close calls with snakes, especially with tree vipers that had fallen to the ground when we cut down the trees they had been living in. There is good news and bad news about rain forest snakebites. The good news is that about half of all bites are "dry." The snake doesn't want to waste venom on an animal obviously too big for it to eat. In about a quarter of venomous snakebites, the snake injects just enough venom to teach the trespasser a lesson. The bad news is that in that last quarter, in which the snake injects full venom, the victims usually experience extreme pain and sometimes die. When they don't die, the residual damage from the venom can dissolve ligaments, cause muscles to atrophy, and create all sorts of other problems that can last for years.

Even a very small *cayata* snake, which looks like a small rattler without the tail appendage, can inject enough venom to make its victim start bleeding from his or her eyes, mouth, and nose within just minutes of striking. Dica, Komi's brother, was bitten in the ankle. He recovered from the bite okay, but the venom ate away the tendons running from his leg muscles to the outside of his foot. Without those tendons, his foot curled under until he had to walk on the side of his foot instead of the bottom. That severely limited his ability to get around, until we found some army boots that laced up and held his ankle in place like ice skates would.

Each day, there seemed to be some happening that made it distinguishable in some way. One day an MAF plane flew over to drop us more machetes and files to sharpen them with. We had asked the pilot to make the drop of precious tools on the sandbar in front of our makeshift camp. The pilot made a low approach, flying right up the river between the trees on each bank. But when he dropped the machetes and files, they sailed past the beach and into the water about midstream. Almost simultaneous with the splash, we heard several more splashes near the bank. Some of the men in our group had dived into the river to rescue the much-needed tools.

They found some of the machetes, but not a single file. That was a disappointment. A dull machete is little better than no machete at all.

Another day, Rick flew out in Bravo Tango Sierra. He simply wanted to see how we were doing, but like the good neighbor he was, Rick brought fresh rolls from a bakery in Shell. He flew overhead and dropped half of his delicious cargo on the first pass. But it missed our clearing, sailing way off into the trees. He turned around and made a second pass. I could see that he was going to miss again.

I tried to warn him, but I was too late. I could almost taste those delicious warm bakery rolls as I watched them sail into the jungle to be lost forever. I wanted that bread, but the Waodani wanted it even more. Some of them had not tasted bread for years; some, maybe never. But if they hadn't, I knew they had at least heard about it—the Waodani love bread. I thought the bread was gone. They just went to find it.

It wasn't quite as light and fluffy as it had been when it left the bakery, but I know we enjoyed those *pansitos* more than anyone in the outside world could imagine.

One day I was introduced to an entirely new form of jungle torture. I was bitten on the little finger by what the Waodani call a *mani*. It looks like a black ant on steroids, measuring about an inch long when full grown. I was helping Mincaye dig out a stump when I felt a searing pain in my little finger. The pain was so powerful that I couldn't tell where it was actually coming from. I grabbed my hand and gasped in pain. Mincaye saw me jerk upright and came to investigate. He did not look at my hand, however. He just looked around on the ground and then batted at my pants and boots. "Mani, wenae, wenae imba," he informed me. He was telling me that I had been bitten by a *mani*. I already knew the "bad, bad are" part.

Mincaye continued, "Babae, de de tee antepoi." I wasn't sure what he was saying, but he kept repeating it and pointing down at the ground. It sounded like he was trying to recite part of the alphabet in Spanish. When he had repeated it enough times, I realized he *was* pronouncing letters. "DDT, antepoi." He wanted me to get some DDT to kill the ants.

We didn't have any DDT, so he suggested another jungle remedy: gasoline. He insisted that I dip my finger in gasoline. I half expected him to light it on fire. No big problem though—it couldn't have hurt any more than it already did.

Each night's supper offered a new opportunity for entertainment. One night it was dark by the time Steve and I had bathed in the river and gotten our bowls of thick soup. We had just started eating when Steve said in a strangely mumbling way, "Hey, can you shine your light on me?" His pronunciation was terrible.

I got my flashlight out and saw that he was tugging at something dark sticking out of his mouth. He pulled it out partway, and then it sprang back. I suggested he just give it a good tug. He did, and out it came. I could see that it was a howler monkey arm that had been smoking for a couple of days. Most of us had been given chunks of pig meat that night, but our cook, Omaka, had saved the last of the monkey for Steve. The part that was getting stuck on Steve's teeth was the monkey's fingers. When he unsuspectingly put the monkey hand in his mouth in the dark, the fingers bent enough to slide in. But when he tried to pull it out because it was too tough to bite, the fingers started to uncurl, making the hand bigger and much more difficult to pull out. Steve just chuckled and gave the hand to one of the men next to him, deciding that he could get by with a granola bar from his stash that night.

After dinner we went to the movies, jungle style. One of the favorites was a promotional video of the farming operation run by Steve and his brothers. The Waodani loved to see the huge Steiger tractor pulling a forty-foot-wide disc. They said, "Babae, tell Namo [Steve] to bring one of those down here, and we will happily watch him do this. Growing fat, we will all live very well." When they saw the combine filling big trucks with shelled corn, they just sat amazed.

I realized that it really was amazing. Steve's farm could more than feed the entire Waodani tribe, which was rapidly approaching two thousand people. That is a small population—but a fourfold increase since the days of anger and killing when they were on the verge of extinction as a people.

I also had a World War II movie with lots of airplane footage in it. I thought they would be interested in the planes, but they wanted to know why the planes kept exploding. I explained that the planes flying behind the ones that exploded had guns in them and were shooting them. They wanted to see that video over and over, trying to figure out how those pilots could tell which plane their personal enemy was in.

One night shy Dyuwi spontaneously started to pray. "*Waengongi*, we used to live hating and afraid and killing all the time. But Your Son *Itota*'s blood washing our hearts clean, now we live well." Then he went around the tribe, praying for each village and everyone in the villages who he knew was sick or suffering. He prayed by name for those in our group who didn't yet walk God's trail.

Actually, Dyuwi prayed for us every night. He could easily go on for fifteen to thirty minutes in a booming voice full of authority and vigor. The rest of the time, he was so shy that I never could get him to work with any of the other men. He always just wandered off by himself.

Kimo was the camp clown. He had a pair of binoculars that someone had given him. In camp, he would back as far away from the group as he could without falling off the riverbank and look at us through those crazy glasses. Then he started giving a running commentary of all the strange things he was seeing. I don't know what he was saying most of the time, but to me he was the Waodani equivalent to Rodney Dangerfield. Just seeing him squatting on his haunches with those old binoculars tied me in stitches.

This was a good time for me. As we worked, I remembered why I loved so many of these people. They were unsophisticated, but they were real. They were afraid of events and influences of the outside world that they had no control over. They had been completely isolated from the rest of the world. Now the isolation was less than it had been, but they felt it so much more. Younger members of the tribe were in an identity crisis. They didn't know who they were anymore, and even I could not assure them that the world would make a place for them in the new era that had arrived.

After ten long, wonderful, wearying days, we headed back upriver with the group from Toñampade. No one was yet prepared to keep the chain saws running, gas and oil mixed, and chains repaired. But Tidi and one or two others were getting close. Steve had taught them a lot with his gringo hand signals. The Waodani really liked him and insisted that I tell him to come back—and bring his *tractodo* to make a big, big garden for them.

Before the plane arrived, I asked Mincaye when I should come back. He said I should come back when the *ebowei* was finished so I could land out there. Based on how much work we had accomplished with a huge crew of more than thirty men and a few women, I figured the airstrip would not be done before the gardens were ready to harvest. I doubted if they could finish a usable runway in less than ten months. The guys at MAF had predicted one to two years based on what they had seen in other communities. And I was sure our big crew would immediately dwindle to just a handful of stalwarts when I left and the rice, sugar, and videos left with me.

Mincaye talked to the others who had told me to come live with them and said, "Again coming, after three moons, the ebowei will be ready and you can land." Mincaye added, "Then we will build houses to live in." Coba agreed, and Tidi said, "Boto tono"—*Myself too.*

There it was: the big commitment. All three men had extended family in Toñampade. Moving would mean building new houses. That would be the easy part. Moving downriver before the gardens were ready would be the real sacrifice. There would be some lean months while our new "grocery store" was developing.

But now I knew I had a core group of people who were really committed to doing what they could to take responsibility for meeting their own people's physical and spiritual needs. I was greatly encouraged. Actually, I never expected non–God followers to make a commitment to be part of this experiment, so I was not surprised when none of them offered to make the big move. What motivation would they have? The Waodani were used to looking out for themselves, not others. It was simply not part of their culture, which taught them to depend on no one outside their immediate family group.

The God followers had a reason to help others. For them, it was an opportunity to express their appreciation to *Waengongi* for revealing the trail He had marked for them with His Son's own blood. Maateo passed on *Waengongi*'s instructions this way: "Minito boto caebo bai adobai caedinque wadani inanite anamai inte ononqe godo caemini aencaedanimpa"—*Give as freely as you have received* (Matthew 10:8).

I left the equipment, radio, supplies, and outboard motor at Aunt Rachel's little shack for my return. I traded my boots in Toñampade for a pair with a large slit in the side. I had a deep yearning to buy everyone working on the project a new pair of boots, a machete, and a new ax. It would have been a huge gift to each of them and a super deal for me. Where else could I get that much pleasure for half the cost of a plane ticket from Orlando to Quito? But I knew I couldn't do it. Hands had been stretching out to the Waodani for decades. They had responded to the temptation by receiving that unending stream of gifts from a variety of organizations, from a number of countries. There is a tendency for generosity and the desire to be significant in the lives of other people to mix with a bit of selfish desire. We like to find a little pond where we can be big fish. This deadly form of altruism ruins the lives of the people we want to help and steals future dignity from them and their descendents.

No one had died or been badly injured during the ten days we had been working on the airstrip. I had made friends and gotten to know men and women I had not known before. And I had established once more, to my own satisfaction, that my only interest was to help my jungle family. Anything else—the airstrip, clinic, school—had to be theirs. I wondered if any of that would actually happen . . . and if it did, how long it all would take. And how long it would last.

14

Get Set

I was speeding down the river on a powerful Jet Ski, carrying a badly wounded warrior behind my seat. A Waodani health promoter, capable of prescribing basic medicines, was monitoring the warrior's vital signs as a bag of plasma dripped into his arm to replace blood he had lost when his chain saw kicked out of a tree and nearly severed his leg.

I made a sharp turn, still at high speed, sending a wall of water spraying toward the far bank as I pulled into the dock beside our house. The health promoter and I each grabbed one end of the stretcher out of the clever stanchions that allowed our powerful Jet Ski to serve as a high-speed medevac craft. We headed up the new concrete steps leading from the dock to the grass-covered lawn extending from our house past Mincaye's house and the clinic.

We had modified a golf cart into an ambulance, which I had left for the health promoter. She would need it to transport our gravely injured patient to the airstrip. I ran down the path that cut across the cable bridge, over the deep ravine, and past both the school and the radio station. I would have the plane almost checked out and ready to go when the makeshift ambulance got there. I knew that this first hour was critical for our victim.

We had received the call from a clearing upriver by walkie-talkie. It had taken only ten minutes in the clinic's high-powered jet boat to get up there, five minutes to stabilize the patient and get the IV going, and another eight minutes to speed back downriver. The modified Jet Ski could do almost fifty miles per hour down the winding river. Once it was moving, it required only inches of water in which to operate. The Teflon runners protected the hull if it happened to run over rocks or logs in the river.

With the five additional minutes needed to get our now-comatose patient to the plane, we had already used up twenty-eight precious minutes of our critical hour. With thirty-five minutes to Shell and a few minutes for the ambulance ride to the mission hospital, we would be just over the proverbial hour until getting medical help to give this man the best chance to live.

In the plane, we were set up to continue the IV. We had a power respirator with oxygen. Our regular radio operator, who doubled as announcer and program producer at our small Waodani radio station, would call ahead to let the hospital know we were coming. The ambulance would be waiting at the MAF hangar when we arrived.

Our emergency medical system was a smooth-running machine.

While I was accompanying the health promoter and patient to the hospital, the Waodani young man who was in charge of supply purchases and organizing return flights would be loading the plane for our return flight.

I was looking forward to watching the Discovery Channel that night on our new satellite television with Ginny and some of our Waodani friends when I suddenly woke up.

My dream had been extremely vivid in its detail. The school, the clinic, the radio station, our house, the medevac Jet Ski, and the plane parked in the taxi-through hangar—it had all seemed so real. But I wasn't in Ecuador; I was still in Florida, getting ready to make this giant leap into the unknown.

I looked at my watch and saw that it was not quite five o'clock. In the afterglow of my dreamworld mad dash on the river, to the plane, and then into Shell, I began to think about what it would take to make those things a reality.

First, it would take a serious investment of capital. The plane would be forty-five to sixty thousand dollars; the Jet Ski and modifications plus transportation to Ecuador, another ten thousand. Equipping a clinic would be about twenty thousand, with another twenty to set up a diesel generator and build a small electrical distribution network for the base. The radio station would require a couple of simple studios and a transmitter of a thousand watts or so.

We would have to build a number of buildings: a clinic, a school, a radio station, a hangar, and a combination generator and maintenance shop. We would also need houses for my family, the primary health promoter, the plane coordinator, and the radio station manager, and a guesthouse for other Waodani who would be coming to train for some of these roles in their own communities.

I was really becoming excited about what I could do for the Waodani. My still-sleepy mind was tackling this challenge in much the same way it had when I was starting my first construction and land-development business in Ecuador after college. I had later refined my abilities by starting a similar business in Minnesota. Then I had helped organize a cadre of professionals from the construction trades in the United States who offered to help jump-start the construction of a new dam and penstock on the eastern side of the Continental Divide in Ecuador. After that, my partner and I sold our construction business, which included a small lumberyard, a real estate office, and a residential development. From there I joined old family friends who were starting a developmental oil production company in west Texas. I was in the middle of that when Mission Aviation Fellowship asked me to trade west Texas for West Africa.

Fortunately, I had always had partners who shared my desire for life to count for more than the bottom line. When I told my partners in the expanding oil exploration company that I had been asked to leave all that and fight the famine disaster in Africa, they were surprised. But one of the brothers who spearheaded the oil and gas operations said, "I think you ought to go. A hundred years from now no one will care how much money any of us made or what we did with our lives unless it serves a purpose that outlives us."

So Ginny and I packed up our four children, and we moved to Mali, West Africa, for a very long year. Ginny and I returned from Africa with a sobered outlook on the fragility of our environment and the people who live in it. I had grown up in the third world, but there was always sufficient food for everyone, no matter how poor they were. In Mali, we saw people dying of starvation and disease by the hundreds. I tackled the job of setting up an air service and radio communications network to get food and medical care to starving communities.

As I was waking from my vivid dream, the harsh realities of our task hadn't completely set in. I was reveling in the idea of tackling a broader task on a much smaller scale. I had not known the political and economic paradigms in West Africa, but this time I was going back to a world I did understand. In Ecuador I had standing, contacts, and a deep, long-term relationship with the People.

I also had my own resources. If I needed a plane, I could buy one. I could pay for buildings and equip the clinic, shop, and radio station with all that we needed. I knew there were people who would join me in this major undertaking of giving the Waodani a chance to control their cultural, material, and spiritual destiny.

When the sun came up that morning, I had already made notes of all the ideas that had been running around in my mind. I have a habit of sleeping with a pen and spiral notebook by my bed. During the night, if I wake up with what seems like a good idea, I write down the thoughts that come to me in the dark and then review them the next morning. Quite often, those nocturnal inspirations are totally bogus when I evaluate them the next day. But some of them have provided solutions to the unending challenges that face all business owners.

In my dream I had envisioned a tribal center that I knew I could build and whose oversight I could organize. But in the reality of daylight, I realized that in building such a base for the Waodani, I would be pounding one more nail into their coffin. Anything *I* did for them would not be theirs, any more than the Toñampade church was theirs. Their schools weren't their own; their territory was theirs only as long as authorities who signed the papers giving it to them did not sign other papers taking it away. Their culture was rushing toward chaos, with marriage patterns breaking down and no system of community discipline to replace the killing patterns that had once served the purpose of conflict resolution—though in an unsustainable manner.

What Mincaye and my Waodani family had asked of me was to teach them to do what only the foreigners knew how to do. They wanted to do it on their own. They wanted to take back some authority for their own future. But to take authority, they would have to take responsibility.

People can't take responsibility for things in life that they don't have authority over. That just doesn't work. That is why, in North America, as the government has taken more authority away from parents, it has also had to take more and more responsibility for the children. The converse is also true. You can't have authority over something unless you are also willing to take responsibility for it.

This was a discouraging realization for me. I would have liked nothing more than to help the Waodani build an efficient center that would astound people. But I knew that in order to put the Waodani in the driver's seat, we would have to sit, stand, and walk before we were ready to run.

I would even have to be careful how I lived out there. If I built a house that exceeded what they could build or afford, I would be raising the bar to the same unreachable standard that many others had demonstrated to the Waodani. I had to prove to them that they "have what it takes." I needed to teach them the skills they needed that their old culture had not handed down to them. I would also need to convince them not to lose the valuable skills that their ancestors had passed on to them.

Perhaps most difficult of all, I would need to figure out some way for them to fund what they wanted to do. It was important that they keep their identity without being forced to live on the crumbs outsiders dropped to them in an attempt to entice them into permanent societal debilitation.

I could not predict how things would go once we started extending this new trail to link the Waodani with the outside world. I only knew that they should not be asked to give up their identity, their territory, or their children. I also knew that Ginny, Jesse, Stephenie, and I should live as models that the Waodani could aspire to copy.

I started planning the house I would build, how to furnish it, and what technologies to incorporate into it, as well as which ones to avoid. Ginny, without going through the hours of analysis I had given to this question, simply told me, "I don't think we can live in a thatched longhouse with a bare ground floor like the Waodani do. But I don't want to have anything they can't have either."

This became my guiding principle in the months ahead, even when it came to helping the Waodani. We would not be content with things as they were, but we would not aspire to make things what they could not be either. I thought of the creed that is often repeated at Alcoholics Anonymous meetings: "God grant me the serenity to accept the things I cannot change, the courage to change the things I can, and the wisdom to know the difference."

/\/\/\/\/\/\/\/\

As a family, we had decided long ago that we would not allow our family to be separated as long as the choice was ours—not, at least, until our children were old enough to marry and needed to be independent. On the Waodani side, culture stipulates that the fate of one will likely be the fate of all. We were ready to step into their boat with them.

Waodani culture does allow one family to distinguish their lifestyle from the rest of the tribe. If someone kills a large animal and has excess meat, he shares it with his extended family and others in his clearing. If a person makes exceptionally nice pots and has a few extras, she is expected to give them to anyone who admires them. I had begun to understand that it could even be dangerous to stand out. I had heard stories of Waodani who tried to be innovative. When someone got sick and the family was looking for a cause, it was standard practice to suspect evil spirit involvement. The spirits were assumed to be acting at the behest of a *wenae bai*, or spirit person. So the People began looking for someone who had been acting strangely, which might indicate involvement with the spirit world.

It is true that the Waodani are incredibly egalitarian. They are free to do whatever they choose, so long as it is within the parameters of what is considered normal behavior, from the time they reach the age that they would be starting school in the outside world. But actions have consequences, even way out in the Amazon. If a Waodani was innovative in his behavior, it would give reason to accuse him of interacting with evil spirits.

If someone was accused of being an evil spirit person, he could deny it, but his behavior would convict him in the suspicious and fearful minds of his neighbors. Waodani culture would not tolerate a Joan of Arc or a William Tyndale. It would probably be better for him to accept the accusation and use it to scare off his accusers by threatening to do them harm too.

So the Waodani people have always done whatever they pleased, but no one tried to get ahead. It was always considered useless to try to improve your standard of living. Besides, in a culture that expected death at any time, what was the use of trying to build a more permanent or more comfortable house? It would require more *cae* (doing), and your enemies would burn it just the same as a standard house.

With the cessation of most of the killing, however, there was good reason to build more permanent houses. In Toñampade, Dayumae and Komi had a board house. So did Aunt Rachel. A few others had some boards for beds and fireboxes, which allowed them to sleep and cook on an elevated platform. The boards of the box contained dirt, which kept the fire from burning the house down.

Living in a house with a thatched roof, however, was like living in a box of matches. If a fire used for cooking or warmth happened to catch the thatch on fire, there was an immediate inferno. We needed a clean roof if we were going to have any kind of equipment such as a computer, radios, or a copier—all things that I felt the Waodani needed to be exposed to. I also felt we would need at least a clean roof if Ginny was to remain sane.

I remembered sitting in Mincaye's house as a boy and having little bits of thatch, crickets, and roaches constantly falling on me. A thatched roof becomes a living organism after a while.

Another time, I was in a Waodani house when a big roach landed in the cooking pot. The man of the house made a terse proclamation, and within minutes everyone in the house grabbed everything of value and fled. Then the warrior took an ember from the fire and touched it to the thatch. The next thing I knew, white smoke was billowing from the roof. When the smoke was so thick it looked like it could be sliced, it suddenly transformed into a ball of flame that burst into the sky. In just minutes, all that was left of the longhouse was the charred frame, half fallen in on itself.

Even as a boy, I had wondered why he didn't build a new house—or at least gather materials for a new house—before burning the old one. This is a perfect example of a fundamental distinction between the way the Waodani think and the way people in technologically advanced cultures think. One way of thinking is not necessarily better than the other. They are just different.

It is true, planning has its advantages. But the Waodani don't get ulcers or suffer from high blood pressure. They laugh a lot more and worry a lot less. By the afternoon of the house burning, that Waodani warrior had a temporary shelter built, and in a few days he had a new house well on its way to completion. He had no mortgage, so he did not have to involve the bank. He didn't need a burning permit or a construction permit, and there were absolutely no tax ramifications to consider. And even if he'd wanted to call the fire department, there wasn't one to call.

/\/\/\/\/\/\/\

I decided to use a Home Depot tarp for our roof. It would be clean like a tin roof, would require very little structure to hold it up, and would be more affordable for the Waodani than tin. It would certainly be a lot easier to transport into the jungle than tin would be. I also hoped that it would not be as hot. There was a time in Tiwaeno when Aunt Rachel had the only completely thatched roof in the village. The oil company had built a camp inside Waodani territory, then quickly abandoned it. So the Waodani helped themselves to the roofing and other useful materials that had been cheaper for the oil company to leave behind than to haul out by helicopter.

Actually, they *had* left behind a helicopter that had crashed at the camp. I remember thinking how cool it was that Komi took the tail cone from the helicopter and attached it to one end of his house. I also remember, however, that the rest of the house was like an oven when the sun came out and started baking that tin roofing.

The need for shelter would be pressing for all of us who were moving our families to the new center. So I decided to build our house high enough that we could use the ground level for additional housing, storage, a temporary clinic, or whatever else was needed before it could be built elsewhere.

We got all our lumber at our own version of "Low's." First we cut down the tree, and then when it was "low" we cut it into boards. I bought nails in Puyo, and I brought from the United States boxes of every size of drywall screw made. I knew I would never remember all the things that we take for granted in the States, but I tried to be as prepared as possible. I became a regular at our local hardware stores and building material suppliers. I would enter each store and arbitrarily pick a side. Then I would walk slowly up and down each aisle, evaluating everything I saw for possible application in our new home and occupation. I know I drove the clerks crazy. They kept asking if they could help me find what I was looking for. Several of them got pretty interested in the process of thinking through our new life with me. When I came in, they would excuse themselves from other customers and accompany me through the store. I even got calls from a couple of them who had brainstorms in the middle of the night.

It made me feel good that I wasn't the only one waking up in the middle of the night with ideas for solving potential dilemmas out in the rain forest. For a while, I was worried about making windows. The answer came to me at three-thirty one morning: I would buy a big roll of window screen as is used to repair screen doors. We would build the house so that the distance between the top of the outside walls and the wall header was just a few inches shorter than the screen is wide. When the house was built, all I would have to do was unroll the screening from a starting point, wrap it all the way around the house, fix it in place with a hammer stapler, and cut out the entry door. In fact, if I built the entry door first, I could just staple the screen around the top of the door and then cut it out from the rest of the screening. Presto! Doors and windows complete!

That idea worked great. Other middle-of-the-night inspirations did not. The idea of using a wading pool fed by a submersible sump pump in the creek behind the house—placed inside a plastic laundry hamper to keep mud and leaves out of it—was one that didn't. The rollable copper sheet with a built-in waterline given to me to use as a solar water heater didn't work either. It might have, but we never got around to trying it.

During the planning stages, I had no way of knowing just how busy we were going to be. As it turned out, I wouldn't even have a chance to put the screening on the windows until we had been in the jungle several months. Ginny and Stephenie convinced me it was time for screens when one of our rare visitors from the outside world had an encounter with an FIOIS (Flying Insect Of Incredible Size) while sitting at our living room table (board) one night.

I knew we would need electrical power. Most Waodani could not reasonably obtain or maintain a generator, which would require that they purchase and transport fuel, add stabilizer if it sat too long, access oil and parts, and possess mechanical know-how. I opted for solar power. Many Waodani already had community radios with car batteries that were recharged by solar panels. That was technology they could more easily copy. The biggest hurdle would be cost.

We could convert the 12-volt power from batteries into 110 volts with an inverter. But first I would have to find out whether I needed a sine wave inverter, a square wave inverter, or a modified sine wave inverter. I found out that the type of inverter would be determined by what we wanted to run with the resulting power.

I figured we needed to run a two-way radio so we could stay in touch with Shell, as well as a shortwave radio so we could stay in touch with Shaun and Jaime when they returned to college after spending the summer with us. We needed a computer so Jesse could teach the Waodani how to use it as a word processor and record keeper. And we needed a tiny printer and copier if we wanted to make any teaching manuals.

I could find no one on the end of a telephone in any country who had ever tried using a copier with inverted power—not even the copy company representatives. So I developed a test lab in our pool house, which we had converted into my office—and test laboratory.

Everyone seemed to offer the same advice: "Just plug it in!" But that wouldn't work in the jungle, where we didn't have anything to plug it in to.

I realized that it would have been far safer and easier for my family and me to just stay plugged in to the good life we had built in Florida and give up on the idea of moving to the Amazon. But there would be danger in that too. If we let the status quo determine what we did with our lives, we would risk living lives of self-indulgence and insignificance. I once heard a radio preacher respond to the question, "What would you do differently if you had life to live over again?" with this answer: "Well, I wouldn't change anything major. But if I could do it over again, I would take more risks, and I would take myself less seriously." Good advice.

I ordered a modified sine wave inverter and connected it to a car battery that I charged with a solar panel. Ginny called my testing method "the smoke test." Once I had the power system set up with the solar panel feeding a car battery, which fed my inverter, I would plug in each piece of equipment, turn it on, and see if smoke emanated from it. If no smoke came out, I would see if it would do whatever it was supposed to do. I thought about trying to sell my methods to the manufacturers, but I was pretty busy "smoking" their equipment, so I just left them in the dark.

As I worked, I couldn't help but realize that time and eternity would put our efforts to a similar smoke test. As so often is the case in life, I had no idea what I was actually getting into. On the other hand, I have accumulated lots of mileage traveling where there are no maps and proven methods. I knew that I didn't know what I was getting us into. I never expected it to be easy, and I never once thought that anyone except *Waengongi*, who knows everything, could predict if this unlikely endeavor would ever justify all the time and effort it was going to require of us.

15

We're Gone

Jesse, Shaun, and I headed down to the jungle on June 5, 1995. It was hard to believe we were already halfway through the year. I realized that Aunt Rachel's body had probably already been reduced to a skeleton in the warm, damp earth of Toñampade. It was a sobering thought. It seemed like only days since I had been in Quito on my last visit to Ecuador before she died.

During that visit, I had talked a camera crew at World Radio Missionary Fellowship into recording Aunt Rachel. I asked a friend to interview her about her life, because when I tried interviewing her, she would start a great story and then say, "But you already know that." So I directed and my friend interviewed. We had recorded over seventeen hours of incredible stories from her life, especially about the thirty-six years she had lived with the Waodani. Her long fight with cancer had drastically weakened her by this time. In fact, the only way I could keep her energy up so that she could record more than an hour a day was to bring in chocolate milk shakes from the local Ecuadorean, fast-food joint. She loved chocolate milk shakes, although she rarely got to enjoy them since there were no milk shakes in the rain forest.

I thought about my final good-bye to dear, stubborn, brave Aunt Rachel. We both knew it was our final visit on earth. Aunt Rachel had loved my dad, and she had been more like a mother than a sister to him. She had been something of a second mother to me, as well. She said I reminded her of my dad, and I knew she loved me a lot. She had always been my closest link to my father, the only one able to tell me the stories of his growing up years and all those exploits that a father usually tells his son himself. She told me how he had built a roller coaster from the roof of their old three-story house in Pennsylvania to the ground outside Grandpa's glass studio. And how at twelve years of age he had taken apart the old family car and put it back together, just to see how it worked. She told me how he had posed for Grandpa Saint as the little boy whose five loaves and two fish Jesus had used to feed the multitude. Grandpa's stained-glass window depicting that miracle, with Dad's image as the boy who gave everything he had to God, still hangs in the Washington National Cathedral near the U.S. capital. It was only one of numerous windows created by Grandpa for the National Cathedral, but as Aunt Rachel told me about all of them, the one with Dad in it was always most special to me.

Just before I said good-bye to Aunt Rachel after our last filming session, she grew uncharacteristically sentimental. "Isn't it something," she asked, "that the Lord Jesus would have used someone like me to do His work in this special place? I was too old by the time I could apply for missionary service. I couldn't help the Waodani much medically, I was not a Bible scholar, and I was never really a superior translator." I wondered why she was revealing her lack of qualifications for what she had spent half of her life doing.

"Well, Aunt Rachel, why do you think God gave you this assignment? What do you think He saw in you that He could use?" Her eyes brightened, and this eighty-two-year-old hero of mine responded with a formula for living: "Well, Stevie Boy, I loved the Lord Jesus with all my heart, and I trusted Him completely." She paused before continuing, "And I guess I just learned to persevere in whatever He gave me to do."

Thank you, Aunt Rachel. Those words still rang in my ears as we headed back down to the jungle to do the seemingly impossible. Our mission seemed crazy, but I knew it really was not. I had business friends who were giving their lives to make money they would never get around to spending—money that might end up ruining their children's lives. Aunt Rachel had "wasted" half her life attempting to be an ambassador of heaven to "savages" whom no one cared about. At the very end of her life, she looked back on her accomplishments as insignificant. She knew what I have just recently begun to realize: God doesn't need us to do His work, or He wouldn't be omnipotent. He wants our love and a relationship with us. It is about "being," not "doing."

I have always been very pragmatic. I hoped that at the end of my life I would be able to look back on what I was about to do in the same way Aunt Rachel looked back on her time with the Waodani.

/\·/\·/\·/\·/\·/\·/\

The last thing we did before leaving for Ecuador was to watch Jaime graduate from high school. An almost junglelike rain caught all the graduates and their family and friends in the open. When Jaime walked to the stage, he was near the top of his class scholastically—and totally drenched. We were really proud of him. The only sad note was realizing that he would be coming back from the jungle without us to start the next major stage of his life. I knew this was really hard for Ginny to think about. But once she felt that she could help contribute to the Waodani cause, she never looked back.

The plan was for Shaun and Jesse and me to head down first and get started on our house, while at the same time helping to get the airstrip ready. I really had no idea what progress the Waodani would have made in the three months since my brother-in-law and I had left. I had asked for a progress report from Mission Aviation Fellowship, thinking that someone flying near the new strip could detour a bit and send me some information. But the only thing I heard back was that I shouldn't expect much to happen in just three months.

At first, I convinced myself that the MAF pilots had not seen how motivated the Waodani were. Then my confidence began to wane as I realized that I had never heard of another airstrip being built by a local community, much less an airstrip for a community that did not exist yet, being built by volunteers from other communities. I also remembered the backbreaking work it had taken just to get started. I especially remembered the stinging sensation as my sweat washed moss and leaf debris into my numerous cuts and scratches, while sweat bees swarmed inside my clothes, ears, nose, and mouth.

I knew it would be better not to expect much progress on the airstrip, though I still held out a glimmer of hope that when Ginny and Steph came down, I would be able to fly them to our new home.

Getting to Quito was like a rerun of the last trip. The three of us had so much baggage that an American agent called out, "Who's the leader of the group with the huge pile of baggage stacked by the first-class counter?" We had about twelve hundred pounds of cargo this time. I informed agent Cindy that it was ours. Jesse and Shaun conveniently disappeared just as I informed her that we were a group of three. I felt conspicuous because we had enough stuff for fifteen.

I asked for Connie, but Cindy said Connie was off that day. *Oh no!* Before I could formulate Plan B, Cindy's face lit up. "Are you the Quito mission group?" she asked. She then informed me that Connie had asked her to handle our "group," and she handed me fifteen baggage tags. I had asked for twelve. American only owed us six. Shaun and Jesse were amazed.

Getting from Quito to Shell with all our baggage was an adventure of its own. A missionary friend loaned us his Isuzu Trooper with a trailer hooked to the back. It took the Trooper, the trailer, and Aunt Rachel's old "Puke" (a 1972 Datsun, which was painted throw-up mustard yellow) to hold all our gear.

Shaun was nineteen, had never driven in Ecuador, could not speak the language, and had little experience with a standard transmission. I asked him to drive the Puke while I drove the Isuzu. Shaun was understandably nervous. Jesse rode with him as his interpreter since Jesse had had two years of Spanish to Shaun's one.

Our timing was a little off. By the time we got packed and on our way, it was after three in the afternoon. We headed south out of Quito, following the Avenue of the Volcanoes on the Pan-American Highway. The road climbs up into the *paramo*, a cold and desolate region above the tree line, before beginning a rapid descent into the rain forests to the east.

By the time we reached above twelve thousand feet and were ready to start our descent, both cars were about out of energy with our heavy loads. Having climbed most of the snowcapped volcanoes we were passing, I remembered how short of gas my own motor would get at those altitudes. At the highest point in the road, there is so little oxygen in the air that a can of gas can be lit while holding it in one's hand. It will light, but it won't explode. Just a bit higher, the atmospheric pressure is so low that liquids boil at a much lower temperature than we are used to. While mountain climbing, we often drank soup or warm Jell-O while it was still boiling. At those altitudes it is hard to get anything to cook without a pressure cooker.

Shaun felt like *he* had been in a pressure cooker by the time we started down out of the mountains. I warned him to keep downshifting to keep the brakes from overheating. Then it started to rain. The Puke had only one wiper. And that one looked like it was original equipment. Just as we passed Baños at the base of a sporadically active volcano, darkness fell.

The road from Baños to Shell is one of the most awesome drives in the world. The Shell Oil company carved the road out of the sheer sides of a deep canyon that starts in the Andes and finally opens up in the Amazon jungle. It is a deep chasm cut by snow melting from the glacier-covered peaks we had just passed. In only fifty miles, that narrow gorge drops from potato-farming hills, where we once saw heavy-coated llamas and bundled shepherds, to the three-thousand-foot plateau where the Shell Oil company built its jungle airstrip and base camp.

The road that winds down the precipice wall is so narrow that there is rarely room for two cars to pass. Poor Shaun—he was in an unfamiliar car, complete with the eccentricities that all twenty-four-year-old automobiles that have lived on cobblestone roads have. He could hardly see out the windshield, and even when he could see, the lights were shining out over the abyss. A tiny miscalculation could send them plummeting several hundred feet into the white-water rapids below. Jesse told me later that it was probably a good thing it was dark when they followed me through that last stretch. It was easier not seeing the huge drop-off.

We were all weary by the time we got to Shell Mera. We spent the night there before catching an MAF plane to deliver us and all our stuff into the jungle.

/\./\./\./\·./\·./\/\

When we flew in to Toñampade to borrow a canoe to head downriver, we had a pleasant surprise. Two Waodani men came by Aunt Rachel's house and handed me a mud-caked piece of metal. When I turned it over, I realized I was holding the altimeter from Dad's plane. They had found it down at the sandbar. Amazing, after thirty-nine years, to be holding this piece of my own history. It still sits in our living room as a reminder of how fragile life is.

Mincaye was waiting for us in Toñampade. I was a little disappointed, because I had been hoping he would be downriver working feverishly to get the new airstrip finished. I assumed he must have spent most of the time since I had left right there in Toñampade. But as we talked, I realized that he had been down working on the new airstrip. When he heard we were arriving, he poled a long day upriver to greet us. He also wanted to harvest his gardens in Toñampade for all those who were still down there working—and for Shaun, Jesse, and me.

On the way down the river with Mincaye, his wife Ompodae, Shaun, Jesse, and several others, we passed a steep bank with a ledge near water level. On that shelf, Jesse spied an anaconda that was at least thirteen feet long. Most of the Waodani no longer talk openly about these huge reptiles as spirit animals, but they are still extremely leery of them.

I thought everyone would want to see it up close, so I turned the long canoe around and guided our big dugout back through the swift current to where the giant snake lay sunning himself. Jesse wanted to poke at it with a pole. The Waodani were all yelling at him not to do it, which of course Jesse could not understand. Half of our passengers would have jumped ship, except that the only place to go was the ledge with the anaconda on it.

I think our snake must have recently eaten. He was totally oblivious to our presence, even when Jesse poked at him a bit. We left hoping that he liked living upriver.

When I finally managed to turn the boat back around again, everyone was jabbering about how scared the others in the boat had been. The Waodani really love to make fun of themselves and each other.

If I hadn't been operating the engine, I would have been tempted to catch that *obe*. Snakes like that make great conversation pieces and often help to get someone talking. They also tend to keep down the number of unwanted solicitors that come by.

I wondered what Jesse and Shaun would think when we rounded the final bend and they saw our new home. They had no discernible reaction. Then I realized that it looked just like all the other jungle riverbanks we had been passing for the past three and a half hours. They did not realize they were seeing their new home.

For the past three months, I had been dreaming about and planning what to build and how to build it, imagining what everything would look like. But Jesse and Shaun just saw dense jungle. They started to help the Waodani build tarp shelters for us to sleep and cook under. I headed for the airstrip to see if any progress had been made.

I followed the trail until suddenly it broke into the open. Stretching in front of me was an almost-finished airstrip! The center of the strip, where the roots had been dug out, was smooth and tamped. The only thing that needed to be done to make it operational was to fill in a couple of depressions and tamp the very center some more. I was amazed, proud, and humbled in about equal proportions. I couldn't wait to tell everyone that the Waodani had done just what they said they would, in the time they said it would take them. No one got paid. They did it as their initial investment in our big—and now clearly mutual—experiment in fighting to become partners with the outside world instead of beggars or servants.

Two days after I started to build our house, we were twice reminded why the airstrip was so important. First, we heard a distress call from a village identifying itself as *3 de Noviembre*. They had a young woman who had been in hard labor for three days but was unable to give birth. They were begging for the plane to come and rescue her. But there was no answer from Shell, and we did not have a plane yet.

The second reminder came almost as soon as the delivery saga was ending. Peque's son burst out of the dense foliage into our small clearing. He had run all the way from Damointado that morning to tell us that Gami had been bitten by a snake and was bleeding everywhere. It was only nine-thirty. He had covered the trail in two and a half hours. I had antivenin with me, but they wouldn't want to wait for me to slog back over that trail. I doubted if I could make it in less than seven hours, even if my life depended on it.

But then Peque's son told us Gami was already dead. That could have meant that he had fainted, was unconscious, or was actually dead. I had the same feeling I had experienced in West Africa when I was told that starving people would die and there was nothing I could do to stop it. In that situation, it was explained to me that the people I felt desperate to help were so far gone that the resources needed to bring them back could save two or three people who were not yet critical. In North America, we are used to having enough of everything for everyone. It's hard for most of us to imagine that there are actually places where there isn't enough food or medicine for everyone who needs it.

Finally, the boy told us clearly that Gami had turned cold and they had already buried him. In this culture, I still wasn't absolutely sure he was dead. But what could we do without a plane? With a plane, I could have flown there in about four minutes with the antivenin. "Why did they not call by radio and tell us Gami was snakebitten?" I asked. I was feeling miserably helpless. "The radio not working, they could not call; so Peque sent me."

It turned out that the solar panel wire to the battery had become corroded, and the battery had run down. Incredible! If the battery had been charged and we had had Bravo Tango Sierra, we could have gotten Gami to the hospital within an hour of being bitten. Now he was dead. Gone forever.

We had barely cleared the site for our house when Shaun, Jesse, and I collapsed in exhaustion. Out in the jungle, you have to fight to keep from getting mud everywhere. Then you have to fight to get the mud cleaned off of you. Finally, you have to figure out how to get dressed again without getting your clothes either wet or dirty. In fact, I think that has been my most enduring frustration in the jungle: trying to keep clean things clean and dry things dry. That seems like a small thing until you spend a night in clothes that are either damp or muddy.

There was one factor of daily life that soon eclipsed all others in terms of the growing distress it caused us *cowodi*. I had forgotten to bring salt. On day one, it was no big deal. On day two, it was a growing disappointment. But on day three, it was difficult for us to eat. By day four, I was craving salt. After that, I began to have dreams about salt. I wanted it as I imagine a heroin addict must crave his fix.

Being without salt in the modern world of prepared foods is not like being without it where we were. All canned, precooked, and instant foods have huge quantities of salt in them. We, on the other hand, were eating wild meat, plantains, and manioc. None of them have any discernible salt in them at all. At first I thought the solution was simply to do without. But I soon realized that we would have to have salt if we wanted to keep working. The boys and I were perspiring so much that I knew we would soon be debilitated by an electrolyte imbalance if we did not get salt.

The only thing we could do was to work in the shade as much as possible and keep from doing the things that caused us to perspire most. I thought about wetting our clothes, but they were naturally wet as soon as we started work each morning at seven.

Fortunately, although I was discouraged that I had forgotten such a critical necessity as salt, I was pleased by how quickly our local "lumberyard" started supplying lumber. Tidi came in from the jungle one day to find out what size lumber we needed next. I tried to tell him we needed four-by-fours to build more of the framework. In Wao-Tededo that comes out as, "Two and two end joints of your longest finger on one side; and two and two end joints of the same finger on the other side; and looooong."

Tidi was confused. Tementa just picked up a brittle vine and cut off a sixteen-inch piece. He bent it every four inches and tied the ends together. "Like this cut them," he said. Tidi gave me a big smile and was gone.

About ten minutes later, I heard a huge tree fall. Tidi did not come in for lunch. But right after lunch, four-by-fours began to arrive with the designated lumber carriers. I figured that most of our lumber went from being part of a living tree to being part of our house in less than three hours.

I had heard people talk about houses that looked like they were built with a chain saw. Ours really was. Rather than ordering lumber to fit the plan, we designed our house plan to fit the lumber. The building materials also set a new standard for freshness. You almost had to wear safety goggles when driving nails to protect your eyes from water squirting from the lumber.

Tementa had come to help with the construction. He always seemed to know where to be at just the right time. He would be out at the airstrip for a while, and then the next thing I knew, he would be in the jungle helping Tidi. Then he would be gently offering me advice on some material I might want to consider for some part of the construction.

One day, when our meat was getting low, I saw him with a gun, walking into the jungle. Fifteen minutes later he walked back into camp. I asked him if he had decided not to get meat. "Doobae," he said quietly, and walked past me. *Already?* I wondered. Then, as he passed me, I saw a huge tapir head tied on his back. Tementa said he had walked down the trail a ways. There, under some big leaves, sound asleep, was this biggest and perhaps most timid of all jungle animals. He told me he shot it in the head so it wouldn't wake up. Men from our crew began running down the trail to retrieve the rest of our new meat supply.

After five long days of work on our house, the structural skeleton was almost complete. I hoped it would rain a lot while we were gone. If it did not rain, I was afraid that this water-saturated lumber would dry and twist, and our structure might self-destruct.

/\./\.·/\·/\./\·/\·/\./\

It was time to go meet Ginny, Stephenie, Jaime, the medical team, "superagent" Connie, and Connie's daughter. Connie was making good on her dream to visit the Amazon. She was a dream come true for us, too. She handled all the travel arrangements for our large group, gave tips at the big packing party Ginny held in Ocala, and led the group through all the little inconveniences of modern-day international travel. The medical group was going to be in Ecuador for about ten days. Connie would stay the whole time they were there.

On our end, it took us half a day to go upriver. Just a quarter mile before reaching the airstrip, we heard a plane take off. The good news was that it wasn't our plane. The bad news was that our plane did not arrive until four-thirty.

We weren't desperate to get to Quito until the next day, but we were desperate to get to salt as soon as possible. We got out of the MAF plane in Shell, bought two cold Cokes in the hangar, and headed to the nearest restaurant. Before our meals were served, we ate two bowls of well-salted and very spicy salsa. The greasy spoon food was delicious. Jesse held up a french fry dripping oil, and we all moaned with pleasure before wolfing down the food in front of us. *It is no wonder we "civilized people" are fat,* I thought. Jungle people, by contrast, don't suffer from high cholesterol or high blood pressure. Fats, salt, and carcinogens are just not part of their diets.

But that food—oversalted, fried in oil, and drenched in hot sauce—sure tasted good! I love jungle fare, but I did wonder if we could genetically alter it to taste like the fatty, salted, and carcinogenic foods we enjoy at home. If we could do that, we North Americans would all be happy and in good shape.

/\./\.·/\·/\./\·/\·/\./\

I couldn't wait to see Ginny, Stephenie, and Jaime at the airport. I expected Ginny to be nervous when she got off the plane, but instead she threw her arms around me and told me she was so glad to be back with me that she didn't care what our circumstances were. It is hard for a guy with a wife like that not to get a big head. But I wondered if Ginny would still feel the same way when she saw her partially finished chain-saw house surrounded by tangled jungle. I thought Steph might be a little nervous too. But she was chomping at the bit to get out of the capital city and down to the jungle.

Rick and Teresa and their two children were part of the group that came with Ginny, but they had decided to stay longer than everyone else. They offered to remain as long as necessary to help us get moved into our new jungle home. More important, Rick offered to help evaluate which medical needs we could teach the Waodani to handle on their own. Rick was actually the instigator of the entire medical training group going to Ecuador.

We spent several days in Quito, where the medical team from our hometown of Ocala, Florida, taught some Ecuadorean surgeons to do knee replacement surgery.

Then, finally, our whole family, along with Connie and her daughter and the medical team, headed for the jungle. They all wanted to see if the Amazon was really as great as Connie had told them it was.

/\/\/\/\/\/\/\

After the medical team and Connie and her daughter left, it was only the Saint family, Rick and Teresa, and their two children.

At this point, the "to dos" on my short list included the following:

Get old Bravo Tango Sierra ready to fly.
Get the house to livable condition.
Move out to our new Waodani territory home.

Bravo Tango Sierra was first on the list. Once we got that old bush plane in the air, I knew everything would be easier.

The expert aviation mechanics at Mission Aviation Fellowship in Shell were backed up with their own maintenance, but I held out hope that they would at least help me do some of the work on BTS.

Here I ran into a situation I had not anticipated. Jungle flying is very specialized. There are no fields in the Ecuadorean jungle for emergency landings. The airstrips are short, narrow, wet, and muddy. They are not fenced, so animals and people use them too. The Waodani have to laboriously cut the grass on their airstrips by hand with machetes, so they frequently let it get very long before they cut it. Then when they do cut it, it lies on the runway like hay waiting to be bailed. Cut grass like that can mound up in front of a wheel and cause the plane to veer off the strip. There is also the possibility on a new strip that roots might have been left to rot, creating holes in the surface.

I had no specialized training, as professional missionary pilots receive. Bravo Tango Sierra was not a modern bush plane with special equipment, such as dual brakes or short takeoff and landing features. The MAF director in Ecuador decided there was a good chance I would end up killing myself. He did not want MAF to be responsible, which he thought they would be if they helped me work on BTS.

They certainly had no obligation to help me. In fact, I had received hints that this might be the case. But I thought they would, because when MAF asked me to go to Africa for a year, I sold my house, packed my things, and went.

The house Dad built when he started the MAF operation so long ago was right across the street. That rough little road that once saw more horses and mules than cars still ran in front of our old house, only now it was paved.

I stood in the large, modern MAF hangar and looked across to the little shed where old 56 Henry had lived until that fateful day Dad took off from this very place, never to return. The place where I stood to watch him leave for the last time is still there between our old house and the runway, which is also paved now.

I guess I just assumed that I was part of the "family." I had no idea I was soon going to have to choose which family I really wanted to be part of.

I felt jilted by the people who, several generations removed, were replacing my mom and dad and the work they had started. The slight I felt, however, turned out to be a blessing in disguise. I have noticed that often happens when I am willing to let God write the story. Having to rebuild my own engine was a good initiation for what was ahead. At least now the Waodani could not accuse me of being a "taker" just before I began my own crusade to convince them that they could do most of what outsiders had been doing for them for so long.

Aircraft engines are a lot like Volkswagen engines. Each of the cylinders is a separate unit that can be removed from the engine case. When I arrived in Shell and went to inspect BTS, none of the cylinders were on the engine. I finally found them in a barrel of diesel fuel.

The plane's owner, Rick, had told me that a couple of cylinders were cracked. I did not want to be in the middle of a takeoff and have another cylinder crack, so Rick and I made a deal. I would put all new cylinders, pistons, and rings on his engine in exchange for using the plane. That seemed to be a good trade.

I had the new cylinders with me, but I was counting on taking the old ones off so I would know how to put the new ones on. Instead, pistons, cylinders, and a myriad of tiny parts were all mixed up in a barrel of diesel fuel. It was going to be like putting a puzzle together without having a picture on the box to tell me what it was supposed to look like when it was done.

I didn't know where to start. Teresa came to the rescue. When Ginny told her of my dilemma, she told me she liked working on their family cars, and she would be happy to help. She didn't seem the least bit intimidated, but then she hadn't seen where I would be flying yet either.

There is a fundamental difference between a car and a plane. An old-timer once told me, "The biggest difference between a car and a plane is not that one flies. The biggest difference is that in a car, if the engine quits, there you is. But in a plane, if the engine quits, where is you?"

Teresa inspired me to get out the overhaul manual I had brought. Then we got out all the new parts that Connie and American Airlines had brought down for me, and we started comparing old and new. I read a little and compared what the book said with what I was seeing, and they seemed to match up.

About that time, one of the MAF pilots from Finland offered to help me in the evenings. He also told me about a licensed Ecuadorean aircraft mechanic who might be available to inspect what I was doing. I had to have a licensed aircraft mechanic to sign off on the necessary paperwork.

The Saint family seems to turn out two models. We get either the mechanical gene or the artistic gene. I got the mechanical one, but I am certainly no professional. On the other hand, I figured, how difficult could it be to put together an airplane engine?

I thought it would be a lonely project, but that was not the case. My boys offered to help first. Then several young Waodani fellows who were in town came by to see me. They offered to help too. The Finnish mechanic stopped by once in a while, and so did the Ecuadorean mechanic. And in a pinch, the MAF mechanics were generous with advice, even though the official policy was "hands-off."

I was thrilled when everything fit. I did have to do a couple of things twice, but in the end we had no parts left over.

I enjoyed the challenge. The overhaul manual was very thorough, which I was grateful for, and the Ecuadorean mechanic was quick to question how the manual said to do certain things. The highlight, however, was my Waodani helpers. They were fascinated with everything. I'm sure they thought I knew what I was doing. After all, I had white *cowodi* skin. I didn't want to tell them I had never done what I was simultaneously doing and teaching them to do.

I did not realize it then, but I would spend a lot of time explaining to Waodani that outsiders don't know how to do everything. I would spend even more time and energy trying to convince *cowodi* that just because someone has beautiful olive-colored skin does not mean that they are incapable of mastering "outsider" skills.

On the third day of engine rebuilding, it was time to see if our awkward assembly of well-oiled parts could make noise and spin a propeller. I figured the Waodani young men would be surprised if it started. Instead, I was the one who was surprised. They just acted like they'd expected it to work. Oh yeah, they didn't know I had never previously done what we had just done.

The engine fired up, and the oil pressure gauge said the moving parts were getting oil. It was time to see if old BTS would fly.

Ginny and the boys came over to join my Waodani pit crew for the big occasion. We had borrowed a few rooms in an old house across the street, so they didn't have far to come. The house where we were staying while I rebuilt BTS's engine had belonged to one of the first missionary doctors at the hospital my dad and his friends had been building when they were killed.

By the time I had made several taxi tests, it was getting dark and the Shell airstrip was about to close. I decided it was time to fly. I had not yet validated my pilot's license in Ecuador, so I asked Capitan Henry, who had rescued me during the war, to do the test flight with me so we would be legal. With everyone watching carefully, as though to fix the location of loose parts they expected to fall off the plane, I gave BTS the go, and we were off.

I took off over the cliff on the west end of the strip, turning left to follow the course of the Pastaza River. Then I circled back for a touch-and-go. I was feeling pretty good, but everyone on the ground was waving frantically at me, so I pulled into our borrowed lean-to and shut down.

Everyone started talking at once, telling me that when I took off, flames shot out from the bottom of the plane. Against the almost dark sky, it must have been pretty dramatic. I had no idea what could have caused that to happen. We were obviously a cosmopolitan group. "Goonga nangi pongandapa, atabopa"—*Fire, lots of it coming; I saw it!* was the Waodani version. "Vimos un fuego tremendo cuando despegaste" was the Spanish version: *We saw fire, tremendous, when you took off!* In English, someone exclaimed, "When you took off, we saw flames shooting from the belly of the plane. You aren't going to fly that thing again, are you?"

I think the English version was meant for Ginny's benefit more than for mine. Ginny just said calmly, "Well, Steve is pretty careful. He doesn't always go by the book, but he won't do anything he doesn't think is safe."

I didn't fly BTS again until the next day. I talked over the various possibilities for what sounded like a flamethrower attached to our little Cessna 172. If I had been grounded by every flying horror story I have heard over the years, I never would have dared to land my J-3 Cub in farmers' fields in college. I would have missed out on meeting some great folks. I would have missed out on a lot of good food too.

On the other hand, when flames are shooting out of a newly rebuilt aircraft engine, it is clearly not something to be taken lightly. I decided that the most reasonable thing was to give it the "again" test. When a piece of equipment does something nonstandard with potentially negative consequences, the pilot does what he was doing when the problem started and sees if the machine does what it did "again."

BTS did not do it again, so I did what I had been doing—flying—again. In fact, I did it again about 2,300 times over the next year and a half. That old, ragged four-seat bush plane, whose history spanned thirty years by that time, became more like a member of the family than simply a means of transportation. It was our family car, our ambulance, our delivery truck, and our recreational vehicle, though it didn't serve in the last category very often.

Now that we had the plane up and running, next on my list was the house. We decided that this would be a project for the "boys." I'm sure Ginny would have been game to go with us, but Rick and Teresa's two children were quite young. And I knew we would have to live under tarps slung a few feet over the damp, creature-infested jungle floor until we could move into the house. I certainly did not want to use up Ginny and Stephenie's pioneering spirit too quickly.

16

It's a Jungle Out Here

When we were building the airstrip, the Waodani had started thinking of names for this new village. It needed to have some significance. While they were discussing the issue over smoked wild pig meat, I thought of naming it after Aunt Rachel. But I didn't want to suggest it, until one of the warriors asked me what I would "see well" to name it.

"Well, how would you all see it to call it Nemo-ompade?" I asked. Mincaye immediately said, "Yes, I see that well." Then he explained to those who weren't from their clan that Dayumae's sister, Nemo, whose name she had given to Aunt Rachel, had once had a terrible fever when they were traveling through this very area of jungle. "Being hot with fever and needing water, they stopped at this very *ompade* (creek), and drinking water from it, she did not die."

So our new home became Nemompade, "Star Creek," named for Dayumae's two sisters: the one saved from the fever and later hacked to death by Moipa, and the one with the ruddy complexion she adopted as the replacement, the one we had just buried upriver.

The next few weeks included a lot of firsts for us. The first flight into the just-completed rugged airstrip of Nemompade—which at that time consisted of one partially finished tarp-roofed house and several temporary thatched huts—was one of the most important firsts. It was also one of the most exciting.

Before that first landing at Nemompade, I flew Jaime, Shaun, and Rick into the nearest established Waodani community so they could walk over to Nemompade and take one last look at the strip for me. The Waodani were perfectly capable of fixing anything that needed a last-minute touch-up, but I wanted someone I could precisely communicate with to check for soft spots and put some markers out for me. We could not afford to take a chance on damaging our flying "family car."

My first landing was fine. The biggest challenge was to get down to the runway. From the ground, the airstrip looked plenty wide. But branches on the huge trees beside the runway spread out over the airstrip so far that from the air it looked more like a tunnel than a place to land. There was enough room to get down, but it was tight. In fact, it was a tight enough squeeze that we couldn't get any other pilots to land at our little community for months; they refused to come until we cut down some of the offending branches. We would have done it sooner, but it was a huge job just climbing those trees—which could easily have a trunk circumference of over twelve feet—much less having to wield an ax or chain saw while balancing on a branch over a hundred feet above the ground.

The Waodani and the boys and I spent a couple more days working on the house before Ginny and Steph headed out. Although it was still just a rough frame with a tarp stretched over it, Ginny had informed me that she was ready to move into her new home so we could all be together. We busily cut enough boards to put down an area of floor about twelve feet by twelve feet. The Waodani made a notched pole so we could climb from the jungle floor up the nine feet or so into our new home.

When I flew Ginny and Steph into Nemompade, they were really impressed with the runway. Their excitement lessened slightly as we walked the dark little trail that led from the airstrip to the few shelters on the river-bank. I still had to duck on the trail to get through. I was hoping that they would be pleased when they saw how much progress we had made on the house, but I didn't hold out much hope: Our "house" had no walls, no windows, no doors, and no floor except in that one little corner.

I have to admit that I was a little nervous as I watched my wife and daughter survey their new home. I explained that the boys and I would continue to sleep under the temporary shelters on the jungle floor. Steph was the first to comment. "No way, why can't I sleep with you guys?"

Then Ginny turned to me and said, "Steve, it is beautiful; I would rather live here, even if the house never got any better than this, than to live in a beautiful home without my boys." I told you she is a girl to ride the river with!

Another first for the girls was learning to bathe in public. All the men in the community simply stripped down to our briefs, or a little further for some of the old guys, who still wore G-strings. The Waodani women stripped to their panties, or even further. Although our sense of modesty would lessen substantially over the next year and a half, Ginny and Steph decided to work down to that new standard slowly. Ginny decided that she would bathe in a sundress, using it like a shower curtain, with her head protruding from the top. It worked fine and had the added advantage of allowing her to visit with the neighbors and do chores while she was taking her bath. While she was getting herself clean, she was also washing her clothes and making friends. Kind of like having a neighborhood party at the public Laundromat while everyone takes a bath together.

I have heard people say that it is a horrible experience to live in a house that is being remodeled. Try living in one that is being built around you! As we put down more flooring, Ginny expanded her household operations to incorporate the new areas. By the time we had the floor half finished, residents in our new house included Ginny and Stephenie, a *cowodi* mother with her two children, about six Waodani women with a couple of nursing babies, a pet toucan, a macaw, and two monkeys. The pet wild pig someone gave us was not allowed in the house. The *odae* couldn't make it up the notched log stairs, but he didn't give up without trying a hundred times.

/\\/\\/\\/\\/\\/\\/\\

We hadn't been there long before Mincaye started bringing me requests from other Waodani communities to make flights for them. Having access to a plane that "lived" in Waodani territory was a new phenomenon that none of the People had ever dreamed possible. I could see that pretty soon I would be flying all day every day if I didn't find a way to distinguish the urgent flight requests from all the rest. I asked Mincaye and Kimo if they would decide.

That made them extremely nervous. Remember, the Waodani don't really have any historic mechanism for dealing with confrontation. Their only means of resolution was killing. If someone asked for a flight, it would be considered confrontational to refuse their request. But I could not be the one to decide. I had come to do what the Waodani wanted me to do. I realized that the answer was to give the decision to the elders.

The Waodani don't appoint leaders. Their culture disdains the idea of one person imposing his will on another person. The Waodani don't even have tribal elders. But we had to have someone to take charge of how and when the plane would be used. So I showed those who had told me to come that God's markings say that within the church *ne anani*, or elders, should be selected to direct and protect the congregation. I asked the Waodani I had known and respected in Tiwaeno when I was a boy who the *ne anani* were. They did not seem to know. I explained that the "elder ones" are the ones who take care of those who need help and make big decisions that affect their group as a whole.

They still could not tell me who the elders were. I was perplexed. Then it occurred to me that Kimo and Dyuwi were right there with us. I reminded them that they had taken me *aepaenigii*—into the water to be baptized. They acknowledged that what I said was true. Then I reminded them that it was the *ne anani* who baptized those who wanted to publicly declare their decision to follow God's trail.

"So," I continued, "you were the *ne anani* when I was a boy. Are you not still *ne anani* now?" They seemed to think that what I said made sense. But it was clear that they no longer considered themselves to be elders, either in the Waodani church or in their communities.

I started to name the various responsibilities elders take and the services they perform. I asked who did those things, and they responded simply, "The foreigners do that; the foreigners do that."

This was our first real crisis. I was determined to help the Waodani do what they wanted to do for their own people and not to do what *I* wanted to do for them. Someone needed to tell me which flights to make and which ones not to make. *They* had to decide if they wanted to build the clinic first, start a medicine distribution service, or build a community school. To make such communal decisions, they had to decide who the elders were.

I brought the issue to a head by saying that I could not make any more flights until they decided who was going to tell me which ones were critical to the tribe and which ones were only of personal benefit. Ginny pointed out that I was about to shoot myself in the foot. "What are you going to do when you want to make a flight for us?" This simple life was starting to get complicated.

Fortunately, Mincaye, Kimo, Tementa, Dyuwi, and Komi, along with Dawa, Dayumae, and a few other women, saw the importance of what I was asking them to do. They got on the radio that Jesse had set up and called mature God followers from the other Waodani villages to come to Nemompade. When everyone arrived, Tementa, the only adult in the group who could read, began to read from the Waodani New Testament that Aunt Rachel, Cathy Peek (another linguist with Wycliffe Bible Translators), and several helpers had painstakingly worked to translate into the Waodani's own language. When the People had clearly in mind what *ne anani* were supposed to be and what they were supposed to do, they began to select those who best fit the description in God's carvings.

They chose Mincaye, Tementa, Kimo, Dyuwi, Dyuwi's son Tañi, Kenta, Paa, Amoa, and Omene. These men lived in six different communities that were fairly representative of the other fourteen or fifteen villages. But they didn't stop there. They also chose some younger men, whom they decided to call *nengcaeca*, or "doer ones." These would be young men who could read, knew a little bit of Spanish, and would be able to help the elders figure out how to do what they decided needed to be done. They also identified a third group, the *piquianani*, or older ones. The *piquianani*, some of whom were not God followers, would not have a vote, but they would have a say in what the elders would decide they should corporately try to do for the tribe.

They wanted me to be a *ne anga*, but I pointed out that I could not function in that capacity because I had not lived there for a long time and did not know well enough what was happening. I also did not have a good grasp of the language, and I wasn't Waodani. Mincaye objected to the last excuse. "Aren't you just like us, having lived with us from the time you were small and helpless? Only your skin looks like a foreigner. And," he conceded, "you don't have ear holes; but then, neither do Tementa, Tañi, and Kenta."

Everyone laughed as the ever-loyal Mincaye went into a long rendition of all the things I could do just like a true Waodani. Finally, when he realized that he couldn't make me a Waodani just by asserting that I was, he declared me to be *Wao-wodi*: not quite Waodani, but certainly not *cowodi*.

The Waodani elders had functioned well, at least within the Waodani church, when I was a boy. It was sad for me to realize that well-meaning people from the outside had so dominated the Waodani that they no longer even saw the need to identify leaders within the tribe.

When Mincaye came to me the next day and told me of several flight requests, he carefully told me which ones to make and which ones not to make. He gave me reasons for each decision and solemnly told me that the *ne anani* had decided this. He was very tense. I could tell that he and the other elders were taking a big risk by deciding that I should not do what other Waodani were asking me to do. But I knew this risk would be worth it in the end if it led to freedom for the Waodani to control their own wood bee.

The only thing Ginny asked of me during those early days was to try to get the house completed enough that we could all live in it, at least for one night before Jaime and Shaun left for college in the United States. The inevitable split-up of our family was weighing heavily on all of us, but Ginny felt it most.

Shaun had been working with Dyuwi and some others on the difficult task of cutting tree trunks to bridge the slough at the west end of our airstrip. It was hot, dirty work that had to be done while sweat bees swarmed over the workers' entire bodies, as well as in their ears, noses, and eyes. But Shaun liked the physical labor. The Waodani were surprised at how strong he was and how willing to work. He would leave early in the morning, and we would hardly see him until dark. He could not speak Wao-Tededo at all, and only a little Spanish, but it was obvious that he liked the Waodani and—equally as obvious—they liked him.

Jaime decided he would work on the house. He is a hard worker but does not like "dirty" to be part of the job description. He and Rick decided that our house should have walls. Under the rustic conditions we were living in, that almost seemed like an unnecessary frill. But Jaime, Rick, and Coba added thirty-inch walls around the perimeter of the entire house. It was kind of nice to know we didn't have to worry about rolling out of bed at night and falling ten feet to the muddy ground below.

Jesse, besides helping on the house, was kept fairly busy getting our communications set up. When we were in the States, Ginny had asked me to make sure it would be possible for us to stay in touch with family while we were in the jungle. I asked Jesse to take that responsibility. Before I knew it, he had taken his test, gotten his radio license, and learned how to make antennae.

Jesse asked the Waodani to help him install several different antennae he had bought or built that would allow us to communicate directly with the United States. Sure enough, the first time he tried, he was able to talk with a ham radio operator in the States, who patched us into his telephone so we could call our family in North America and let them know that we were all well.

Stephenie seemed to make her biggest contribution by simply fitting into the tribe. At about five feet eight inches, Steph was taller than everyone in the tribe, I think, except maybe Kenta. With her fair complexion and long blonde hair, she did not exactly blend with the Waodani physically, but she certainly did emotionally. Within days, she was beginning to speak Wao-Tededo, spending hours playing with Waodani children, and learning Waodani crafts from the Waodani women. The more obvious it became that she wanted to learn to be Waodani, the more the People treated her like she was one of them.

The teenage girls loved to spend time with Steph. While they helped her to learn their language, she taught them to play her little keyboard and explained to them what her life had been like in the outside world. I knew she was acclimating well when she started going barefoot. I had to make her wear her jungle boots so she would not get *niguas*, a type of worm that can enter a person's body through even tiny cuts in the feet. I also did not want her to be laid up like I had once been when I stepped on a thorn that practically went through my foot.

I flew Rick, Teresa, and their kids into Shell the day before Shaun and Jaime were scheduled to leave for Quito and eventually the United States. That night, for the first time, it was just us in our Nemompade house. Ginny finally got her wish, and we spent our first night together in our jungle home. It would have been a perfect night if Shaun and Jaime weren't leaving, if our new night monkey had not kept us awake by pouncing on us from the rafters, and if a driving rain had not poured through the cracks between the rough boards that made up our short outer walls.

I told myself I would need to put battens over the growing cracks that the drying wood produced. I also made a mental note to trim the branch that kept slapping against the post on the outside corner of Ginny's and my room. Each time it hit the house, it sprayed us with rainwater. Once the branch was trimmed, our broken-winged pet macaw would no longer be able to climb up it and screech at us at five-thirty in the morning.

It really was hard watching Jaime and Shaun leave. We would not see them again until their Christmas break. We did not know it, but by the time we returned to the States, they would both be making plans to get married. Our family would never be quite the same again. That was true, in more ways than we could have known at the time.

Finally, Nemompade was down to Mincaye's family, which included "Wild Pig," one of his sons-in-law, and his family; Tidi and his growing family; Wato, the widow of my old friend Toñae, and her son, Gaba; Coba, by himself because his wife, who was Mincaye's wife's sister, had not been willing to leave Toñampade; and Jesse, Stephenie, Ginny, and me. We expected that things would quickly settle down. That almost seems laughable now.

A constant stream of visitors from other villages started coming through Nemompade. We had chosen the location for this village because it was centrally located. That meant that Waodani traveling between other villages stopped by to see what was happening in our little village with what seemed like planned regularity. Everyone just assumed that all visitors would stay with us. That way they would get not only free room and board but also free entertainment—watching us live a cross between Waodani life and *cowodi* life.

We also had numerous *cowodi* who wanted to visit us. It was entertaining even for us to watch people from the outside world interact with the Waodani on the Waodani's home court. One day, after we'd been there for a while, a woman with a Dolly Parton–like hairdo came to visit us. She spent Sunday with us, so we joined the Waodani in the longhouse they had built for a meeting place. When the Waodani get together to discuss "God's thing," they don't have a formal program. They just let what happens, happen. Sometimes people will tell how their lives have changed since they started walking God's trail. Other times someone will lead chants or translated songs with outsiders' melodies—or rough facsimiles of those melodies. Others tell stories from God's carvings about God followers from long ago. No one is ever in a hurry to end the meetings, which often go on for hours.

Of course, the congregation does not sit stiffly in pews while all this is going on. Men whittle darts; women make string and nurse their babies; children play quietly while they listen. The congregation usually includes quite a menagerie of animals too.

In Nemompade, we were usually joined by a couple of dogs, our pet wild pig that thought it was a dog, birds that flew back and forth through the longhouse or roosted on the rafters, and a monkey or two. On this particular day, Wato's woolly monkey, Macho, came to see what was going on at church. He climbed onto the rafters and sat quietly on a crossbeam—right above our guest with the big, platinum blonde hairdo.

When the pig got bored, he began to nip at the dogs, who bit the pig's ears to get even. That was the signal for the *boogie* monkey to join the fray. Macho got excited and started to urinate. His aim was unfortunate: right into our guest's big hair. She must have thought it was an insect, because she started waving her hand above her head as if she was trying to shoo away a pesky insect.

Right then, one of the dogs bit the pig a little too hard. It jumped up and shot stinky musk from the gland on its back onto the offending dog. Several of the Waodani scolded the pig and threw dirt clods from the floor at him. This increase of commotion was too much for Macho. He ratcheted up his activities from "level 1" to "level 2." When the monkey's "business" landed in our visitor's hair, she still thought it was an insect, so she decided to dispatch it before it could do her damage.

Her coup de grâce was right on target, but what she hit was obviously not what she'd expected. She took one look at her hand and then one look straight up. What she saw verified her worst fear. I'll have to hand it to her: She did not scream or throw up. She just wiped her hand on the log she was sitting on and tried to act as if nothing out of the ordinary had happened.

/\/\/\/\/\/\/\/\

Our house was divided into three sections. To understand our house plan you can take a regular piece of paper and fold in both ends so they meet in the middle. That divides the paper into one quarter on each end with half left in the middle. Now divide each end into two rooms so that each one has an outside corner. Make one of those rooms the storage room and prospective bathroom, the other three into bedrooms, and the center into a kitchen/ eating area/hammocked library (stocked with years of editions of *National Geographic*)/local theater, and you have our house plan.

Ginny and I took one bedroom, about ten feet by ten feet. Steph took another one, which doubled as the schoolroom where Steph and Jesse would teach themselves the essentials required for their respective sophomore and junior years in high school.

Jesse slept in the radio room/office/jelly bean repository. I never did figure out where Jesse got so many jelly beans, but I have these vivid memories of Jesse and Mincaye constantly disappearing into Jesse's room and emerging with jelly beans in their mouths and smiles on their faces.

The fourth end room was where I planned to put a bathroom. In the meantime, it served for storing parts and expendables for the canoe motor, construction tools, airplane parts and tools, and the few staples we bought in from Shell to supplement our diets until the gardens started to produce.

The middle room was where Ginny used her little propane camp stove to cook for us and to wash our few dishes. It was also our dining room. Rick had built us a hand-planed board table, which was mounted to the storage room wall, and two benches. We all learned to love that little table. We ate there, did homework on it, and talked around it at night while our candle wreaked havoc on jungle insects that could not resist its allure and flew into its flame to sizzle and die.

The rest of that room was strung with hammocks. It served as the Nemompade bed-and-breakfast, local clinic, dry goods store, and video viewing room. I don't think there was a single night that we didn't have one or two or twenty or thirty people sleeping with us on their way through Nemompade. We usually had a lot more who wanted to watch a video, such as *Little House on the Prairie*, *Zorro*, or *Star Wars*. The questions they asked were as fascinating to us as the videos appeared to be to them. We tried to explain that some things we watched were true; other things were *like* true but were just people acting like other people. It was difficult to explain "make-believe," which does not translate easily into Waodani culture.

I can just imagine Waodani in the communities around us saying, "Hey, it's Friday night. What do you say we pay Babae and Ongingcamo a visit and see what strange things they are doing and have to eat, and see what is showing on their little 'bee-day-o' thing?" (Except that the Waodani do not distinguish Friday from any other day of the week, so any night could be video night.)

We still had the little twelve-volt TV/VCR that had made such a hit with the Waodani while we were building the airstrip. Every night those who lived in Nemompade would ask Stephenie or Jesse to put on a video "for the visitors to see." They were fascinated by war movies. They would comment back and forth about how violent foreigners were. They also loved wildlife shows and asked to watch them over and over so they could memorize the habits of these animals they didn't know but wanted to hunt. Jesse and Steph, though they loved the Waodani, got desperate once in a while for just a little time to themselves. They tried to bore our movie crowd with some chick flicks, such as *Anne of Green Gables*. There is almost no action in those movies, and the Waodani could not understand any of the dialogue. But no one got bored; they loved them! It did not take them long to figure out what all the relationships were and to create their own version of what was going on.

They also liked videos such as *Jurassic Park, The Jungle Book*—any version was fine—and *The Princess Bride*. Their comments about those shows would make great books. During the opening scenes of *Jurassic Park*, one of the old women scooted nervously away from our little video screen and asked nervously, "What are we going to do if that thing comes here?" Dawa just laughed. "We'll send these lazy men out to hunt it. If they can kill that thing, we'll have meat for a looooooooooong time!"

If we didn't have a video going, those from other communities were happy just to watch us. We had no doors on our rooms. And when the wet boards in our interior walls dried, huge cracks were left in our walls. You could see almost as well through the walls as through the doorways.

Finally, however, the total and constant lack of privacy became overwhelming. I realized it was unnecessary to give up all our privacy. When our Waodani neighbors wanted to be alone, they went home. We were the only ones who couldn't do that, because there were always other people in our house/community center. Unfortunately, I could not think of any way to get some privacy without offending our Waodani family or distancing them from us. On the other hand, I felt like I needed to protect Ginny at least in this little area.

I offered to build a door with a latch on it for the opening to the porch and stairs. Ginny said no. She wanted privacy, but she did not want to offend any of the Waodani. Instead, she cut up some bed sheets, weighted the bottoms, and hung them in the doorways to our rooms. After I put slats over the cracks between the boards in our walls, we felt as private as possible in a house with thirty-inch walls and no windows, no curtains, and no blinds. I did build a simple screen door for our outside entrance, but it didn't have any kind of latch on it. It banged open and closed a hundred times a day as our Waodani family, friends, and neighbors came and went as they pleased. I was grateful Ginny and Steph and Jesse wanted to be as open and accessible to the Waodani as I did.

Our house also became the Waodani clinic. Ginny was a registered nurse when we met, and I have always wanted to practice medicine. With no other regular medical service available inside Waodani territory, the need for health care was so great that we had a constant stream of people coming to us for treatment of everything from snakebites to problematic deliveries of babies. We also saw patients with parasites, machete cuts, broken bones, and systemic infections. Several members of the Nemompade community had been trained as health promoters. Ginny and I encouraged them to handle whatever they could. We invited medical people from a mission hospital as well as occasional visitors with medical training to put on medical training courses for the health promoters and us. Before long, we could take care of most of the nonsurgical medical needs that came our way. The Waodani also asked me to help them start a medicine house (what we would call a pharmacy). Mincaye's daughter and her teenage son, young Mincaye, took responsibility for that.

The medicine house became hugely popular. A missionary nurse helped us keep it stocked with affordable medicines that the health promoters knew how to use. Pretty soon, I could tell that there was much less sickness in the villages I flew into on a regular basis. But the whole system broke down a couple of times when the oil company sent bags of free medicines into one of the Waodani villages they wanted to win favor with. Word spread throughout the jungle that the oil company was going to give everyone free medicine. So none of the health promoters came to buy any more. They knew it was useless to try to sell medicine if the oil company was giving it away. When they did come, they begged us to buy their little stocks of medicine back. What was worse was that the free medicines the oil company sent were not meant to treat the medical needs we had. They were mostly painkillers and older antibiotics. They did send some snake antivenin. Unfortunately, it did not work for most of the snakes we had to deal with. I wondered how many people would suffer or even die because someone in the outside world carelessly gave the Waodani one more handout.

The Waodani who served as health promoters could prescribe basic medicines, but they rarely had what they needed when they needed it. The only alternatives up to this point had been to let the patient suffer or to talk a missionary pilot into taking the sick patient to the edge of the jungle to one of the hospitals there. Now if the elders thought someone needed to go to the hospital, they would ask me to take them. Our only costs were fuel and oil. The pilot and airplane were free.

∿∿∿∿∿∿∿

The availability of the airplane created probably the biggest change of all. As we started settling into our totally unpredictable routine, I found myself flying almost every day. Sometimes it was just one or two flights. Some days I flew all day. As I sat down one night to log the reams of information the government required for each flight, I realized that I had made twenty-three flights that day. Twenty-three times I had loaded the plane, unloaded it, buckled in passengers, and delivered medicines, messages, and even a baby. My average flight was about eight minutes long. But to travel the equivalent amount I had that day with old BTS would have taken two hours on the trail for every minute in the air. It would have taken about three or four Waodani to carry the cargo I had delivered. Doing the math, I realized it would have taken one person, walking forty hours every week, over a year and a half to do what I did in just one day with an old twenty-five-thousand-dollar airplane.

I loved the challenge of every takeoff and the thrill of every muddy, adrenaline-inspiring landing. And I absolutely loved being able to help the people whose "gopher" I had become. The only sour note was that I realized we were all becoming too dependent on the plane.

What would happen when we left and the Waodani no longer had the plane or the money to replace it?

The tribe needed an economy as much as it needed anything else. The

Waodani are hard workers when they need to be. They are clever and good with their hands. But they simply had no skills or education that were marketable in the outside world. And anything we tried to make in the jungle for sale outside had to compete with other native tribes who could take their products to market by road: a much more affordable option that we did not have. We would have to fly ours.

The flying not only began to consume my time but Ginny's as well. I was flying over some of the most rugged and sparsely populated territory in the jungle. So just as I had watched my mom do for my dad, Ginny monitored the radio whenever I was in the air. I told her where I was and where I was going, who I had on board with me, and when I expected to land on the other end. I used an incredible little GPS to navigate my trips. I always flew along the straight line on my moving map display so that if someone had to come looking for me they would know where to look.

I really did love the flying, and I loved working together with Ginny. But I knew that I would do the Waodani a lot more good if I spent less time flying and more time teaching one of them to fly.

While I was out trying to make the Waodani world a better place for them to live in, Ginny spent the majority of her time—when she wasn't writing down my coordinates or giving me weather reports—trying to figure out how to keep three-day-old meat from spoiling without refrigeration and coming up with delectable recipes for monkey, tapir, exotic birds, turtle eggs, giant catfish, and ROUS's (Rodents Of Unusual Size, for those who have never seen *The Princess Bride*).

Jesse and Stephenie spent some time most days doing schoolwork. But they were passionate to learn the Waodani way of life and to help these people whom they were learning to love as much as I did.

They started a school for the village children and served as the teachers until the Waodani elders hired one of Mincaye's grandsons, a sharp young man with a fairly decent education, to take over.

When I realized how little time Steph and Jess were spending on their schoolwork, I thought they might not be allowed to move on to the next level. I should have saved my worry. They not only passed the year just fine, but they also became functional in two new languages and a couple of cultures while they were at it.

The most discouraging and dangerous problem we faced was dealing with the constant tensions between the government, oil companies, anthropologists, environmentalists, and missionaries, who all had desires to influence the Waodani and to control their destiny in different ways.

As I look back on it now, I can understand, to a certain extent, why each of those powerful entities wanted to influence the Waodani. I can't say that if I worked for any of them I would have had a different perspective on how to handle the "Waodani problem." That's how most outsiders view the Waodani, who claim a huge expanse of game-rich land. They are also sitting on potentially huge oil reserves, which the Ecuadorean government claims for itself and which the oil companies want to get for their own financial benefit. Most anthropologists want to roll back the clock and lock the tribe into a culturally controlled environment with one-way glass walls so the rest of us can look in and observe these egalitarian nomads without them being able to look out and change. Environmentalists want to keep Waodani territory pristine, regardless of the Waodani's desire for more modern means of transportation or some industry to provide them with jobs so they can buy their own clothes and medicines.

Of all of those groups, the only ones who actually seemed to care about the Waodani were the missionaries. But none of them had to share the Waodani's temporal fate. I believe Aunt Rachel came as close to identifying with the Waodani as anyone from the outside ever will. She became so Waodani in her heart and in her way of thinking that during the last hours of her life, when she was terribly weak physically, she started speaking Wao-Tededo to the kind pastor's wife who was keeping her company as she slipped into eternity. In such a weakened condition, all multilingual people tend to slip into their mother tongue.

But even altruistic missionaries often wield a great deal of influence that I believe rightfully belongs to indigenous people themselves. We all know that choices have consequences. The choices rightfully belong to those who have to face the consequences. I felt it my duty on numerous occasions to take exception to the government, oil companies, environmentalists, and aid organizations when I believed what they were doing was hurting the Waodani's long-range viability as a unique people group and as individual and equal humans with certain inalienable rights. I also felt that I needed to object to members of the missionary community at times, from my unique position as a *Wao-wodi*. I never fooled myself into thinking that I was Waodani or that I could see the world exactly as they did. I never claimed to speak for them unless they specifically asked me to. But I honestly don't know of any other person without Waodani blood in his veins who loves and respects the People more than I do. And as fate would have it, there is no other "outsider," as far as I know, who has as long and intimate a history with them as I do.

/\·/\·/\·/\·/\·/\·/\·/\

The Waodani fell in love with Ginny right away. Ginny is very capable, but she is not driven to take charge. She sympathizes with whoever is on the bottom of life's heap. There is only about one thing that really gets her riled: abuse of the down-and-out. That, and the threat of harm to those she loves. In fact, whenever Ginny got upset with me in the jungle, it was usually because she thought I was taking unnecessary chances at hurting myself. She is fiercely loyal.

The Waodani women loved to sit and watch Ginny prepare food in her "modern" kitchen. They cooked over open fires, but Ginny had a four-burner camp stove. Ginny also had a sink cut into two chainsawed boards, although she had to carry her water up from the creek behind the house in a bucket. Then she would carry the dirty water outside to dump it.

Ginny rarely complained, but she did grumble a bit about having to dump the "pee can." I had built a frame for a toilet seat when my mom and stepdad came to visit us, because it was difficult for my stepdad, Abe, to navigate the high steps down to the ground and the trail out to our outhouse. The frame held the seat, and we could slide a one-gallon can underneath it.

That improvised pot saved a lot of hassle. To go to the outhouse, we had to put on our boots, grab a flashlight, and completely wake up. We never wanted to be less awake than whatever we might run into along the trail to the outhouse. Once there, it was advisable to check the thatched roof for tarantulas or snakes. We also checked around the seat for ants and scorpions.

After Mom and Dad left, I continued to use our improvised stool. Jesse and Steph must have been using it too, because the can was usually full by morning. I heard Ginny scream just outside the house one morning. I ran to rescue her but found her just standing on the ground, holding our chamber pot. She had tripped, and the still-warm contents had splashed all over her hands.

I started emptying it myself, which proved to be just the motivation I needed to finally install a used RV toilet I had been given in Shell.

Ginny's other complaint was about not having screens on our windows. She said it made her feel vulnerable to have bats and huge night insects flying through the house. I agreed that it could be annoying, especially since our candles attracted so many insects. Some of them were large enough to put out the candle flame. Others got caught in the pool of wax and just sizzled as they burned while trying to get free. The smell was bothersome once in a while, but I really liked the open feel.

Ginny finally told me she would install the screening if I would not. It wasn't going to be a major project, but I continued to procrastinate about it. In reality, I simply didn't want to feel cooped up. However, late one night, Ginny won the ongoing discussion. We had guests visiting at the time, a couple who obviously had not done much camping. We were all sitting at the table talking when a huge grasshopper was attracted to the candles on our table. For those who consider fried grasshopper a delicacy, this one would have made a meal. It had awesome spikes all over its legs and back, and it chose our female guest's thin silk blouse to land on.

The hopper hitting her back was not nearly as startling as its digging its spikes into her back to hold on after landing. I jumped up and pulled it off, ruining her blouse in the process. Without thinking, I dipped the insect's head into the flame to make sure it would not repeat the performance—and because its spikes were digging into the palm of my hand. The sound and smell of that grasshopper's head burning really stretched our guest's sense of propriety. I don't know if she was more frightened of the grasshopper or offended that her blouse was ruined. They never asked to visit us again, so I couldn't ask.

As soon as those guests left, I put up the screens, even though I did feel sort of closed in after that. Our pet macaw was disappointed too. He was used to walking out on a branch that brushed the house by the corner of our bedroom each morning so I could scratch his head. Although those days were gone, we didn't have to worry about enormous insects or vampire bats after that, so there was some benefit to it.

The Waodani women always wanted Ginny to go to the creek with them.

Some of my fondest memories from the wonderful year and a half we spent in the jungle were of watching Ginny washing our clothes with the other village mothers. Ginny would pull her long, full sundress up and tuck a fold into her panties to keep the bottom out of the water. Then she would scrub away at the mud and mildew with a bar of soap and a lot of muscle. I can still remember hearing her and the women laughing and carrying on. Ginny never learned much of the language, but she certainly had no problem communicating. I never could figure out what Ginny and the Waodani women talked about. Considering how much fun they were having, I knew it was probably best to just leave it alone.

The Waodani women seemed concerned that Ginny had not mastered the art of proper scolding. So whenever they thought she should be scolding me, they never hesitated to take up her cause and give me a good-natured scolding for her.

One day I could see that Ginny was excited. The women had asked Tementa to plant four short poles into the middle of the pool where they washed clothes. After that, Ginny used them to hold her wash and to serve as a washboard. She was so excited about this new convenience that I felt like a worm for not realizing how much effort it would save her. I should have built her a washboard myself. On the other hand, it was just one of the many proofs that while we were watching out for the Waodani, they were also watching out for us.

One of the women was especially devoted to Ginny. Marga was only half Waodani. Her father was one of the last living full-blooded Zaparos, another small tribe that had gone much the way the Waodani tribe was going. Married to hardworking Tidi, Marga was very sharp. Just over thirty years old, she already had seven children. Because she wasn't fully Waodani and felt a bit ostracized, Marga was sensitive to Ginny's needs. Ginny learned to love a number of Waodani women, but her relationship with Marga was unique. Marga, in return, lavished Ginny with care and attention.

Whenever someone brought Ginny a bleeding slab of pig, bristles and all, or a sixty-pound catfish with its guts hanging out, she would smile brightly. But inside, Ginny felt desperate. It took me a while to figure this out, but Marga realized it right away.

Ginny never asked Marga to bail her out. Marga simply wanted to. She would take the meat and bring it back, washed and wrapped in banana leaves.

Ginny and Steph frequently visited Marga's house, and her whole family knew they were always welcome in our house. I guess that wasn't unique—the whole tribe knew that. Our door was always open, literally.

One morning, before it was light, I felt someone climbing the steps to our house. I grabbed my flashlight and went to see who it was. Marga's oldest daughter, Nemonta, was standing at the top of the steps, holding something that she promptly handed to me.

"This is for Ongingcamo and Nemo, my mother sending it to them," she said.

It felt like some meat wrapped in cloth. I figured Tidi had gone night hunting. But when I went to set it down by the sink, it made a sound. I unwrapped it and found a beautiful newborn baby. It had obviously just been born. It had not even been washed yet. I called Ginny and handed the precious bundle to her. She squealed in delight, and Steph came running from her room.

I should have known this might happen. When Marga got pregnant, I had asked her, "Your baby, when is it coming?" But she answered, "Not my baby, but Ongingcamo and Nemo's baby is coming." I didn't take her seriously at the time. Now I realized she had meant it.

It is not unusual for the Waodani to share their children with couples who don't have any. Parents often give one of their children to the child's grandparents. It was obvious that Marga knew we would leave one day, and she never wanted to be completely separated from Ginny. Marga wanted this baby to be a tie that would bind her to Ginny for life.

This was a major development I had not counted on. I knew I couldn't just sit down with Ginny and unemotionally discuss what we should do. She is the consummate mother. Four children of our own seemed like too few once they started to grow up. Living in the jungle, surrounded by mothers constantly nursing their contented, olive-skinned babies, Ginny felt her mothering instincts quickly resurface. If Ginny was excited to have a baby in the house, Stephenie was ecstatic.

Word about our new baby got around Nemompade quickly. The people were obviously curious to know what we would do. If we said no, they would know that there was a limit to how much we wanted to be a part of them. If we said yes, we would have a child to rear. We would have to figure out a way to bring her up so she would feel at home in the United States and in Latin

Ecuador, as well as part of the Waodani tribe. We would have three languages to teach her.

Besides all that, we would probably have a daughter just slightly older than our grandchildren. Mincaye would have liked that. He has a number of grandchildren older than his last three children.

The biggest factor was that Ginny and I had actually talked about having more children. But we had decided that if God wanted us to have more children, He would have to make it happen. I had forgotten that conversation, but Ginny told me she had made it her prayer, even here in the jungle. If this precious little girl had come in answer to Ginny's prayer, I certainly did not want to stand in the way.

Right from the start, Stephenie was excited about raising Marga and Tidi's baby. Ginny tried to act neutral, but her performance was totally unconvincing. Worse yet, I began to desperately want this "peace child," a precious daughter to tie us to the Waodani forever. We finally agreed that if we could get through the necessary red tape, we would raise this beautiful little girl.

Marga and Tidi understood that we would not be able to stay in the jungle forever. In order to get our new baby into the States, we would need a U.S. visa, which would first require written permission from the tribunal in Puyo.

I told Marga and Tidi that we needed to take the baby to Puyo to register her and take the matter before the tribunal. As far as they were concerned, she was our child. If we could get the necessary papers, we were ready to accept that responsibility. I knew there would be a lot of paperwork and that no one in Puyo would understand what we were attempting to do. Although sharing children is appropriate and traditional in Waodani culture, it is not commonplace outside the jungle.

We went to register the baby right away. When the registrar asked the baby's name, Marga and Tidi just stood silent. The registrar again asked Marga for the baby's name, and she told him to ask me, that I was the father. I didn't explain, though I thought later that maybe I should have tried.

Ginny and Steph had decided to call her Ana Beth, for Ana and Elizabeth, our mothers' middle names. So our cuddly bundle of soft, contented joy was registered as Ana Beth Nenkimo. It was time to visit the tribunal.

Only two of the three members of the tribunal were in town. One agreed to meet with us. When he found out what we wanted, he asked Marga why she would want to give away her child. She did not understand. She wasn't giving her baby away, she said. She was giving the baby to us. She explained that we were family. She had seven children and could have plenty more. But Ongingcamo had no babies. She asked him if he knew how sad it is for a mother not to have a baby.

I explained to the tribunal member our relationship to the Waodani and to Marga and Tidi. He remembered the story of my father and had just seen a television special about us living with the people who had killed part of our family.

But then the tribunal told us that it would be impossible for them to allow a baby with a healthy mother and father to leave the country. He explained that there had been several cases of Ecuadorean babies being sold into adoption. For every such case there were many more rumors. Ecuador was extremely sensitive to the accusation that it could not take care of its own children.

I tried to translate what he said for Tidi and Marga. Marga, who understands a bit of Spanish, already understood, and she wept softly. She did not take little Ana Beth from me, however. She would be the baby's wet nurse, but as far as she was concerned, Ana Beth was our baby.

In the months that followed, Ginny and Stephenie fell in love with our little girl. And so did I. The Waodani still consider us to be Ana Beth's parents. Whenever I go down to visit now, even without Ginny, Ana Beth stays with me. She is shy with all other visitors, but it is clear that she considers me her cofather and Ginny her second mother.

The Nemompade community understood that without papers you can't do anything in the "outsiders' place." They knew we would have taken Ana Beth and raised her as our own if the *autoridades* had seen it well. Thankfully, Ana Beth still ties us to them in a special way.

17

The Fateful Day

One of our children's favorite books when they were young was *Alexander and the Terrible, Horrible, No Good, Very Bad Day*. We had had our share of those days in Nemompade, for sure. But there were other days when hope for the future of these people seemed to buoy me up. In the erratic world of the Waodani, some days started out one way and ended another.

One such day served as the turning point for our lives with the Waodani in Nemompade. The elders had gathered in Nemompade. Tañi and Dyuwi had walked from Tiwaeno to Toñampade and then came downriver with Amoa and Paa. Omene walked over from Tzapino. Kenta had the longest trip. He and his wife, Ana, canoed one day and walked one and a half. They had just moved from Tiwaeno to the southern boundary of Waodani territory to keep an eye on the oil companies that were beginning to penetrate the region from that direction. Kimo poled Dawa up from where they were now permanently living at the confluence of the Tzapino and Ewenguno Rivers. Mincaye and Tementa were, of course, already in Nemompade.

I had encouraged the elders to get together every other month. The free-spirited Waodani culture makes it difficult to get nine specific people together in any one place at a given time. The fact that many of the old people do not think in terms of numbered days and months adds to the complexity of having get-togethers like this. So does the fact that the call has to go by trail rather than telephone or e-mail. Meeting together would not be easy, but I knew it would be necessary in order to care for the needs of the ever-growing number of Waodani communities.

Getting together was difficult, but it was not unprecedented. In the old days, the *ne anga* in the tribe was responsible for getting the people together for parties. This was the mechanism by which the tribe members renewed their relationships with one another. In fact, it was a lazy *ne anga* who had first caused all the killing to start, as Mincaye had told me, counting back on his fingers ten generations to when that man had lived.

He said this "grand marshal" of the jungle was supposed to call the people together for fiestas, where new couples could be married and families could dance together and renew their relationships. When this *ne anga* did not call the people together for a long time, many of them assumed that the fiestas were still being held but they were not being invited. This led to suspicions that others in the tribe had it in for them.

In their isolation, they stewed over being left out, trying to figure out who their enemies were—who had taken them off the "list." Instead of waiting for those people to come and do them harm, Mincaye told me, "Being afraid, they became angry and speared their enemies first."

The Waodani term for the biblical concept of church elders came from this sole Waodani office. The *ne anani* (plural for *ne anga*) now came together to discuss how they could go to the People rather than getting the People to come to them. Since the cessation of vendetta killings, the tribe had grown rapidly. The only time the entire tribe gathered in one place now was when money from the outside was available to buy rice and sugar and other food. The Waodani are like North Americans in this, at least: Without a lot of food, they cannot have a good party.

The *ne anani* had gathered together, nine warriors all sitting in our house in deep discussion. I sat apart from them so they would know I was interested in what they were doing but that I was intentionally not part of the decision-making process.

In a culture such as ours in North America, in which people like to be elected to leadership positions and actually campaign to be chosen, it is difficult to understand the Waodani aversion to standing out. The Waodani take offense at someone who draws attention to himself or herself. That, in fact, was a good way to get speared. The *ne anani* had not run for this office. They had chosen themselves, not to be "big men," but to take on the responsibility of caring for others—an unusual, sacrificial, and gutsy move.

The discussion went on and on. Finally, they left for a while to drink manioc and plantain at Tementa's house. When they had gone, Ginny came into the room and said she had something to tell me. I could see it was a big deal and recognized the telltale signs of building pressure on her face. I reviewed my recent activities to figure out what I might have done to upset her. I couldn't come up with anything.

"Ginny," I said, "there is obviously something on your mind; why don't you tell me what it is before you explode?" I was trying to ease her tension, but it did not work. Ginny started to cry.

"Steve, we have to leave before we become part of the problem instead of part of the solution," she said through her tears. I wondered if Ginny had missed the fact that the *ne anani* had just spent half the morning in discussion about how to help their people—and I said as much to her.

Ginny answered carefully, but determinedly, "I saw what happened. The *ne anani* were sitting there all tense, trying to come up with a solution to whatever problem they were discussing. Poor guys, most of them were actually perspiring from the effort. I couldn't tell, of course, what they were really saying, but I could tell that at one point they had come up with a solution. Then they looked over at you. Remember when Odae walked by with chicken feathers in his mouth?"

Yes, I remembered seeing our silly pet pig with feathers in his mouth. He loved to chase the few chickens that the tree boas had not eaten at night. The Waodani had warned me that he would soon start killing and eating the chickens instead of just chasing them and pulling their feathers out. But I could not imagine what that had to do with the *ne anani* and Ginny's concerns.

"When you saw Odae with the feathers in his mouth, the *ne anani* were watching you. They were obviously hoping that you approved of their decision, whatever it was. You were looking at Odae, and you scowled. They couldn't see the pig and must have thought your disapproval had something to do with the conclusion they had just come to. When they saw your disapproval, they clearly went back to their discussion. I'm sure they thought you disapproved of their decision, so they are now trying to come up with a different decision that you will like."

Ginny was right. I was so pleased with myself for not dominating the Waodani the way everyone else seemed to that I had become blind to what was really happening. The Waodani would make decisions they thought I would approve of. Then they would watch carefully to see what my reaction was. If I did not like it, they would come up with other solutions until they found one I did like.

They weren't really taking authority for their own affairs; they were trying to copy me. The foundation of democracy is that the guy who has to live with the consequences should get to make the choices whenever possible. Authority should be delegated to the government only when it is impractical for the individual to make decisions and enforce them.

Ginny had thought there was nothing she could do for the Waodani and was sure she could not take care of me the way she wanted to in the jungle. She was so wrong. It was obvious, though mystifying, that she deeply loved me. It was also clear that she had opened up a new section of her heart for the Waodani. But she could not engage in much of what was going on because she did not understand the Waodani way of doing things and she could barely understand their language. Fortunately, this left her just far enough removed from the details to see the big picture.

I realized that I had not seen the jungle for the trees. The only way the *ne anani* would really test their ability to make decisions was for me to get far enough away that they could not access me. I had to be distanced enough that I could not bail them out immediately if they made what seemed like a bad decision to me.

We had to leave. Ginny was right. It had been only a year and a half since Aunt Rachel had died and the Waodani had told me to come back. By the time we left, we would have been living with the Waodani for about fifteen months. That isn't long, but it came on the tail end of thirty-eight years of Waodani contact with and growing dependence on the outside world. I did not want to leave too soon, but I was pretty sure that staying too long was even more dangerous.

As soon as Ginny told me what she had observed, I felt as if a huge weight settled on me. I thought I would be relieved when the time came to leave. The Waodani world was like living in a soap opera on fast-forward. Chaos reigned. How could it not when everyone did whatever he or she pleased, when the only authority was the pressure of subtle community disapproval?

I realized that in my being here, it was as if I had been holding the pilot light button on the Waodani furnace. If I let go of the button too soon, the pilot light would not stay lit. But as long as I was holding the button down, the furnace couldn't come on and do its thing. As in many areas of life, here, too, timing was everything.

I went through the curtain into our bedroom and sat on the floor. That was as close as I could get to being alone. I was worried for the Waodani, but I was even more worried for myself. I wasn't simply worried about what they would do without me. I was more concerned about what I would do without them. I was no longer a businessman, and I had little desire to go back to a life focused on making money. It had been achingly painful to break out of the role I had played for so many years in which my success was based on my level of busyness. But now I was no longer part of the world that measured my worth, not by what I contributed to the community, but by how well I looked out for number one.

So many years ago, I had left the life of mixed cultures I had grown up in to study in the United States. After Ginny and I were married, I had chosen to live in the United States and had painfully learned how to function in that complex, fast-paced world. But then I had wrenched myself away and returned to a world of the opposite extreme. Now I realized I didn't fully belong anywhere.

I experienced the most incredible sense of loneliness I can ever remember feeling. I had just been voted out. Not by the community, of course. They would have been happy to go on living as we had been in our inadvertent charade. No, I had to vote myself out. My deep love and respect for the nomads of the rain forest—people who had made me as much a part of their world as they could—compelled me to do it.

Sweet, sensitive Ginny came into the room and sat on the floor beside me. She hugged me and we cried together, hoping that the *ne anani* would not come back and catch us. I knew I needed to tell them that it was time for us to plan our leaving while they were all together.

By realizing that I had to kick myself out, I knew that I finally understood the Waodani dilemma in a personal way. I wanted the Waodani to be their own people and to never change. But to remain unchanged meant they would disappear. To change meant huge risk and possibly decades of painful experimentation and transition.

At the present, the old people were in a daze. They could not understand all the dangers that were waiting to devour life as they knew it. The young people were more like me. They didn't belong anywhere. They couldn't be part of the old ways and didn't want to be. But the outside world would not accept them. They were hanging between the Stone Age and the twentieth century. They grabbed for any opportunity that happened by, like a spider waiting in his web on a trail. Some things that came down the trail were simply too big for the spider to catch and hold. In the same way, whenever the Waodani young people tried to grab onto the "big things," they found their flimsy webs broken and their lives smashed in the process.

I finally felt the full helplessness and hopelessness that enveloped this strange and wonderful world, a world that seemed so simple when observed from the outside.

/\/\/\/\/\/\/\/\

That afternoon, we heard small monkeys in the trees near Nemompade. So rather than reconvening our meeting, we grabbed our various weapons and went "grocery shopping." With my glasses constantly fogging whenever I looked up, I had a hard time seeing the wily little creatures. But when I saw them, I was still the best shot in the community with a .22 rifle. I was the only one who had ever been able to afford target practice.

Amoncas don't have much meat on them, but they add flavor to the soup, and the hunt gave me a chance to temporarily forget the awful task of telling the elders of my decision. In all honesty, I realized I had known all along that this day was fast approaching. Ginny had simply pushed me to admit what I already knew to be the truth.

When Waodani visitors came to Nemompade, we had a little ritual we would go through. Someone would ask Stephenie or Jesse what we could do for the visitors. "Not seeing videos for a long, long time," they would begin, "how will they ever know how the foreigners live?" Steph and Jess would reply, "Do you see it well that we should show them a video?" To which they would gleefully reply, "Seeing it well and your father saying yes, we will happily watch it with them tonight."

On this particular night in late May 1996, before we watched *The Jungle Book* for the 150th time, I made my sad announcement to the *ne anani* and those closest friends and family who had left their homes and lives in other communities to start this little community of "Star Creek"—Nemompade.

There is seldom an easy way to do a hard thing. "Iñanani," I said. "My People, you telling me to come, I have come with my nanicabo to help you learn how to do foreigners' things, like you taught me how to do the ancient ones' things when I was young. Now, you having learned to do some of their things, I must go to the United States place again so you can do these things, if you see it well." When I finished speaking, the people just sat on our floor in silence, typical for the way Waodani show deep emotion. Marga and Ompodae made the first move to react to my shocking announcement. They both moved to Ginny and put their arms around her. Softhearted Ompodae began to cry.

Jesse was sitting in his usual spot in the hammock with Mincaye. He grabbed Mincaye's ear hole, a surefire way to start Mincaye cutting up under normal circumstances. Mincaye just sat there without noticing. Only when he saw that Jesse was crying did he react, comforting this big boy whom he obviously loved deeply.

In North America we sometimes observe a moment of silence, but we don't really know how to be quiet together. The Waodani do. That night we all sat there in silence for a long time. Then without saying anything, they just began to drift off into the night. No one even asked for a piece of candle to light the trail home.

Finally, Kimo broke the silence among those of us who remained. "Ongingcamo, goo-nite," he said, and then left. Those few words that had become a little tradition between Ginny and Kimo opened the emotional door. I heard a few chuckles, followed by more sniffles and soft weeping.

My heart was breaking, and I couldn't keep the tears back. There was no question about it: Leaving was going to be far more difficult than coming. We had felt we needed to come, but now we knew we *had* to leave. If we stayed, we would soon begin to undo all we had worked so hard to start.

Finally, with the house still about two-thirds full, someone asked, "Babae, your thing, who will be doing it now?" I had wondered if anyone would ask this question. I was afraid that everyone would just revert to a life of dependence on *cowodi* benefactors. We may not have made progress toward self-sufficiency in ways that the outside world would notice. But many of the Waodani had realized that it really was up to them to take responsibility for their own people and for their own futures. You can't fix forty-five years of problems in a year and a half, but every new course starts with a little turn. I thought many of the Waodani had started the turn to a new course. If they made it, my role would be insignificant. But if they didn't make it, I wouldn't have to wonder what I could have done and should have done to help them save their future.

I chose my words carefully. "Now you have to decide who will do the things you gave me to do, *Waengongi* showing you." There were some faintly audible intakes of breath. At least some of them understood and agreed.

Finally, everyone who wasn't sleeping on our floor left, and Ginny and I went to bed. Kenta and Ana put their blanket on our rough-hewn floor just on the other side of the boards that separated our room from the open living room.

My saddened mind was whirling, wondering what the future would bring. In the midst of my pondering, I heard Ana start to say something. Her head couldn't have been a foot from Ginny's and mine. Ginny poked me inquisitively because Ana was speaking very haltingly, one struggling syllable at a time.

Every once in a while she would pause, and Kenta would say something in reply. I leaned out of bed and looked through the crack between our curtain door and the door frame. Ana had a little candle in one hand and her big Wao-Tededo New Testament in the other hand.

Ana was sounding out each word with great determination. Then, after she had gone on this way for a while, Kenta would repeat back to her in normal conversation what she had been so brokenly reading to him. I realized this was how they read the Bible together each night. Ana read the sounds while Kenta added them together in his mind. Then he would repeat each thought back to Ana. She was struggling so hard to read that she could not make out the meaning from the individual words until Kenta gave it back to her.

The Waodani God followers were not a majority in the tribe. They numbered only about 20 percent. Every once in a while, when the *ne anani* got together, they would go community by community naming everyone who was following God's trail. Those who had made a public statement that they were following His trail rather than their own, who had been baptized, and who proved their conviction by the way they lived were considered God followers.

The number would have been much higher if they counted everyone who claimed to be a God follower without evaluating the evidence.

The God followers were not the only people in the tribe with whom we had relationships, but they were the only Waodani with motivation to help others at their own expense. It did not make sense to deny oneself for the benefit of others under normal circumstances. But those who wanted to follow *Waengongi*'s trail understood that the Book of His markings showed them the new way they should live.

The next morning, the entire community assembled at "God's house." We were informed to come.

No one was in charge, so nothing happened for quite a while. We all just sat there quietly, thinking. Finally someone asked, to no one in particular, "Well, how about if Tementa does what Babae has been doing?"

I thought Tementa was the obvious choice. But I knew that this was a big decision and needed to be made carefully. When a corporate decision has to be made, the Waodani feel tense. The only way to relieve the tension is to quickly arrive at a consensus. No one dares to oppose a direct recommendation, so no one can just come out and nominate someone. Instead, the question is always asked benignly: "How would you see it . . . ?" or "How about . . . ?" A gentle suggestion can then be countered without opposition by someone else asking the same questions about an alternative.

Usually, everyone just agrees on the first suggestion made, although that's probably because some polling is often done privately before the question is asked in the first place.

When they asked what I thought, I suggested that the God followers who made up most of the assembled group ask *Waengongi* about who should do this. They concurred, and the meeting broke up. We then headed from the church to the clearing by the river, where most of the houses were. When we got there, someone said almost authoritatively, "Now, I say, let's talk to *Waengongi*." We formed a circle, and the Waodani spontaneously began to hold hands. That wasn't like them, but then again, neither was it normal for someone to pronounce that we should pray.

One by one, each of the Waodani prayed that God would show them what to do. By the time everyone prayed, my hand was numb, but I really began to feel hope. This brave little group had accepted the news about my leaving with palpable sadness. But they had moved ahead to make a decision on their own. It wasn't natural for them to do this, but they were demonstrating that they knew how to do it. They asked God to show them what to do, and then they unanimously chose Tementa.

Once that decision was made, we began to pray for Tementa. We sat down on some logs for this prayer service. By the time the meeting was finally over, my hand was fine, but everything from where I was sitting on down was numb.

The people went on to appoint Omanka, Mincaye, and Ompodae's oldest daughter, to officially run the tiny pharmacy the community had built under our house. They said Tementa and Nemonta would run the combination store and trading post also located under the house. Marga, Omanka, and a couple of others would share responsibility for taking care of sick people who came to Nemompade for medical help. This group had been given some initial medical training and had also been part of numerous training courses that a doctor friend of ours from West Virginia had given us in Nemompade.

Ginny, Stephenie, Jesse, and I said we would concentrate on helping these few Waodani learn whatever skills they would need to tackle their new roles.

/\·/\·/\·/\·/\·/\

Before the end of this memorable day, we got a message by radio that Mincaye and Ompodae's one-year-old grandbaby was dying. I jumped in the plane with Mincaye and Ompodae and flew upriver to Toñampade. As soon as we landed, I was told that Mincaye's grandson, whom we affectionately called "Chubby," was dead. Mincaye, Ompodae, and I ran to the house where Mincaye and Ompodae's daughter, Sada, and her husband lived.

Chubby was lying in a little box all dressed up in a jumper. He had a blanket around him and looked as adorable as ever. I was relieved to see that he was asleep, not dead. The Waodani use their word for dead just as we do. We say things like, "He was dead asleep" or "You mess with me and you're dead." In Wao-Tededo, "dead" can mean anything from passed out to unconscious to actually dead.

Sada watched me as I entered their little house. I reached down to touch Chubby's fat little cheeks. He had been born with a heart defect that required specialized surgery to correct. His little lips were always bluish in color. But now as I looked down at him, he actually appeared to be better. When I touched his face, it was warm.

Sada continued to watch me closely. I'm sure she must have hoped I had an outsiders' trick to save her little boy. But as I looked at him closely, I could see that Chubby was no longer sleeping. He was dead. In the entire year of this little boy's life, I had never seen Sada without her baby. When she saw my reaction to finding Chubby dead, she must have known that it was too late. She began to sob in a grief that no one can know until losing a child of their own. At the time, I could not yet fully understand the depths of her pain.

How does one console a teenage mother who is looking at her baby lying lifeless in a crude wooden box? How does one dare to suggest that one day she will be able to think of things other than his sleeping by her side and nursing gently at her breast, or his soft little hand reaching up from the carrying cloth, where his weight would press him into her side all day long?

Ompodae was crying for her daughter and grandson. As I watched her grieve, I realized that when Ompodae was Sada's age, Waodani mothers sometimes took babies like sweet little Chubby and killed them, burying them to keep a dying family member company in the afterlife. It was not uncommon for fathers to bash their babies' heads in if they cried too much, since crying could attract enemies who might be searching for them. Or if a baby came too soon after another one, a father had sufficient reason to throw it into the river or leave it out in the jungle.

While Sada sobbed, Tidonae got Chubby ready for burial, expressing his grief in a different way. He placed a nice transistor radio in the box with the baby. Next he put in a pair of baby shoes and all the little toys he had saved for so carefully to buy for his little boy. He splashed cologne all over the box and then got out the talcum powder. He was determined to put the powder on Chubby, so I helped him unwrap the precious little body.

When Sada saw Chubby's tiny hands, she began to kiss him all over. Tidonae finally took him away from her, and we wrapped his little body again, placing him back in the little burying box. Tidonae put a padlock on the box. At first I was confused by the lock. But then I remembered that in

Toñampade everyone had to lock up his valuables. Chubby was Tidonae's most valuable possession, and he wanted to put a lock on the box.

Months earlier there had been an opportunity to help Chubby, but I had decided against it. Chubby's heart defect was treatable, and I had the money to pay for the surgery. I was considered part of Mincaye's family, so I could have helped them without technically being expected to pay for other expensive medical services. But I knew it would be wrong to do it.

The cost of Chubby's surgery would have covered the costs of treating hundreds of people with chronic malaria. It would have paid for medical exams for hundreds of others, with enough money left over to have provided each community with antivenin. With what it would cost to pay for Chubby's surgery, a number of other lives could have been saved. And there was no guarantee that Chubby would have survived the surgery. He would have needed the surgery at a very early age; if he had died then, I would not have been able to explain to Sada and Tidonae why my help had taken their little boy from them so much sooner than if I had left them alone.

The *real* reason I had not arranged surgery for Chubby, however, was that his mom and dad did not want to go through the painful uncertainty that surgery required. They did not want strangers to take control of their baby or their own lives. And that, it seemed to me, was their decision to make, not mine.

In our sophisticated world, Chubby might have been taken away from his parents because they didn't want him to have surgery. In this other, more advanced world of ours, the government thinks it knows what is best for all of us. And as a people, we tend to think we know what is best for everyone else in the world.

For example, I ran into a man at a major hospital just before we left for Ecuador. His arm was bandaged and in a sling. Just to be friendly, I asked him what he was in for. He told me he had been having problems with his little finger, which had been severed in an accident. He was rushed to the hospital, where he was taken to surgery and his finger was reattached. He told me he had spent five years in and out of hospitals. He was in constant pain and had not been able to go to work in all that time.

I wondered what more could be done for him. "So what are they going to do for you this time?" I asked.

"I'm going to have them amputate it," he said. "This little finger has ruined my life for five years. I'm going to lose the finger. I want my life back!" Now the insurance company was going to spend twenty thousand dollars more to get him right back to where a motorcycle accident had taken him five years—and about a million dollars in medical expenses—earlier.

I got the impression they had reattached his finger without his consent. This was just a small picture of how the outside world tended to make major decisions that would seriously affect the health, welfare, and future of the Waodani. I yearned to be able to help defend them. But I knew that what they needed most was an opportunity to help themselves.

/\/\/\/\/\/\/\/\

We knew we needed to pass on a number of skills to the People before we left. Tementa learning to run the store was a good example. We had been operating under the idea that all these tiny enterprises were to benefit the tribe, not for profit. On the other hand, each enterprise had to be profitable enough to pay its own way.

I had been buying the merchandise that the Waodani came to Nemompade looking for. We stocked necessities as well as a few luxuries. The first group of necessities included machetes, axes, files, and grindstones. Luxuries included soap, rubber boots, matches, string, nails, backpacks, and a few edible treats, such as sugar, salt, rice, lard, and cooking oil.

I had been trying to teach a couple of people how to bargain for better prices in Puyo, but most of them were too timid. Shop owners could ask whatever they desired, and if the Waodani buyer wanted the item, he would just hand over his money. The older people could not count and were especially vulnerable.

Some enterprising merchants flew into Waodani communities every once in a while. When we first arrived, it was not unusual for one of these merchants to exchange a four-dollar pair of boots for a beautiful hammock or full-size blowgun. A quality hammock takes up to a month of steady, if not full-time, work. But before we set up shop in Nemompade, these merchants were the only way many of the Waodani could get things from the outside world unless they sent their young people to trek to towns on the edge of the jungle to buy things for them.

But even there, they usually paid exorbitant prices and were often taken advantage of in much worse ways. A favorite trick for outsiders to play on unseasoned Waodani boys was to offer them something alcoholic to drink. They did not know that they could refuse the offer, so they usually drank. Sometimes their money was stolen once the liquor got to them. More frequently, the crowd that pressed them to drink left them to pay the tab.

When young men lost the money that had been entrusted to them by members of their community to buy merchandise, they hesitated to return home. They generally ended up sleeping anywhere they could find, and after a time, began to prey on the new arrivals themselves. Because it is very un-Waodanilike to be stingy, the new arrivals felt obliged to buy meals and colas and bread for those who were already in town.

Once one of Dayumae's sons-in-law was in a town on the edge of the jungle. He was simply walking down the street when he passed a bar where a fight had broken out. The fight spread onto the street just as he was passing. One of the belligerents mistook him for another combatant and slashed his throat with a broken bottle. He never returned home.

For girls, the fate was often much worse. They loved to go to town to see all the pretty things and to get away from the stigma of being "Aucas." What they didn't seem to know was that outside the jungle they couldn't just build a shelter to sleep in. Nor could they harvest food from the garden or gather it from the wild.

When the girls got hungry, they were an easy mark for *cowodi* boys, who often talked the girls into sleeping with them in exchange for a meal or a cheap dress. There was no great stigma among the Waodani for being sexually active before marriage—unless the girl got pregnant. Then life became much more complicated. By the time Aunt Rachel died, I was seeing mixed-breed babies in many communities. In Toñampade, where the teachers had access to Waodani girls, it was almost epidemic.

So the Nemompade store offered a lot more to surrounding Waodani villages than just being a convenience store with big discounts. It offered a safe alternative to the dangers of buying in the outside world.

I explained to Tementa that in town, if he bought an item in the market, he should ask for a lower price than what the merchants wanted. He knew the basic concept of bargaining. But Tementa, though extremely sharp, was also quiet and reserved.

"After you negotiate a very good price for just one, tell the merchant you want a lot and negotiate for a still better price," I explained. I could see that most of the Waodani thought I was being unreasonable. Tementa, however, concentrated on everything I told him and made notes about it in a little notebook.

Next I explained that he should record what he ended up paying for each item. That required dividing the cost of, say, a box of soap by the number of bars in the box. This gave us our cost per item. Then we would add a percentage of that cost to cover wastage and the expense of flying it out to Nemompade.

The idea of percentages proved to be a stumper. Tementa was perplexed by the concept. I showed him how to do it with some beans from Ginny's food shelf. If you have a hundred beans and you want to add 20 percent to cover the cost of the flight, you just count out twenty additional beans and add them to the hundred beans. That was easy for him. But when the base number was only fifty, I could not figure a way to explain that 20 percent of fifty was only ten, not twenty. "How could twenty percent be the same as twenty beans one time and only ten the next time?"

Numbers are a fairly easy concept for *cowodi*, whose lives are governed by them and who study them in school for years. But take a *cowodi* and ask him to make a rain shelter in the jungle. He doesn't know a strong stick from a weak one and has no idea how to distinguish a tying vine from one that will break with the slightest twist or tug.

The solution to percentages turned out to be a little solar-powered calculator I had. Tementa could do percentages easily on the calculator. He still did not understand the concept, but he quickly learned to put in the actual cost of a box of soap, divide the total cost by the number of bars in the box, and then multiply the resulting price for one bar by 1.20.

He did not have to learn the concept behind percentages if he was not going to build on that concept. He wasn't going to become a math teacher. He just needed to figure out how to price merchandise.

One thing Tementa understood instinctively, which seems to elude a majority of North Americans, is that if you spend more money than you make for long enough, you end up with problems of the financial, marital, and sometimes even the medical sort.

As Ginny, Jesse, Stephenie, and I concentrated on teaching Tementa and others the outsiders' skills they would need to take charge, I began to ask how other tribes in the jungle were solving these same problems. The almost universal answer was, "They aren't." They relied on outsiders to teach them, heal them, transport them, provide them with communications, and sell to them.

I began to see that the need the Waodani had was not unique to them. Dependence was a major affliction for people groups all over the world in frontier areas. I wondered who would help all those other people groups. If someone believed he or she was capable of mastering the skills required to meet their own changing needs, maybe the quagmire of dependence could be avoided. It is not easy to avoid dependence, but it is far easier to avoid it than to heal it once it has become systemic.

I knew that education is not the solution to all the world's problems. I could see that when we were building the Nemompade airstrip. We started out with a number of young boys in camp. A couple of them worked right along with the grown men. They could work hard, but they would only work a few hours and then, after a couple of days, they left. Others just stood around arrogantly, disdainful of even getting dirty. The only thing they did enthusiastically was eat.

I realized that the amount of work these young people put out was inversely proportional to the number of years they had spent in school. Their education was drastically out of line with the world they were part of. I tried to explain the concept of percentages to a couple of bright young fellows who had been in school for years. They did not know what I was talking about. In the process of getting a theoretical education, they had given up much of their ability to garden, hunt, and gather. Some of them knew how to do these things but were unwilling to do them. It now seemed beneath them.

It would have been one thing if the blame for their predicament was all theirs. But it wasn't. Much of the blame belonged to outsiders who think everyone has to be like us to do the things we do. Why not change the way things are done to fit the culture and natural abilities of those needing to learn?

When I was in Mali, West Africa, my loyal friend and office assistant, big "teddy bear" Abou, showed me how far indigenous frontier people think outsiders will go to change them to fit an established way of doing things.

Abou was a giant in Mali. His feet were so big he could not buy any shoes that fit. I asked friends to send him a pair from the States. It was a big day when they came.

At size thirteen and a half, the shoes looked like boats. Abou was thrilled. He tried them on and said with a huge smile, "Dees ao goooot boss, I'm shua!" But they didn't look good. I could see that Abou's toes were all curled up. Everyone in the office realized they were too small. I was disappointed for him, so to lighten the disappointment I asked him to take them off so I could make them fit better.

Abou got a huge grin on his face. He was obviously confident that I had some mysterious secret to stretch shoes. I took my pocket knife out of my pocket as he took off his new shoes. But when he handed me the shoes, I went for his feet with my knife.

All the expatriates laughed at my stupid little joke. It helped cover the disappointment that had some of them on the verge of tears. But not Abou, nor the other Malians who were with us. I realized from the looks on their faces that they actually thought I might cut Abou's toes to fit his new shoes.

That would have made more sense than some of the changes we force on people and their cultures before we pass on to them the skills they desperately need to live as partners in our increasingly complex world.

18

End of the Beginning

Jesse and Stephenie needed to be back in the States to start school in August. That became our target date for leaving. It felt as if there was a somber cloud hanging over us as we worked toward that date. I always look forward to new challenges, but this was different. The only challenge I could find in leaving was to do whatever I could to get us all ready for it.

Ginny seemed to feel the same fundamental sadness that was wrapping its dark tentacles around my heart. Fortunately, Shaun decided to come back to spend the second summer with us. That gave us all something to look forward to, especially since Jesse had decided to go back to the United States ahead of us to get a job for part of the summer.

I hated to see Jesse go. He was completely at ease with the Waodani, and they felt the same with him. Although he was much bigger than they are, the Waodani realized that he was cutting his hair like them and beginning to act more and more like them. This seemed to greatly endear him to them. That, plus the fact that he was always making them laugh. He and Mincaye provided constant entertainment.

One night while we were watching an old video everyone had seen before, Mincaye fell asleep in one of our hammocks. Jesse snuck up behind him and tied a string to the big hole in of his earlobes. The usual crowd in our house completely ignored the video to see what Jess was going to do this time.

Jesse ran the string from the first ear, around the hammock, and then through the big hole in Mincaye's other ear. When he was finished, he shook Mincaye in mock excitement and exclaimed in a loud whisper that everyone in the house could hear, "Mincaye, night monkeys! Let's hunt them and eat them!"

Jesse grabbed his gun and ran for the door with Mincaye right on his heels. When the string around the hammock began to pull on his ears, Mincaye already had too much momentum to stop. He was still, no doubt, half asleep. As the string pulled tighter, Mincaye realized what was happening and fell backward to keep from pulling his earlobes off. Fortunately, the string swung the hammock toward him and he landed dramatically back into it, swinging wildly and yelling as if his ears really had been pulled off.

Everyone roared with laughter and immediately started developing their personal renditions of what had happened. Early the next morning, this new adventure story of Jesse and Mincaye would go out via radio to most Waodani villages. Within a few days, people started arriving just to hear the Nemompade crowd tell their various versions of Jesse almost pulling off Mincaye's ears.

I suspect that Mincaye knew what was happening all along. In fact, I wouldn't doubt that he and Jesse had planned the whole thing.

I was going to miss Jesse, but I knew it might take him a while to adjust back to our old world. Better to start the transition during the summer while working than in school surrounded by almost two thousand other students. Jesse and Stephenie's classmates would have no clue that they had just returned from a place almost as strange to their world as Mars is to Earth.

I knew from experience how excruciatingly lonely it can be to be surrounded by people who don't even have the ability to understand the major life experience you have just been through. I'm sure that is why many of my friends and peers were never able to integrate back into their previous worlds after they returned from the Vietnam War.

Right after Chubby's funeral, I flew back to Nemompade to get Jesse. He had asked me to take him to Terminal City for a visit before he had to leave. Jesse rarely flew with me, because he always had a lot to do in Nemompade. I often relied on him to watch over things while I was gone; I had complete confidence that he could handle almost anything that might happen. And the Waodani had become extremely loyal to Jess. Anyone who messed with Jesse or his family was going to have to answer to a small army.

But Jesse really wanted to see Terminal City, so I flew the few miles over to Damointado. As we flew up and down the narrow gorge a couple of times, I pointed out to Jesse where Gikita and Mincaye's clearing had been, as well as Nenkiwi's and Dabo's. Then I simulated Grandpa Nate doing the bucket drop, making tight circles between the huge ridges that wedged the two little rivers below into their narrow confines. Dad had wanted so badly to be friends with those people below. And here Jesse and I were, the next two generations, doing the same thing. But this time, the people we saw waving up at us were our friends.

Sadly, I realized that out of the more than two thousand flights I had made during our time with the Waodani, this was probably the only flight I made just for Jesse. After just a short while in Nemompade, I had realized that my family was just as critical to our work there as I was. If it hadn't been for that, and the fact that they gave themselves to this trying adventure so readily, I think I would have been guilty of neglect. I spent so much of my time, effort, and emotion on the Waodani and their children that there was little left for my own wife and kids.

I felt sad as Jesse and I flew back toward Nemompade. I realized that this might be the last time I made this flight.

Just for fun, I glided past the end of the airstrip and into the river channel, I gave BTS full throttle as we roared around the bend of the river and down the straightaway toward the house Jesse had worked so hard to help build. Just before flying into the bank by our house, I pulled up in a steep climb, wagging the wings in a salute to the people who had come running to see what was going on. The look on Jesse's face told me that the People below us had taken root in his heart just as they had in mine.

$$\diagup\!\!\diagdown\!\!\diagup\!\!\diagdown\!\!\diagup\!\!\diagdown\!\!\diagup\!\!\diagdown\!\!\diagup\!\!\diagdown$$

The next day was God's day. This was going to be a special one. Shaun, Jesse, and Stephenie had asked to be baptized before we left Nemompade. The three men who had baptized Dad into death and then baptized me as a symbol of Life more than thirty years ago were in Nemompade for the elders' meeting. I asked them to help me baptize my children like they had once done for me. They all said they saw it very well to do so. A group of Waodani young people found out what we were going to do and asked to be taken *aepaenigii* too.

The Nemompade group gathered in their *Waengongi onco* around eight o'clock and sent word for us to come. Tementa or Mincaye were usually the ones to call the people together to "talk to *Waengongi* and to learn about Him." Tementa was the primary teacher, usually reading a portion of God's markings and applying it to some practical challenge we all faced in our daily lives.

The service lasted nearly five hours. The only break came when Odae, our pig, got loose from the vine someone had tied him with and came to join us. All our hunting dogs, a few monkeys, and various tame birds were already in the building. When Odae showed up, a fearless dachshund named Dobson chased him through the longhouse. A minute later, they came tearing back with Odae chasing Dobson. The dogs all started to bark and then began to chase the pig, Dobson, and each other.

The people jumped up on the benches and started scolding the animals. Wini had been taking his turn at preaching when the melee broke out. He just kept talking. I figured that most of what he was saying was probably still getting through. The Waodani are used to carrying on multiple conversations in the middle of chaos.

But the excitement was too much for Macho, our pet woolly monkey, way up in the longhouse pole structure. As he always did when he was nervous, he began to urinate. We quickly moved to avoid the shower from above, as well as mud and fleas from the dogs and pig below. By this time, Odae had also become excited and was ejecting nasty, smelly musk from the gland on his back. The men were all laughing, but the women were not. They grabbed vines and started swinging wildly at the animals. I think a few swings were intended for the men as well.

Wini just kept on preaching.

When things finally calmed down, the women passed around plantain drink and wild pig soup with boiled manioc. Tementa stood to address the crowd, which by now included folks from other villages. He began by talking about the villages where there were no God followers to teach the people how to walk His trail. These villages—such as Dicado, Cacatado, and Bameno—were far downriver and would take days or even weeks to reach by trail. These and other villages had asked the God followers to come teach them, but no one had gone yet.

Then Dyuwi's son, Tañi—who had lost an eye playing the Waodani version of cowboys and Indians, with blowguns and real darts—and Tementa began to teach about the importance of baptism for those who are following God's trail. After a little over an hour of instruction, Tementa said we were ready to take the ten young people *aepaenigii*. I had, of course, already talked to my three children.

We got into canoes and made our way across the river to a large beach just upstream. I had asked Mincaye, Dyuwi, and Kimo if they would help me baptize my three children. Jaime wrote from the United States that he wished he could participate as well. I also asked if each one of them would pray for Shaun, Jesse, and Stephenie. I think what they understood was that they should instruct them, rather than pray for them.

"*Itota* happily died for us, so we should die for Him now," Mincaye said to Jesse. "You go on God's trail. Don't go over here or there; just keep always, always following God's trail!"

Kimo spoke quietly to Stephenie for just a minute or so, gently but also intently. He leaned toward her dramatically, watching her face closely. Then he turned to me and said, "She understands; it is enough." Together Kimo and I lowered Steph into the water, as Mincaye and I had done with Jess, in symbolic death to self. I was glad it was only symbolic. Steph was so intense in her zest for life that I couldn't imagine life without her. I was incredibly pleased with how she had learned the Waodani's language and many of their customs. She was practically a blonde Waodani. Besides learning from the Waodani, she had truly opened her young heart to them. She understood the helpless, hopeless plight of the tribe's teens. Whenever I got terribly discouraged, she was the one who reminded me that we had not come for results. We had come for love and to be obedient to what we were convinced God wanted us to do. She was a lot wiser and more mature than sixteen years of age could account for.

Gentle Dyuwi chose Shaun Toñae. Dyuwi is a marathon pray-er. He likes to pray about everything. I sometimes wished that Dyuwi's prayers were shorter, but I always felt special when he prayed for my family. This occasion was extraspecial.

Oncaye, who had been baptized with Kathy and Iniwa and me, was with us on this significant day.

We all wished Jaime could have been with us, but he was planning to be married and felt he should stay in the States and work for the summer. Jesse did get us in touch with him via ham radio just before we went to the baptismal service. Hearing his voice made us miss him even more during this memorable ceremony.

With so many Waodani visitors in Nemompade for the elders' conference and with friends visiting from Shell, we were quite a crowd. The Waodani and the father of a family visiting from Shell had gone pig hunting. I was jealous when this friend had shot a pig just a short way from Nemompade. I had tramped through the jungle around Nemompade and had not gotten a single pig the entire time I was there. But I was glad we had plenty of meat to make the gathering a real party.

That evening we showed the *JESUS* film, a dramatic film of the life of Christ. More than one hundred people gathered in our house to watch our little thirteen-inch, twelve-volt TV/VCR. The movie was in English, but no one seemed to mind. Those who knew the story, which was taken from the Gospel of Luke, gave a running narration for those who did not.

/\/\/\/\/\/\/\/\

I had cut down as much as possible on my flying the last couple of months before we were to leave. But there was still rarely a day when I didn't make one or two flights, and sometimes there were days when practically all I did was fly. I loved it.

Almost every takeoff was at full weight. "Full" was different for every strip and every condition. I had to vary my load for wind, water on the runway, and long grass. I had made over two thousand flights in and out of these precarious Waodani airstrips while we were living there. I had kept meticulous records about each strip so I knew just how much weight I could carry under each set of circumstances.

I kept the weight light enough to clear the trees on takeoff but heavy enough not to waste any potential from this incredibly useful tool the Waodani still called the *ebo*, or wood bee.

One night we got a call to go to Tzapino to check on a woman who had been in labor all day without success. They said she was bleeding a little. This was her third or fourth child, so Omanka and Marga told me the baby should have come easily. I never could figure out why they always wanted me to handle the problem births. But they told me to go *baneki*, or "as soon as there is light." So I did.

When I started my takeoff roll, the usual nightly mist was just rising from the jungle floor. I needed to get to Tzapino before it covered the trees and the airstrip. I had enough fuel to fly around until the mist burned off, but the Tzapino people wanted me there as soon as possible, so I wanted to beat the mist.

When I gave BTS full power, the low pressure just outside the prop blade tips caused the air to cool and the water vapor to condense. It formed a perfect tunnel of clouds that enveloped the plane until I reduced power after clearing the trees. It was like flying through a round passageway of fluffy clouds, with the front of the tunnel always just in front of me.

I turned toward Tzapino and saw one of the most incredible sights I have ever seen. Below me the jungle was covered in a mantle of soft clouds just delicate enough to appear to be tearing on the tops of the tallest trees as it gently moved over them. Off to the northwest were six majestic snowcapped mountains rising into the dark blue early morning sky. They looked near enough to reach out and touch. Usually the rising mist obscured these beautiful mountains that I had climbed in high school. This morning I was in the air just ahead of the mist. I was actually glad I did not have a camera with me. Some exceptional sights are best remembered in the mind. I can still see those mountains clearly in my memory.

There wasn't time to gawk, however. Tzapino is only about a three-minute flight from Nemompade, and the airstrip is unusually short. I never got higher than the ridge on this short flight. I just flew through a convenient V in the top of the ridges, and I was lined up for landing. The warmth of the river that crossed right in front of the tiny airstrip seemed to be keeping the air above it clear.

Crossing the river, I skimmed the marsh reeds between the river and firm ground. I touched down in the first fifty feet, just before the airstrip climbed a short but steep hill. There was no go-around on this strip, so the hill helped stop the plane. I really liked that hill.

The Waodani woman I had come to see was so weak that she was still lying in the bottom of the dugout, which her husband had used to pole her to the airstrip, when I landed. I asked a lot of questions and gave her a brief exam before reaching the conclusion that she was not in effective labor. But I'm no midwife, and I didn't want to take a chance. I called Dr. Patton, my personal medical trainer at the hospital in Shell. When I told him what I had found, he agreed that she was probably not in real labor even though she had had several babies and thought that she was. He suggested I fly her to the hospital. When we got there, he confirmed my diagnosis and asked me if I wanted to do the honors. I usually got my instructions by radio when I didn't know what to do. Here I had a trained nurse to help, a sterile chair and instruments, and an instructor giving tips.

The mother's amniotic sac felt as if it had been made by Goodyear. Once it was ruptured, however, labor progressed just as the mother had expected. She pushed once and I made the catch, suctioned the little fellow's nose and mouth, and handed him to the nurse so I could tie and cut the umbilical cord. It took about five minutes for the placenta to deliver, and I was off to do a few errands before picking up the mother and her new son to fly them home. North American mothers would have expected a little more time to rest. Jungle mothers would probably like more rest too, but out there I have seen mothers heading out to work in their gardens within an hour of delivering a baby.

One mother who was helping her husband pole their canoe up to Nemompade couldn't make it. Her husband stopped on a sandbar for her delivery. Five minutes later they were back in the canoe, and a half hour later they arrived at Nemompade. The mother was poling sitting down. I don't know if that was because it hurt to stand up or if it was because she had to hold her new baby while she helped pole.

Four days later, I had another exciting flight that also ended up at the Shell hospital. I had flown to pick up Ompodae, who had been visiting her daughter and Odoki in Huamono. The airstrip there is wide and unusually flat. But it is short and ends against a steep hill. I tried to talk the Huamono Waodani into extending the strip up that hill to a level spot about a hundred feet up. The runway was fine as it was for landing, but it was so soft that it was hard to get the plane to even start rolling on takeoff. I could take a full load into Huamono, but I could not take off with much.

After delivering some things and loading Ompodae and her gifts of plantains and smoked meat—which I planned to make a serious dent in during our flight back to Nemompade—I prepared for takeoff.

I glanced to the right and then to the left to make sure everyone was clear. One of old Bai's sons, Gaba, was standing on the side of the strip. When I called out, "Libre," he looked right at the plane's engine area and called back, "Libre." I was clear to start the engine. I did.

The prop started to swing toward the first compression stroke, where I expected it to fire as it usually did. Instead, I heard a solid clunk. I sat there for a second and looked out at the people by the side of the strip. They all just stood there—no gestures or anything.

Then it hit me that the prop had struck something where nothing should have been. I jumped out and started toward the nose of the plane. There on the ground under the prop was a teenage girl with blood pouring out of her head. I reached her and fell on my knees. My first thought was that I had killed her. I pulled her scalp apart where the fountain of blood was exiting her head. The prop had cut through her scalp and the tough lining between the scalp and skull. I was relieved to see that her skull was still intact. I had almost expected to see her brains.

She woke up and tried to run away. Blood was running down her face and into the neck of her dress. She appeared to be dazed, but she knew who she was and who I was. I asked her how she had gotten under the prop. That piece of information, she could not remember. I checked to make sure her pupils were dilating properly.

Someone who saw what had happened told me that the girl had been standing behind the right door looking at Ompodae's smoked meat. When I looked over to the right, she had ducked her head to run under the strut, trying to get to the other side of the airstrip. When Gaba called "Libre," she was just going under the strut, and he didn't see her.

People in jungle villages might feel awkward around cars, but they are familiar with airplanes. She knew better than to run under the prop. If that first cylinder had fired, I'm sure it would have cut her head in two. Fortunately, this time all we had to worry about was keeping her from bleeding to death and getting her to the hospital to make sure she did not have a severe concussion.

I flushed the wound with water I carried in the plane. It wasn't sterile, but it was cleaner than my prop, so I used it. Then I bandaged her up with supplies I always kept in the plane for situations such as this. We had to leave Ompodae and her plantains behind, but the smoked meat was still in front with me. I tried to get the young woman to talk to me so I could verify that she was okay and to keep her awake. I had put her in the backseat to keep my center of gravity back, allowing a shorter takeoff run. I could not see how she was doing behind me. Finally, I reached around and squeezed her leg just above the knee.

That got her attention. She reflexively grabbed my hand and held on so I wouldn't squeeze her leg again. We finally worked out a solution. Since I wanted to keep her awake and she didn't want me to squeeze her leg again, I would hold up some fingers on my hand and she would grab my hand and squeeze that number of times. If I held up fingers and she didn't squeeze, she knew I would squeeze her leg again. I really wanted to eat some of Ompodae's meat, but I would have had to share with my patient, and I did not think chewing jungle jerky would have been advisable in her current condition.

Back at the hospital once again, I got an advanced lesson in suturing. I was greatly relieved when the professional medical staff at the mission hospital verified that she would be okay.

I have done a lot of flying in a number of different countries and in a variety of conditions. In the United States, most flying consists of following rules and pushing buttons. In the jungle, however, the plane was my car. I usually flew with the window open and my elbow sticking out. It could get really hot under that big Plexiglas windshield, so I usually didn't latch the doors until just before takeoff. That gave me some needed ventilation.

It wasn't a big deal because at takeoff speed, no one could have opened the door even if they had tried. But it made my fairer-skinned passengers nervous, so I usually pulled the doors shut before takeoff for their peace of mind.

Landings usually made outside visitors nervous too. My standard landing procedure at Nemompade was to lose altitude as I neared our clearing. I would drop down below the ridges on either side of our little valley. Then I would turn toward a giant dead tree about halfway up the ridge on my right. I would fly toward that tree until I was about fifty feet above the trees and a football field distance from the dead tree on the steep ridge directly in front of me.

At that point I made a steep left turn and lowered the nose. To the uninitiated, it looked as if we were going to fly right into the ridge. And when I made that last left turn, it looked as if I was going to dive into the trees below. What I could not see until I made that last turn was the narrow channel that cut through the trees right in front of us. The trees were so tall, and the airstrip swath so narrow, that from the side you could not tell that there was anything ahead but more rugged jungle.

I always made the same mistake when I flew with visitors. I assumed that when my passengers finally saw our airstrip, they would relax. That wasn't usually the case. When they saw the narrow chasm between those huge trees with two little muddy tracks down the middle, they were frequently more scared than ever.

Bush pilots have a reputation for doing things by the seat of their pants, but that isn't usually the case. Bush pilots who survive have very definite boundaries that they never cross. When they fly in rough conditions on a daily basis, they learn to differentiate between those things that are critical and those that are simply cosmetic. To the casual observer, some of my flying techniques probably seemed high risk, such as brushing the landing gear in the bushes on landing at Quiwado. But the bushes on the approach end were not the danger. Going off the other end of the short trip into the swamp and stumps was.

Every time I took off from one of those short strips, I was taking a significant risk. It was a calculated but justified risk. People have to do that every day, all over the world. The flyboys in the early days of World War II had a life expectancy of just a few hours in the air. For a while, bomber crews could expect an average of two missions before they were killed; they went anyway.

When we were in the jungle, I often had to do things that aren't written in any standard operating procedures book. One afternoon when I landed and unloaded at Nemompade, Ginny was waiting for me at the strip. She frequently did that so we could walk the trail back to the house together. There was so little privacy at the house that we were more alone on the trail than in our bedroom. We got caught kissing several times, but the Waodani just giggled.

Ginny watched me unload my passengers. She finally asked, "How many people did you have with you, anyway?" I had to think. There was a man in the copilot's seat with his little boy on his lap. I had two mothers in the back with children on their laps, and a ten- or eleven-year-old boy under a lap belt between the two women. Eight people in a four-seat plane. That wasn't usual, but it wasn't really unusual, either.

I was meticulous, however, about my fuel handling. We stored the fuel in drums under a thatched hut next to our thatched hangar. I showed Tementa how to suction the fuel from the barrel into a clean five-gallon container, from which we poured it into a funnel and through a chamois skin that would separate any water that might have condensed inside the barrel and dripped into the airplane fuel.

I was making an average of one takeoff and one landing every eight minutes of flying time. That is really hard on a plane. If I wasn't careful, things could start to break, and I had no margin for error where I was operating. Only one time in twenty-three hundred flights did BTS's engine skip a beat. It was just that: one instant when a couple of cylinders didn't seem to fire. My heart instantly jumped, my adrenaline surged, and my mouth went dry. It was probably just a drop of water in the fuel. But where there was one drop there could be a few more—or a cupful. On takeoff, that could be fatal.

Once Tementa started fueling the plane, I felt as comfortable putting my life in his hands as in my own. He didn't have as much experience yet, but he had fewer distractions to contend with.

When I had first told the Waodani that I needed to leave, they had a difficult time handling the news. As time went on, they became resigned to it. But as it seemed to get easier for them, it became more and more difficult for me. I kept thinking, *We are happy here, and we feel significant. I have finally gotten over feeling that I am what I do, and I know I wasn't meant to be a "big businessman"—so why leave?* Then I would remember that we were leaving for the Waodani's good, not ours. I must have had that little question-and-answer session with myself a hundred times.

Ginny and Stephenie were struggling with the same issue. Living with the Waodani was not fun in and of itself. But those people in the tribe who loved us and trusted us did so with a gusto that made it difficult to imagine not being able to give them a piece of candle at night, or watch videos with them, or have them sleep on our floor or sleep on theirs from time to time. It was hard to think about a life in which we did not hunt and fish with them or have the up close and personal joy of doctoring them and flying for them and being family with them.

19

Another Spearing

Colonos—people moving in to squat on Waodani land—had been a problem ever since the oil companies penetrated Waodani territory with a couple of roads. Just before it was time for us to leave, the problem flared up again.

The authorities called for a meeting in Cononaco Texaco, a growing oil company camp on the Cononaco River. Several of the younger men in the tribe knew that many of the *colonos* were Colombians who were used to disobeying Ecuadorean laws in order to get what they wanted. These young people thought it would be good publicity if all the Waodani attending the conference were to show up in modified native dress, carrying spears.

Dayumae wanted me to take her and some of the other *piquianani* (old ones) to the conference. I agreed to take them, but I tried to explain that I could not bring all of them back. The oil company strip was designed for helicopters and special STOL aircraft. I could land with all the seats full, but I could take off with only one person. And even to take one person out, I would need to fly down a river channel until I could clear the trees.

I never personally attended conferences such as this unless the Waodani invited me. And even when I was, I hesitated to go. I knew that my presence there would strongly influence some members of the tribe to look to me for leadership. That was not what they needed.

After dropping off Dayumae and the others, I flew back to Nemompade and waited for news. It came almost immediately, but it was not what we had been expecting.

We got a radio message that old Babae had speared a *colono*. The report said that everyone had fled except the old people, who were crying for me to rescue them. I took off as soon as I could get out to the airstrip.

When I arrived, Dayumae told me in dramatic Waodani style what had happened, with a lot of sound effects and gestures.

Apparently, the *colonos* had outnumbered the Waodani about two to one at the gathering. Well-armed soldiers were there to keep the peace, even though no one expected any trouble. The *colonos* also had guns, but that was not unusual. In the jungle, almost everyone carries a weapon.

The group was ushered into a typical jungle building with a tin roof and rough board siding. It was a colorful and packed house. A minor government official had just started to welcome everyone when Babae suddenly exclaimed about something.

Before anyone could do anything to stop him, the old "killer" lowered his spear and rammed it through the abdomen of one of the *colonos*. He threw the weapon with such ferocity that it impaled the *colono* and stuck fast to the board wall behind him.

Dayumae told me that Dyuwi immediately grabbed Babae's spear and started pushing it hard toward the wounded *colono*. That didn't sound like Dyuwi. But when she told me that Kimo started pushing the spear as well, I knew something was really wrong. Then she told me that Babae was tugging at the spear to pull it out. He wanted to spear the shocked man again, but he had only one spear. I expected her to tell me that the soldiers started to spray the whole assembly with their machine guns.

"No," she said. "The soldiers were scared. They ran away with the *colonos* and just disappeared. Knowing they would come back to kill, I called to tell you to come get me. I don't want to be here anymore, where all the people fight and more people will die."

She was obviously referring to an ongoing saga of confrontations between Babae on the Waodani side, and all outsiders on the other.

The Waodani had told me that when Texaco pushed its road inside Waodani territory, Babae had wanted to see the *cowodi*. He built a longhouse next to the oil company road and planted his gardens. But he got hungry before the gardens were ready to harvest. Although he had never seen their gardens, Babae knew the foreigners had plenty of good food. He watched as they drove their big *autodi* to bring food to their workers. One day he told the *cowodi* that he wanted some food too.

They did not understand his language, but eventually, they got the message and gave him some food. I'm sure he must have thought it was only right that they share with him. After all, they were taking his land; the least they could do was give him food.

When the dry season hit, the gravel road got dusty. Babae did not like the dust, so he stood by the road and told them to go slowly. Not only could they not understand what he was saying, but they could not even hear him as they whizzed by in their noisy pickups on that rough gravel road. All Babae knew was that "the *cowodi* did not listen." So he took a rock and threw it into the *autodi* so they would stop and listen to him. They stopped, but they shouted at him rather than listening.

So Babae felled a tree over the road. When the next truck came by, he jabbed all four of its tires with his spear so that it would go more slowly.

Someone from the oil company must have decided Babae needed to be taught a lesson. They couldn't have an old "Indian" intimidating oil company workers. So, the Waodani told me, the oil company sent a Colombian *colono* to burn Babae's house down. Babae tried to find the arsonist to avenge himself but was unsuccessful.

During the opening speech of the conference, however, Babae saw the man he had been looking for. It was a perfect opportunity to get even, and he even had a spear to do it with. So he speared him. We never heard what happened to that *colono*, but I hope he lived, and I hope he spread the word not to mess with the Waodani.

For weeks, as we got ready to leave, rumors flew wildly about *colonos* coming to kill Waodani. I didn't think it would happen, and I desperately hoped it wouldn't. The *colonos* had fled from one old warrior with a single spear. The soldiers with automatic weapons ran away before the *colonos* did. I doubted any of them wanted to take their chances against the notorious Waodani inside the tribal territory, where the unfamiliar terrain would put them at a terrible disadvantage.

There were some areas where the Waodani seemed almost helpless to protect themselves. Politically, they were like nursing babies. Economically, they were reduced to begging. But there was no question that in their own territory, they were—and still are—the supreme masters of guerrilla warfare. Like some of the warrior tribes of North America, they are in much greater danger of being subdued through dependence than by armed invasion. The Waodani do not live in wide-open spaces where they can be attacked en masse. Every Waodani from childhood on up knows how to disappear into the dense foliage of their Amazon homeland. The only thing they need to survive for an extended period of time is a piece of knife stone they can find in almost any river. The *colono* spearing scared many of the older Waodani. But in a strange way, it reassured me. The Waodani had not completely given up.

/\\/\\·/\\·/\\·/\\·/\\·/\\/\\

Jesse was leaving on the last day of May. I dreaded seeing him go, partly because Ginny and I would miss him greatly, but even more so because he would have to say good-bye to Mincaye. We knew that would be painful for both of them.

As I loaded the plane, I caught sight of Mincaye and Jesse standing under the wing on the other side of BTS. They had their hands on one another's shoulders and were leaning toward each other like they were in a huddle. Then I saw that both were crying. I had never seen a Waodani man cry before. It was both a heartbreaking and moving sight.

Mincaye had, in some ways, replaced Jesse's real grandfather—the one Mincaye had speared to death. Jesse's real grandfather could not have loved him any more than this adopted one did. Mincaye could not have been more loyal. I hoped my dad was watching.

Finally, it was time to go. Jesse got in the plane, and Mincaye disappeared. I found out later that he had run back to his house to be alone in his awful grief. He had lost two grandsons in quick succession: one buried in a cheap box and the other lost to a mysterious world from which he might never return.

Poor Jesse didn't stop crying until we were almost to Shell.

After Jesse left, I began to think more about my own upcoming departure. I was scared for the Waodani. I knew that I had not done much for them, materially, that would last. I expected most of the projects, such as the store, the clinic, the church structure, and the tribe-controlled medicine distribution, to wind down as everything else that required money and management seemed to do.

And I was equally scared for myself. I had spent a long year and a half unraveling my personal identity as a busy businessman. In return, I had exchanged it for true living in an environment that valued spending time with people more highly than hoarding and building a net worth to leave behind.

I expected unprecedented loneliness and wondered how I would ever find something meaningful to do back in the United States. I was physically weary. In the midst of constant tensions among the Waodani, oil companies, missionaries, government authorities, and outside meddlers, I probably should have looked forward to leaving. Instead, I found myself dreading it.

I felt like a man without an identity. My jungle family had no way of even imagining what my "foreigner's" life was like. In the United States, I had a plane that carried twice as much as Bravo Tango Sierra and flew about twice as fast. I had once owned heavy equipment powerful enough to clear the Nemompade airstrip in a few days. I had earned more money in a year than all the Waodani people combined.

But during my time in the jungle, I realized the absurdity of trying to prove my value or establish my identity with possessions or money in the bank. The Waodani had shown me love and acceptance of greater consequence than the powerful equipment and busy importance I had left behind in that other world—a world I no longer really felt part of.

One night I got home very late—late enough that Ginny met me at the airstrip with a flashlight. It was the only time I remember landing without a reception committee at the strip. Ginny and I tied the plane down as tree frogs and insects began their nightly concert.

A full moon was coming up as we began a slow walk down the trail toward the houses. I put my arm around her and felt her familiar body under her flowing sundress. I loved this world that was so free of pretense. Even our clothes were free. I felt that freedom as I ran my hand down Ginny's back and around her waist.

The intense infatuation I had felt so many years ago for this one-in-a-million girl was still alive. We were still deeply and passionately in love. But over the months we had lived together in this pristine rain forest, I had come to view Ginny as my hero as well as my partner. I had enticed her to "another planet," away from everything familiar and comfortable. And Ginny had repaid me with admiration and respect. While I was floundering around trying to make sense of our radically new existence, she took my side in every battle and found enough energy to make sure she still tantalized me.

One of the priceless treasures I would take home was the jewel my incredible Ginny had become. She had been my wife and lover first. She became my best friend, trusted confidant, and encourager later. Now she really was my hero too.

When we reached the clearing, I saw that Ginny had placed a bar of soap and a towel for me on top of a stump by the trail to the river. As I bathed in the river with the moon reflecting off the quietly gurgling river around me, I realized I did not want to trade in this world, where people delivered babies and bled and died right in the open: a world where people weren't ashamed of their nakedness; a world that did not require contracts to enforce relationships. The authenticity of this culture had sunk roots deep into my soul.

My love and infatuation for Ginny had reached a climax I didn't even know could exist. We had seen Stephenie's and Jesse's horizons explode beyond a single culture and grow to encompass three very different worlds. Shaun and Jaime had proven that we no longer needed to enforce the principles we had taught them. They were perfectly capable of governing themselves and had made almost seamless transitions to manhood.

This had been the richest year and a half of life that I could remember, and there was no tax to pay on it. How could I exchange this for fast food, fast relationships, and fast cars? How could I go back to banking through a speaker, communicating by e-mail, and eating food out of boxes and cans? How could I return to paying a fortune for insurance just so my car would get fixed, my illnesses would be covered, and my family would get a bit of money to remember me by when I die?

I knew that when we returned, this past year and a half would quickly become a media event. We had been so isolated in Nemompade that we were beyond the reach of most media exploitation. I didn't mind explaining what we had done or why we had gone back to live among the people who had killed my dad. But I was afraid that if we were asked to tell what we had seen and felt and how we had changed, it might dull the edge of this incredible experience.

/\/\/\/\/\/\/\/\/\

The day we had all been dreading finally arrived. On July 21, 1996, I was going to have a full flight out to Shell with Ginny, Shaun, and Stephenie on board. Shaun had spent most of the summer doing the backbreaking work of helping the Waodani fill a swampy stream so we could extend the Nemompade airstrip, but it was still not completed.

We had decided that I would take Ginny and the kids out first, then come back to spend one last night with the Waodani by myself.

When we started for the airstrip, the entire community appeared out of nowhere, along with visitors from five or six other villages nearby. Some of the visitors were just curious. Many of our Nemompade neighbors and family were sad. A few, however, looked emotionally devastated.

The mood seemed to affect the small children and even the animals. The children clung to their mothers' legs. The babies were quiet. Even our wild pig seemed to know that this was not the time to chase dogs or kids. He just lay in a puddle, expressing physically what the rest of us felt emotionally.

The women hugged Steph and Ginny again and again. Everyone said good-bye to Shaun. Ompodae started to cry, and that opened the floodgates for everyone else. Ginny carried Ana Beth out to the strip. As she handed the baby back to Marga, it was more than I could bear. I busied myself by repeatedly inspecting the plane, putting off the inevitable.

Finally Steph said bluntly, "Pop, if we don't leave right now, I can't ever leave." She was right. We made our final preparations, but as we did, I realized something was wrong. Mincaye was not at the strip. I couldn't take Ongingcamo and Nemo and Toñae away without allowing them to say good-bye to Mincaye. I could not imagine anything except a fatal accident that could have kept him away.

Ompodae saw my concern and explained why Mincaye was not there. "Like a little one, he is crying down by the river by himself." Then she started to weep all over again. I realized that Mincaye's good-bye with Jesse had been so painful that he could not bear the pain of saying good-bye to three more members of his "family." He was not coming.

I fired up the engine, almost hoping that some mechanical problem would force us to wait until the next day. But everything was fine, so I gunned the engine to break the wheels free of the mud floor of our thatched hangar, and we taxied down to the end of the strip. I had done this so many times that I just went through my checklist by habit. Over the intercom I asked, "Everyone ready?" Only Shaun could answer. We were off.

Just before we reached flying speed, I noticed white leaves on the jungle borders flashing past us. A slight wind had picked up from behind us, blowing the leaves so their white bottoms were showing. I was breaking my own cardinal rule of never taking off until the only thing I was thinking about was taking off.

By the time I thought about cutting the power and aborting the takeoff, I saw the three-quarter marker pole zip by on my side. I was committed.

I got into the air okay, but BTS would not climb efficiently until I was showing seventy on the airspeed indicator. The trees at the end of the runway were growing larger by the second. I checked my flaps—ten degrees. I pushed the throttle in a bit harder; any more and I was going to break something. Our old bush plane didn't need more throttle; it needed more horsepower.

Dear God, I thought, *don't let all this end with me hurting or killing my family.* It was all I could do to force myself to keep from pulling back on the control yoke. Slowly we began to climb, but I knew it was not going to be enough. I had one trick left. I knew that the first trees I had to clear were taller than those behind them.

Before we hit the trees just ahead, I could add more flap and BTS would balloon up about twenty or thirty feet. But then I would be going slower than seventy, with more drag. I would have to give away a little altitude to maintain flying speed until I made it to the river. Then—if we made it that far—I could dive into the river between the trees and get my flaps up so I could climb out.

No one said anything, but Shaun was staring at me as I watched those fast-approaching trees. I knew Ginny and Steph could tell I was not playing around.

And then suddenly the slight tailwind turned to a slight headwind, and we climbed like an elevator. We cleared the trees by at least fifty feet. Fifteen seconds more and I don't know if we would have made it. It crossed my mind that "gratitude is the shortest-lived human emotion."

Crashing would have been such an absurd ending to this story that I started to think I shouldn't have been concerned. Surely God would not have let us end up impaled on a tree in the middle of nowhere. But then it occurred to me that my dad and Jim and Pete and Roger and Ed might have thought the same thing.

An old Bible proverb says, "The mind of man plans his way, but the LORD directs his steps" (Proverbs 16:9, NASB). I was sure hoping so, because even as we were heading toward this new chapter in our lives, I still did not have a plan. We were going "home," but it sure didn't feel like it.

Ginny told me she thought I should keep working for the Waodani from a distance—that I would probably be asked to speak a lot and that I should spend some time writing. *Sure,* I thought. *Who will I speak to, what will I write about that anyone who can read cares about, and what can I do for the Waodani from thousands of miles away?*

In addition to everything else she was to me, Ginny turned out to be prophetic too.

I left Ginny, Shaun, and Steph in Shell and headed back into Nemompade for my last night. I had one last load of supplies to deliver for the store.

/\/\/\/\/\/\/\

I wondered if it had been a good idea to go back by myself. *Maybe we should have started earlier—I could have made an extra trip with our bags first and then returned for Gin, Steph, and Shaun,* I thought. Maybe the Waodani would pressure me to change my plans and stay with them. Maybe I hoped they would.

When I landed, Tementa, Tidi, and several others started to unload the plane. Mincaye took my hand and gently led me toward the path to the houses. This was strange. I had never left the plane until it was unloaded, checked over, fueled, and tied down. Tementa was capable of doing all that, but I did not want to copy the typical Ecuadorean bush pilot pattern of having others do all my hard work. I had always felt like I was working for the Waodani, not the other way around.

But Mincaye was holding my hand, and I didn't want to pull away. After all, we were marking a major change in our relationship. So I walked down the path with this old jungle warrior who had taken me into his family when I was a fatherless little boy. What an improbable situation. Here we were, walking down a muddy trail side by side, holding hands.

After we'd walked awhile in silence, Mincaye, ever the diplomat, began talking to me in a soothing voice. "Babae, don't cry. *Waengongi*, knowing all things, I say don't cry. You going to the foreigners' place for a little while, come back soon, and I will go hunting and bring lots of meat." I was leaving Mincaye in a disintegrating culture in the middle of a world that still thought of this man I loved as a savage. Yet here he was comforting me on my way to live again in the land of Disney World.

I was shocked when we got to my house and Tementa's wife and six daughters were in the house. *Couldn't they wait even a day before taking over?* I wondered. The term "vultures" crossed my mind.

The three oldest daughters were taking down the curtains Ginny and Steph had made with Marga on her old sewing machine. Ginny had run a piece of string along the top of the window screen and another along the bottom all the way around both ends of the house. Then she took flowered sheets that matched our bedsheets and sewed a little circle hem into the ends. She put one hem over the top string and one over the bottom string so we could pull the cloth across the screen to keep wind and rain out or push them back when we wanted the windows clear.

While I tried to overlook their insensitivity, Nemonta carefully informed me, "Taking down Ongingcamo's cloth, we will wash it and save it for when she comes back." I should have realized they weren't being offensive. The Waodani had built this house with me. I had told them over and over that I did not want a house or an airstrip or a clinic or a store in their territory. I had told them I would help them only if *they* wanted to have those things.

The old people had asked me specifically what would happen to my house when I left, and I told them I did not have a house. I told them they should decide what to do with *their* house. I hoped that they would allow Tementa to live in it, and that is exactly what they decided to do. Now here I was, getting my dander up because they were coming in to protect the things they wanted Ginny to have when she came back.

One minute I saw them as interlopers in my house; the next I was trying to convince them that Ginny and I wanted them to use everything: the dishes, the sink, the camp stove, the toilet, the rough warped board beds, and the cheap foam mattresses. We wanted them to use them, just as we had.

When I had decided to spend that last night in the jungle alone with the Waodani, I told them I would use the room we had built for patients' families in the little clinic building next door. They already had it fixed up for me with my favorite hammock. Ginny and I never mastered sleeping together in a hammock, but when I was alone, I much preferred a hammock to a bed.

Everyone seemed to have agreed that from now on, whenever I was in Nemompade, Dawa and Kimo would travel to Nemompade from their clearing downriver, where Kimo had taken me when I first trekked from village to village. It was decided that they would look after me and sleep with me. But Nemonta would feed me. That night, when we ate, she gave me the first bowl of soup, the one reserved for the oldest member of the family. She knew that Ginny often made Tang for me, so Nemonta had mixed some of the orange drink and served it in one of our cheap plastic mugs instead of in a quart bowl as they usually drink from.

After dinner, I fell asleep while Kimo prayed for me and each member of my family, including my mom and "Dad Abe."

The next morning it hit me. This was the real, final, no-backing-out-now day for me to leave. I told Dawa and Nemonta, "Gobopa"—*Go I am doing.* They quietly relayed the message to someone outside. In an instant, I could hear the message being transmitted to all the houses in the Waodani's long-distance falsetto voices.

When I started down the trail, little Dawa, Mincaye's beautiful four-year-old granddaughter, was waiting for me. As I walked by, she reached up and took my hand. A few feet later, Ongimae, the daughter of my martyred friend Toñae, handed me her naked little boy, Koni.

Everyone else hung back for some reason, following at a distance. Little Dawa kept asking, "Babae, gobi?"—*Babae, going you are?*

"Ooo, gobopa"—*Yes, going I am,* I would reply, and we would walk a little further.

Koni, his soft little bottom resting on my arm, just rode along quietly. The crowd followed at a distance, no one laughing or carrying on boisterously as the Waodani usually do.

As I walked to the airstrip, I found myself longing for the walk to last. I had made that walk hundreds of times over the last year—to pick up a little boy impaled on a stick in a muddy jungle river, to deliver store goods to Waodani who had no access to salt, candles, matches, or medicine. I had taken that walk in a lot of different conditions: sometimes sad, sometimes scared, often lonely, even confused once in a while . . . and almost always tired. But this last trip was the only time that was really hard to face.

One of life's greatest blessings for me is knowing what God wants me to do and then being able to give myself completely and unreservedly to it. My time in the jungle had been one of those special times. I loved the Waodani and had felt as at home in our little clearing in the jungle as any place I'd ever lived.

I had watched Ginny rise to meet challenges most women with her background couldn't even imagine: from finding scorpions in the laundry hamper to scrubbing clothes by hand in the same stream where she bathed and retrieved water. She averaged anywhere from twenty to a hundred guests a day with no privacy whatsoever. She had difficulty communicating and was often unable to even guess why the people we lived with did what they did.

I thought of all these things as Tementa was loading the plane, tying everything down, and checking the fuel. This was the only time I'd ever taken off without dipping the tanks to see with my own eyes how much fuel I had. Tementa would not have minded, but I wanted to show him in a critical way that I trusted him.

I started to say good-bye, but before I could get the words out, everyone gathered around me and Mincaye started to pray. "*Waengongi*, don't let Babae hit the trees, don't let a snake bite him, don't let him get mosquito fever, don't let an *autodi* kill him . . ." and on and on. He prayed for protection for me from every danger he could think of.

I climbed into the plane and called, "Libre." But no one answered. I called "Libre" again, but no one seemed to want to be the one to give me permission to start up and fly out of their lives. Finally, Tementa nodded to me. If he was feeling as choked up as I was, maybe he just couldn't get the word out.

As I taxied down toward the end of the strip, I saw our pet pig take off after me. Just what I needed. I decided to outrun him. I was doing almost thirty miles an hour, but I still hadn't passed him. Then I caught sight of him right in front of me, running like lightning. If I hit him, we would have a good dinner, but I would probably have to wait for another prop to fly to Shell with. I reached to pull the power, when Odae made a high-speed, ninety-degree turn and headed into the jungle beside the strip.

That pig had kept things lively in Nemompade long enough. This time he had crossed the line. I decided that when I came back, I would have to shoot him. Once he messed with a running airplane, he had to go!

The Waodani must have come to the same conclusion. When I returned two months later, our pig was gone. I asked some people what had happened to him, but no one seemed to know. When I asked Ompodae, she looked like I had caught her with her hand in the cookie jar. "I didn't eat any," she blurted out. I'll bet that old pig was in the pot before I reached Shell.

20

Between Two Worlds

The hours spent packing our final supplies in Shell, traveling to Quito, and finally getting to the international airport for our flight to Florida passed like a blur in my mind. I woke up early the first few mornings outside the jungle wondering why no roosters were crowing.

When we went through the airport, a couple of men dressed as airport employees helped us move our carry-on bags out of the way at the ticket counter. When they left, we were short one camcorder. They didn't get much—that video camera had been dying a slow death out in the jungle and actually had quit working altogether just before we left. But we still felt violated and exposed. It was a preview of what we were all going to feel for a while back in the land of the free and the home of the brave.

We had one other little surprise at the Quito airport. Quito sits in a high valley almost ten thousand feet up in the Andes. At normal weights at that altitude, a plane requires a lot more runway to take off than at sea level. American Airlines decided it needed to reduce the weight on our flight and asked for volunteers to be bumped. No one wanted to stay in Quito, until they offered eight hundred dollars and a free ticket to anywhere they fly as the enticement for a few passengers to stay behind.

Shaun needed money for school, but he had friends and a special girl waiting to meet us in Orlando. It was a tough decision, but he finally decided he couldn't pass up American's offer. I knew how much Shaun loved Anne, and I couldn't wait to meet her. Shaun had made it clear that if we gave our blessing, Anne would soon be our daughter-in-law. Ginny and I had always told the children that marriage is a family affair. While we were happy to let them choose their spouses, we wanted veto power. Or we could choose and they could veto. "But," we told them, even before they were interested in marriage, "no one gets married until everyone is happy."

Of course, we didn't really expect that idea to work, but Shaun was actually putting it into practice. Poor Anne. I'm sure she didn't know what to think of the Saint family when we marched off the plane without Shaun! On the bright side, we really enjoyed getting to know her. Anne's father died when she was just a girl, and I found myself relishing the idea of getting to be something of a father to her. We were pleased to be included in Shaun's romance. Or, rather, I was pleased; Ginny and Stephenie were ecstatic.

Before we left for the jungle, Ginny and I had told Jaime that we thought he should try to get to know a girl named Jessica Shea, whose family we knew a little bit from church. By the time we got back to the United States, Jaime and Jessica were in love, and we were thrilled for both of them. I hoped he would ask her to marry him and that she would say yes. Ginny, as usual, was way ahead of me and acted as if it was a done deal. As always, in matters of love, she was right. Jesse was so impressed with Jaime's glowing reports about Jessica that he asked Jaime to set him up with her sister, Jenni. Jaime wrote to Jesse while we were still in the jungle and told him, "Don't worry, bro. I've got everything set up for you." I doubted that even silver-tongued Jaime could convince Jenni to marry his brother. Wrong again! Ginny and I knew Jenni. She came to our house with a group of young people every Wednesday night to let me talk to them about what life is all about and how to find God's trail through it. As Ginny, Stephenie, and I considered each of these girls, we were thinking we might end up batting a thousand.

Steph's romance would come a little later. She did not have to be convinced that dating was a poor way to find a partner for life. She hated the whole idea. She didn't dislike boys, but she thought dating was just a game of emotional Russian roulette. When boys asked her for a date, she would say, "Sure, but you have to ask my dad first." I found this out when one frustrated would-be suitor finally got up the courage to ask me if he really had to have my permission to date Steph. Steph saw me talking to him, and I saw a smirk cross her face, as if to say, "Okay Pop, how are you going to handle this one?"

What could I say? If I said it wasn't true, he would feel rejected by Steph. If I said yes, he would think I was old fashioned and possessive of my only daughter—which I was.

∧∧∧∧∧∧∧∧

I had been physically away from the land of "bigger and better" for only a year and a half. But emotionally it felt like I had been gone for a decade. I couldn't have imagined how difficult it would be for me to slide back into our old life.

Jaime and Shaun had been using our station wagon at the University of Florida. Now we all piled back into it to head for home. A single mother with two children had used our home while we were gone. She had left it clean and welcoming for our return. Our bank accounts were at the same bank, and our little city was struggling with the same tremendous growth it had been experiencing when we left. Everything was pretty much the same as we had left it, but it did not feel the same. I began to realize that we were the ones who had changed.

Now that we were back in the *cowodi omae*, we realized how much easier and more comfortable life here is. We could have anything to eat, anytime we wanted it. Everything seemed so straight and clean. Life was more orderly than I had ever noticed before. People even stopped for stop signs and red lights. In Ecuador, traffic signs were more suggestions than absolutes.

In the first couple of weeks we were back, Ginny made it a point to thank me over and over for her refrigerator with an ice maker that delivered cubes or chips through an automatic dispenser in the door.

When we mentioned to friends how surprised we were that most of the foods in the grocery store were preprepared, one said, "Maybe the rest of us should leave for a while so we could appreciate what we have." Another friend chuckled and said she had recently seen a woman pull a couple of TV dinners out of the store freezer and put them back with the comment, "No, I don't feel like cooking tonight."

One of the downsides of the "good life" is the difficulty we have in continuing to appreciate it.

/\\/\\·/\\/\\·/\\/\\·/\\

Our transition back to life in the States was going to take much longer than we thought. It was like sitting down to an all-you-can-eat steak dinner after nearly starving to death. I actually found myself wanting to trade the megabar at Ryan's Family Steak House for a whole smoked fish. And when I was drinking a decadent cookies-and-cream milk shake at Steak n Shake, I found myself wishing I could trade it in for a gourd full of chewy plantain drink. Everything just seemed too rich, too easy, and way too fast.

The biggest difference of all was that we did not have a hundred or fifty or even twenty people in our house every night unless we invited them. Neither Ginny nor I said so, but I think we both missed having friends wandering in and out all day and having a crowd of them hanging around at night to watch a movie or just be together.

In the jungle, I actually started to expect daily disillusionments, accompanied by unexpected personal rewards. That was one thing we had not left behind. We had asked a friend to invest some money from the sale of our business for us while we were away. He tried to make a home run for us with our funds, even though that was not the investment strategy we had agreed on. While we were gone, the stock market had gone up almost 30 percent. That was the good news. The bad news was that he had invested our funds heavily in technology stocks. While everyone else's net worth seemed to have gone up about 30 percent, ours had gone down about the same amount.

This created a spiritual as well as an economic crisis for me. I would not have said so openly, but part of me had believed that if we were looking after God's business, God would be obliged to look after our business. I really struggled over this financial loss. It ate at me. I considered trying to have my investment manager's securities license taken away, trying to convince myself I owed it to the community to protect others from him. He had agreed to invest in conservative companies with a proven track record. It isn't my normal tendency to be cautious, but I didn't want anything to go haywire while I was gone. I had never let anyone else make financial decisions for me, and now I wondered if I would ever trust anyone to do it again.

Finally I had to admit that it wasn't my sense of responsibility that was gnawing at me. I simply wanted revenge. I wanted to get even with this man I had trusted who had let me down. I had the same dark nature as the Waodani did. I just lived in a cleaner environment. I didn't have to take a spear and run my enemies through; I could just call up the SEC or an attorney who knew the system and send them out to do in those who had crossed me. Regardless of whether my stockbroker had done what I asked him to do or not, I began to have a sneaking suspicion that there were some more life lessons I needed to learn in order to live in the United States if my life here was going to benefit others, and not just myself.

It took a long time to get over the feeling of betrayal, but this financial loss also served to steady me. It was like a sea anchor on a boat in a storm. It dragged behind me. It slowed my progress and kept me from running erratically in various directions. I needed that, because I honestly felt like I no longer had an identity.

Jaime had enjoyed the freedom of being on his own while we were gone. He assumed that I would take over as family policeman as soon as I came back, and he chafed when it seemed like I was taking away his ability to make his own decisions. I was oblivious to his struggle. I wasn't trying to control him at all. In fact, I was proud of the way he had handled himself and all his affairs like a man. I was relieved to realize he was taking care of himself. I was struggling to order my own life, or at least find a sense of significance in it again.

It had not been easy living in the chaos of Waodani life. But I desperately missed being so obviously needed and so intensely loved by them. I had to remind myself constantly that I had left for their good, not mine. Otherwise I might not have been able to resist going back to live in Nemompade again. Stephenie also seemed to be feeling what I was. I overheard her telling Ginny, "I am going to go to school here, but I don't think I can ever live in the States permanently. I just don't fit in anymore."

Slowly, we began to reacclimate. Jaime took it upon himself to start looking for cars. We were all going separate directions. We had one car to share among six of us, and we really needed at least four, maybe even five. The rest of the world thinks it is unimaginably luxurious for North American families to have more than one car. What they don't realize is that we don't have public buses or plenty of taxis waiting to be hailed. And in the United States, things are so spread out that you can't really walk from place to place. In this other world of mine, cars aren't a luxury; they are an expensive necessity.

I kept a journal the entire time we were living in the jungle. Writing down what was going on in our lives helped me keep perspective. It let me get things off my chest and helped me think through what we should do to carry out the Waodani's requests for help.

I quit writing shortly after returning to the States. On the last page I wrote, "Six thousand dollars a year for insurance because we have teenage drivers, even though not one has ever been drunk, all are excellent students, and they have never gotten tickets. We pay for many people who don't care, aren't responsible, and have little to lose." I realized that we were spending more for auto insurance than for our complete living expenses in the jungle.

My journal entry went on: "We fill our days with entertainment and activities, buying appliances and gadgets to cook, wash, bake, compute, and generally relieve us of living, so that we can spend more time exercising to get in shape because the gadgets and machines are doing all our work. It is hard to live here and not go along, but I am more and more pleased with how we lived in the jungle. Very nice to be all together as a family, however."

Not a very bright note on which to end about six hundred pages of journal notes.

Shortly after returning from Ecuador, I had an experience that seemed to tie my two desperately different worlds together. Mom called me and asked me to run over and do her a favor. Mom and Dad Abe lived just a mile from us in Ocala.

When I got there, Mom told me she had found some old reels of sixteen-millimeter movie film. She had borrowed an old projector, but she could not figure out how to thread it. One of my first businesses as a boy in Quito had been renting old cowboy movies of Roy Rogers and Gene Autry and showing them with my partner, Steve McCully. He collected the money at the door to his mom's living room, which we frequently made into a theater on Friday nights. I was the projectionist. So I knew how to run even the most recalcitrant of projectors.

When Mom closed the curtains and I started the first reel, I wasn't expecting to be interested in whatever was on this old film. I couldn't have been more wrong. It was a copy of the original footage my dad had taken on Palm Beach.

Shortly after Dad and his friends were killed, a documentary film had been made using a lot of Dad's original movie footage. It was titled *Through Gates of Splendor*, the same title that had been previously used by Aunt Betty Elliot for a book about this story. The other widows had asked her to write it in response to the continuing demand for more information about the killing of Dad, Roger, Jim, Ed, and Pete.

I had watched the *Through Gates of Splendor* movie many times. Everyone who visited us seemed to want to see that half-hour film. But every time I watched it, one question always remained in my mind. The film showed Dad making an actual landing on Palm Beach. It shows the plane appearing around the upriver bend as it descends between the thick jungle on both sides of the river. By the time Dad needs to make the turn to line up with Palm Beach, where Uncle Pete or Uncle Ed is standing with the camera, he is too low to bank the wings. Instead, he slides into the turn, dropping closer and closer to the water until suddenly, just as his wheels are about to touch the water, he crosses the edge of the sandbar.

Anyone who knows how to fly watches that approach with amazement. I always had! But I had started to wonder if Dad was actually making a landing or just a touch-and-go for the camera. Touching down within a plane's length of the end of that short sandbar after a twisting and skidding approach down the Curaray River just seemed too perfect. I had always yearned to know if Dad was really that good or if this had just been a touch-and-go, which would have made it much easier to touch down right at the water's edge. I couldn't tell from the documentary, because that clip had been cut just as old 56 Henry's wheels touched the sand. No one seemed to know what had happened to the original footage, so I never found out if there was more footage from that scene. Now here it was again: that same amazing landing that had represented the incredible difficulty of building a bridge between the "Auca" world and the rest of humanity. For me, that footage represented my yearning to really know my dad.

This time the footage did not cut off. Finally, forty years after the fact, I got to see the rest of the story. Dad does touch down just as his tail wheel passes over the edge of the beach. The plane doesn't bounce even a little. I don't imagine it is of much consequence to anyone else, but to me, it felt as if I had just had a brief exchange with my long-lost dad. That was the most difficult and dramatic landing I have ever seen on film. I wondered if I would ever have occasion to test my flying skills in a similar situation. Little did I know that I would get to reenact that very landing on an even shorter beach when this story was made into a movie ten years later.

I knew when I left Nemompade that the Waodani would wonder if I was flying out of their lives or just leaving temporarily. Although I told them I would be back in two moons, I knew many outsiders had made them promises that they did not, or could not, keep.

I made my first return visit just two months after leaving. I was really looking forward to seeing our Nemompade family. I wondered how they would react to seeing me again. I wondered who would even be there.

When I did return two months later, everyone seemed to be waiting for me when I landed on that familiar airstrip. But they didn't give me the usual jovial welcome that thinly veiled the constant tensions and complexities of their new lives.

No one said so, but I got the feeling that someone had just died. That would explain why all the elders and many "old ones" from other villages were also there. I wondered who had died. It had to be someone from Nemompade, I figured, because so many people were there.

The Waodani did not even let me go to the house to put my things away. My backpack and a couple of duffels filled with rifles and other much-anticipated supplies were taken from me at the plane. Instead of taking me to the house, they led me to the *Waengongi onco*.

When we got there, there were even more people waiting. *Maybe several people died,* I thought. I mentally started to check off everyone from the Nemompade group. They seemed to all be there.

When we were all sitting together, I noticed that they had put a cement covering on the dirt floor in this special meeting house. Outside of that, and the fact that there was a really big crowd of really tense people, everything here seemed to be the same.

Finally, Tementa said, "The old ones thinking something, they want to speak to you." More waiting. There was a lot of throat clearing going on.

One poor dog tried to sneak in, and someone whacked the mangy cur. He let out a yelp and was gone. I could hardly contain the growing anxiety that was building in me. "Someone tell me what is going on and why everyone is so morose," I wanted to blurt out. But that wasn't the way we did things here. The thing to do was just to wait.

I grabbed someone's baby to help distract myself from imagining all sorts of calamities that might explain this solemn gathering. But the first sign that I was not the cause of whatever was on their corporate mind was when one of the kids came running into the silent meeting and brought me a plastic cup full of *Yupi*, a cheap powdered jungle substitute for Gatorade. (I think it got its name from what happens after you drink it.) Another kid gave me a bowl of soup with a big piece of wild turkey breast in it. No, I wasn't the bad guy. As I ate, I wondered who was.

Finally, very dramatically, Mincaye stood to his feet and cleared his throat. He stretched a little and cleared his throat some more. By this time, we had been sitting for probably fifteen minutes without a single word being spoken. I had had time to get nervous, grow bored, play with a baby, and eat lunch.

"Babae's father coming long ago," Mincaye began very slowly, followed by some more loud throat clearing, "he went very fast from place to place in the wood bee. Some of us, seeing him with our own eyes, know this happened. Then a loooong time later, another plane coming, we saw it too. Who was in that wood bee? Well, wasn't it Babae himself? He, too, went fast from place to place; taking the elders to teach the people, bringing people to the medicine house, and taking medicine and bread to the other living places."

The topic was either me or the airplane. We were starting to make progress.

"What about now?" Mincaye was warming to his topic. "Amoa being bitten by the snake, how could he get medicine so he wouldn't die? When Awani broke her arm, how could we get it fixed without the wood bee to fly her to the hospital? In Huamono, the People all having mosquito fever, how could we get *biimo* for them to get well?"

Okay, all his rhetorical questions were aimed at the airplane, not me. But maybe I was being held responsible for leaving and taking the plane that the tribe had started to think of as its own.

I started to feel defensive. I started to carry on my own internal conversation, attempting to defend myself against all the terrible things that had happened in the two months I had been gone because the Waodani no longer had their own airplane and their own pilot: *It wasn't mine. I had to return it. And I had to leave for your own good.*

Mincaye finished his speech without ever suggesting what he thought I should do about all the calamities the airplane could have solved. He just sat down.

I don't remember the order in which they spoke, but every elder and most of the old men and a few women followed Mincaye with their own speeches. Kimo, Dyuwi, old Dabo, Amoa, Paa, Tomo, Dayumae, Kenta—he had the only short speech, at about ten minutes—Cobadi, Cogi, Peque, and on and on the speeches continued.

I sat. I slumped. My legs went numb. Finally, I fell completely asleep leaning against one of the big posts. When I woke up, my legs were so dead I knew I had to move. I tried straddling the log I was sitting on. My legs started to wake up and tingle with that special pain that comes with renewed circulation.

I longed for the distraction of our pet pig and the dogs and monkeys and birds that always joined these meetings. I wondered what could have kept our pig away. (I didn't know yet that he had long since been dinner.) One pet wild turkey flew through the building and out the far end. It was followed by some parakeets that squawked and jabbered as they flew. That was better than no distraction, but it wasn't much.

It would not have been so bad, but everyone was saying the same things Mincaye had said. Dad came flying the wood bee. I came flying the wood bee. Now they had no wood bee, so this one could not go to the foreigners' hospital, and this other one died, and no one had medicine, and Dyuwi went to teach the people at one village and, when they would not feed him, he had to turn around and walk two days without food to get home.

The meeting was an amazing and confusing event. It went on for more than four hours. And I sat every minute of it on a rock-hard log. I tried sitting on the floor for a few minutes, but my leg started to cramp. I had just finished almost two full days of traveling: by car to the Orlando airport, commuter plane to Miami, 757 to Quito, bus to Shell, BTS to Nemompade. I had been sitting for two days—and now an additional four hours. I started fantasizing about the luxury of a sculpted folding chair. My overstuffed recliner back home was beyond imagining.

Finally, finally, finally, there was no one else left to repeat the wood bee speech.

Toward the end of this ordeal, I started to suspect what this solemn assembly was about. *Oh no!* I thought. *They can't want me to get them their own airplane and pilot.* But that was exactly what this marathon meeting was all about.

Tementa finally stepped in to bring the convocation to a head. "The old ones thinking we need our own plane, Babae, what do you think?"

I had to nip this one in the bud. They were talking about a very expensive and complex proposition. I had explained over and over that when foreigners gave them money for things, foreigners would control those things: the secular Golden Rule. Translated into Wao-Tededo, it went something like this: "He who gives *tucudi* paper (money) for something, gets to think what he wants to happen. Because he has the *tucudi*, everyone has to see what he thinks well." In other words, "He who has the gold, rules."

They had seemed to understand this. I gave them examples to illustrate how the oil company called the shots when they paid for school buildings to be built. The government paid the teachers in most communities, so the government decided what was taught, who the teacher was going to be, and when school would start and end. Most of the communities had radios that had been paid for by mission organizations. If it was used for unapproved purposes, the mission could punch in a number that would turn the community radio off so it couldn't be used until the Waodani agreed to abide by "the rules."

And really, that is the way it should be. I hated everyone else controlling the Waodani's lives even more than many of them did. But I know that in the real world, "he who pays the piper calls the tune." If those paying the piper take the money away, the piper goes hungry and there is no music.

"It takes *nangi, nangi, nangi tucudi* to buy an airplane," I told them. "You telling us what to do," someone volunteered, "we will work very, very, very hard and buy one." At about a dollar a day working for the oil company, which was the going net wage and the only real employer for Waodani labor, it would take every adult in the meeting who wasn't nursing a baby or pregnant about ten years to buy a thirty-year-old plane such as Bravo Tango Sierra.

Someone else suggested, "You showing us how, we will build our own wood bee!" They were as serious as a heart attack. The suggestion was so preposterous that I didn't even know how to answer. I remembered my brother, Phil, taking his dead pet canary to the missionary radio tech to be fixed. He was so sure Uncle Krecky could fix it, none of the rest of us dared tell him it couldn't be done.

"God seeing it well, maybe someday we can have a truly Waodani *ebo*. But who will fly it and fix it?" I asked them. "If a foreigner flies it, then it won't really be yours. Only flying it yourselves will you truly tell it where to go and when to come back."

They already had an answer to this. They were determined to have their own plane and their own pilot. They just wanted me to work out the details. They had chosen the pilot: Tementa. I could choose the plane.

When they had asked me to show them how to start a store and school, build buildings, work on engines, and do dentistry, use a computer, connect lights to batteries, write checks, make uniforms for school, grow rice, be tour guides, keep track of basic accounts, and all the other things they had asked me to help them master, I believed it could be done. But now they were asking me to help them jump from the Stone Age to the Space Age in one gigantic leap.

I just didn't think it could be done. I had told them they could do anything the *cowodi* could do. But they could never afford it. Unless we did regular "genuine experience tours" such as the one we had done for a group of our friends from Ocala. That might make it economically possible. Tementa could not master a Cessna 172, however. He was smart enough, but he wasn't big enough.

I had already tried teaching him to fly. He did everything well, except to fly a straight line. When I would point out a distant landmark and ask him to fly to it, he would inevitably drift off course. I finally figured out that he couldn't see the landmarks over the dash. Stature can be a problem. The Waodani didn't cut down trail obstructions high enough to clear my head. Cessna did not make planes for men five feet two.

We would have to design our own plane.

The government would never give Tementa a license, however, unless he first got a high school diploma. That would take years. He couldn't even start training until he had it.

I said, "You seeing this well, and me thinking about it, if *Waengongi* sees it well, then we will do it." There was no question in my mind: This would take a miracle.

The Waodani God followers had more faith than I did. They told me that they were going to speak to *Waengongi* "always, always, always" about this.

He answered sooner than I thought. On my way out of the jungle, I ran into bad weather and had to divert to Tena, another town on the edge of the jungle with an airstrip. While I waited there for the weather to clear, I noticed an ultralight aircraft tied down beside the strip. It had two seats, which actually made it a light aircraft. I hadn't thought about the possibility of a light aircraft for the Waodani. I was inspecting it when the owner showed up.

He asked if I wanted a ride. I wanted to see what it would do, so I accepted. When the weather cleared, we took off with the little two-cycle engine screaming just behind our heads. I yelled over the engine noise, "¿Qué licensia tienes?"

"I don't have a license," he replied in Spanish.

"Have you ever crashed?" I asked next.

"Claro que sí," he responded, and started pointing out a tiny beach, a pasture, and one or two more places he had made forced landings when his engine quit.

I immediately offered to take him for a ride in BTS. I wanted to get out of that wire-braced little flying machine flown by an unlicensed, crash-proven pilot. But I had found out an important fact: An ultralight might be just what we needed.

/\\/\\/\\/\\/\\/\\/\\

One year later, with the help of a couple of friends and Jesse and Jaime, I fitted an Australian aircraft engine to a unique kit airplane. We put rugged landing gear on it, changed the fuel system, and modified it so that the whole machine could be disassembled in just a few hours. All but two parts of the entire aircraft could be taken to Ecuador as accompanied baggage.

Several volunteers and the boys and I had built one plane as a proof of concept. The second one we packaged up and checked on as baggage with our official air carrier, American. We flew the parts into Nemompade, and I showed Tementa and several other Waodani how to bolt together the parts we had prefabricated. Then we began to cover the frame with a special cloth. Finally, we flew the parts back to Shell, where we could cover the wings, assemble the major pieces, and do our test-flying.

The Waodani were excited. When we got the fuselage together in Nemompade, they wanted to push each other around in it in the little clearing in front of our old house. Two would get in and hold out their arms like wings, one or two others would push, and someone else would make engine sounds to make the test run official.

There were setbacks, of course. We pinched one of the tire tubes when we bolted the wheel halves together. Then we needed a patch, glue, and a compressor. I just had to run to the local hardware store and grab everything we needed—don't I wish.

While assembling the plane, we started to attract visitors. The grapevine carried the news that the Waodani were building their very own airplane. This would be the equivalent of hearing that the Starship Enterprise was coming to town for a demonstration and that Scotty was going to select a handful of people to beam up to the ship for a quick tour.

A group of Quechuas came by one day and hinted to me that they had heard a preposterous story. They had heard a rumor that some Waodani— "the same people who were once called 'Aucas'"—were building an airplane. I told them it was true and took them behind Rick's house in Shell to see for themselves.

Tementa and several other Waodani were working with an experienced airplane builder, a couple of other volunteers, and me to assemble this little airplane. A couple of fairly high-ranking air force officers had even come by to watch and couldn't resist getting involved. It was incredible for me to see one of those officers working side by side with Tementa. I could not imagine anything else that could bring two men from opposite ends of the Ecuadorean class structure together as equals.

Finally, the Quechuas motioned for me to follow them. They backed away from the project and asked, "Are the Waodani really building this airplane themselves?" I pointed to Tementa and the other Waodani. Tementa was showing several other workers what to do and then checking their work.

"If they can do this, why can't we?" they asked. I told them they could. I remembered when I was in kindergarten and I was talking to some friends in

first grade. They said, "Aw, kindy-garten, is easy-peazy. But wait till you get
to big school." Then it was, "Wait till you get into junior high" . . . and then
senior high, and then college. The Quechuas, like the Waodani and Shuar
and thousands of other people groups all over the world, were struggling to
be taken seriously. But they kept being told they just didn't have what it
takes. That is a debilitating form of discrimination that pushes capable people
into a unique kind of poverty: poverty of the soul.

"You can do this too," I said. "Ver es saber"—*To see is to believe.*

"Will you help us?" they asked. I couldn't help them, but I told them that
they could find someone else who would help them. They just laughed
dejectedly. "Who would ever help us do such a thing? We're just *Indigenas*."

After they left, the Waodani confronted me. "Why do you say yes to helping us, but to the Quechuas you say no?"

"I did not say no. I just told them I could not help them, being very busy
helping you," I explained defensively. But they weren't finished with me.

"Thinking like a foreigner, you think you have to do everything. We don't
say you yourself should teach them, too, but teaching us, together we can
teach all the other ones who don't know."

Sure we will, I thought. That was as likely as . . . the Waodani building
their own airplane.

That night I could not get the idea out of my head. It really did not make
sense to design dental equipment or aircraft or unique power-generating
equipment for just one small group of people. It would make sense, however,
if the research and development could be amortized over a large number of
indigenous groups who could possibly use them.

That night I-TEC, the Indigenous People's Technology and Education
Center, was born. Instead of giving medical care and dental care to the poor
and uneducated people of the world, why not teach them how to care for
their own people? Instead of giving them a fish to eat, why not teach them to
do their own fishing? And then why not teach them to make fishing tackle
and teach others like themselves to do the same?

It was the most unlikely idea I had ever grabbed hold of. Instead of educat-
ing people to be like us so they can do the things we do the way we do them,
I realized we needed to reinvent the tools and training methods to fit the
people who needed to use them.

When personal computers started to proliferate, I refused to learn MS-

DOS. I knew the computer companies would figure out sooner or later that there were millions of people who wanted to buy and use their products but who weren't going to become computer geeks in order to do so. I was right. Instead of millions of us learning to think like computer experts, they started making their computers think like us.

This was, in some ways, the same thing. The big difference was that our market was even bigger. The only drawback was that most people such as the Waodani don't know that it is possible for them to take care of themselves and their people. They don't know what they could do with a little training and equipment designed for their way of thinking and their way of life. And then, of course, there were a few other small matters. Many, if not most, of these people have no money, and they don't know how to read and write.

The Waodani had initiated a concept that could revolutionize their lives and the lives of thousands of other technologically primitive people groups. But I knew it would be an uphill struggle against great obstacles. The indigenous people themselves would have to be convinced that they are capable. Outsiders would have to be convinced of the same thing. Our chances of success were slim, but the potential benefits of success for the Waodani and people like them was incredible.

I felt a little like the farmer who won the lottery. When asked what he was going to do with the millions of dollars he had just won, he responded, "Shucks, I guess I'll just go on farming until it's all gone." I knew I had a great idea, but I did not know what to do with it yet.

21

The Foreigners' Place

We had been back in the United States for a year, and it was almost time for Jesse to graduate from high school. He and Stephenie begged me to bring Grandfather Mincaye to the United States for Jesse's graduation. If we could get him up here for the graduation, he could stay for Jaime's wedding. This would be especially meaningful since Mincaye was Jaime's tribal namesake. I thought it was a great idea, but I knew it was impossible.

Mincaye had no passport. To get one, he needed military papers. He also needed to prove that he had voted in all recent elections or get an official excuse for not having voted. After all that came the really tough hurdle: a United States visa.

I had just spent a year and a half trying to renew my Ecuadorean passport. I even had an Ecuadorean attorney friend working on it. I can read and write, and I have contacts in Ecuador. Mincaye had nothing but me. But Tementa already had an Ecuadorean passport. *Maybe,* I thought, *I should take Tementa and Mincaye to Quito with me when I leave after finishing the assembly of their airplane.*

We actually got the plane built in a couple of weeks, and then we assembled it and got it ready for a test flight in one additional week of very long days and nights. Our backdrop was the active volcano Sangay—about thirty miles away—which was spewing smoke and lava over the jungle. One of the volunteers and I were sitting on lawn chairs for the first flight, so we didn't dare do more than take a couple of short hops—about like the Wright brothers' first flights.

I thought I should at least try to get Tementa a visa so he could come and do some flight training with me in Florida. But with Mincaye, the situation was hopeless. I would only have one day in the capital to try to get him the years of paperwork he needed. But I at least could show Jesse and Steph that I had tried.

We arrived at the U.S. Embassy in Quito when they opened at ten o'clock on a Friday morning. We paid the fee for an interview and were given a number—a very high number. I hoped they gave out sequential numbers all week. I knew there was no chance of getting an interview if our number represented our place in line for just that day.

I realized the numbers were daily when I saw the waiting room. Some people had waited all night to get their place in line. I overheard one woman say that all her children were in New York. She had been trying to get a visa for almost five years so she could visit them. We were obviously wasting our time.

When I filled out Tementa and Mincaye's visa forms, I was even more convinced of the hopelessness of our cause. Almost all the information they wanted was not applicable to Mincaye and Tementa.

Telephone number: "Not applicable."
Address: "No one delivers mail to us" or maybe "The ninety-first sharp right bend in the river downstream from Toñampade; we're on the bank to your right."
Bank: "Mincaye's only bank is the place he ties his dugout canoe."
Car: "Will 'airplane' work?"
Next of kin to notify: "Although Mincaye has thirteen living children, about forty-some grandchildren, and a handful of great grandchildren, notifying them might be a challenge for the consular staff."

Finally, I got to one blank that I figured I could fill out. The form asked for the applicant's occupation. I wrote "hunter-gatherer" on both of the forms.

I handed in the forms, and we waited and waited as one by one those who were ahead of us were called up to the thick interview windows—and rejected. I was about to suggest we leave when I heard one of the consular officials say to a colleague, "Hey, get a load of this. 'Occupation: hunter-gatherer,'" and they laughed. I figured this was our chance. I motioned for Tementa and Mincaye to follow and walked up to the window where the officer had made the "hunter-gatherer" comment.

When I asked if he had called for us, he looked at my number and told me to go wait our turn. But the consul himself was in the room and had heard the comment about Mincaye and Tementa's occupation. He took the form from the junior officer and told him he would conduct our interview himself.

He asked me if I was the one who had filled out the form. "Yes, sir." He asked if I knew these men. "Yes, sir, all my life."

Then he began to tell me about himself. He had been in Ecuador years before in the Peace Corps. He told me he had read a book about a man who was killed with four friends by an indigenous tribe in the Ecuadorean jungle. He wanted to know if I knew anything about those people.

I told him, "Yes, and one of the men who killed those missionaries is looking at you through this bulletproof glass."

Oops. I had forgotten that I had checked no by the box that asked if Mincaye had a criminal record. But the consul didn't notice. Instead, he asked, "The missionary in the book had your same last name; would you by any chance know who I'm talking about?"

I told him I did. "That must have been *Jungle Pilot*, a biography of my dad's life."

Next, he wanted to know why I would want to take the man who had killed my father to the United States with me. I tried to explain that he had "sort of adopted me," and we were now family and my son was graduating and . . .

He cut me off and told me that he had a meeting to attend. "If you'll come back this afternoon at three o'clock when the consulate closes," he offered, "I'll give you a one-time visa for these two men, on the condition that you travel with them. But I see only one passport here. Where is the other one?"

I told him I would try to bring it that afternoon. I now had the most difficult and unlikely piece of the impossible puzzle. All I needed now were a passport, ID pictures, military papers, an exoneration from voting, and a reinstatement of Mincaye's full citizenship rights.

I had started at the most difficult hurdle so I would get turned down quickly and could give up. Instead, I was now under pressure to get about two years' worth of red tape pushed out of the way in five hours. The various offices we had to visit were scattered all over the city, and the word *expedite* has no equivalent in Spanish. If you want to talk of love, Spanish is wonderful. If you want to be precise and fast, Spanish is the wrong language.

I decided to go for the next most unlikely piece of the puzzle: Mincaye's military papers. At that office, the line was backed all the way down a long corridor that started deep in the bowels of the ancient building. Our place in line was right in the doorway that led into the building from the street.

All Ecuadorean males are required to do a year or two of military service. The only way out is to make a petition to be excused. To be exempted, one would have to have a good reason and pay a fee, which is supposedly used to compensate someone else to serve for you. In a society that loves bureaucracy and a system that expects gratuities to move the lumbering wheels of government at every level, getting out of military service has no fast track.

I was just trying to figure out what to do when a gruff little man with a uniform covered in gold braid with prominent epaulets on the shoulders pushed past us as if we were little more than obstacles to be shoved out of his way. He then turned toward Mincaye.

"Why do you have those big holes in your ears?" he asked belligerently in Spanish. "They make you look like an 'Auca' or something."

Mincaye gave the little guy his usual disarming smile. He had no idea what the officer had said. I answered for him. "He has earplug holes because, well, he is an 'Auca.'" I did not want to take time to explain that the term he had called Mincaye was demeaning. It no longer applied to Mincaye, and considerate people no longer use it.

"Why is he here?" he asked.

"Because he has been offered a visa to visit *los Estados Unidos* and needs his military papers to get a passport," I replied.

"Come with me," the little general commanded. He announced, "An 'Auca' is going to visit the United States," to everyone in the large room and led the way to the front of the long line.

When we got to the harried secretary who was processing everyone's requests and directing them to the various officials who could process them, the general told her, "I have a meeting for one hour. When I come back here at the end of that hour, I want this man to have his military papers. I will sign them personally."

The young woman looked terrified. I knew that if she failed to carry out the officer's demand, he would lose face in front of this room full of people. He would lose face, and she would probably lose her job. She begged me to help her fill out forms while Mincaye just watched us scurrying around. It is not easy to fill out documents for Mincaye. For example, no one knows when he was born or where. He has only one name, but Ecuadoreans always have one or two or more given names, plus their mother's last name and their father's last name. Mincaye's mother and father didn't have last names.

But one hour later, Mincaye had everything he needed. They had exempted him on the basis that he was too old to walk. I tried not to laugh. I would have put him up against anyone in the room, no matter their age—other jungle natives excluded.

It was now one o'clock. All we needed was a voter exoneration; some pictures; fingerprints; and one tiny red passport, filled out, stamped, signed, and sealed.

A few minutes before three o'clock, after we had witnessed two or three more miracles, a final official was waiting for Mincaye to sign his name. I had taught him how to hold a pen, which he had been diligently practicing. I had invented a signature for him that required him to make only six little vertical lines side by side. He was supposed to then connect the first three lines with top arches and the bottoms of the last three with similar arches. This crudely formed the letters *M* and *W*. To make the signature official looking, I tried to teach him to make a bold circle around the two initials with a slash down and across them.

Mincaye grabbed the pen so determinedly I thought he would break it. He was concentrating so hard, trying to remember how to sign, that he broke out in a sweat. He just froze. He couldn't do it.

Something had to be done. Finally, I carefully reached around him and put my hand over his. I began to make the six lines, and Mincaye relaxed. As I made Mincaye's official signature on his passport, I hoped the passport official would not object. While I used Mincaye's hand to sign his passport, Mincaye just looked at the official and smiled.

By two minutes to three, we were back on the street hailing a taxi. We still had to get back across town to the Embassy. I hoped the consul wasn't going to give up on us for being ten or fifteen minutes late. He didn't.

/\/\·/\·/\·/\·/\·/\/\

Mincaye and Tementa sat proudly in the stands while we watched Jesse receive his diploma. Mincaye wanted to sit with Jesse and the graduates, but after some explanation, he agreed to sit with the rest of us.

It had been an incredible adventure taking my family to live with the Waodani in the Amazon. Now we began that adventure in reverse.

Tementa had been to the capital city of Quito a number of times. By Waodani standards, he was fairly streetwise. He knew what money was, and he felt comfortable wearing a full set of outsiders' clothes. Mincaye was a different story.

When I returned with Mincaye and Tementa for Jesse's graduation, I knew I needed to prepare Mincaye for the high-tech world, just as I'd had to get my family ready for the Amazon.

Jesse had taught Mincaye a few words of English during our time there. Every time I would try to explain something about the foreigners' world to Mincaye, he would just pat me on the back or put his arm around me reassuringly and say, "Oooo kaay." And he would give me a huge, encouraging smile.

He had also learned the thumbs-up sign, which he began to use on me all the time. I knew he was totally unconcerned. He had taken care of me and taught me how to survive in his *omae*. Now I would make sure he survived in my other *omae*.

The comedy began as soon as we began to board the airplane in Quito. Mincaye had been in plenty of bush planes. But the largest one probably never held more than ten people. The American Airlines 757 was gargantuan by comparison. As we climbed the stairs to the giant *ebo*, Mincaye was ahead of me and Tementa behind. That was a mistake. The passengers ahead slowly moved into the plane to find their seats. Mincaye got to the turn by the front galley and had to stop. I was thinking about other things while I waited. It seemed to be taking an awfully long time for the line to start moving again.

Finally, I leaned over Mincaye and looked down the aisle to see what the holdup was. There wasn't any. Everyone in front of Mincaye had already sat down. I was embarrassed that we were holding up all of the passengers behind us. I said, "Mincaye, gocaimba"—*Let's go.* He just stood there with a huge smile on his face. "Look, Babae," he said, "these foreigners see me very well."

Sure enough, the passengers who were already in their seats were looking at this stranger with his feather headdress and big plugs in his ears. They could not help but emulate his infectious smile. I encouraged Mincaye to move ahead. I was glad he didn't feel a need to greet all these new friends. No doubt, he thought they had all been waiting for him. After all, they were all expectantly sitting there, facing right at him.

When they started serving breakfast, Mincaye smelled the food. He asked, "Babae, is there a cooking house on this big *ebo*?" I decided to show him. Eating is important in all cultures. To the Waodani, it is central to all other activities.

I was sure that Mincaye would be fascinated with the galley. Instead, he acted nervous. He kept looking over his shoulder as though something was bothering him. Finally he asked me, "Babae, where are these foreigners going?" I told him, "We are all going to the Miami place."

"No, not those foreigners." He lifted his chin to indicate the passengers who were sitting down with their backs to us. "The *cowodi* who just went outside." He was leaning over a passenger to see out the window.

I did not know what he was talking about, but I assured him that no one could leave while we were thirty thousand feet over the Caribbean Sea. "Yes," he countered, "seeing them myself, two foreigners just went through those doors." He pointed to the two bathroom doors.

When I showed him what was behind the doors, he forgot all about the passengers he was sure had just plummeted to their watery graves. "Babae," he exclaimed, "this *ebo* has a 'going place'!" He crossed his legs and squatted slightly in the internationally understood sign language for having to "go." He pronounced, "Babae, every time I ride with you in Bravo Tango Sierra, I always have to pass water very bad. Why don't you put a going place in our *ebo*?"

When the in-flight entertainment began, they showed *101 Dalmatians.* Mincaye was confused at first. Then he got excited and started looking up and down the aisles and under the seats. He saw all those beautiful hunting dogs, and he wanted one. His antics finally caught the attention of the flight attendant. She figured out pretty quickly that she wasn't going to be able to carry on a conversation with Mincaye. He was much too agitated to talk to her. He was trying to find out where all those dalmatian puppies were. His best hunting dog had just been killed by a wild pig, and he wanted a replacement.

She asked me if I knew Mincaye. I was tempted to say no, just to see what she would do. But then she told me that she was going to have to sedate him or restrain him if he didn't settle down. I started to explain that he was looking for the puppies, but I thought better of that and just told Mincaye that she was a very angry woman and we'd better not try to get a dog on her plane.

Going through immigration, picking up our suitcases, passing through customs, and making our way through the crush of people in the Miami airport, Tementa just watched what I was doing and followed suit. Mincaye was a different story. He was like a seventy-year-old kid in a candy store. Everything was fascinating and new. He wanted to inspect all the new things and even examine some of the people. He especially seemed to be fascinated with heavyset people. That fascination would prove to be long lasting.

I had rented a car for the drive from Miami to Ocala. I led the way through the Miami terminal and out to the rental car shuttle. I heaved a sigh of relief when we got in the little bus and I could relax. But Mincaye did not sit down with Tementa and me. He just stared at our driver, getting closer and closer, until I could see that the driver was getting nervous. Mincaye was dressed in fairly normal clothes, though he did not look at home in them, but he still had on his headdress and earplugs.

I was just about to say something to Mincaye when he let out a big sigh and said, "Babae, I see this foreigner very well." I told the driver that Mincaye was from out of town and had just told me that he liked him. Mincaye just kept staring at the poor man. He was shaking his head back and forth, one of the ways he shows he is building up to something. "I see this foreigner very well," Mincaye repeated. "Waiting for us for one moon, maybe he has not even eaten."

I realized why Mincaye was impressed. I had been down in the jungle for almost a month. Obviously Mincaye figured this driver was a friend of mine. Mincaye reasoned that he could not have known precisely when we would arrive, so he must have been waiting for us the entire month. That, Mincaye thought, took real loyalty.

When we got to our rental car, Mincaye decided he liked the red one better than the white one we had been assigned. Tementa said teasingly,

"Mincaye will drive the red one, and Babae will drive the white one." Mincaye immediately changed his mind and decided he liked white even better than red.

As we left the Miami airport, we got on a huge expressway. Mincaye was quiet for a while and then asked a question that gave me a look deep into the soul of this man I had come to love so much. He asked very softly, with deep emotion and a sense of urgency, "Babae, is this *Itota's weca?*"—*Is this Jesus' place?* I wondered what he was getting at.

I thought back to something I had read in Aunt Rachel's journal. Shortly after she, Dayumae, Aunt Betty, and Valerie had gone to live with the Waodani, Dayumae told her Mincaye was threatening to spear her. Then one night Aunt Rachel heard someone prowling around in the dark outside the little thatched hut Kimo had built for her.

The Waodani had wanted an unrestricted view of this strange foreigner with white skin and long, light brown hair. So Kimo built her a thatched roof on tall poles with no thatch or split bamboo for walls. She was completely exposed for everyone to see.

Aunt Rachel was not scared, but she wanted to know who was prowling around her little shelter. She called, "Acano-imi?"—*Who are you?* Mincaye answered from the dark that he was just going to urinate. A few minutes later, he came and squatted by her hammock next to the little fire.

He asked Aunt Rachel if it was true that *Waengongi* was strong enough to clean anyone's heart. Aunt Rachel confirmed that *Waengongi*'s carvings said He could. Then he asked if even his heart could be made clean from hate and fear. Aunt Rachel confirmed it. Then he got up and left. The next morning he returned and announced that she had been right. "Talking to *Waengongi* and asking him," Mincaye said, "He has cleaned my heart." The incredible transformation had begun.

I knew Mincaye really wanted everyone else to walk the "good trail" that finally led to *Waengongi*'s place when we died here on the dirt. He thought foreigners from the *Estados Unidos* never hated or killed anyone. But he was about to realize that foreigners need to learn to walk *Waengongi*'s trail, just as Waodani do.

I desperately wanted to tell Mincaye what he wanted to hear: that all the foreigners followed God's trail. But I had to tell him the truth. It was the same here as it was among the Waodani. Some people had heard that

Waengongi cared about them and had marked His trail for them. Others still had not heard or understood. Some of those who did understand decided to walk the Creator's trail; others chose to follow their own trail.

Mincaye had been through the Miami airport, where a nice man had been faithfully waiting for us for a month. Now we were in the middle of six lanes of traffic all moving in an orderly way toward a common destination. I realized that Mincaye thought this must be the kind of place *Waengongi* would have sent His Son to be born. He was hoping that this was the Holy Land.

I was overcome with emotion. Mincaye, an old Amazon warrior who had once killed his enemies, was now a kind and gentle man. He loved me and my family. And I loved him genuinely and deeply. I couldn't wait to deliver him—and Tementa—to my family.

∧∧∧∧∧∧∧

Every time someone came to our house for a visit or we watched a video or went out to do something, Mincaye and Tementa's presence made it an adventure. I couldn't possibly recount all our experiences, but I can't help telling a few of them.

The afternoon we arrived in Ocala, Ginny asked me if I would run to the grocery store to pick up some things for supper. Some of the people who had gone to the jungle on our first "Wao Tour" wanted to come over and visit Tementa and Mincaye.

I took Mincaye to the store with me. Halfway through the fruits and vegetables, Mincaye stopped, his mouth gaping as he marveled at the piles of food on display. "Whose is all this food?" he asked. I said it was for everyone. He could not believe it. He must have thought he had died and gone to heaven.

A woman saw Mincaye marveling at and touching all the food. I was watching him too, so she sidled up to me and confided, "I don't suppose he's from around here."

"No," I confirmed. "He is from the Amazon jungle." She thought for a moment and concluded, "I'll bet he doesn't even speak English."

I confirmed this conclusion too.

Just then Mincaye saw me talking to the woman. He looked right at her and said, "Hi," and gave her the thumbs-up sign. She looked at me as if I had lied to her, and took off.

Mincaye insisted that we walk up and down each aisle. He wanted to know what was in each box and can and package. He kept putting things in our shopping cart. He wanted to please Ongingcamo by taking lots of food back to her. As he filled the cart, I quietly put most of the things back onto other shelves. I'm sure we made a lot of work for someone who had to put all those things back in their proper places.

Mincaye was especially impressed with the bakery and the meat section. I told him what each package contained: cow *bang*, pig *bang*, chicken *bang*, fish *bang*. He really wanted to take some live lobsters home with us so we could play with them and then eat them. I told him they were not good—not good for the pocketbook, at least.

At the checkout counter, Mincaye watched everything the young lady behind the counter did. Then he insisted on carrying the big bags full of food out to the car. He hefted them onto his shoulders as we do in the jungle, and off we went.

Ginny had sent me to the store for potato chips, dip, and a loaf of bread. I came home with over a hundred dollars' worth of groceries. I just could not say no to Mincaye when he so badly wanted to take the food to Ginny.

Later, when we got back to the jungle, Mincaye told the people all about the foreigners' big food houses. "Now I know why the foreigners are all so big and fat. They don't walk, and they don't make gardens or hunt." His wife, Ompodae, exhaled explosively. She wasn't going to buy that. How did the people get around? How did they get food? Mincaye had his opening. He was going to milk his incredible revelations for all they were worth.

"It is true that the foreigners don't walk. They go everywhere in their *autodi*. Even when they go by trail, they don't move their legs. They just get on the trail, and the trail moves." He was obviously thinking of the moving sidewalks we had seen at the airport. The People were having a difficult time believing what Mincaye was telling them, but Tementa had been there too, so it must be true.

Mincaye went on to explain the foreigners' food houses. "They are so big that lots of people can live there at the same time. If I ever have to live in the foreigners' place," he told them, "that is the house I want to live in."

He told them that no one brings food into the food house. He had watched carefully, and everyone was taking food out. A couple of people might have had their doubts, but they all knew that *cowodi* could make heavy airplanes fly. They could talk over long distances through little boxes, and they could show people in another little box so we could watch them at night. In comparison to that, how hard could it be to make an inexhaustible supply of food appear in a food house?

He went on to say that anyone could take as much food as he wanted. He explained that they even gave us little cars with wheels so we could take a lot.

"The only thing you have to do," he explained, "is when you are leaving, you have to go by the place where the young foreigner girls stand. They look at you very seriously. But if you just stand there and smile, when they smile back, you can take all your food and go eat it happily."

I felt I should explain. I knew what was going to come next. They were going to ask me to build them a Winn-Dixie or a Publix so they could all grow fat too. I wanted to explain that you had to pay for the food. But most of Mincaye's audience were older people who really didn't have a good understanding of money. I pulled out a credit card and said, "Only giving the young foreigner something like this, can you take the food and go."

No Waodani knew what a credit card was, but at least they would realize that something special had to happen before you could take food from the food house.

Mincaye just waved his hand as though what I had told them was of no consequence. "Don't worry," he explained. "They just give that thing right back to you, and then you can go and eat all your food!"

Ompodae wasn't ready to accept all that Mincaye was telling them. She tried to catch him. "You said you and Babae went all over the *cowodi omae* in an *autodi*. How did you get food when you weren't near the food house?"

Mincaye laughed and then began to explain. He was enjoying telling of his adventures in the foreigners' place. "Babae has friends everywhere," he explained. "Whenever we are away from the big, big food house and my stomach hurts, telling Babae, he just stops at one of his friend's houses. They open the little windows in their walls and hand us food. Those people really like Babae, just like we do."

/\/\·/\·/\/\·/\/\

In the smorgasbord of new experiences, one event really sobered Mincaye and Tementa.

They loved to watch videos. When we watched *My Fair Lady*, Mincaye started mimicking the old guy who sings "I'm Getting Married in the Morning." The Waodani have no music tradition other than chanting. When they try to sing, the result is usually absolute chaos. They sing with different rhythms, in numerous simultaneous keys, and at different tempos. I had assumed that they just couldn't do the music thing.

When Mincaye started to mimic the musical, we realized that he really has a very nice singing voice. He was especially entertaining as he high stepped around the living room in nothing but his underwear. Dress code was not an issue around our house, but several people who came to our door unexpectedly were sure surprised. Mincaye is quite the dude in nothing but his Skivvies and his matching earplugs.

One night we were watching a World War II documentary. Mincaye and Tementa both watched with fascination. But when Allied planes began dropping bombs over Germany, Mincaye grabbed Ginny and asked for an explanation. He was worried that the things falling off the plane would make it crash.

"No," we explained, "those things are like dynamite. They are dropping them on purpose." Mincaye asked, "But look, they are flying over the living place. People on the dirt might die if they drop those dynamites." We had to explain that that was what the pilots were trying to do.

Mincaye could not believe it. He wondered why they wanted to kill those people. "They are their enemies," we said. He wanted to know how they could see from so far away that those were their enemies. "They aren't looking to see that they are their personal enemies; hating them all, they want to kill everyone."

Mincaye commented, "We used to kill for no reason. But we only killed our own enemies. We let the other people live unless they were foreigners."

At the end of the documentary was footage from a concentration camp. Mincaye was fascinated by fat people. He was horrified to see the walking skeletons coming out of the concentration camps. When we explained that these people had been intentionally starved, Mincaye said. "We lived very badly, our hearts being dark. We killed our enemies, but we would never, not feeding them, make them live."

He and Tementa got up and walked into their bedroom. I didn't know what to say. They had just realized that the fundamental difference between their people and the foreigners who had showed them the good trail was not the Waodani's violent culture. They were discovering that foreigners are violent too—even more so, in their opinion, than their people were. Both the Waodani and the *cowodi* needed to find a good trail to walk in life. They were beginning to realize that the three of us could tell foreigners how we learned to walk *Waengongi*'s very good trail.

22

On the Road

Right after Jesse's graduation, I had several speaking engagements scheduled. Instead of flying there, I decided to drive so I could take Tementa and Mincaye with me. Jesse would fly up and join us in Pennsylvania for the trip back. We were going on a road trip!

One of our first stops was in Waxhaw, North Carolina. A large organization that supports Bible translation missionaries such as Aunt Rachel is located there. A number of pilots and other technical support people from JAARS who lived there had served the Waodani. I had never visited the JAARS center and thought Tementa and Mincaye would like it too. I tried to explain who we were going to see, but they did not understand until we walked by the hangar and saw a Helio Courier sitting there. Tementa and Mincaye both recognized the plane and became excited. They asked who the plane belonged to. These were the people who had flown in supplies and helped them make peaceful contact with their downriver relatives. These planes and those of Mission Aviation Fellowship had flown sick Waodani to the WRMF mission hospital and had delivered medicines.

We met a couple of the JAARS staff members who had been in Ecuador and knew the three of us. While we were visiting, one of the men who was listening in told me that the account of my father's and his friends' deaths had convinced him to commit his life to God by serving others. I asked if he would tell Mincaye and Tementa what he had just told me.

For four decades, Mincaye has been referred to as "one of the 'Auca' warriors who killed the five missionaries." Thousands of people from all over the world have told me that what happened on that Amazon headwater sandbar in 1956 was a turning point in their lives. Tementa's father had lied about my dad and his friends, which led to their being killed. I wanted him to know that what his father had meant for evil had turned out to be a powerful force for good in the lives of many people—many times more people than the number of people in their entire tribe.

I translated while this man told how his life had been marked by the story that encompassed all three of our lives. I could tell that Mincaye and Tementa were moved by what he was telling them. Then he asked if we would speak the next day at their weekly assembly. We agreed.

The same man introduced us the next day. He explained that it was because of what Tementa's father and Mincaye had done that he had spent his career with JAARS. Then he asked if there were any other members of the JAARS staff who were helping people such as the Waodani as a direct result of this story. He asked them to stand.

I translated what he was saying for Mincaye and Tementa. To my amazement, almost half of the entire audience stood to its feet. I know this story has powerfully affected a lot of lives. It certainly has affected mine. But even I was surprised.

I couldn't tell what Mincaye and Tementa were thinking until we were introduced and began to speak. I was going to translate for Tementa first. But he just stood there. His eyes were full of tears. He was so emotional that he could not speak. That was not like him. In fact, in contrast to Mincaye's gregarious and dramatic personality, Tementa is reserved and even seems a bit cool, until he gets to know someone well. We affectionately call him "Ice T."

That morning I saw that what had cost some so much had paid huge dividends in the lives of many people. I thought this was probably the most powerful demonstration I would see of this amazing story that *Waengongi* had made us part of. I was wrong.

/\./\./\./\./\./\./\

On our way from North Carolina to Pennsylvania for our next speaking engagement, we drove through the mountains of West Virginia. Tementa wanted to know what the huge piles of black rocks stacked up near the road were for. I told them it was *dica gungungu*—"rock that burns." This was another of those difficult-to-believe mysteries in the outside world, like "hard water" (ice). I could see that they couldn't quite picture burning rocks, so I stopped and picked up several pieces of hard coal that had fallen off the trucks I had seen hauling it. Back on the road, I was telling them about this amazing stuff when I looked in the rearview mirror and saw a police car following me with its lights flashing. I pulled over and went back to explain to the officer that I was telling my passengers about "burning rock" and had not been paying attention to my speed.

I got the idea the highway patrolman thought I was being smart, so I started to explain that my passengers were from out of state. He cut me off and told me to get my car title and registration. I had to ask Mincaye to get out of the car so I could get the papers.

By the time I found the papers, Mincaye had gone back to meet who he assumed was a friend I had stopped to talk to.

Mincaye was pushing closer and closer to the officer while petting his patrol car and telling him how much he liked all the colored lights that were twirling and flashing on it. The officer had one hand on his gun while he fended Mincaye off with the other. I was thinking, *Oh no, how will I ever explain that Mincaye got shot by a West Virginia highway patrolman?*

The officer seemed as anxious to be rid of us as I was to get out of there so I could explain to Grandfather Mincaye what not to do around people with guns. The officer just gave me a warning and asked me to drive more slowly so my friends would live to make it back to the jungle. He should see how we drive in Ecuador, where most places don't have speed limits or hard-and-fast rules.

/\/\/\/\/\/\/\

As we were preparing to speak at the event in Pennsylvania, Mincaye asked what the people needed to know. I suggested that he just tell them what life was like before and after he started walking *Waengongi*'s trail.

Another guest spoke first. He had just been released by Colombian guerillas after being held by them for months. It was a fascinating but long story.

By the time he got done, it was time for the meeting to be finished. I was hoping that they would just let us give a greeting and sit down. But they wanted us to speak.

I spoke by myself first to set the stage for Tementa to speak. Then Tementa told them how he and other God followers in the tribe did not want to always have to ask for help. He asked them, "Don't *Waengongi*'s markings say that all His followers should tell others how to follow Him?" He told them that he had been chosen to learn to fly and that he and others had learned to fix teeth. He also said that they were teaching their people how to follow *Waengongi*'s trail.

By the time it was Mincaye's turn, it was really getting late. But as soon as he began to speak, none of the people in the audience were looking at their watches. Mincaye explained how he and his people had lived in a constant turmoil of fear and hate. Then he put his arm on my shoulder and explained how my dad and his friends had come to teach them "the good way to live." He explained that when he was a young man, he and his people lived by killing. "We killed the others, and they killed us."

He was not sure that the sea of foreigners in front of him understood what he was saying. I was struggling to take Waodani thoughts and put them into the very different thought patterns of North American English. Tementa was helping me in his rough Spanish once in a while.

Mincaye decided to summarize what he had been telling them. He stated, "We acted badly, badly until they brought us God's markings. Now, seeing those markings and walking *Waengongi*'s trail, we live happily and in peace." Then he put his arm around my neck and pulled my face down by his. "Manenke," he said. That was all he had to say.

Mincaye is an old Amazon warrior. He cannot read nor write. He doesn't even know the concept of celebrity. But after that talk in Pennsylvania, he was destined to become one. An Oklahoman businessman and his wife were in that Pennsylvania meeting. When Mincaye talked about going from hating and killing to a life of peace, that businessman yearned for the same message of reconciliation and transformation to reach his culture. This was just shortly after the massacre at Columbine High School, so North Americans were thinking about violence in our society too.

Mincaye and I ended up visiting Columbine on another speaking tour.

Later, that visit played a pivotal role in Mincaye and other Waodani giving permission to Mart Green, the businessman from Oklahoma City, to make a movie of the story Mincaye, Tementa, and I had told.

Mart asked me to give him permission to make the movie. I told him that I could not speak for the Waodani, but I could introduce him to the Waodani and he could ask them himself. I was sure the request would not go any further. I was wrong. This businessman and a group of friends and associates were passionately determined to tell this story to as many people as they could.

I took them down to the jungle and introduced them to the people who had been part of the Damointado group that had killed Dad, Jim, Ed, Pete, and Roger. I was surprised that busy professionals would take time to meet the Waodani. I was even more pleased with how respectful and warm they were toward these people who had made me part of their lives.

At first, the Waodani said no. A lot of people had been taking pictures and video of them but not telling their story. I had reservations too. But when I explained what had happened at Columbine, the People did an about-face. They said, "That is just how we used to live, killing for no reason." Mincaye added, "If the foreigners need to see how we lived before and how we live now so that they, too, can live in peace, I say yes." The others agreed.

When I cautioned them that they might be shown naked as they used to live, Ompodae just whipped off her blouse and skirt and said, "Then let them show us how we were—living angry and hating and killing, we were just like animals." Mincaye, Dabo, and Kimo had speared Ompodae's brothers and mother and little sister. The people who had wiped out a good part of her family, including Mincaye, who had taken her for a wife, were sitting right there with us. Kimo had killed the family of his wife, Dawa. They had speared Tementa's father. They had speared my dad and uncles.

"Now look at us," Ompodae said, and she smiled. But Mart Green and his wife and the film team were all looking elsewhere. They weren't used to having people rip off their clothes in meetings.

After five long years of work, the feature-length documentary (*Beyond the Gates of Splendor*) was released in 2005, and the movie (*End of the Spear*) was released in early 2006.

/\/\/\/\/\/\/\/\

I had been getting requests to speak before Mincaye, Tementa, Jesse, and I had made our little road trip. But after speaking in Pennsylvania, requests started coming in from all over. Mincaye loved living with us, and we loved having him and Tementa in our home.

Tementa was much more at home with foreigners' technical things than he was with crowds of foreigners. In fact, I showed Tementa how to drive my car, and he could do it by himself—turn signals and all—after just two lessons. Mincaye, on the other hand, had little interest in technology. He was a people person. He loved everyone, and everyone loved him.

Several things that happened on our first two or three speaking tours illustrate this perfectly. When we returned our rental car on Tementa and Mincaye's first visit to the land of Disney World, we saw a colorful parachute rising and falling behind a row of trees. My two buddies were curious, so I drove us over to see what it was.

A couple of young men had come up with the idea of pulling a ski parachute behind their old pickup truck. They were planning to charge for rides. We were just there to watch, but while we were watching, Mincaye became interested in a little boy on a riding mower who was cutting a takeoff pad in the scrubby old pasture we were in. Tementa and I watched the guys figuring out how to work the parachute. Then, out of the corner of my eye, I saw Mincaye walking beside the boy on the mower. Suddenly, I realized what he was doing.

Mincaye saw that in front of the mower the grass was long. Behind it, the grass was nice and short. And no one was sitting on his haunches swinging a machete as they do to cut grass in the jungle. Mincaye was trying to reach under the mower to feel whatever was making the grass short. I took off to lend a hand before Mincaye lost one.

While we were examining the mower, I heard one of the men yell, "Hay'it ee'it!" I turned to see the maiden flight. Oh no! They had Tementa strapped into the chute, and the truck was starting to move. It was too late to save "Ice T," but I was determined to be there when he crashed so I could explain to his wife, Nemonta, what had happened.

I dove into the back of the pickup as it passed me. The "flight manager" was yelling instructions in backcountry English that even I couldn't understand. Tementa wouldn't have a clue. Finally I caught, "Pull the steering lines or you'll hit the truck." I was going to pass it on to Tementa, who was now about seventy feet in the air. But just then the pickup stopped, and I went flying backward against the cab. We had reached the end of the field. Besides that, I didn't know how to say "steering lines" in Wao-Tededo.

Tementa landed about two feet from the trailer hitch on the back of the pickup. He was unfazed. "How did you learn to do like this?" he asked me. I told him, "I don't know how to do this thing." He looked at me as if to say, "Well why did you want me to do it?" I felt bad about it for about five minutes. I would have to be more careful not to allow Tementa and Mincaye to infer things from my actions that could get them into dangerous situations.

I felt bad for only five minutes because, while I was showing Mincaye that the mower had dangerous machetes underneath it, I heard the flight team yell "Hay'it ee'it" again. They had a two-hundred-foot rope on the contraption this time. They were really going high. But they were sticking with their same test pilot. This time, Tementa was on his own.

/\/\/\/\/\/\/\

On another trip, Mincaye, Tementa, and I stopped in Washington, DC. Someone had suggested that we visit the Human Rights Caucus of the U.S. Congress. We were driving right by the capital, so I figured I could at least make a couple of telephone calls. Besides, I wanted Tementa to see the Smithsonian National Air and Space Museum. We would just let Mincaye watch people. He liked that even better than planes and rockets and other machines.

We enjoyed the museum, but we also got two appointments in congressional offices. One was with congressman Frank Wolf's office, from the tenth congressional district in Virginia. He was on recess, but his office manager said she would meet with us.

About halfway through the meeting, as I was explaining some of the problems the Waodani were facing—problems such as being required to vote but not having anyplace in Waodani territory where they could vote—the young lady we were meeting with suddenly put her hand over her mouth. I thought she had forgotten another appointment or something.

"Oh my goodness," she said. "I know who you guys are. You're, like, talking about Jim Elliot and Nate Saint and Ed McCully and those missionaries who were . . ." and she stopped. "Oh my goodness! Wait until Congressman Wolf and my dad find out who I met with!"

A moment ago, she had been professionally distant. Suddenly, she began treating us like family.

Just before we left, Mincaye did his dramatic throat-clearing thing to make sure we knew he had something important to say. He told the office manager, "We have come to see your place. Flying from Nemompade to Shell and riding on the *autodi* to Quito . . ." He wanted to explain all we had gone through to get to see her. "Now," he continued, "I see it well that you should come and see us, in our place."

She looked at me. "Could I?" she asked.

"Sure," I told her. "You have Mincaye's invitation."

But she didn't come. When Congressman Wolf and her father found out about the invitation, they wanted to go instead. So they visited us in the jungle. When word got out that a U.S. congressman was visiting Ecuador, the U.S. ambassador and the Ecuadorean government asked for meetings with him. But Congressman Wolf's office told everyone that they were going to visit the Waodani. We were in charge of the itinerary.

After their visit in the jungle, Congressman Wolf and his office manager's father had me accompany them to Quito, where we met the ambassador, Ecuador's equivalent of secretary of state, and the Ecuadorean president himself.

/\/\·/\·/\·/\·/\·/\/\

Mincaye was a born public relations man. But he didn't like bathrooms. On our first speaking tour, we stayed mostly in people's houses. I had taught him about faucets in Quito. One is for the *yogiti* water, and the other one is for the *ocoya* water that can burn you. Mincaye said they both hurt. But I showed him that if both faucets are turned on, the water comes out *waemo*—"very good." When he went to take a shower in the first house, nothing happened for quite a while. Tementa and I hadn't showered yet either, and we were running out of time, so I went in to check on Mincaye.

Mincaye did not know what to do. This tub had only one faucet, and he did not know if it was the very cold one or the very hot one. I showed him that this particular kind of faucet gave both cold water and hot water. He just had to turn it past the cold water to get to the hot.

At the next house nothing happened, because in that one the faucet had to be pulled out to make the water come. Mincaye was getting almost paranoid. I had told him foreigners always did things the same way, such as driving on the same side of the street and stopping when the light is the color of blood and going when it is the color of leaves.

He was not going to believe my talk about standardization anymore.

Finally, when Mincaye went into the bathroom at one house, I heard the water come on. I was elated. Mincaye was catching on. I was watching the news with our hosts when we heard a terrible banging coming from the bathroom. It sounded like Mincaye was trying to break down the wall. The man of the house looked a little nervous, so I decided to check on Grandfather. I looked in the door, but no one was in the shower—or anywhere else in the bathroom, for that matter.

Then I heard the banging again. Mincaye was lying down, all curled up in a ball, trying to get his body under the tub spout. When I pulled the shower door back, he looked up at me with this helpless look and asked, "Babae, the foreigners all being big and fat, how do they get under this little thing?"

Mincaye's bathroom experience got worse at the Orlando airport. We were in a large men's room with a long row of stalls. Mincaye was afraid to go into one. He was worried that he might open the door and find a foreigner in it. "What if there is a foreigner in there and he gets angry?" he asked. I showed him how to look under the door to make sure no one was there.

He cautiously walked up and down the row all bent over, looking under each door. I should have had a video camera. Finally, he picked a stall and went in. But almost as soon as he went in, I heard the automatic toilet flush, and Mincaye came running out. His eyes were like saucers. He had not seen anyone in there, but someone *was* in there and had flushed the stool.

He said he didn't need to "go" anymore. He just wanted to wash his hands. Tementa and I were talking about something, so I just watched Mincaye. He walked up to one of the sinks and gave it a once-over. No faucets. He looked at the men on either side. They were getting water just fine.

Mincaye watched them more carefully. One of the men was nervously scooting his foot back and forth while he washed. Mincaye watched him, then looked over at me and gave me the thumbs-up sign. But when he rubbed his foot, still no water. Finally, in exasperation, he just held out his hands and presto—water came out!

/\\·/\\·/\\·/\\·/\\·/\\·/\\

One of our least favorite things to deal with has been airport security. I have tried to explain to the security people that I can interpret for Mincaye. One young lady told me she would handle it. She gave me her best "teacher look," as if I were back in third grade. So I went back to wait my turn. She got Mincaye to hold out his arms, fine. It took her a while longer to get him to take off his shoes. He thought she wanted them, but he could see that they were much too big for her. They were much too big for him, too. His feet are so wide from walking barefoot all his life that we had to get shoes about four sizes too big before they were wide enough for his feet.

By the time the frustrated young woman got Mincaye to understand that she wanted him to raise his foot and hold it there, she was ready to just pass him, regardless. She just couldn't get him to turn around. She would point to herself and turn around. Mincaye would just point at her and look at everyone else waiting in line with a big smile. He thought this young foreigner was very clever. The security agent was not smiling, but the growing line was. I guess we had all been treated like cattle long enough. We didn't dare mess with security, but we were enjoying watching Mincaye do it. He was getting away with it too, while all the rest of us were trying not to laugh out loud.

When the young lady finally tried to walk around behind Mincaye, he just turned with her, lifting one foot and then the other. Finally, a supervisor came, and to his surprise, everyone groaned with displeasure when he passed Mincaye and cut our entertainment short.

Another time, I went through the security arch and set off the buzzer. I had checked all my pockets. The guard said he thought it was my military-style belt buckle. I tried to unclip just the buckle, but it wouldn't come off. So I started to pull off my entire belt. A guard behind must have misunderstood what I was doing, because he said with urgency in his voice, "Just the belt, just the belt!" I wondered what he could possibly think I was going to do.

That was when I remembered that Mincaye was behind me. He had come through after me and set off the buzzer too. The guard tried to tell him that it was his buckle. Mincaye didn't understand, so the big guy pointed in the vicinity of Mincaye's buckle. This made Mincaye nervous, so he looked over at me for a clue as to why this stranger was getting so familiar with him.

When he saw me taking off my belt, he thought he understood. By the time I saw what was happening, he had his pants almost to his knees. I whispered, "Caedamai, mamae, caedamai!"—*Don't do it, Grandfather, don't do it!* I was too late. He had already done it.

Everyone behind us was watching this little drama unfold. At first, they just froze when Mincaye started to take off his pants. Then, when he realized that he had goofed, he just turned around, typical Mincaye, and smiled at everyone. They started chuckling and laughing with Mincaye, who by now had let go of his pants. He was having fun laughing with all the foreigners. His pants were headed to the floor.

I tugged his pants up while he just smiled and kept Orlando International Airport at a standstill for a few more seconds.

I actually lost Mincaye at O'Hare Airport in Chicago twice. He was following me when we passed under the huge dinosaur skeleton. When I got to the gate, he wasn't with me. I panicked and started a desperate search for him. Then I remembered the dinosaur skeleton. Sure enough, that is where I found him. I knew I had better start putting my address and cell number in several of his pockets on each trip.

On another trip, Mincaye and I were flying with a friend. He got us upgraded to first class. I sat with the friend so he could fill me in on what was going to happen after we arrived. Mincaye was sitting with another passenger right in front of us. The flight attendant brought each of us a nut cup, which he set on the wide console between the seats. He came back two or three times to Mincaye's row. Finally, when he came back with nut cups for the row in front of us a third time, I looked over at Mincaye's seat to see what was going on.

The attendant handed an extra cup to the businessman but didn't offer one to Mincaye. Then I saw why. Mincaye had four of them on his lap and was busily downing them all. I knew what had happened. When the flight attendant put the original nut cups down between the seats, he looked at Mincaye. Mincaye took that to mean they were for him, so he had taken both. When the attendant brought two more back so as not to embarrass Mincaye, he just smiled and took both of them, too. Finally, the attendant just handed one to the businessman next to Mincaye. That was the way we would have done it in the jungle. Mincaye must have just figured that the flight attendant liked him best.

Then the same attendant started passing out drinks. Again, he kept going back to Mincaye. I finally paid attention and heard Mincaye saying with great earnestness, "Idaewa, idaewa"—*It is enough, it is enough.* I told the flight attendant what Mincaye was saying, and he replied, "I should hope so; he is on his fifth can of Coke."

Poor Mincaye was about to explode after eating four nut cups and drinking five cans of Coke. Mincaye did not want the attendant to feel bad, so the more he brought, the more Mincaye tried to drink. Mincaye had probably been trying to get him to stop for the last several cans. But as long as he was drinking them, the nice man kept bringing them.

23

Now I See It Well

In the summer of 2000, Mincaye and Tementa and I were invited to speak at a conference for Christian evangelists from all over the world. Amsterdam seemed like a long way to go, but the conference was being hosted by the Billy Graham Evangelistic Association. I had first met Dr. Graham at a crusade in Quito when I was a boy. I had grown up respecting men such as Kimo, Dyuwi, Mincaye, Toñae, and Tementa. I looked forward to meeting people such as these men from all over the world. I was also eager to do anything I could to encourage men and women who were giving their lives to offer spiritual hope to hurting people in their own parts of the world.

I also thought it would be a great opportunity for Tementa and Mincaye to see that the three of us are just a tiny speck in the big picture of incredible things *Waengongi* is doing all over the world.

I told Mincaye and Tementa that I saw it well to go, and they both said, "Ough"—*Yes*.

Before we left for Amsterdam, we were looking forward to a special family event. Stephenie was coming home after a long year of traveling with a Youth for Christ music group. They had toured in the United States and India. Finally, Steph's last stint was to help lead a group of high schoolers to Trinidad. She flew from there to Minneapolis to deliver her group before finally coming home to us.

Stephenie was tall, with long blonde hair and her mother's dark eyebrows.

She was beautiful to look at but even more fun to have around. She was intense, uncompromising, and unyielding on matters of principle. I had missed her terribly while she was away.

Steph was special for many reasons. First, she was our only daughter. In fact, she was the only Saint granddaughter in our family. My sister, Kathy, has two boys; my brother, Phil, has three boys; and Ginny and I had three boys and then, finally, Stephenie.

When she was small, I asked her to promise me she would never grow up. She promised, but I couldn't hold her to it. Ginny and I loved every stage she went through. Every one, except perhaps her leaving home to go to college, where she studied piano performance. Even then, she came home every weekend and often on Wednesdays. That was pretty nice, except that we missed her on Mondays and Tuesdays and Thursdays and Fridays. We had always been a close family. Ginny was our glue, and Steph was our spark. Shaun, Jaime, Jesse, and I added the fuel.

When Steph was asked to put college on hold to travel with the YFC group, I tried to talk her out of it. I wasn't ready for her to leave. I wasn't scared; she was a smart girl and had a lot of experience handling tough situations. She had lived in Africa and North America and the Andes Mountains and the Amazon. She was young, but she had broad experiences in living and plenty of travel savvy.

The bottom line was that I just wasn't ready for our little girl to leave home. I told Steph that there would be other adventures. She said she wasn't considering it for the adventure. Finally, I told her that it just didn't make much sense for her to pay thousands of dollars to work her tail off living out of a suitcase on the road. I tested her resolve by suggesting that I did not think they would really have a major impact on many people.

Steph came back by asking me, "If I take a year of my life and if it only benefits one person in a significant way, isn't that enough?"

I said no, but I knew she had me.

Just before my dad went to make friendly contact with the Waodani, he had written an open letter to friends. He knew that there was a chance he would be killed. And he knew that people would question the wisdom of his going.

In that letter, written only twenty-one days before he died, Dad wrote about risk and return in life. He wrote, "As we weigh the future and seek the will of God, does it seem right that we should hazard our lives for just a few savages?"

He wasn't just risking his life; we would all be in a vulnerable position. If something happened to Dad, what would become of me—of us?

A little further into the letter he wrote, "As we have a high old time this Christmas, may we who know Christ hear the cry of the damned as they hurtle headlong into the Christless night without ever a chance."

Then Dad wrote, "Would that we could comprehend the lot of these Stone Age people who live in mortal fear of ambush on the jungle trail . . . those to whom the bark of a gun means sudden, mysterious death . . . those who think all men in all the world are killers like themselves. If God would grant us the vision, the word 'sacrifice' would disappear from our lips and thoughts; we would hate the things that seem now so dear to us; our lives would suddenly be too short; we would despise time-robbing distractions and charge the enemy with all our energies in the name of Christ. May God help us to judge ourselves by the eternities that separate the Aucas from a comprehension of Christmas, and Him, Who though He was rich, yet for our sakes became poor so that we might, through His poverty, be made rich."

On Christmas night Dad wrote his last letter to all my grandparents. In it he wrote, "It has been a wonderful Christmas for us here. . . . Rachel had retired early. . . . Marj and I sat on the daybed in the living room watching the lights on the Christmas tree and reflecting on the goodness of the Lord. It wasn't long until Kathy and Stevie were curled up with their heads on our laps. They looked so good to us in that softly colored light. They were soon fast asleep, as was Philip, already in bed."

If Dad had risked his life and Mincaye was the only reward, I wondered, would that have been enough? Yes, if I believe in eternity, it would be. The way things were now, in eternity I get Dad back and still get to live with Grandfather Mincaye and good old Kimo and sweet Dyuwi and Epa and Ompodae and Tementa and old Dabo and Wiba and Toñae. . . .

Was it worth it to give up my only little girl for a whole year just to give someone I didn't know the chance I had been given to walk God's trail? Not if this life is all there is. But I had to grudgingly admit that I do believe this life is only the opening exercise to the next life that will last forever. And yes, with that in mind, it would be worth Steph's leaving, even if only one person decided to follow God's trail as a result.

/\./\./\./\./\./\./\./\

But all that was in the past. The day had finally arrived for Stephenie to come home to us. We had two new granddaughters, whom Steph was desperate to get to know and love on, and one more on the way. The price was paid, and life was going to be complete again in a just a few hours.

Mincaye was just as excited as we were. We started making preparations for meeting Steph at the airport and planned a small but happy welcome-home party to celebrate her long-anticipated return to us.

I decided to make some "welcome home" signs. I knew Stephie would act outraged if I called attention to her in public, but I also knew she would secretly be pleased. She had been e-mailing us almost every day while she was traveling. Well, at least she was e-mailing Ginny almost every day. Ginny and Steph were not only mother and daughter; they were best friends.

Stephenie was intense like me; Ginny was calm. Steph and I were always analyzing things. We set goals and then drove toward them with determination. Ginny picked out the crucial things in life without really analyzing them; she just instinctively knew who was genuine and what was important. She did not have great ambition to accomplish things. Family was central to her world. No doubt that is why Stephenie and I both found it so impossible not to adore her. She was our fan club, our cheering squad. While we set out to accomplish objectives, Ginny loved us unconditionally. She loved us whether we were getting As or Cs in life.

As a family, we had been having a lot of comings and goings. We were used to being apart and then picking up where we left off with little hoopla. But this was our only daughter, the boys' only sister, and Grandfather Mincaye's only blonde granddaughter, and she was coming home after a desperately long separation. Our level of anticipation was so high it could almost be bottled.

Every time a big plane taxied by us on the apron outside, Mincaye would grab me and say, "Nemo pompa"—*Star is coming.* I kept telling him, "Waca"—*Another one.*

And then, suddenly, it was there: Steph's plane was pulling up to the gate. My grandmother used to say, "The watched pot doesn't boil." Yes, and it seemed like the watched Jetway would never get into position to let our much-missed and finally-returning little girl get off that big *ebo*.

I gave Mincaye a little jab and told him, "She comes." He grabbed his sign and started waving it over his head. He was too short to have any chance of seeing over all the foreigners who were surrounding us.

Finally, he started jumping up and down with the sign. He did not want Star to miss us. Other people were watching Mincaye too. It is not every day that you see someone at the airport with a feather headdress, a pig-tooth necklace, and earplugs, jumping up and down and holding a big sign—an upside-down sign, no less.

I saw the look on Stephenie's face when she saw us. She put her hand over her eyes and bowed her head in mock shame. Having Tementa and Grandfather Mincaye with us was a total surprise. Stephenie must have figured out that it was Mincaye with the sign. Who else would be willing to make such a spectacle of himself, and who else would hold a sign upside down?

She pretended she didn't see us and started to walk right past us. Mincaye caught sight of her through the sea of people and darted between and around people like a dog going for a bone. I could follow his progress by what seemed like a shock wave going through the crowd as he pushed his way to Steph.

He reached her and grabbed her and started jumping up and down again.

I realized I was not the only one watching Mincaye. When the waiting crowd saw the old warrior grab the beautiful, tall blonde, I could see big smiles spreading through the crowd around us. They could not have guessed what made the little man in the strange outfit and the stately young woman in the jeans and black leather jacket so special to each other, but they were pleased that they were.

Everyone else went to the car while I waited with my big little girl for her luggage. We were just standing there when a girl about ten years old walked up, pointing at Steph and yelling excitedly, "Here she is, Mommy. Look, I found her." A woman came up to us and said, "Thank you, young lady," then quickly left with the girl.

Steph's face immediately turned dark and brooding. "Pop, it isn't right that parents make kids miserable just because they can't get along." I could see that my little girl was seething inside. She recounted what had happened on the plane, the words spilling out of her in a rush of emotion.

It turned out that Stephenie and the little girl had been seated together. The girl was put on the plane by her father and stepmother, who didn't like her, she said. She was returning to live with her mother and her boyfriend, whom the girl was afraid of. Suddenly, without warning, Stephenie threw her arms around me and began to cry. "Thank you, Poppa, that I always know you and Mom love each other and that you love me, even when you are dorky." She had slid one hand down my back and gave me a big pinch when she said "dorky."

My exciting, excitable, wonderful daughter was really home!

When we stopped to pick up Jesse and Jenni's car just south of Ocala, Steph asked if she could drive the rest of the way home. She hadn't driven for a long time. I thought about suggesting that we drive by the airport so I could take her for a quick ride in the Waodani's new powered parachute. Steph really liked to fly, and I had anticipated her excitement when she experienced the thrill of shooting into the sky under a piece of paper-thin cloth, with only a couple of tubes and a seat between us and the earth below. But I figured the timing wasn't good to take Steph flying.

Everyone wanted to catch up on a year of separation in the shortest time possible. I knew Ginny, especially, would want time with Steph right away. So we decided to save the flying for another day. When we got home, Steph grabbed Jesse Joy, one of the two new nieces who had just been added to our family. Our little Joy was the first representative of the next generation. When Stephenie saw our tiny baby, she announced determinedly that we had had our turn with Jesse Joy for a month. It was now her turn to hold the baby. And she let us know she was not planning to share for quite some time.

Steph actually felt slighted that we had not arranged for the babies to be born after she got back. The important thing to us was that she finally, unbelievably, was back.

During the welcome-home party, the house was crowded. We had not officially invited anyone outside the family to join us, but besides Ginny and myself, there was Tementa; Mincaye; Jesse and his wife, Jenni; their baby, Jesse Joy; and Jaime and his wife, Jessica, who was due to have our third grandbaby in a few months. There were also a number of family friends who kept stopping by to welcome Stephenie Rachel home. The only time I got to be alone with Stephenie was a chance meeting we had in the hallway in our house. Steph stopped me, put her arms around my neck, and put her head on my shoulder. In only four words, she let me know that she reciprocated all the feelings that were threatening to blow my heart apart with thankfulness and joy at finally having my little girl home.

"Pop, I love you!" I knew I needed to remember that moment. Life would never be more complete, I figured, than it was right then.

Before we parted in the hallway, Steph told me she had a headache. That gave me a few more precious minutes to have her to myself as I rummaged through my jungle medicine kit to find some pain pills.

A few minutes later, Ginny grabbed me conspiratorially and told me Steph was back in her room. She wanted to know if I wanted to go back with her. She said Steph's head was really hurting and Steph wanted me to pray for her. I could tell Ginny also wanted to have some alone time with just the three of us.

/\/\/\/\/\/\/\/\/\/\

When we got to her bedroom, Stephenie told us that her head was pounding. I decided the lecture about bodies needing sleep, even at twenty years of age could wait. Instead, Ginny sat on the bed and pulled our much taller daughter onto her lap. I sat next to these two precious girls of mine and wrapped my arms around them. I began to pray that God—*Waengongi*—the Creator of the universe who was busy solving millions of major crises around the world, would add my little girl's headache to his concerns and take away her pain.

I was still praying when Stephenie's body tensed and she let out a little yelp of pain. I opened my eyes just in time to see her eyes roll back into her head.

Everything seemed to go into slow motion then. Ginny laid Stephenie on the bed while I pulled out my cell phone and dialed 9-1-1. An ambulance was at our house before we could even tell anyone else what was happening. Besides, what would we have told them? Steph was tired and maybe dehydrated from being in the hot summer sun in Trinidad. We were used to taking care of our own medical needs. I had just called for help because I did not want to take any chances.

I rushed down the hall and met the paramedics at the front door. When they got to Steph's room, they lifted her onto the wheeled gurney and started for the door. Steph was unresponsive. Her head was limply bouncing on the gurney, so I held it as best I could, following the three paramedics out the front door and into the ambulance waiting in our driveway, its lights reflecting off our trees and house and cars.

There was no time to plan, but I was not about to let three strangers take off with my daughter without me. I jumped into the ambulance too.

We arrived at the hospital emergency room in no time. It had only been a few minutes since Ginny and I had been sitting there holding our precious girl in our arms. I could not imagine what was happening. I just kept waiting for Steph to sit up, shake her head, and accuse me of trying to embarrass her twice in one afternoon.

Then Jesse, Ginny, and Mincaye showed up. They had followed the ambulance in our car. They saw me standing next to Steph, who was stretched out on an emergency room rolling bed. She looked just like she did when they took her out of our house—like she was sleeping, except that she had an IV tube in her arm and a breathing tube to keep her airway open.

Ginny and Jesse wanted to do something to help, but we all knew that the emergency personnel were doing much more than we could for Stephenie. So we just stood out of the way with that terrible, helpless feeling common to everyone who has had a loved one in the hospital.

Mincaye's reaction was different. As soon as he saw Nemo unconscious, with tubes and wires connecting her to strange boxes while total strangers did even stranger things to her, he grabbed me and pulled my face to him with his hand behind my neck. He had a horrible look on his face that I had seen only a few times in my life—and up to this point only in the jungle.

"Babae, who is doing this thing?" His eyes darted around the busy emergency area of the large hospital, trying to make sense of what was happening. I was too slow in responding. He repeated the question with even more intensity. The look on his face was beginning to frighten me. His hand on my shoulder and neck was squeezing so tightly that it was starting to hurt.

I realized that Mincaye must have been extremely confused. Right in the middle of the party, he had seen a strange vehicle with lights on it drive up to our house. This had never happened before while he was visiting us. Strange people burst into our house and ran out with Steph, and now they were sticking her with needles and tubes. These people were doing something terrible to Grandfather Mincaye's girl, and he wanted to defend her.

Mincaye had killed who knows how many people with his own hands. I realized he was ready to do it again to protect my daughter, whom he desperately loved. He knew I did not know how to kill, so he needed me to tell him who was hurting Steph. Maybe he thought someone had sent evil spirits to do this. It was clear he was ready to defend her.

When I realized what was going on in his mind, I wanted to explain. But I didn't know what was happening either. All I knew was that I had been asking God to take away my little girl's headache and now they had her intubated and were scurrying around, getting her ready for a CAT scan.

"Waa, ininamai," I told Mincaye—*I don't know.* "No one is doing this." That was all I could think to tell him.

Ginny's sweet mother had arrived. She reassured us, saying she was certain Stephenie would be okay. But I felt this huge, dark storm beginning to envelop me. I wanted to pull the tubes and needles out and run away to a quiet place and hold my precious daughter until she was all better.

Everything seemed to be happening in slow motion as my mind raced at an adrenaline-induced warp speed. My heart was no longer bursting with joy as it had been a half hour ago. Now it was beginning to shatter and crumble. I had a terrible, growing feeling that I would never hear my daughter tell me she loved me again or have her lay her head on my shoulder. What could ever take the place of that?

Ginny looked at me with pleading eyes. I didn't know what to say or do. When she needed me most, I was helpless, confused, and paralyzed by my own fear. I needed to comfort poor Ginny. Whatever I was feeling had to be only a part of the agony she was experiencing.

As my mind was attempting to process the blur of activity around me, I saw the look of fury leave Mincaye's face. It was replaced by a totally contrasting look of peace and confidence. He was focused totally on me now.

"Babae," he said with a big smile, "now I see this well. Don't you see, *Waengongi* is doing this Himself, taking Star to live in *Oneidi* with Him." He pumped his head up and down to emphasize what he was telling me.

Mincaye was making no sense. A loving God would not do this to us. He owed us. When He had asked us to give up our lives and live in the jungle, we did. Now all I was asking was to have Stephenie back.

Grandfather held me with one hand and started reaching out to members of the emergency room staff who were scurrying past us. Ours was not the only drama unfolding in their little world of unexpected hurts. Mincaye had forgotten that they could not understand him.

"People, people," he was saying, "don't you see what is happening? *Waengongi*, loving Nemo, He is taking her to live with Him now. Being an old man, I will go live there too, very soon. If you will only walk *Waengongi*'s trail, then you dying, you will come to His place, and Stephenie and I will be there waiting. Happily, we will greet you."

As the black cloud of despair shrouded me, I could feel my faith slipping away. But Mincaye was wrapping his arms and his faith around me. How strange the information Aunt Rachel had given him must have sounded so long ago. She told him that if he would give up killing those he hated, as *Waengongi* wanted him to, *Waengongi* promised to protect him. Mincaye knew that was nonsense. If he gave up killing, he had every reason to believe he would be speared and die. And still, he had given up his vendettas and hatred, based on the information he had received from my family.

As I felt my lifeline of trust in God's power and protection slipping through my numb fingers, this old warrior was trusting God for me. Could I trust an illiterate "savage" who only knew what we had told him? I had no choice. The great blackness was covering me. The cord of faith I had trusted and followed since my dad had been jerked from my life was running out. The end would soon pull through my hand, and I would be lost.

It was not a physical thing, but as I felt myself sinking into despair, it was as if I let go of my lifeline and grabbed onto Mincaye's. Standing there in the emergency room, a picture popped into my mind of a beautiful lawn of green grass under a live oak canopy that ended in a retaining wall at a calm, flowing river. I had passed a site like this several times when I had taken the family down the beautiful Oklawaha River near our home. I saw Stephenie and Mincaye sitting on that retaining wall, swinging their feet as their toes brushed the spring-fed water below.

Ginny was standing a few feet away from me in the ER. Her anguish was acute as we watched Stephenie being wheeled past us so her head could be scanned for clues about what was happening to her. I already knew that Steph was gone. I felt I had to prepare Ginny for what was going to happen. I said, "Ginny, I think Steph is dying. I don't think she is coming back."

Ginny recoiled. "No, no, we can't give up hope." She was right; Mincaye had just helped me see that. We did not have to give up hope, even though our precious and only daughter was dying. We could hold on to the confidence that was now washing over me in a way I had never experienced before. We could believe that we would see her again, along with my dad and Ginny's dad and Gikita and Aunt Rachel and the baby we had lost before Jaime was born and Dyuwi's wife, Oba, and all the other people we loved who had died while following God's trail.

The doctor came out of the CAT scan room and started to explain, "In major injuries like this . . ." Injuries like this? Steph had not been injured. I could feel the anxiety rising again. I had to either take charge of this dreadful situation and assert myself or let go in faith. I let go.

The doctor told us that a blood vessel, or vessels, in Stephenie's brain had ruptured. It was possible to operate, but the bleeding was so massive that her brain had swollen and quit functioning. I already knew we did not want to rely on professional heroics to hang on to our daughter. We would have been happy to keep her, even in a permanent coma, but I did not want our will to take priority.

The doctor told us the situation was hopeless. I knew he was wrong. He told us he had a daughter just a little bit younger than Stephenie. He told us that if this were happening to his daughter, he would not operate. There were tears in his eyes. Those tears meant more to me than he possibly could have known.

They took Steph up to the ICU. Ginny and I went with her. A machine was breathing for her as the waiting room filled with people who cared about us. Our son Shaun and his wife, Anne, arrived from Birmingham with our granddaughter Elizabeth, who had also been born just before Steph came home. *Oh no,* I realized, *Steph didn't even get to hold her.* I wanted to at least be sure that when Elizabeth grew up, we could tell her that she had met Auntie Stephenie.

Shaun, who was just finishing medical school, brought Elizabeth into the ICU, and we took her picture with Steph. I almost thought Stephenie would sit up and hold her for the picture. Right then I had an incredible thought. I knew that in the Bible there had been several instances when Jesus had raised people from the dead. One man whose little girl had died received his daughter back from the dead. At the time, I couldn't remember if Jesus had performed the miracle or if it was a prophet or one of the disciples. What I did know was that it had been done with God's power, and I believed God could do the same for me.

I pictured Steph sitting up on that gurney. She would ask why we were at the hospital, and then we would pull out the needles and tubes and go home to finish our party. I believed that all I had to do was to beg God for this miracle, and He would do it. I was sure it could happen.

But then I thought, *If God is all-powerful and all-knowing, none of this is happening without His knowledge or permission.* This had to be part of His plan for Stephenie and for us, just as Mincaye had been trying to explain to the people in the emergency room. This had to be part of the story God was writing with our lives. It was an excruciating chapter in our story, but I suddenly found I believed that somehow—beyond our ability to comprehend—this terrible trauma would eventually and mysteriously prove to be a cornerstone of God's plan for our lives.

If I asked God to change things and He gave in to me, how would my change alter the rest of His plan? I did not want to ask God for what I desperately wanted in the short run, only to find it had cost us what God wanted for us in the long run.

Maturity sneaks in on us while we aren't watching most of the time. I realized that as much as I yearned to take Steph home with us, I was not willing to risk giving up God's Plan A for something less.

Immediately, my resolve was tested twice. First Ginny said, "Oh, Steve, feel Stephenie's body." She lifted up the sheet that was covering Steph and took my hand and rubbed it over our precious daughter's smooth, warm skin. This child was the finest expression of my deep and intimate love for Stephenie's sweet mother. Feeling that body that I knew I would give my own to save, I was tempted in a terrible way to beg for Plan B. But I just couldn't.

Just then a close friend came into ICU from the waiting room. He told Ginny and me that everyone was praying that God would heal Stephenie. I felt a wave of appreciation sweep over me. People of faith were praying with us. But wait: Lew had said that they were praying for Steph to be healed. That prayer was not theirs to decide. My mind was made up. We would trust God and let Him write our story. I heard my own voice explaining to our friend, as though I were at a distance, overhearing the conversation. "No, Lew, ask everyone to pray that God will do whatever He thinks is best. And ask Him to give us the courage to accept it until we see why He wanted it this way."

Then a young man entered the room. Before he even spoke, a feeling of dread swept over me. This was something I could not face. I stepped between him and Ginny. I wanted desperately to stop this conversation before it began.

It is one thing for someone to tell you there is no hope. It is another thing to accept it. I knew the young man who was approaching us was about to ask us to give up all temporal hope. He was going to ask us to allow him to take Stephenie's organs to keep other people alive. I just couldn't face this. I did not want Ginny to even hear him ask.

Just as he opened his mouth, however, an additional wave of peace came over me. I could see it happen to Ginny, too. He started by explaining how sorry he was to have to ask. . . . Ginny and I both simply said, "Yes, it is okay." But then Ginny whispered to me that she didn't want them to take Steph's heart. Neither of us knew how to express that reservation. We would just trust God for that too.

Before we knew it, the nursing staff informed us that Stephenie's vital signs were falling fast. They would have to take her to surgery right away. I remember walking with her gurney down to surgery. At the big double doors, Ginny and I watched them wheel our still-warm child out of our lives forever.

A close friend offered to stay with Stephenie during surgery. It was a comfort to know that someone who cared would make sure that her precious body was treated with respect. As our precious daughter's organs were taken so others could live, Ginny and I walked out of the hospital holding hands and at peace. It was a totally absurd reaction to what was happening in our lives.

/\/\·/\/·\·/\·/\/\

The church was packed for Steph's memorial service. There were hundreds of people there. Mart Green, who was just starting to make his movie, came and brought his entire family. There were other people there from out of town. Jesse made a slide show of Stephenie's life. Everyone laughed when they saw a picture of Steph holding a Waodani baby while a big-eyed little monkey rode on Steph's head.

During the memorial service Tementa prayed, "Oh Father, Creator, you always do well." He went on to express his confidence and appreciation that God had prepared a place for all those who walk His trail to live forever. I realized how difficult it must be for him to remember the many members of his tribe, including his father, who had died at the end of the spear without ever hearing that there is a radically different trail that leads to a place where we can live forever with *Waengongi*, the Creator.

At the cemetery, a member of the musical group that Stephenie had been traveling with sang "How Great Thou Art" in English and his native language of Hungarian. He had fallen in love with Stephenie. The most difficult call of my life was the one I had to make to tell him that he would never get to ask Steph to marry him. I could only imagine what must have gone through his mind in the huge silence that followed. Now he was singing:

> *O Lord my God, when I in awesome wonder*
> *Consider all the worlds Thy hands have made.*
> *I see the stars, I hear the rolling thunder,*
> *Thy power throughout the universe displayed.*
> *Then sings my soul, my Saviour God, to Thee;*
> *How great Thou art, how great Thou art.*

Mincaye wanted to sing too, or at least chant. He led, and Tementa and I followed his lead. He chanted:

> Waengongi *created everything*
> Waengongi *created everything*
> *Blue and scarlet macaws, He created them*
> *Blue and scarlet macaws, He created them*
> *Stars and sun He created them, stars and sun He created them*
> *He has made a place we all can live, He has made a place we all can live*
> *Believing and following we all can go,*
> *Believing and following we all can go.*

I realized that faith and death are the great equalizers in life. People are born into a plethora of different circumstances. Some people are born into opulence that is unimaginable to those who are born into abject poverty. Some, like many of the Waodani, consider themselves rich, even in poverty. My family was born with the right to receive blue passports. We were ensured many freedoms. But I know people in Africa who were born into slavery.

What makes us equal is that we all have to die. After that, it makes no difference where we were born or how rich we were.

This life is only the opening exercise. The only fundamental, long-lasting aspect of life is deciding which trail we are going to walk in life. I translated what Mincaye said about this many times: "If we follow our own trail, at the end, where are we? But following *Waengongi*'s trail, at the end we come to His place. He has made us a place where we all can live happily and in peace." He really believed it too.

We lowered Stephenie's body into the sugar sand of Hillcrest Cemetery in Ocala, Florida. Then we went home to be together and reflect on the great tragedy that had befallen us. It was so heavy, we should have been crushed. Instead, everyone seemed happy. It sounds terribly inappropriate now. But it almost seemed as if we were finally continuing the party we had started four days earlier when Stephenie came home to us.

We all seemed to be okay. Sad, but okay. As long as we stayed together, I felt that we would survive. But I was supposed to leave for Amsterdam with Tementa and Mincaye the next day. I didn't want to go. I knew Mincaye and Tementa would not want to go either. I was sure the family would agree that we should not go, so I asked them while we were all together.

Ginny, uncharacteristically, was the first to speak. "I know we are all fragile right now. The safe thing to do is to stay put, take no chances. But I also know that what you three will say at Amsterdam could be a real encouragement to people who think that North Americans never have anything bad happen to them."

Mincaye and Tementa had probably thought that too. They had seen people die for want of pills and antivenin. Some died because the radio didn't work to call the plane or because the weather was bad and the plane couldn't come. Sometimes medicine did not come because the people controlling it heard the calls for help but did not believe the need was urgent. Other times, they were busy helping other people. But I had my own car and my own airplane. I had money to buy medicine and a son who was a doctor. And still Stephenie had died.

Ginny said, "Don't forget: We have a spiritual enemy. What if the devil wants to use this to keep us from doing something God wants? It isn't worth the risk. I think you have to go!" Without a single dissent, our three sons and our three daughters by marriage agreed.

I did not want to go, but I was proud that my family wanted us to go. Mincaye said he would stay at our house. Then when I explained what Ongingcamo had said, Mincaye said, "I say too that we should go and speak *Waengongi*'s talk to those people living over the big, big water."

24

Cloud of Witnesses

A member of the movie team, Tom, decided to go to the Amsterdam conference with us to help with arrangements. He had already proven his friendship by taking it upon himself to organize a speaking tour for Tementa and Mincaye and myself. He had seen that I did not have the fortitude to limit the number of speaking engagements we took on as we traveled. We frequently spoke four, five, even six times a day. He also saw that we did not ask for any kind of financial consideration. He and his family had traveled with a stage show, so he knew the ins and outs of touring. He started insisting that if someone wanted us to speak to their school or church or civic group, they should make a contribution to indigenous people such as the Waodani through our Indigenous People's Technology and Education Center.

He wanted to look out for us on this trip too. On the way to Europe, Tom and I were talking. I told him what had happened in North Carolina when all those people stood up to show Mincaye and Tementa how much this ongoing story had affected them. Tom immediately said, "Oh, wow, you have got to do the same thing at this conference."

We couldn't. In the plenary session we had been allotted only ten minutes. We were speaking right after a queen from some exotic country and right before Charles Colson, the former chief counsel in the Nixon administration who had done prison time for his role in Watergate. He was a now a God follower who had started a major ministry to other prisoners.

I did not know what we were going to say. What could we say in ten minutes, divided three ways, with interpretation for two of those thirds? What we said had to be easy to understand. What I was speaking or interpreting into English would be simultaneously translated into a number of other languages. The conference delegates would listen to what we said using small headphone radios that they could tune to a language they understood.

All the speakers at the conference were supposed to write out and time what they were going to say. The interpreters would use the manuscripts to practice conveying the speakers' thoughts in their assigned language.

I could not imagine what we could say in a few minutes that would make a significant impact on the lives of delegates from all over the world. I had just buried my only daughter. *That* was what was on my mind. I knew many of these delegates had faced far tougher tests. Some of them, I knew, were coming from places where they faced persecution and even the threat of martyrdom. Some of them had been the victims of genocide. Others lived in countries that had been decimated by famines and plagues. Some delegates were from such out-of-the-way places that they had never worn shoes before. Very few of them could pay their own way. For most of them, this was the biggest happening of their entire lives. And we were going to take up ten minutes of it.

I was told that there would be over eleven thousand delegates at the conference. They were coming from 209 countries—more countries than even the United Nations had ever assembled in a single place at one time. When we arrived at the conference, I realized that what we had been told to expect was not an exaggeration.

Our internal clocks were way off by the time we landed in the Netherlands. We were tired and emotionally drained. But I told Tom I thought we should go to that evening's plenary session so Tementa and Mincaye would be prepared for what was going to happen the next night, when it was our turn to stand in front of that huge "rainbow" coalition.

I noticed right away that no one paid any special attention to us. With eleven thousand delegates all dressed in their native costumes, wandering around the section of the city where the huge auditorium was located, we just blended in.

In the plenary session, we sat by several delegates from Zimbabwe. Mincaye was impressed right away. He consistently reminded me that the Waodani once thought that outsiders with light skin lived inside logs, like white termites and other pale-colored insects that seldom see the light of day. Mincaye also reminded me frequently that his skin was dark. But in comparison to our seatmates from Zimbabwe, Tementa and Mincaye looked a little like they might have come out of a log too.

I got a little nervous when they asked us to join in small groups to pray. I kept my eyes open when one of the Zimbabwe men began to pray. Sure enough, Mincaye couldn't help himself. He reached out and began to pet the arm of the man next to him. He just had to feel that wonderful black skin. I distracted him before he began to pinch and make other tests. Fortunately, innocent touching between men seems to be taboo only in Western countries. The man next to Mincaye didn't even seem to notice.

Later, Mincaye asked me if it was true that when we go to God's place He would give us new bodies. I said, "Yes, *Waengongi*'s markings say that is so." He thought a minute and then said, "When I am living in *Oneidi*, I want skin like those men from the Africa place and hair like the foreign woman on the airplane." He wanted black skin and red hair. That would fit Mincaye!

Mincaye and Tementa went to sleep as soon as we got back to our room. I just tossed and turned. We had traveled across six time zones, I think. That threw me off, but so did being away from home during this difficult time. I felt as if I was abandoning the rest of my family, even though they were the ones who had said we should go. I waited for an inspiration. None came.

Finally, as the sun was coming up, I realized I had to get some notes down on paper. And I needed to coordinate with Tementa and Mincaye. We were going to do a one-hour workshop the following day. We'd been asked to explain to other delegates why the Waodani wanted to learn to meet their own medical and dental needs and fly their own airplane. They wanted us to demonstrate to people from other countries what can be done when the tools and training are designed around the end user rather than the other way around. Most of this would fall within Tementa's area of expertise.

I asked Tementa how he would see it if Mincaye and I spoke this day, and he would speak the next day. I did not want to offend my good friend Tementa. He understood the time limitation and agreed that I would just tell the people about him and why his people had wanted him to learn how to fly.

Mincaye was different. He likes to wear a watch, but it has nothing to do with time. He doesn't know numbers, and he thinks of time only in periods of the day: early morning, morning, the sun straight up, and so on. Ten minutes would definitely not compute in Mincaye's thinking. I was also a bit nervous about how Grandfather would react when he realized how big the audience was. I should have realized that because he doesn't think in terms of numbers, the number of people in the audience would not bother him. There would just be a lot of them. He would probably tell his wife, Ompodae, that there were enough foreigners to fill their house as many times as he had fingers and toes. That would be about four hundred. Close enough.

Tom suggested we get our costumes ready. That was easy for me, but Tementa and Mincaye had been seeing all the other delegates in flowing robes, curl-toed slippers, pajamas, and all sorts of bright colors. We finally decided on khaki Dockers with sleeveless black T-shirts as a base. Mincaye and Tementa would add their toucan headdresses, pig-tooth necklaces, armbands, and tribal net bags, and Mincaye would also wear his earplugs. Tementa's ears had never been pierced and stretched.

I made some notes for introducing Tementa and Mincaye, and a few more to set the stage for whatever Mincaye wanted to say.

Normally, when Mincaye and Tementa and I would speak, we were given between thirty-five minutes and an hour. I had gotten used to several variations of what they would say. Sometimes, if I did not understand a word or phrase in Wao-Tededo, Tementa would try a Spanish word to give me a clue. But Mincaye speaks only Wao-Tededo, and he speaks very fast. If I ask him to slow down, he just drops the volume. The speed stays the same.

Mincaye's narratives also jump around a lot, in typical Waodani fashion. When telling stories in the jungle, the Waodani start anywhere they want and jump back and forth in the sequence of events. They always plan to tell the same tale numerous times. Eventually, those listening are able to put the pieces together in sequential order. This time, however, we would have only a few minutes, and there would be no opportunities for clarification.

We were introduced to Franklin Graham, who was representing his father, Billy. We were also introduced to people who were responsible for the technical aspects of that evening's plenary session. The sound engineer told us he wanted us to use the podium microphone. Mincaye and I would have to take turns leaning into it. There was a hooded light on the podium, so I would be able to see my notes. At the last minute, the program director told us that they had received requests that we be given more time. Chuck Colson had agreed to shorten his talk, so we should take two extra minutes. What to do? I decided that I would take that as an indication that I should do what Tom had suggested I do: ask for a public demonstration of our story's impact on the worldwide delegation. I was sure hoping someone would stand or wave.

The program director told me that they had made up an introductory video. I had not seen it. That could be a problem: I had been blindsided a number of times when canned introductions covered the same material I was going to speak on. Too late to worry about that now.

We were about fifty feet from the nearest part of the audience. I wondered if Mincaye would realize that we were talking to all the people past the edge of large platform, way off in the distance. That is when I noticed that the podium was quite high. They had a step for shorter speakers, but I did not know if it was movable or not.

As the introductory video began to play, I whispered to the platform manager that we could not use the podium since it would block the audience's view of Tementa and Mincaye. They would not even know who was speaking to them. He said we could just stand on the platform beside the podium and use a mike on a stand. But that would not work well either, because Mincaye and I are so different in height.

I led the way onto the dark platform just as the video was finishing. I took the microphone out of the stand and thought, *Well, it will all be over in twelve minutes or so, one way or another.*

The lights came up—right in our eyes. I could not see the audience or my notes. Nothing left to do but wing it. I would simply have to tell everyone what was in my heart, just as Mincaye would.

"Thank you! It is a high honor and an extreme pleasure to be able to address all of you God followers from all over the world tonight," I began. "I am here with two of my dearest friends in the whole world. Tementa is an elder in the Waodani church. His father was the only man in the tribe whom my father ever met. When he came to the beach where my father and his four friends had landed their small plane, he was fascinated by the airplane and showed through sign language that he wanted to ride in it. Finally, my father decided to take him for a ride. After they landed, Nenkiwi, Tementa's father, didn't get out. He made it obvious that he wanted to see his village from the air, so my dad flew him over the village. The door was off, and my dad later wrote in his journal that as he flew over the village, he realized that Nenkiwi didn't want to see the village from the air; he wanted the people in the village to see him in the air. To be sure that they would see him, he tried to climb out the open door onto the wing struts. My dad didn't want him to fall, so he reached over to grab him. But the Waodani didn't wear clothes except for a G–string, and Dad wasn't sure if Nenkiwi would be offended if he grabbed that."

It took a few seconds for the translators in all the different languages to catch up. When they did, nervous laughter rippled through the huge audience. I went on to explain how the Waodani elders had asked me to teach one of them to fly, and how we had chosen Tementa, Nenkiwi's son, to be the first Waodani to learn to fly.

"Last Saturday, Tementa flew an aircraft by himself," I said. The audience responded to this with enthusiastic applause.

Now the audience in Amsterdam knew who Tementa was. I went on with our extemporaneous address. "And now I would like to introduce to you *Maemae* Mincaye, who will be speaking to you in just a minute. *Maemae* means 'grandfather.' I call him that because my children call him that. They love him dearly," I said. "Most of us know that God works in mysterious ways, don't we? It just happens that in God's economy, this man whom my children call Grandfather is the 'new grandfather' who replaced their grandfather, a man whom Mincaye killed when I was a little boy."

I paused and then continued. "Last week at this time, Mincaye's only blonde granddaughter—my daughter, Stephenie Rachel—was called home to heaven." I told the crowd how Mincaye had helped me see God's hand, even in Stephenie's death.

"When we rushed to the hospital, he didn't know what was going on, but when I explained, he was excited," I told the crowd. "'Now I see this well,' Mincaye told me. 'God is doing this. I'm an old man, and soon I'm going to heaven too. When you come, living very well, we will be waiting for you in God's place.'" Now there was sustained applause throughout the arena.

"May I present to you," I finished, "one of my dearest friends and your brother in Christ, Maemae Mincaye?"

Up to this point, I had been telling the audience what Mincaye had said to me at the hospital. Now I would interpret what he wanted to say—live. This is a daunting task because the Waodani's language and culture are both unique. In this instance, the task was made much more precarious than usual because what I interpreted from Wao-Tededo into English was going to be simultaneously translated into all those other languages, which for many in the audience would be their second or third language. I needed to stay true to what Mincaye was saying while making it simple to interpret and understand.

"I am a True Person," Mincaye began. "My ancestors lived angry and hating each other—that's how they lived. They didn't know any other way. The older people, my ancestors, went to the Coca River [Napo River], and they would just spear them. When we saw them, we speared them. But not only the foreigners; we also speared our own people. That's how we lived." For clarification, I added, "He's wanting you to truly understand that they lived hating and killing each other."

Mincaye went on, "It was a bad way to live, but they didn't know any other trail. My ancestors didn't know God's carvings. How could they walk God's trail if they didn't see God's carvings? I didn't know either, until somebody came to teach me God's carvings, and then I began to understand.

"When I killed Steve's father, I didn't know any better. Nobody had come to tell us, and we didn't know that his father was coming to show us God's trail. And that's why we speared him.

"Then Dayumae came back to us, and she began to teach us God's carvings. But when we asked her questions, she said, 'I don't know any more, but if you see it well, I will invite my sister. She's a foreigner with white skin. I will tell her to come here and she can teach us how to follow God's trail, seeing God's carvings.'

"My heart was black and sick in sin, but then I heard that God sent His own Son. His blood dripping and dripping, He washed my heart clean. *Now I live well.* Now you—God followers from all over the dirt—now I see you well because you are truly my brothers, God's blood having washed your hearts clean too." There was no question that our extremely cosmopolitan audience was hanging on every word Mincaye was saying. They applauded vigorously now. There were shouts and whistles from some of the less restrained members.

At this point I was quite sure that our time was up. I was feeling under terrific pressure to stay within our time frame, but I knew that Mincaye was totally oblivious to a schedule. So I asked him quietly, "Idaewa?"—*Is it enough?* He leaned into me and whispered back, "Ayae!"—*More!* My mind was spinning. I respected Mincaye too much to cut him off, but I understood the complexity of the conference schedule, which included multiple speakers, workshops, staggered meals, and transportation to dorms all over the city. I didn't know what to do, and standing in front of eleven thousand delegates from around the world is not conducive to careful contemplation. The audience had seen our quick personal exchange; so I explained, "Grandfather says he has one more thing to say."

Mincaye finished up: "Leaving in just a few days, I may never see you again here. But I will see you there" (meaning heaven). "Speaking God's carvings all over the world, let's take lots of people, following God's trail, to live with us in heaven, God's place." At this point Mincaye was greeted with thunderous applause. It went on so long that I realized it was using up our precious allotted time! I knew I had to draw our short talk to a conclusion.

"Thank you," I shouted into the microphone.

Then I remembered that we had been given two extra minutes. I could not see my watch, so I did not know how much time we had already used. But the audience had been so responsive to Mincaye that I decided to try what Tom had suggested. I had not planned how I would do this, but there certainly was no time to think it through now. I had to do it on the fly.

"There are things in this Western world that the Waodani don't understand," I said. "Mincaye can't understand why 'foreigners' cut so much grass to go look for little white round things they can't eat. He says, 'Maybe they should cook them more.' I don't understand golf either, so I couldn't help him. And Tementa wonders, 'How is it, eating so much grass and leaves, that the foreigners are all so fat?'

"They also don't understand that what they meant for evil so many years ago, God intended for good. I hope I'm not imposing on you, but I have never been able to explain to them that God has used them, as well as my father and the four other missionaries to spread His gospel around this world. If what we call the 'Auca Story' has affected you in some significant way, would you quickly stand so they can see that God has worked good from what they meant for evil?"

I had hoped that maybe several hundred delegates would stand. I was sure there were many language groups represented who had probably never heard this story. But from experience, I was sure that there would be at least a few who had.

Nothing in my lifelong association with this story prepared me for what happened next. A smattering of people all over the auditorium stood immediately. That was only the beginning. It may have taken just a second for my request to be translated and understood, because just an instant after the first people stood, thousands of delegates began rising to their feet. They gave a thunderous applause, not for us, but for the amazing story God has written using such diverse and unlikely players.

∧∧∧∧∧∧∧

Most movie scripts start with people at peace. Then an offense, usually based on greed, is introduced, leading to violence. The climax is the violent vengeance of the good guys against the bad guys. Guns blaze, explosions destroy, and the terminator walks into the sunset, soiled and slightly wounded, but victorious.

This story started with tragedy and violence and worked from destruction to peace. It is a script too far-fetched to be believed—if it weren't true. But it is. And I have watched from a front-row seat as it has been written over these last fifty years.

I recently returned from a visit to the jungle. The Waodani future is still tenuous, and their culture is sliding down the slippery slope of disintegration. Many of the young people are struggling to find an identity. But at least they get the opportunity to struggle to define their future. I take hope in that. I yearn to raise funds and organize a quick escape for the Waodani—for a fairy-tale ending. But I know that isn't the answer to their current dilemma. So I'll go on loving my jungle family who first loved me. And I'll enjoy seeing my grandchildren, the fourth generation now, loving and being loved by them too.

This isn't the end of the story. As long as there are players willing to accept their parts and a Master to write the script, it will go on. After all, life is a story. It just happens that Mincaye's and my chapter included the end of the spear.

Epilogue

Maybe They Knew

I have said more than once that if I could go back and change this story that has inextricably intertwined my life and those of my family with the Waodani, I wouldn't change a thing except the dire circumstances that now face this unique tribe of people. Not only have some of them made me feel like part of their family, but I have loved, admired, and respected them for as long as I can remember.

But there is one other thing that I have always longed to change. It has long hurt me to think that my dad, whose gentle hands smelling of airplane grease and fuel were never too busy to tousle my hair or help me build something, died on a lonely sandbar in the middle of nowhere, feeling that he had failed.

When my own boys were little, I wondered how I would have felt if I was dying and realized that I was going to leave them fatherless—with no dad to teach them the complex skills necessary to grow up to be productive members of society, to follow God's trail, and to be good husbands and fathers. I have always thought that would be even more painful than dying.

My dad and his friends never knew that the very men who were mercilessly spearing and hacking them to death would one day receive their wives and children warmly into their thatched jungle homes. Nor did they know that I, as a representative of their five families, would actually get to live with these same men and do many of the things that Dad, Pete, Ed, Jim, and Roger had so hoped to be able to do for them.

Knowing that they died with no inkling of the thousands of people who would follow in their footsteps because they lived and then died well has been a sore in my heart for fifty years. But something incredible happened just a couple of years ago that has soothed that emotional hurt.

It started a number of years ago when Olive Fleming visited Palm Beach to see the place where her first husband, Pete, had been killed. Obviously, she had questions about the events of that day. My aunt Rachel had been translating for Dawa as she answered Olive's questions. During the exchange, Dawa pointed to a place over the jungle canopy along the ridge behind Palm Beach and informed Olive matter-of-factly, "That is where we saw the foreigners who were chanting after the other foreigners were speared."

Olive had been confused, thinking that either she had misunderstood what Aunt Rachel had translated or Aunt Rachel had misunderstood what Dawa had said. There were no other foreigners. Not on Palm Beach, anyway. Not on that terrible day.

How could anyone have been above the trees?

Dawa didn't know who they were or how they got there. She said, "They were all dressed in the same *weicoo* (cloth)," and she went on to explain that they looked like the choir she had seen in a church when she and her husband, Kimo, had visited the United States with Aunt Rachel long ago.

Olive wasn't going to let the subject go. Her second husband, Walt, a longtime professor of theology, wondered if perhaps it might have been angels.

Olive was in the process of writing a book and decided to include Dawa's account of seeing "angels" above Palm Beach in her manuscript. But there were people who objected to the inclusion, so while our family was living with the Waodani in the mid-1990s, Olive asked me to try to verify Dawa's account with the other members of the spearing party who were still living.

I asked each of them individually. They all agreed that they had seen something. None of them had ever seen anything like it before. They did not know what it was, but they all heard *amitamini*—chanting. Mincaye and Dyuwi saw whatever it was from the top of the ridge on their way back to Damointado as they helped Nampa, who was still unsteady from the bullet that had grazed his head. They said it looked like lights floating above the trees, but they both agreed that what they saw was located right where Dawa had told Olive and Rachel she had seen the foreigners above the trees.

During my interviews with Dawa, Kimo, Mincaye, and Dyuwi, I asked them again to describe what they had seen after they had killed my dad and his four friends. Their accounts were all too vague for me to feel comfortable encouraging Olive to include it in the book.

Several years later, I was down in the jungle helping some friends make a feature-length documentary of the Waodani story. A good friend of mine, Steven Curtis Chapman, was with us to make a music video for a song he had written about our life story. Just after he arrived, we were sitting in the cooking house next to the longhouse with thatched walls that extended from a high peak to the ground behind us. Kimo was sitting next to us, trying to carry on a conversation with our film director's brother, Dave.

But then, while Steve Chapman and I were conversing and Dave and Kimo were trying to carry on a conversation in sign language, we suddenly heard orchestral music coming from the longhouse behind us. I was surprised, because we have no electricity there, and no one had played any music during the two weeks we had been there. Steve noticed my puzzled look. "It sounds like the CD of the original sound track for the documentary," he told me, explaining that a member of the film team who had just arrived with him had brought a portable CD player and had let him listen to the new sound track. Mystery solved.

Kimo and Dave seemed oblivious.

Then, without warning, Kimo jerked dramatically as he reflexively turned his head to try to see through the thatched wall behind him. He listened for a minute and then looked intently at me and said, "Manamai iñindabopa"— *Just like that I understood (or heard) it.* The verb he used can mean either "understood" or "heard."

Steve lifted his eyebrows and gave me a look that said, "What was that all about?" I had no idea. Something had obviously startled Kimo, but he went back to trying to communicate with Dave as if nothing had happened. So I let it go as one more little unexplainable incident that didn't translate between cultures.

But then, a minute later, Kimo jerked violently around again when the same theme in the same cut played again. He repeated the same intent look he had just given me and said, "Your father and the other foreigners dying, that is what I heard."

I suddenly understood. Less than a half hour before, I had again been talking with Kimo about the foreigners he had seen floating above the trees after killing my dad and the others. When he said, "Just like that I heard it," he was referring to our conversation earlier. I called in to whoever was playing the music and asked them to hold the place on the recording. Then I asked Kimo if he wanted to hear it again. He agreed enthusiastically, and Steve, Dave, and I accompanied him into the dark interior of the longhouse. Unfortunately, it was so dark that the friend who was operating the CD player could not see which piece had been playing. So I sat down in a hammock to listen while the other guys tried to find the cut again. Finally, they just started playing the brand-new recording from the beginning.

Kimo had developed a taste for classical music listening to the BBC on a shortwave radio my mom had given him years earlier. He just sat and contentedly listened as one piece after another played. Then, on cut number 6, Steve, the musician in the hut, said, "I think this is the one he reacted to."

Sure enough, Kimo sat bolt upright and started giving me a long narrative about what he was hearing.

"Your father and the other foreigners who came here to give us God's carvings, being speared and dying, this is what I heard." He went on, "Hearing this and seeing the foreigners chanting, I knew that we had done badly, badly."

When he paused, I asked who the foreigners were that he saw chanting. Kimo responded, "I thought they were evil spirits, and I was afraid."

My mind was in a whirl. Kimo had clearly said, "While your father and the other foreigners were dying, this is what I heard." He'd said "dying," not "dead." What he was listening to was orchestral music with no voices. The Waodani have no musical instruments other than hollow bamboo tubes, which the men sometimes play when they dance, that sound like someone blowing into a Coke bottle.

No wonder no one could give me a good description of what they had heard. They didn't have the necessary terms to describe it. It wasn't really chanting. The "foreigners" they had heard were singing a melody. And they were backed by orchestral music.

People who don't live with a daily awareness of the spirit world find what Kimo heard and saw difficult to believe. But for me, it had huge significance.

I know Kimo and Dawa and Mincaye and Dyuwi too well to even consider the possibility that they would lie about something like this. They have seen foreigners fly heavy machines through the air. They have seen foreigners talk into little boxes that people far away can hear. Foreigners put people and animals into a little box where we can watch them over and over, and they have giant food houses that never empty even though everyone takes food away. They have little rooms in big houses that close and then open in a different place, so those inside don't know where they are.

Why would it have seemed noteworthy to the Waodani that they once saw foreigners singing above the trees? And why make something like that up when there was no reason to believe that we didn't already know about it? They certainly would have had no reason to believe that anyone would be impressed with this minuscule event tucked into the panorama of significant events that finally broke down the wall of separation between them and the outside world.

But this was not an insignificant detail to me. I believe in a spirit world. I have experienced it, both on the good and the evil side. I choose to believe that men have actually walked on the moon. I choose to believe that the earth goes around the sun. There have been times in history when many people have not believed the things that I believe—and many still don't.

I also believe that the best explanation for what the Waodani saw is that they were angels. And if Kimo saw them and heard them singing and as a result decided that the killing coup was a bad thing, then I believe that maybe my dad and Jim and Ed and Pete and Roger heard it too.

If the spirits convinced Kimo that what he had done was bad when everything in his culture said it was good, then I believe those five brave men could have understood the same message to mean that they were not dying in vain. What happened to them that day, and what happens to you and me today and tomorrow, is all part of an epic story that God has been writing since the beginning of time. What I have related here on these pages is not my story. It is just one infinitesimal chapter in the great story of man and his quest for God and God's quest for man. This is part of God's story.

For reasons beyond my comprehension, this part of the story has captured people's imaginations and has inspired many to trust God to write their stories too. It gives me great comfort to think that the precious fathers that Steve, Mike, Matt, Beth, Jerome, Valerie, Kathy, Phil, and I longed to know and have missed so much knew that God had a purpose in His Palm Beach script. Others—including Beth Youderian Kachikis, Marilou McCully, my mom, Aunt Rachel, Nenkiwi, Gikita, Nampa, Akawo, and our precious Stephenie—now all know what the true purpose of life really is. The rest of us will certainly know very soon.

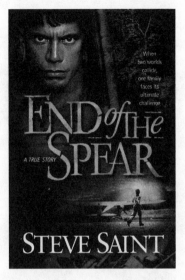

FREE Discussion Guide!

A discussion guide for
End of the Spear is available at

 ChristianBookGuides.com

---

SaltRiver Books are a bit like saltwater: Buoyant. Sometimes stinging. A mixture of sweet and bitter, just like real life. Intelligent,
thoughtful and finely crafted—but not pretentious, condescending, or out of reach. They take on real life from a Christian perspective. Look for SaltRiver Books, an imprint of Tyndale House
Publishers, everywhere Christian books are sold.

SALT**RIVER**®

Intelligent. Thought-provoking. Authentic.
www.saltriverbooks.com

Also available on eight CDs from Tyndale Audio

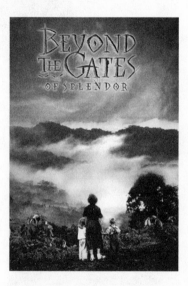

Even people who can't read or write can learn to deliver babies, treat malaria, and repair teeth. . . .

INDIGENOUS PEOPLE'S TECHNOLOGY
AND EDUCATION CENTER

Mincaye
demonstrates
oral surgical
techniques
during an
I-TEC training
session
in India.

The Waodani have proven that anyone can learn to perform medical and dental work, fly aircraft, and rise to many other challenges. When they asked Steve Saint to teach them and other indigenous people, he knew he couldn't fulfill this mission by himself. In 1996, Steve founded I-TEC, an international organization whose goal is to develop new technologies and equip indigenous people to meet the needs of their own communities.

For more information or to find out how you can
contribute to I-TEC's work,
visit www.itecusa.org,
email itec@itecusa.org,
or write to
I-TEC
10575 SW 147th Circle
Dunnellon, FL 34432.

Also from Tyndale House Publishers

An international best seller!
Experience the thrilling story of missionaries Gracia and Martin Burnham and their horrific year as hostages of the Abu Sayaaf terrorist group.

Available in hardcover and Living Book editions

Gracia Burnham reflects on her year of captivity in the Philippine jungle and the amazing lessons she learned about God's grace and constant care.

Available in hardcover and audio editions

In January of 1956, five men entered the jungle in Ecuador to make contact with a savage tribe . . . and never returned.

Through Gates of Splendor, the best-selling missionary story of the twentieth century, was first written in 1956 by Jim Elliot's wife, Elisabeth. Decades later, this story of unconditional love and complete obedience to God still inspires new readers.

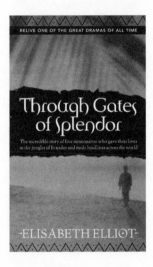

Mass Paperback

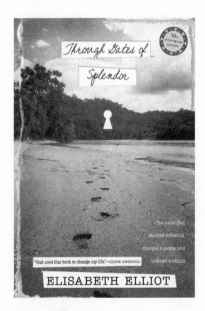

50th Anniversary Edition

"To know the street children is to have one's life transformed."

When Dr. Chi Huang took a year off from Harvard Medical School to work with orphans and street children in La Paz, Bolivia, he had no idea it would take only that one year to change his life forever.

Through his own story and the stories of Gabriel, Mercedes, Vicki, Daniela, and beautiful little Rosa, "Dr. Chi" gives us a glimpse into the shocking world of children who, betrayed by those who were supposed to protect them, are left to the dangerous freedom of the streets. And he gives us a fleeting glance into his own inner world, where he is forced to confront his past and reexamine his future.

When Invisible Children Sing is an amazing story of faith—faith ignited, challenged, almost abandoned, and ultimately restored. Journey with a remarkable man through a remarkable year and allow your own faith to be ignited, challenged, and renewed.